ERROL & OLIVIA

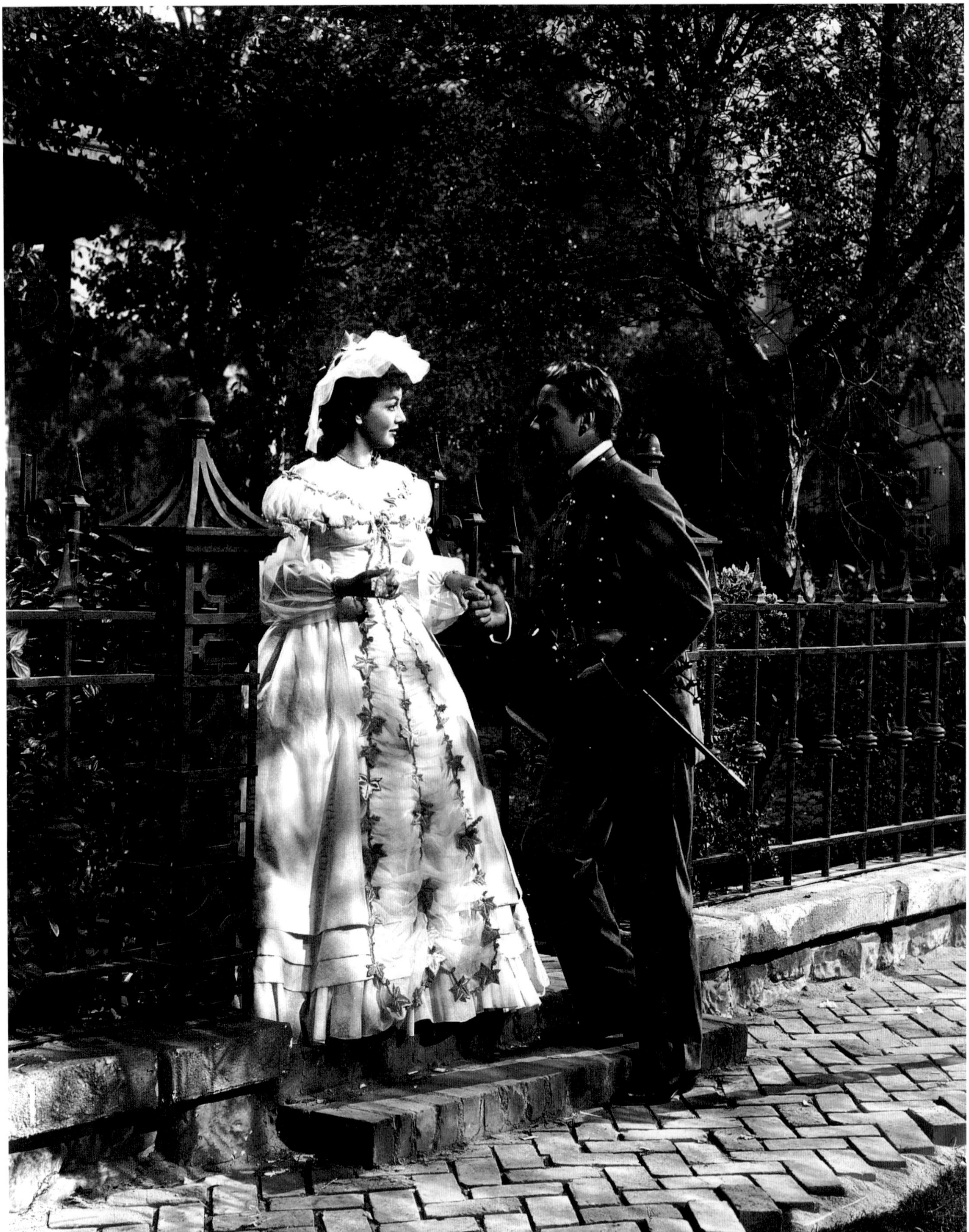

ERROL & OLIVIA

Ego & Obsession in Golden Era Hollywood

Robert Matzen

GoodKnight Books
Pittsburgh, Pennsylvania

GoodKnight Books

© 2010 by Paladin Communications

All rights reserved. No part of this book may be reproduced or transmitted in any form or by any means, electronic or mechanical, including photocopying, recording, or by any information storage and retrieval system without permission in writing from the publisher.

Published by GoodKnight Books, an imprint of Paladin Communications
Pittsburgh, Pennsylvania

Printed in the United States of America

First Edition

Library of Congress Control Number: 2010907549

ISBN 978-0-9711685-8-9

All photographs not otherwise credited are from the author's collection.

frontispiece: Olivia de Havilland and Errol Flynn in *They Died with Their Boots On*.

CONTENTS

Acknowledgments vii
Prologue: Chasing Legends ix

1 Voyages to Port Royal 1
2 The Coup de Foudre 15
3 Flashman and the Lady 31
4 The Big Dance 47
5 The Sure Thing 77
6 Gone Hollywood 87
7 Dysfunction Junction 111
8 Bored to Death 131
9 Life Is Full of Surprises 147
10 Lovers in Exile 173
11 Life After Flynn 193

End Notes 197
Selected Book-Length Sources 201
Index 203

Acknowledgments

As with *Errol Flynn Slept Here*, this new adventure in biography wasn't written in the past year or two but has been percolating in my head for a generation and a half. So, in thanking those instrumental in its creation, I have to start with some fascinating people who have passed on, people who gave of their time, talent, and memories to help me better understand Errol Flynn, Olivia de Havilland, and Golden Era Hollywood. They are Errol's second wife, Nora Eddington Flynn Black; Earl Conrad, the ghostwriter of *My Wicked, Wicked Ways*; actors Victor Jory, Patric Knowles, and Robert Stack; and the prolific Hollywood writer Tony Thomas, who set the standard for scholarship on Flynn and cinema in general. In some cases I was a college student when I sought these people out, and all were patient and supportive of my various projects.

The following individuals and groups were instrumental in helping to shape the story of *Errol & Olivia*: Rudy Behlmer; Stacey Behlmer, Barbara Hall, Faye Thompson, and the staff of the Margaret Herrick Library at the Academy of Motion Picture Arts and Sciences; Jason Brantley; J. Robert Cullen; James D'Arc; Olivia de Havilland; Dave DeWitt; Scott Eyman; Josef Fegerl; Bill and Karen Figilis; Robert Florczak; Joan Fontaine; Steve Hayes; Sheila and Warren Heid; Bruce Hershenson, the staff at emovieposter.com, and the Hershenson/Allen Archive; Louis Kraft; Sandra Joy Lee, Jonathon Auxier, Ned Comstock, and the staff of the USC Warner Bros. Archives; Joan Leslie; Jack Marino; Mike Mazzone; J. McCrary; John McElwee; Tom McNulty; Trudy McVicker; John Hammond Moore; Mike Orlando and the Hollywood Canteen in Toronto; the Tour Department at Warner Bros. Pictures; Mike Pappas; Andrew Parks; and Carole Sampeck, curator of the Carole Lombard Archive and expert on Clark Gable.

Special thanks go to Robert Florczak, Mike Mazzone, and John McElwee, not only for sitting for interviews, but also for investing time in a critical evaluation of the manuscript, suggesting needed improvements, and ensuring that I got the facts right. And thank you, Earl Williams of McComb, Mississippi, for spending 50 years creating a compendium of information pertaining to Olivia de Havilland, including personal letters from the actress.

I would also like to recognize the team that helped to produce this book, including designer Sharon Berk of Cake Creative in Phoenix, Arizona; graphic artist Val Sloan; Tom Maroudas for his fantastic artistry on the dust jacket stills; and editor and production manager Mary Matzen.

Prologue: Chasing Legends

As my co-author Mike Mazzone and I were writing *Errol Flynn Slept Here*, I knew that the mysterious relationship of Errol Flynn and Olivia de Havilland wasn't a topic to be covered in a book about Flynn's home, Mulholland Farm. By the time Errol had built "the Farm" in the autumn of 1941, he and Olivia were finishing their last picture together, meaning there was little to say about the pair in the context of *Errol Flynn Slept Here*. But there is a volume to say about their six years and eight pictures together and the way they lived their lives and approached their stardom during those years.

I never knew Errol Flynn, who has been gone more than 50 years, but I've known many people who knew him, including one of his wives and some of his colleagues and confidants, and they have helped me understand the guy and paint what I hope is a vivid portrait.

I can't say that I know Olivia de Havilland either, although for 30 years we have communicated on occasion via letters from my home in Pittsburgh and hers in Paris. When I approached her with the idea of this book, I heard nothing—Olivia does not respond to communications with alacrity, which is part of her makeup. She lets things sit because, to Olivia, there is always time. She keeps her growing collection of fan mail in a metal file cabinet. She intends to answer each and every piece…in time. She is truly the mistress of her domain.

About a year after my query to Olivia about the book, by which time I had begun to churn out words in earnest, she wrote back, out of the blue—and on blue stationery, which is her custom. It was a long and beautifully composed letter, emblazoned with her signature, and I began to have hope that Olivia would soon be helping me tell her story. Mary (my editor and wife) and I dusted off our passports because we figured we were on our way to Paris to interview my favorite actress, a two-time Academy Award® winner and participant in the most famous motion picture of all time (*Gone With the Wind*, for those too young to have lived through the ballyhoo of the production, the initial release, the many re-releases over the years, or the splashy broadcast-television presentations).

Immediately upon receipt of Olivia's blue letter, I wrote and mailed a response, and proceeded to hear nothing. I attempted on repeated occasions to call her in Paris, to no avail. After another couple of months, I was contacted by a mutual acquaintance who had spent the Fourth of July 2009 with de Havilland in Paris, and sat with her as she held *Errol Flynn Slept Here* in her lap and spoke of Flynn and also of the new book I was attempting to write. By chance this friend of Olivia's is also a writer working on a Flynn-de Havilland book, and it hit me then that her blue letter to me was not what I had at first thought. It wasn't a letter offering help to write my book; it was a "fishing expedition" on behalf of her friend; she was getting the scoop on how far along I was. It was a friend helping a friend.

At first, the realization that we weren't going to Paris, that Olivia wasn't in my corner, disappointed me. At the same time, I admired the fact that she chose to be loyal to her friend. Had I been in her position, I may have done the same thing. And then I reasoned that if I had secured her help on the book, making it a work "authorized by Olivia de Havilland," then I might not be free to explore all avenues of research. In her day she was involved in some controversial and downright unflattering moments, and I realized that she might not want to see these episodes recounted, which might leave me hamstrung by her participation in the project. In some cases she remembers things the way she wants to remember them, which is a benefit of outliving all her co-stars and all the studio executives of Hollywood's heyday. She is the last surviving star from the Warner Bros. stable that included not only Errol Flynn but also Humphrey Bogart, James Cagney, and Bette Davis. And that is saying something.

So, as I was writing this book, on the one hand it seemed incomprehensible to me that Olivia would still be alive and not participating in the creation of *Errol & Olivia*, and on the other hand I didn't believe that she *could* participate in a book that told it like it was.

Ultimately, Olivia would have no direct, collaborative involvement in my work. Luckily for me, however, she is on the record all over the place speaking about Flynn and Warner Bros. over the course of 75 years of interviews. Flynn stopped writing and giving interviews in 1959 when he shed the mortal coil, but Olivia has never stopped, so there is a great volume of material available, much of it recorded in the 1930s and '40s when the memories were fresh and in context and, therefore, more reliable than stories recounted 60 or 70 years after the fact.

Then I got to thinking that there is another great star from the Golden Era still alive who could provide a unique perspective on the subject of Olivia and Errol—Academy Award winner Joan Fontaine, who happens to be Olivia de Havilland's younger sister by 16 months. Joan lived with Olivia during many of the years that saw production of the Flynn-de Havilland pictures. Joan also worked on radio shows with Errol and visited Mulholland Farm. Joan even turned down the role of Elizabeth Bacon in *They Died with Their Boots On* before Jack Warner and Hal Wallis offered it to Olivia. All this seemed to make Joan the perfect subject for an interview, if only I could reach her and convince her to participate.

It took six weeks, but Joan Fontaine did return my call. Our conversation was pleasant but, in the end, unhelpful. Basically, Joan went on the record to tell me that she couldn't go on the record. "If I were to talk to you about Olivia de Havilland," she said in that meticulous and strong Joan Fontaine voice from her home in Carmel, California, "it would be like an atomic bomb going off." That might have been true once upon a time, when the world was fascinated by the feud between Olivia and Joan. But by 2010, the generation that grew up on their pictures is passing, and a couple of generations since then have flourished without ever having heard of either Olivia de Havilland or Joan Fontaine. By 2010 they had become the John Adams and Thomas Jefferson of our age—past titans whose rivalry once caused them anguish but ultimately fueled their survival, as each remained resolute in a determination to outlive the other. To those of us hurrying to document Hollywood history before all the stars large and small have winked out, both Olivia de Havilland and Joan Fontaine still matter. We want to hear what they have to say, and their words are powerful. And speak they will—just not about each other.

So here I was writing *Errol & Olivia*, with Errol Flynn in repose at Forest Lawn in Glendale saying nothing, and 93-year-old *grande dame* of the cinema Olivia de Havilland living three thousand miles in one direction in Paris and saying nothing, and 92-year-old *grande dame* Joan Fontaine living three thousand miles in the other direction in Carmel and saying nothing.

What's a writer to do? Well, write. As with my prior lengthy biographical work on young George Washington (who was similarly resolute in remaining locked away at Mount Vernon and saying nothing), and as with the development of *Errol Flynn Slept Here*, I went back to the primary sources and got the story as straight as I could. I plowed through the Warner Bros. Archives at the University of Southern California, looking at memos and production notes and call sheets and personal letters and photos, and through the Margaret Herrick Library at the Academy of Motion Picture Arts and Sciences in Beverly Hills, studying letters and transcripts and original manuscripts and scrapbooks. I uncovered a treasure trove of information on de Havilland from an ardent fan named Earl Williams of McComb, Mississippi, who started following her career in 1941 and kept at it into the 1980s, and corresponded with her on occasion. I talked to people who knew Errol and/or Olivia and to film historians and, in all, spent two years separating wheat from chaff, determining what was fact and what was legend, and who were the real Flynn and de Havilland versus who the PR people wanted us to think they were.

In the end I learned that Flynn was pretty much the guy I had come to know—brave, reckless, insecure, lecherous, easily distracted, and often depressed. But de Havilland—there's a fascinating personality who was, back in the day, not what we assume she was. Not at all. For the past couple of decades, every mention of Olivia de Havilland in print gushes with accolades about Olivia the "great lady." She is a white-haired matron now, an elegant woman of exacting diction and precision memories of her 93 years of life. But a young starlet didn't beat Jack Warner in court by being a great lady; she did it by being one tough broad. An ingénue didn't rise to stardom with her name above the title by being dignified; she did it by playing a man's game and using her brain and her looks to get ahead.

Forty-five years ago Jack Warner accused Olivia de Havilland of being a cunning woman with a "computer brain," and that microprocessor remains formidable. Improbably, she may be sharper than ever.

De Havilland may have best described herself in 1958 by saying, "I have a man's mind in a woman's body." And no doubt about it, she does. She also said at one point that she grew up loving to read biographies. Well, I sincerely hope she enjoys reading this one, because this is the chronicle of a remarkable and hard life marked by ambition, accomplishment, and the guts to endure. The fact that she will scrutinize this book has made me keen to stick to the facts and keep my documentation handy. In fact, I am looking right now at a photo of de Havilland wearing a wry expression and looking right at me, and I crafted a dialogue bubble beside her mouth that reads, "Is this *really* what you mean to say?" It is my way of making sure I get it right.

Here then is the story of Olivia de Havilland, Errol Flynn, and three other main characters critical to the lives and careers of Errol and Olivia: Jack Warner, Hal Wallis, and Lili Damita. It is also the story of wild, crazy days at the Warner Bros. Studios in Burbank. Flynn and de Havilland were an improbable pair who, in point of fact, entered into their partnership with an improbably high number of things in common.

Robert Matzen
Pittsburgh, Pennsylvania
June 2010

ERROL & OLIVIA

Just turned 18 years of age, Olivia de Havilland of Saratoga, California, strikes a serene and delicate pose as she is about to embark on a grand adventure: working for legendary German stage producer Max Reinhardt in a new version of Shakespeare's *A Midsummer Night's Dream*. As her little sister would be quick to point out, the real Olivia is anything but serene...or delicate.

1 VOYAGES TO PORT ROYAL

The parallels are startling and have never been explored. Both born in the lands of the Pacific Rim—the south for him, the north for her. Both sired by tall, detached, thinking men with eyes for the ladies. Both reared by strong, flirtatious, histrionic mothers, one named Lily and the other Lilian, who berate and dominate their children. Both grow into beautiful young adults who are capable of looking after their own skin. Both take indirect roads to Hollywood and fall backwards into acting careers, at the same studio, at the same time. Both rise to the heights of fame while other hopeful stars and starlets fail, burn out, or, worse, commit suicide. Both are groomed within the studio system, grow rich and powerful from it, and then use their power to rebel against the same studio system as personified by one man, tough-talking, no-nonsense Warner Bros. Studios head Jack L. Warner—J.L.—the Boss. One brings J.L. to his wit's end through mindless antics; the other brings J.L. to his knees through guts, a congenital air of unhappiness, and cold logic. And right about here, with the two stars in court during World War II, the parallels end.

Errol Flynn and Olivia de Havilland grow up in far-flung lands, leading early lives that harden them and warp them. They meet at just the right moment, learn about the picture business together, fall in love, fall in hate, reconcile, and part—all in the span of six years.

But before they meet, they must be born. Errol Leslie Thomson Flynn enters the world on June 20, 1909, in Tasmania, the appendix of Australia. The "lusty infant" has been conceived illegitimately after a shy but womanizing college professor meets the sexy, flirtatious daughter of a master mariner. As discussed in a number of biographies and in Flynn's memoirs, *My Wicked, Wicked Ways*, through Flynn's infancy and into his later childhood, Professor Theo Flynn remains aloof, leaving Lily Mary Flynn, whom Errol will refer to later as "Mother," to run the show with an iron fist. Early on, young Errol learns to be loud and obnoxious, or he won't get any attention because of the carrying-on and mirror gazing of Mother. The pathological way he will deal with women for the course of his lifetime serves as evidence of an unhealthy relationship with Mother, and the fact that his first wife is a dead ringer for Lily Mary, even down to the name Lili, hints that as much as Errol will rail against Mother, she still has her seductive qualities.

Around 1916, according to accounts that Flynn will tell, not just at the boozy end of his life, but in 1933 as a young man, the Flynns move to Australia where little Errol will be cajoled by an older neighbor girl to show what he's got *down there*, as she does the same. No seven-year-old boy is going to know what this means, although the girl seems to know. Her mother walks in on them and goes light on Daughter; Errol catches hell, takes a beating, and, when forced to tell of his misdeeds to his father, refuses. Mother is enraged. "She flew at me again," he recalls. "I screamed. He stepped in. He was never any match for her, either in words or action, and Mother followed through with a torrent of invective. This is no place for me, I decided. I'd leave home, get a job. The next morning I went out of doors, ostensibly to play. I walked off, a long walk, into the farming country. Jobs weren't plentiful. There was a great deal of unemployment in the seven-year-old ranks."[1]

Walter and Lilian de Havilland strike a happy pose with baby Olivia and members of the support staff in Tokyo. The manner of "support" offered by the staff would become a problem for everyone down the road.

At just about this time, farther up the Pacific, Olivia Mary de Havilland makes her grand entrance in, of all places, Tokyo, Japan, on July 1, 1916, seven years and ten days after the first appearance of the Tasmanian Devil. Like the Flynns, the de Havillands are well-to-do and popular in their social set—Walter is a patent attorney; Lilian is a socialite. When Olivia's baby sister, Joan de Beauvoir de Havilland is born on October 22, 1917, each girl has a day nurse and a night nurse. Such are the high times in Tokyo.

Olivia recalls, "My mother became interested in amateur theatricals in Tokyo," and before long participates in productions that entertain the visiting Royals.[2]

Joan says, "Mother's whole attention was absorbed in us, in amateur theatricals, and in entertaining the European social set. Father felt slighted and sought other playmates. Soon Mother's breakfast trays were being served by an upstairs maid who was wearing increasingly beautiful and costly kimonos. Though Victorian, Mother was no fool. It was Yoki-san who had to go…or us. It was us."[3]

"They then decided," says Olivia, "that my mother had to find some place, preferably outside of Japan. There were several possibilities, and the final decision was that my father would buy some land near Victoria on Vancouver Island."[4] They sail to San Francisco but make it no farther north and never see Canada because Olivia contracts tonsillitis, and out come the tonsils in the latest of an ongoing string of health crises for the frail little girls—especially Joanie, who isn't outgrowing her sickly infancy.

Already, there is tension between the sisters. "When Joan got sick," Olivia says later, "it was an immense drama—and for an imaginative, hysterical child that was bad. If she got chickenpox, it was a drama of state. When I had it, I went to bed and was told to keep still and not scratch."[5]

Olivia will see the attention that Joan gets for her illnesses and develop a psychosomatic streak of her own that will stay with her through her career, so that it becomes difficult to separate real from imagined illness and real from imagined exhaustion.

Meanwhile, Down Under, Professor Theo Flynn pursues his doctorate at the University of Sydney and then goes on to other academic endeavors, including studies in London in 1922. Young Errol, feeling the influx of testosterone, tags along to London. He is placed in a boarding school in Barnes, Richmond Upon Thames, where he makes friends with a boy his age—and falls in love with his friend's elder sister, named Mary White. Flynn documents his precocious exploits in love letters to Mary in which he says of her kisses, "they are all right when they are real, by jove." In another he says, "I will be glad when I will be able to go out with you, of course once we have been out it will be easily managed another time…. Will you come up to the football pitch on Saturday?" When classmates, including Mary's brother, tease young Flynn for his ardent pursuits, he reports to her that he "slapped their gobs and told them that they were talking out of their necks." He also laments in the letters that he never hears from Lily Mary: "Mum has not said anything since the last blue moon; probably the stamp supply round her way has run short or something."[6]

Gloomy, insecure, feeling cut off from Mother and in the grip of hormones, Errol becomes a charming, self-absorbed bully. No school can hold the Devil, who is expelled from Barnes in 1924 and heads back to Australia and then Tasmania. School after school greets him and then gives him the boot. By 17, gripped by what would today be labeled Attention Deficit Hyperactivity Disorder, or ADHD, marked by a short attention span, restlessness, forgetfulness, and then a spiraling lack of self-worth, he runs out of schools. In all his years of education, he excels only at tennis and other sports. For the Errol Flynn who will one day be labeled by some as an intellectual, his classroom career is hardly academic.

Out of options and still only 17, he does what any young hellion would—he gets in good with the monied social set and lands a department store job, which he loses in a year because he, apparently, is siphoning funds. At 18, Errol Flynn is proving not to be a hard worker. He has learned to use his charm in place of applying himself, but again he runs out of options and heads for the gold fields of New Guinea in anticipation of a quick strike and a Count of Monte Cristo-like return to Sydney.

For Errol, the awakening is rude. According to author John Hammond Moore in the exhaustively researched (in Australia and New Guinea) *The Young Errol*: "…the handsome youngster who arrived in Rabaul, New Guinea on 1 October, 1927, spent the following 25 months in a number of jobs, frequently getting the boot or suddenly quitting after only a few weeks. Part of his problem was undoubtedly endemic teenage restlessness, but this urge was complicated by well-developed laziness, contempt for authority and—very frankly—failure to get enough sleep each night. Involved with cards, drink, or perhaps some romantic exploit…employers got short-shrift indeed."[7]

Juxtaposed against the sweaty cesspool of 1920s New Guinea is the picturesque, refined hamlet of Saratoga, California, population 800—"Our telephone number was number seven," says Livvie. Little Saratoga, nestled in mountain foothills and in the shadow of the redwoods, serves as backdrop for the American adventure of Lilian de Havilland who has found herself a new husband. He is George Milan Fontaine, a high-collared, stuffed-shirt department store executive who treats the de Havilland children as a gunnery sergeant would treat Marine recruits. A classic stepfather, and not in a good way, Fontaine runs a tight and humorless ship. "Perfection was the least expected of us," says Joan. Livvie and Joanie take to calling him "G.M." or the more apropos "Iron Duke."[8]

G.M. builds his new-found family a two-story, Tudor-inspired stucco house on La Paloma Avenue in Saratoga. Here Joan first starts to call her big sister "Livvie," and here the girls grow up, each of them an oven-forged, curious mixture of fanciful imagination and competitiveness. Olivia remembers, "Our house in Saratoga…was homey and cozy but quite small. So that we had to share the same room whether we liked it or not. And we didn't like it at all.

"Those periods of being the stray dog around the house were numerous…those days when I was told, 'Run along and play, Livvie, Joanie is asleep,' or 'Don't bother me now, Livvie, Joanie wants me to read to her'…and at the same time there was Joan, feeling pretty limp, no doubt, even

In 1926 Errol Flynn, age 17, lounges with the society crowd at a cottage owned by the family of one of his friends. The girl at left partially obscured by shadow is Naomi Dibbs, to whom Flynn would later become engaged. (Courtesy John Hammond Moore)

Above: To escape an unhappy home life, Olivia de Havilland finds a creative outlet with the Saratoga Community Theatre. Here, at age 16, she plays Alice in *Alice in Wonderland*, her first acting role. Below: At about the same time, halfway across the world, sex-obsessed Errol Flynn lounges on the *D'Artagnan*, a steamship, in Saigon Harbor. With Errol is a young woman identified only as "Sakai." Since she is fixing her hair and he is smiling triumphantly, it seems that they have been satisfied by some diversion or other. (Copyright by Josef Fegerl, Seb. Kneipp-Gasse 1/13, A-1020 Wien)

though she was so petted and pampered, and doubtless green with envy of me, all strong and well…and so, you see the seeds which were to develop…were already planted and growing."[9]

A dozen years later when Olivia de Havilland and Joan Fontaine arrive in Hollywood, they will not be stars created and groomed by "star school" at the studios. The traits they share, the beautiful diction, calm demeanor, ability to memorize complex dialogue, graceful movement, and above all, the savvy, result from life in G.M. Fontaine's home on La Paloma Avenue. Joan says that according to their stepfather, "Real education was at home, not at school." The grueling curriculum includes regular lessons in manners, diction, walking, dance, piano, and domestic science. There is no such thing as downtime in the Fontaine home and no such thing as fun—except for Saturday evening trips to the picture show *if* conduct has been exemplary through the week.[10]

In a magazine article years later Lilian will call her daughters' upbringing "just old-fashioned guidance of right and wrong," like the time the little girls argue in the back seat of the car and Lilian makes them walk home—on opposite sides of the street.[11]

Or the time when Lilian discovers that third-grader Olivia has told a fib at home. Enraged, she barges into her daughter's classroom and announces the misdeed in front of all her classmates, adding, "Prevaricators should be shunned." Rebellion is inevitable under the yoke of oppression, and 12-year-old Olivia becomes "ringleader" of a group of A students who bedevil their teachers. Underneath, however, she has become by this time and will remain a shy and uncomfortable introvert and a lonely, lonely soul. Like Errol, Livvie yearns to be in control, he by charm and she by force of a strong and wise-beyond-her-years will. They are also by now each exhibiting a sadistic streak born of the cruel treatment they have received from their closest authority figures. Errol will reveal this streak in cruel practical jokes; Joanie will later cite big sister Livvie's meanness by chapter and verse.

The sisters' central authority figure, G.M. Fontaine, is a dark man. Joan says, "Mr. Fontaine bathed us little girls in the tub each night. The washcloth would tarry too long in intimate places. Olivia and I, never given to confidences, did agree that something was odd."[12] It is a telling admission, and perhaps the tip of an iceberg; neither of them will have anything to do with the Iron Duke as adults.

By the early 1930s, first Livvie and then Joanie begin participating in theatricals, like their mother. This diversion suits the histrionic personalities of all three women. And make no mistake: histrionics rule on La Paloma Avenue.

Several thousand miles to the west, Errol Flynn, now at the age of majority, is on his third stint in the wilds of New Guinea, as overseer of a five-acre tobacco plantation in Laloki using black laborers. The facility exports more than a ton of cured tobacco in 1932, but the product is declared to be faulty due to bad curing. In fact, Australian tobacco growers don't want competition from New Guinea operations that use native labor, and Flynn's efforts there are sabotaged. Were he successful here, Errol Flynn probably would never make his way above the equator or follow the strange path that will lead him to worldwide fame.

As it is, the weary adventurer washes out of the tobacco business and returns to Sydney and his old posse of the social set, including the fiancée he had left behind, elegant, dark-haired, dark-eyed Naomi Dibbs, whose appearance is not dissimilar to a beauty he will meet three years later during the casting of *Captain Blood*. Amongst this crowd, Flynn is one of those cads and bounders who go by the name Reggie or Percy and populate upper-crust social comedies of the day. Their occupation is always in question, but they show up in skimmer and striped blazer with utter charm and deliver the funniest lines in the show.

Above: Errol Flynn sits for his first studio portrait in 1934. (Robert Florczak Collection) Flynn had plotted to meet statuesque and curvy older woman Lili Damita (below) in Paris, and was shocked to find that she stood barely five-two. The chemistry between the two was instant and incendiary.

One day, while on the beach with his friends, Flynn the cad catches the eye of established filmmaker Charles Chauvel, who is casting a documentary about Pitcairn Island called *In the Wake of the Bounty*, which includes a retelling of the mutiny on HMS *Bounty*. In one of those moments that seem incredible because, after all, what are the odds, Chauvel happens to be at the beach the same day that Flynn is at the beach and believes that this striking but anonymous young fellow could portray Fletcher Christian in his picture—not knowing that Errol Flynn really and truly is descendant not only of Christian but of another *Bounty* mutineer, Edward Young. In fact, Lily Mary Flynn's maiden name is Young, of those particular Youngs![13]

So, at just about the time that 16-year-old Livvie is impressing audiences on the stage as Alice in a well-mounted Saratoga production of *Alice in Wonderland*, Flynn is chewing up the scenery on a Sydney soundstage as his own ancestor, Fletcher Christian, in a documentary travelogue.

Finally, at the age of 23 and lacking any experience, Flynn finds something he wants to do and something he has a gift for—pretending to be someone else. He actually gets paid to stand around and use his charm, and with a built-in audience!

Finally, at 16, Livvie can feel some semblance of control and lose herself in a new character. From Saratoga, *Alice in Wonderland* goes to the Palo Alto Community Theater. Livvie will later often say with pride, "The best review I have ever received—at the age of 16—was from George C. Warren of the San Francisco *Chronicle* reviewing *Alice in Wonderland*."[14]

Just now, Livvie has fallen deeply in love, establishing a pattern that becomes more pronounced as she matures. She will later identify her beau only as Peter. He is a year ahead of her at Los Gatos High. They have known each other since first grade, and he is an intellectual on his way to Yale, and a sensitive guy. She calls their relationship an

Olivia de Havilland (second from left) and Evelyn Venable (second from right) struggle to keep their cumbersome headdresses upright as they pose with cast members in a still publicizing the Hollywood Bowl edition of Reinhardt's *A Midsummer Night's Dream* in September 1934. (Photo Courtesy of the Academy of Motion Picture Arts and Sciences)

engagement, and it is indeed serious. She invests everything in Peter and lives and breathes the part of a girlfriend. But when Livvie scores in *Alice*, and now has two loves, both *extremely* passionate, Peter feels as if the rug is being pulled out from under him.

"He began to be possessive and demanding," she says. "He insisted I be with him at times when he knew I had to be at the theater rehearsing." She had seen him as a god and now his behavior is "less god-like" and not in keeping with young Olivia de Havilland's fantasy world of life in general and boys in particular. It is a place the sisters are driven to, a Wonderland *not* ruled by the Iron Duke. Young gentlemen who seek to romance either of them must be tall, older, distinguished, intellectual, commanding, and self-confident to the point of smugness, but as gentlemen, they will allow the girls to engage in their individual pursuits.[15]

In other words, these gentlemen must in many ways resemble a benevolent version of the very man they despise, George Milan Fontaine.

For posterity Olivia will say that Peter's demands are "damned unreasonable" and states that she is forced to give Peter his walking papers, but it may well be that Peter knows what a Yale man has to offer, refuses to play second fiddle to a girl chasing footlights, and dumps Olivia, crushing her in the process.

De Havilland is already, by her senior year in high school, quite a complex personality, and so is Flynn, and the next moves in their lives are dramatic, and each makes that move in the name of acting. The bug infects Flynn so badly that, in short order, he dumps poor Naomi the fiancée, takes up with a rich older woman, and steals her jewelry so that he can fund his voyage from Australia, heading for England and the stage. In the grips of dark influences, he attracts the most nefarious character of his life, Dr. Hermann Friedrich Erben, on a tramp steamer heading west, establishing a friendship that will threaten Flynn's career later on and lead his legacy to near ruin by circumstantial evidence 21 years after his death.

Early in 1935, Nan Grey, June Travis, Olivia de Havilland, June Martel, Maxine Doyle, and Dorothy Dare line up for a photo, having been "recently designated by studio officials as the lucky girls to be developed for stardom in 1936 and 1937." All will appear in multiple pictures during these years; only one will become the love interest of Errol Flynn and go on to earn four Academy Award nominations and two Best Actress Oscars®.

For Livvie, the fateful moment is not unseemly, as Flynn's had been, but it's no less dramatic. She tries out for Elizabeth Bennet in *Pride and Prejudice,* her high school play, and lands the role. She keeps it a secret, but in the Fontaine household, secrets have a way of being revealed. When the Iron Duke finds out that she is appearing in a play without permission, he confronts Livvie at the front door. Joan says that the ultimatum to big sister is that if she leaves the house to work on the play she will never be welcome again. Says Joan with seeming admiration, "Unable to let the school or her classmates down, she left forever."[16]

But there is more to it than that for Livvie. Acting is as essential to her as breathing. She is "painfully shy," a tremendous introvert, and a loner. "I really like people," she says, "but panic always stands between me and them." And as she will admit later, "By representing someone else, I was relieved of my own personality." She will say in another interview, "I'm like a snake—I like to put on a new skin with every role."[17]

When faced with the choice of having shelter or going on the stage, even in a high school play, she leaves home to be able to do the thing that is as essential as breathing—the thing that relieves for a time the ongoing ache of loneliness.

Livvie relies on her social network for food to eat and places to stay and writes to her wayward father in Japan, Walter de Havilland, for support. Walter, who has married his geisha, Yoki-san, dutifully sails to California to meet with Olivia and Joan. He agrees to provide $50 per month to support Livvie, who has won a scholarship to Mills College for Women, a small liberal arts school in the Oakland foothills, on the shore of San Francisco Bay. She will say later: "I thought…at least I will have these four years, sort of sequestered from life and studying, and I will take this major in drama and speech arts and hope to win a scholarship for the following year, because the only way I can get through college is by doing that, but I hope I'll find what I really should do in life."[18]

Flynn knows what he wants to do, and he will use whatever means necessary to become an actor. In Paris, still on his way to England, he manages to meet up with Lili Damita, French picture star (real name Liliane Carre—yet another Lilian in the story). According to one credible report, Errol—whose tastes at this time run to older women (who remind him of Mother)—has been enamored of Lili since seeing her in the picture shows while a youth in Australia.[19] Of all people to meet now. So it can be said with reasonable certainty that Flynn seeks out Damita to further his would-be acting career. He gets her in the sack in a matter of moments (or does she get him in the sack?) and *voila!* Flynn secures a bit part in a musical comedy picture in England called *I Adore You!* at Warner Bros. Teddington Studios.[20]

But Flynn can only seduce his way so far. When other acting parts prove scarce, he invents for himself a fictitious resume and takes an ad out in *The Spotlight*, the British theatre magazine, in which he claims to be the star of non-existent plays and also an Olympic boxer (later he will add Olympic swimmer to his resume). Soon he is performing with the Northampton Repertory Theatre and playing London's West End. Give Flynn credit: provided with this opportunity, he more-or-less cleans up his act and works six days a week without a beef, playing a variety of roles and channeling his charm into modest acting success. He remains with Northampton for six months until the dark side takes over. A mean drunk all his life, one night he knocks a member of the crew, a woman, down some steps

Lili Damita, star of moving pictures in France and Germany, was brought to the United States to be paired with heartthrob Ronald Colman in the 1920s. It didn't work out, so back to Europe she went. In Paris she first laid eyes on (and then laid) young stud Errol Flynn, who had arranged to meet her accidentally on purpose. Lili was just Flynn's type: older, leggy, and hell-on-wheels in bed.

with one punch, and out he goes, despite his morning-after horror at what he had done.[21]

Even now Flynn lands on his feet, and for this he can thank a few British chaps—chief among them Leslie Howard and Robert Donat. Howard has just scored big as the mincing Sir Percival Blakeney in the talking picture *The Scarlet Pimpernel*, and Donat has impressed as Edmund Dantes in *The Count of Monte Cristo*. Bottom line: British leading men are all the rage, and the studio where Flynn has worked in a bit part, Warner Bros., needs to find some.

Nobody likes it when Mr. Warner isn't happy. Jack is the youngest of three brothers; the fourth, Sam, next to the oldest, had died suddenly of blood poisoning days before bringing *The Jazz Singer*, the first feature picture with dialogue, to the screen. Jack's older brothers, Harry and Al, are quiet, dignified businessmen and gentlemen. But not Jack. No, no, not Jack. J.L. is brash, loud, outgoing, pushy, and a ladies' man. He had grown up on the streets; he had grown up in Vaudeville. It's no coincidence that Tom Powers (the *Public Enemy*) and *Little Caesar* had been introduced on J.L.'s watch—they are tough, ruthless men with no small amount of charm, just like the boss of Warner Bros.

Into this setting steps Errol Flynn, who has worked on the stage for months and takes his now-more-reasonable resume back to Warner Bros. Teddington, to the office of studio executive Irving Asher. Supposedly, Asher's wife knows of J.L.'s rant—Burbank needs to find English leading men!—and happens to see the young fellow sitting there waiting and proclaims to her husband that there waits a star to be born. In short order Asher is cabling the home office at Warner Bros. Studios in Burbank, California, in telegram shorthand: "Signed today seven years optional contract best picture bet we have ever seen. He 25, Irish, looks cross between Charles Farrell and George Brent. Same type and build. Excellent actor, champion boxer, swimmer. Guarantee he a real find."[22]

Either Flynn is one charming fellow indeed, or Asher is trying to score points with the Boss. Either way, three days later, Asher casts Flynn in a British picture called *Murder at Monte Carlo*. J.L. orders all his creatives to take a look at film of the new guy. One of those creatives watching *Murder at Monte Carlo*, a studio-bound mystery, is director Delmer Daves, who calls Flynn's performance "self-conscious" and

A TALE OF TWO DWELLINGS

Prior to Flynn's sudden May 1935 elopement with Damita, the scandalous couple had already moved into this fortress-like home on Appian Way, shown (above) in a spring 2009 view. The house featured an enormous living room with fireplace, narrow hallways, low bulkheads that caused literal headaches for the six-foot-two Flynn, and spectacular views all the way to the ocean from the upstairs picture window and the downstairs balcony. The house also included a secret room off the master bedroom—a feature Flynn would design into his dream home on Mulholland Drive (for nefarious purposes).

As Errol and Lili were busy turning each other inside out sexually, Lilian and Olivia de Havilland were sharing an apartment in the Chateau des Fleurs in Hollywood (below) where they would be picked up in the morning for the drive to Warner Bros., and returned in the evening. Younger sister Joanie moved in shortly thereafter and became first Livvie's personal servant and then an actress. Both roles helped to fuel the growing enmity between the young sisters.

yet the kid's got *something*. There's only one way to find out what it is and that's to bring Errol Flynn to California.[23]

The future closes in upon Olivia de Havilland at about the same speed. Not long after *Pride and Prejudice* gets her locked out of her home, Livvie hears that the great Max Reinhardt is going to direct *A Midsummer Night's Dream* at the San Francisco Opera House, and she believes that if she can simply watch the great man direct, the knowledge gained will assure her of a sophomore scholarship as a drama student at Mills College.

At age 60, Max Reinhardt is the impresario—the Andrew Lloyd Webber—of his day, for 30 years a great producer at the Deutsches Theatre in Berlin. In 1927 he had first brought *Midsummer* to America, and now he would do it again in anticipation of filming a version of the play at Warner Bros.

The devil's in the details. Her nails could have been cleaner and her eyebrows less wolfmannish, and those teeth would need some fixing—studio executive producer Hal Wallis later ordered her to do so at her own expense—but this is the rough draft of Olivia de Havilland that was seen in the Warner Bros. screen version of *A Midsummer Night's Dream*. (John McElwee Collection)

Livvie uses her modest connections in Saratoga to arrange dinner with Felix Weissberger, Reinhardt's general manager and casting director. After dinner she enacts Puck for him in an impromptu audition, which earns an invitation to San Francisco the next morning to read for the role of Hermia, and in 24 hours young Olivia de Havilland is offered an opportunity to understudy the understudy for Hermia in the Reinhardt production when it reaches the Hollywood Bowl in four weeks. "Can you imagine what that meant?" she will reminisce much later. "Incredible news! I was now going to be an official member of the Reinhardt company."[24] But it also means that she will miss the fall term at Mills, which she must do, and which Mills must understand.

Hermia will be Gloria Stuart, who more than 60 years later will be Oscar nominated for her role as elderly Rose in *Titanic*. In the summer of 1934, Stuart is a busy Hollywood leading lady with almost 20 film credits, including creepy productions like *The Old Dark House* and *The Invisible Man* at Universal and the service picture *Here Comes the Navy* with Pat O'Brien and James Cagney at Warner Bros. Stuart's understudy is Jean Rouverol, who suddenly lands a big part in her first film, the W.C. Fields comedy *It's a Gift* at Paramount, and drops out of the Reinhardt production, which bumps Livvie up to first understudy to Gloria Stuart. "I took all the rehearsals, all but three," says de Havilland, "and I started receiving Max Reinhardt's direction." The company now relies on this 18-year-old unknown for the grunt work of keeping rehearsals running—a chore for a screen actress like Gloria Stuart. Olivia loves it. As she says, "I had this huge responsibility toward this company, and Herr Professor Doktor Reinhardt."[25]

The responsibility is about to get much grander. Five days before opening night at the Hollywood Bowl, Gloria Stuart announces to Reinhardt that she must withdraw from the production—she has just landed a new picture at Warner Bros., *Gold Diggers of 1935*, with Dick Powell, and it starts immediately.

The impresario turns to Livvie and proclaims, "You will play the part!" And on September 17, 1934, Olivia de Havilland does portray Hermia before a packed crowd at the Hollywood Bowl. On opening night, standing there in an immense headdress and heavy costume, stage fright washes over her and she throws up behind some bushes on the set, and at that moment "the first assistant had to take me by the shoulder and say...'You're on!' and he pushed me on the stage."[26]

So begins Livvie's run in *A Midsummer Night's Dream* on Reinhardt's multi-city tour of autumn 1934. In his memoirs, J.L. recalls receiving a call while in New York from his right-hand man, executive producer Harold Brent "Hal" Wallis, that the studio needs to sign a young girl in the Reinhardt production, prompting the Boss to TWA hedge-hop his way back to California to see Olivia. Wallis has an eye for talent and when he speaks, J.L. knows to listen. Warner and Wallis are what James Cagney calls "front office." Never their names; just "front office." They are a unified force and a hell of a team, both savvy of the picture business, with Wallis often the good cop to J.L.'s bad cop.

Just a couple of weeks earlier, de Havilland had been spotted by Fred Datig, a casting man at Paramount Pictures. Datig is looking for talent to appear in director Cecil B. DeMille's upcoming screen spectacle, *The Crusades*, and calls de Havilland in to the studio in Hollywood for an interview. But the kid's too green, with no experience on film at all, and Datig is certain that DeMille will pass.[27]

Upon sight of de Havilland at the Hollywood Bowl, however, Warner feels that Wallis is right again, and that Paramount has missed something. Olivia de Havilland is offered a starting salary of $200 per week, a small fortune in the Depression, to be afforded the opportunity to continue to work with Professor Reinhardt on the screen version of *A Midsummer Night's Dream*. But there is a catch. A Big one. Studios like Warner Bros. sign actors to exclusive contracts that call for employment 40 weeks a year for 7 years in any role in any picture deemed appropriate. In the end Livvie opts for the security of a paycheck that will provide her freedom and, ultimately, independence from her mother and stepfather.

When underage Livvie (she will not reach the age of maturity in California for three more years) signs on the dotted line of a seven-year contract on November 12, 1934, at the executive offices in Burbank, she becomes the breadwinner of the family, but also the property of the Warner

Flynn does his best impression of suave Brian Aherne in an early Warner Bros. Teddington photo session. Long before the idea germinated to put the young Aussie in costume pictures, Warner Bros. groomed him to be a drawing-room romantic, like Aherne, Robert Donat, Warren William, and others.

Bros. Studios—just like the lights, soundstages, and grip trucks. Her first assignment as studio property is not *A Midsummer Night's Dream*, which is still in pre-production. Rather she takes on the role of girlfriend to comedian Joe E. Brown in the baseball comedy, *Alibi Ike*, which de Havilland biographer Tony Thomas describes as a rude shock for Livvie, "to be transported from the euphoria of the Reinhardt milieu to the workaday business of routine movie product."[28]

For de Havilland, the shocks keep coming. The screen version of *A Midsummer Night's Dream* is overseen by Reinhardt and directed by another native German, Wilhelm "Bill" Dieterle. Warner Bros. executive producer Hal Wallis, age 35, is perhaps the most talented motion picture craftsman in Hollywood and personally oversees the progress of every picture being made by reviewing the dailies—the film that has just been processed. Wallis is one of those earnest, straight-shooting guys who spends 40 years looking middle-aged. He has been sitting in the "first officer" chair since Darryl Zanuck left Warner Bros. in 1933 (two years later Zanuck would form Twentieth Century-Fox). Wallis operates according to Zanuck's blueprint. "When the baton was passed to Wallis," says Rudy Behlmer, author of *Inside Warner Bros.*, "he picked it up and was doing extremely well. He was definitely a heavy hitter, no question. He was tough, but he also knew the business and he was on board totally...the story aspects, the casting aspects, the production, the cutting notes, and he had been a publicity man. So there wasn't anything in the business that was alien to him."[29]

Wallis says, "The script is sacred to me," meaning that the script represents the approved story and no one had better deviate from it.[30] He keeps the script in hand as he sits in projection rooms and watches the dailies of every picture in production, pictures like *A Midsummer Night's Dream*, assessing the work of cast and director alike and tracking the story for viability. Then inevitably he fires off memos, once in a great while with praise for the director or actor, but more often fixing problems. And a problem he identifies early on is "the de Havilland girl," his moniker for young Livvie.

It was a stretch to imagine the 42-year-old rubber-faced comedian Joe E. Brown as a big-league pitcher, and (to say the least) a bigger one to imagine that de Havilland, age 18, would be attracted to him. The film is *Alibi Ike*, released in June 1935. (John McElwee Collection)

"Watch that de Havilland girl," he writes to director Dieterle on February 15, well into production. "She has a tendency to breathe very hard and to gasp for breath between lines and this gets to be very annoying." In general Wallis grouses that these people are reciting all this Shakespeare and can't be understood. In the same memo he again speaks of "the de Havilland girl, with her gasping for breath and burying her face in hollowed shoulder and talking at the same time so that her voice is muffled and everything else."[31]

Two weeks later after reviewing the dailies Wallis writes to the picture's line producer Henry "Heinz" Blanke, another German émigré: "Am just looking at the 'Dream' dailies of the scene with Olivia de Havilland and Ross Alexander running into the foreground where the girl is crying and hissing and drawing her breath in, and everything else. We'll just have to put explanatory titles in the picture, because I can't understand what the hell she is talking about, and no one else will."[32]

As Livvie matriculates through the school of hard knocks, upstart Errol Flynn blows into town, having made the passage from England to the Port of New York on the SS *Paris* and traveled cross country by train to Southern California. His arrival in Burbank is a huge letdown. He expects newsreel cameras; he expects a welcome from Jack Warner; he expects to be put to work. Instead, "I was just a spare wheel on the Warner Bros. lot," says Flynn. "I did nothing."[33]

He kicks around for a while before finally being cast in bit parts in a pair of Warren William B pictures. He collects weekly paychecks for practically no effort, which usually Flynn would find appealing, except that by now he had led himself to believe that given half a chance he will take Hollywood by storm. Why doesn't Hollywood understand?

Into this picture of idle discontent rustles international screen star Lili Damita. "Lili always seemed to rustle," Flynn will say in an uncharacteristically warm remembrance; "it was one of her wonderful traits. No one could rustle an entrance into a room better than she."[34] Damita invites him to her villa at the Garden of Allah at

Sunset Boulevard and Crescent Heights in Hollywood. There they take up their wild sexual relationship where they had left it in Europe, and both are hooked on the physical pleasure and the…well, both are hooked on the sex. Outside the bedroom, they can barely stand one another, but Flynn needs Damita to work her connections and find him parts in pictures—and not just any pictures, but good pictures; Damita needs Flynn to stand there handsomely as her escort while she attempts a Hollywood comeback because her appeal, perhaps because of a heavy French accent, is on the wane.

"What began as an affair went far beyond that," says Flynn. "We decided it would be a good idea to take a house. We found one with a fantastic view."[35] This old-world, low-ceilinged fortress on a hairpin street called Appian Way above Laurel Canyon is discovered and secured by Lili and reminds her of the dwellings of a youth spent in France and Germany. The house sits solidly in rockface overlooking Hollywood and sports a magnificent view that reaches easily to the Pacific. Warner and Wallis get wind of the cohabitation of the tempestuous lovers. Unfortunately, Flynn and Damita are not married, and that won't do for a studio contract player, so after some saber rattling to the tune of breach of contract, the naughty sackmates are married, in Yuma, Arizona, on May 5, 1935.

By now, Lilian and Olivia de Havilland have taken an apartment at another European-flavored structure, the Chateau des Fleurs on Franklin Avenue in Hollywood, where a studio car picks them up in the morning for Livvie's long day's work up in Burbank. The months pass with the young ingénue toiling on pictures assigned by the studio. Says her biographer, Tony Thomas, "Olivia felt she deserved to be given more elegant material and complained to production executive Henry Blanke, who put in a word for her to that effect with Jack L. Warner. Mr. Warner's view was that she was under contract, being paid a weekly wage, and needed to be seen."

Next, she is plunked into a James Cagney-Pat O'Brien comedy, *The Irish in Us*, as the female lead. Says Thomas, "It was already beginning to dawn on her that the main function of a fledgling contract player was to turn up for work, where and when told."[36] By now Livvie is gripped by second thoughts—having signed a long-term contract, she now understands that she will *not* experience college or a stage career. She has become the chattel of the Warner Bros. Burbank Studios and is forced to work long days in front of hot lights, with a collection of leading men not to her liking.

"It was a six-day week, and Saturday night," says Livvie. "Women had to report at 6:30 [a.m.] on the set, ready, dressed, up on your lines, and ready to shoot. You would work until 6:00-6:30 at night, six days a week."[37] She lives among the palm trees, warm sunshine, and dramatic landscape of Southern California, but she does it in a sweatshop surrounded by older motion picture professionals, many of them cynical and unhappy.

"Film work is much too hard for an 18-year-old," she will say later. "Your nerves and physical strength are easily exhausted and it does great injury to one emotionally."[38]

At the Chateau des Fleurs, she often ponders the fact that she should *not* have followed Reinhardt from stage to screen. Seven years is an eternity, and she has missed the chance to become a legitimate stage actress, just as she has missed the life of the college student. Oh, sure, how many 18-year-olds make $200 a week? But this is not the life she wanted. Bottom line: she signed the contract and now she is stuck.

A couple miles away as the buzzards fly, Errol Flynn wonders what the hell the future holds for him. He is engaged in sizzling bedroom gymnastics with Damita on Appian Way, but soon realizes that Lili is insecure to the point of insanity and possessive to the point of smothering. In their low-ceilinged bedroom on the main floor of the house, he can lock eyes with his hellcat as they make love… or he can let his gaze wander out the glass patio doors to the panorama of Hollywood and Los Angeles below, miles and miles and miles of lights and women and freedom, and the sea off to the west, warm waters stretching back to the horizon. He tells himself that he can walk away from this strange new life at any moment, but he knows he's trapped. Flynn is at the whim of the Man, and at the whim of a woman, and he cannot be comfortable with a situation in which anyone is in charge of him but *him*.

These two young, lonely people are adrift in a strange place, and out of their own control. They are two dreamers suffering sleepless nights. And it shows no signs of getting better for either Errol Flynn or Olivia de Havilland.

Jack Warner said that his new discovery Errol Flynn "showered the audience with sparks," and Hal Wallis said that Flynn "leapt from the screen...with the impact of a bullet." After six months studying dailies of Errol and Olivia, Warner and Wallis will feel safe to gamble on a heavy publicity push at Christmas 1935. It didn't hurt that these kids looked like a matched set. (Image courtesy of Hershenson/Allen Archive)

2 THE COUP DE FOUDRE

Fickle Americans! They keep wanting different kinds of pictures, and the studios struggle to keep pace. At first, right after the Crash, audiences seek dramas with grotesque mansions and high ceilings and rich society dames in shimmering gowns, chased by men with their hair slicked back who play polo and call the dames "dahling." But audiences are also craving characters like Count Dracula, Frankenstein's Monster, and the Mummy—wretched creatures who reflect the true horror and the life-and-death everyday struggle of the times. And the crowds want cheap social thrills as well, watching wide-eyed the exploits of Little Caesar and The Public Enemy to better understand the Capones and Dillingers of their day.

By 1934 tastes change. Escapism is the thing. Alexandre Dumas' brilliant *The Count of Monte Cristo* is brought to the screen with Robert Donat as the young hero, falsely imprisoned, who escapes, finds his fortune, and wreaks a terrible vengeance. It becomes the first swashbuckling hit of the talkie era. That same year, *Treasure Island* shows the world hard-core pirates seeking hard-core treasure, and *The Scarlet Pimpernel*, starring Leslie Howard, depicts a secretly dashing British hero risking his life to save French aristocrats bound for the guillotine. By mid-1935 two more big-budget swashbucklers go into production, *The Three Musketeers* at RKO and *Mutiny on the Bounty* at MGM. By June Warner Bros. stands ready to start production on its own adventure picture, *Captain Blood*, based on the Sabatini novel, but J.L. finds himself in the unenviable and somewhat embarrassing position of having no leading man or leading lady to play in it. The Boss believes in the economical business model of growing his own talent and has gone after established outsiders only with William Powell and Kay Francis. But Warner hasn't thought to home-grow a swashbuckler; the new wave of costume pictures has caught Jack L. Warner with his pants down.

The plot of *Captain Blood:* Dr. Peter Blood is minding his own business one night in 1585 when a rapping at his door by a fellow named Jeremy Pitt takes Blood to the farm of Andrew Baines, where followers of the rebellion of the Duke of Monmouth are seeking refuge after a clash with King James' troops. Knowing only his duty to his fellow man, Blood treats the rebels and is arrested for treason and sentenced by the court of the King to enslavement along with Pitt, Baines, and the rest on the British colony of Jamaica. The governor of the island, Colonel Bishop, takes an immediate dislike to the slave Peter Blood, but Bishop's niece Arabella purchases the impudent Blood on a whim. Before long, Blood and his band escape to become feared pirates of the Caribbean. Later, Blood's confederate, Captain Levasseur, captures a ship carrying Arabella and Lord Willoughby, who has been ordered to Jamaica to offer Blood's pirates amnesty if they will fight for the newly crowned King William and Queen Mary against Spain, with which Britain is now at war. Before long, Blood and Levasseur are dueling on an island beach for the rights to Arabella. Blood wins and sails to Jamaica, where his ship defeats the Spanish in a battle for Port Royal, and Blood is named the new governor, replacing Colonel Bishop. Peter and Arabella declare their love, and Bishop must bow before the man he had sought to hunt down and kill.

For the role of doctor-turned-pirate Peter Blood, the studio turns to Robert Donat and offers the part of Arabella Bishop, Blood's love interest, to controversial Marion Davies, whose career has been financed by publisher William Randolph Hearst. But Donat is a frail fellow plagued by asthma, and Davies isn't interested in playing in an undignified pirate picture. Four months drag by with no stars chosen. Harry Joe Brown of the pre-production team tosses a wide net, declaring that "no man in the business is too big to go after for *Captain Blood*."[1] The front office wishes for the Scarlet Pimpernel himself, Leslie Howard—but Howard is an accomplished stage actor who doesn't want to tarry too long in the adventure pictures.

Warner and Wallis then blue-sky potential Peter Bloods—Fredric March, Clark Gable, and Ronald Colman—all A-list stars of the day. But the Boss possesses neither the patience nor the budget to negotiate with other studios for their hottest contract players, so he settles on the usual course: testing lesser knowns within easy reach at Warner Bros. and selling the public on the spectacle of a pirate picture rather than big-name stars.

By April the screen tests are piling up in Projection Room #5. Warner players Bette Davis, Anita Louise, Jean Muir, and the new girl, Olivia de Havilland, have all tested for Arabella. Brian Aherne tests for Blood, new guy Errol Flynn for a member of Blood's crew, Hagthorpe, and Colin

Life on the set of the epic in the making, *Captain Blood*. Among the group photographed on Stage 3 at Warner Bros. in Burbank are a docile-looking (don't let him fool ya!) Michael Curtiz at left and an ill-at-ease Errol Flynn next to him. Holding a gun on himself and also threatened with a cutlass (no jury in the land would convict his attacker) stands the Boss, Jack L. Warner. (John McElwee Collection)

Clive and Ross Alexander for Captain Blood's lieutenant, Jeremy Pitt.

The Boss sees no progress and he hates that. On April 16 he fumes to Hal Wallis: "I noticed that there are 24 reels of tests for *Captain Blood* accumulated up here in the projection room. I would suggest that instead of you going to Palm Springs for the next weekend that you stay here and run these 24 reels, as it is important for us to know who we are going to cast in this picture."[2]

Two more months go by, with no discernable progress made on casting. The second week in June, desperate to get the Boss off his back, Wallis orders screen tests for the studio's two British imports for the role of Blood—leading man George Brent and the new guy Flynn. Flynn passes this round, but Brent suddenly seems old and bland. *Hmmm, the new guy…his name is kinda catchy. Errol Flynn. We don't even have to change it. He is good-looking, agile as a cat, and yet he's humble and deferential…until he walks on the set and the camera rolls. Then he becomes a pirate captain.*

Wallis kicks the decision up to J.L., and Warner realizes that *threatening* to pull the trigger on a previously unknown leading man is a lot easier than actually pulling it. As far as the Boss is concerned: *We'll look like a couple of boobs for sure if this kid doesn't work out.* They watch the tests and run them over and over and remain unsure.

They bring Flynn back the next week and give another British import, Ian Hunter, a shot at the Blood role. Directed by Mervyn Leroy, both Flynn and Hunter work with Jean Muir, a candidate for Arabella. And director Michael Curtiz oversees one more round of tests of Flynn. This time Wallis wants to see Flynn interacting with the Levasseur and Arabella characters and barking orders on the ship.

"Please let's not have any slip-ups on this series of tests," Wallis memos Curtiz, "as the result of them will determine whether or not Flynn is to do the part."[3] *And whether or not J.L. ends up looking like a dope—and I end up in the soup line.*

Curtiz is an interesting character in his own right. Harry Warner had traveled to Europe personally to sign Michael Curtiz (birth name Mano Kertesz Kaminer), so big had been the Hungarian's reputation, and by 1935 he has already returned the investment many times over, directing some of the studio's most important pictures, including *The*

When asked by her new co-star, Errol Flynn, what she wanted out of life, Olivia talked about recognition for work well done. When she asked the same question of him, he replied, "Fame and success." Livvie was put off by the answer, which she found shallow, but Flynn had already failed at so many jobs, he knew this one could end at any moment, so he had better take what he could get. He will soon start hinting that he might quit the picture business before it quits him. (Robert Florczak Collection)

Mad Genius with John Barrymore and *Doctor X* and *Mystery of the Wax Museum* with Lionel Atwill and Fay Wray and *The Cabin in the Cotton* that broke Bette Davis through and *The Kennel Murder Case* with William Powell and *Mandalay* with Kay Francis and *Jimmy the Gent* with Cagney and *British Agent* with William Powell and Kay Francis and oh by the way *Black Fury* with Paul Muni. Off the set Curtiz is quiet and deferential and loves to learn new things. On the set he's a whirlwind whose trademarks are a passion for hard work and a mangling of the English language.

Curtiz brings a mastery of composition to his pictures, filling the foreground with interesting props, shooting his talent at mad angles, and at every opportunity, throwing a giant shadow into the background for atmosphere. He loves the art form and what a camera can do, but he isn't so gentle with actors; he whips them like nags coming down the home stretch. He is disliked by most performers, and he dislikes many of them right back—he is loathe to shoot close-ups of the ones he doesn't like.

Curtiz is one complex guy, all right. Hal Wallis and his wife Louise are close friends of Curtiz and his wife Bess, and Wallis knows that involving Mike in *Captain Blood* will mean headaches because the man is almost impossible to

Looking like a kid being tutored in trigonometry, Errol studies his dog-eared script and listens to the direction of Michael Curtiz on the set. Hal Wallis tells Curtiz that Flynn appears to be "scared to death" in the dailies and appeals to his director to "work with the boy a little."

control once he gets going. Wallis calls Curtiz "a demon for the work," and he's not sure Mike is the right guy to break in young Errol. The new boy will need some reassurance—not the pressure of a relentless taskmaster.

Curtiz had worked with Flynn earlier that year, and only briefly, on *The Case of the Curious Bride,* a Perry Mason mystery in which Flynn had played a corpse and is seen in a flashback that reveals how he had gotten to *be* a corpse. At the time Curtiz had griped to production supervisor Harry Joe Brown about being forced to use the rookie Flynn. When J.L. had gotten wind of this tirade, he fired off a memo to Hal Wallis that read in part: "I think it is a shame to let people like Curtiz and Harry Joe Brown even think of opposing an order coming from you or myself and…when we bring a man all the way from England he is at least entitled to a chance and somehow or other we haven't given him one. I want to make sure he is in the picture."[4]

Now, in the final round of tests for *Captain Blood,* Curtiz is *still* horrified by what he sees out of Aussie Flynn. Even by actor standards, this fellow stinks. His range is from A to… Well, A is all he's got. Curtiz grumbles that no way can he make a picture with this fellow who stinks and the best thing he can play is a corpse!

But this time Mike knows enough to lay off the griping, because when you have been strong-armed by the Boss, it tends to make an impression.

By the second week in July, it becomes clear to Warner and Wallis that Peter Bloods aren't falling off the local lemon trees and that Flynn is as good as it's going to get. J.L. has talked himself into this fact. He must trust what he keeps seeing in the tests—and J.L. has watched the tests so many times that he has memorized them. This Flynn boy has zero in the finesse department, but he takes up a big space onscreen, all broad shoulders and electric presence—it is a sight to see. "Actor or no actor," Warner says later of new discovery Errol Flynn, "he showered an audience with sparks when he laughed, when he fought, or when he loved. He made people feel young and alive."[5]

Hal Wallis will say, "He leapt from the screen into the projection room with the impact of a bullet."[6]

OK, kid, you got the part. Don't screw it up!

Conventional Hollywood history will imply decades later that Lili Damita wields her influence to secure for Errol the title role in *Captain Blood,* but two facts contradict this notion: First, an impressive string of memos circulating within the front office chronicle the dyspeptic casting process and the desperate feeling of Warner and Wallis, who believe that Flynn is the least offensive of the options at hand. Second, Damita is a fading star at this point who has gambled on Flynn to revive her own career—her position is so tenuous that she can't even find roles for herself, let alone for her husband.

The selection of Flynn changes the dynamics of the cast around him. Tall, blonde Jean Muir is no longer in the running for Arabella; Warner and Wallis take a second look at the young girl from the Shakespeare and comedy pictures, Olivia de Havilland, this time with Flynn. "I was called for a test," says Livvie, "simply a silent test, just to see how the two of us in costume would look together, and that's when I first met him. And I walked onto the set, and they said, 'Would you please stand next to Mr. Flynn?' and I saw him. Oh my! *Oh my!* Struck dumb. I knew it was what the French

18

call a *coup de foudre*." If ever there is a god-like specimen, it is the man she beholds now.[7]

Warner and Wallis, and even Curtiz, take notice of the fact that the lean, commanding six-foot-two Flynn nicely contrasts the delicate, five-foot-three de Havilland. Both have what Hollywood historian Tony Thomas will label years later, "classic good looks, cultured speaking voices, and a sense of distant aristocracy about them."[8] *And both these kids give the feeling that they know about sex. It's the damnedest thing.*

The bosses know about chemistry. They have seen it over the years, yet find it difficult to commit a million-dollar budget on the notion that magic will just happen. But what choice is there? So, de Havilland lands Arabella, interested to be part of something grand, with costumes and thrilling action. She has just turned 19. When Jack Warner knows Flynn better, he will understand never to leave good-looking 19-year-old girls lying around the soundstage, no matter how well bred they are.

One aspect of the casting of Flynn and de Havilland is often overlooked: This picture will be a Cosmopolitan Productions release. Says Flynn historian Michael Mazzone, "Cosmopolitan was a William Randolph Hearst company that produced Marion Davies pictures. Hearst took Cosmopolitan to Warner Bros. in 1934 to continue the career of Davies in pictures like *Cain and Mabel*. There were also some side deals in which Hearst had a vested interest, and *Captain Blood* was one of those."[9] And J.L. knows that as a Cosmopolitan Production, his pirate picture will benefit from the clout of market saturation in Hearst's newspaper and magazine empire totaling nine million readers—readers who will find the sexy young stars and their globe-trotting life stories interesting.

The Flynn that Livvie begins to work with is clearly lost in the sea of soundstages, his brown eyes wide and his jaw set. She is on her fourth picture, so she does what she can to help. He is so tall and lean, graceful as a panther. When he speaks, there is the barest hint of Aussie in his voice; she finds it enchanting. And he doesn't say much; when he does, it's a quiet observation, a quip, sometimes self-deprecating and always charming, and every word heats up her heart to the point of melting. But she also senses his worldliness, so she must remain aloof.

Her official opinion of him is rose-colored: "He has so much humor and charm and vitality, and he really is all of those things that a hero is supposed to be.... He can ride and swim and play tennis and sail, and...fence and fight."[10]

Young, impressionable Olivia de Havilland falls for Errol Flynn hard, as she will always fall for men. "Somebody walks into your life," she says a couple of years later, "and before you know it, you are in love with him. You want to be with him all the time, you are thrilled by his very presence, worry about him, have his happiness and interests at heart. It's fearful and wonderful. And it's blind. The ancient Greeks were wise enough to make Cupid blind. Love has no rhyme or reason."[11]

But there *is* a reason, in that each learns through their conversations the astounding number of things they have in common, not the least of which is a brutal childhood

Errol visits Lili on the set of *Frisco Kid*, the feature she is making with James Cagney across the lot. This will be Damita's last hurrah in pictures, with much of her footage on the cutting room floor.

At least de Havilland had been the female lead in three pictures by the time *Captain Blood* came along. Flynn had only been a bit player in Burbank up to now, but he *had* spent years bluffing his way through jobs and did it again now. "We would sit very quietly in our canvas chairs, saying very little to each other," said Livvie of their experience on the soundstages. Here Guy Kibbee, playing Hagthorpe (the role for which Flynn originally had tested), mugs for the uncomfortable pair during a break on Stage 8. (John McElwee Collection)

lived under the rule of a smothering parent. So the cultured girl from Saratoga falls for the Australian roustabout, and Flynn is knocked loopy as well. He has had many women and he has come to understand that when a woman has had many men, the seducing is mutual. A proposition is made by one or the other, usually by her, and they retire to the nearest bed or quiet corner. This is different, because young Olivia gives the impression that she has *not* been around, and Flynn doesn't know what to do. She will open up for short stretches and flirt with him, but always she will back off, and he is forced to stammer; worse, he is reduced to politeness!

To Flynn, de Havilland is a puzzle. She is wide-eyed, with a radiant smile, and her handshake is firm, like a man's. Her laugh is the peal of church bells. She blushes easily, and it's utterly charming. Her hair is baby fine and always a mess under a scarf when she arrives in the morning. She brushes her teeth obsessively, after she eats anything or nothing. She sketches quietly as she waits for her calls. She can withdraw as she sits there and suddenly be lost over the horizon, a hundred miles away. The way her eyes get sometimes, and the way she withdraws sometimes, it's as if she has been off to the wars and is now back home living with dark remembrances. On Olivia de Havilland, the ol' Flynn charm doesn't work, and he simply finds her distant. She is a closed book.

Livvie has a secret that Flynn doesn't know; one that takes her years to figure out herself. As she puts it in retrospect: "I have a fear of being unloved, or of believing I'm loved and finding out that I'm not." She traces it back to her father's move with the maid when Livvie and Joanie were infants. "It has profoundly affected my life."[12] Especially now, when she is knocked off her pins by Errol, the second male of the species, after Peter, to have such an effect, her psyche will *protect* and keep a guy with such potential power over her at arm's length.

As a result, Flynn is alone at Warner Bros., a newly minted leading man with no friends, no advisors except Damita—and there are already cracks in that relationship. Now that he has landed the role of Blood, his wife (he can't believe he has been cursed with a wife!) has grown unpleasant, short-tempered, and often just plain angry. He has no idea what this is about. He thinks back to Mother and her similar moods. Beatings. Recriminations. He recalls a vague awareness of other men about, as if to punish the child and break up the family with extramarital sex.

Livvie sees the intimidating little French diva at the studio, casting dark-eyed daggers. Damita is making a picture on another soundstage, so she has ready access. The youngster backs away, failing to understand what goes on, but knowing on instinct *not* to become involved. It seems she has walked in on adults speaking a different language, looking past her, over her head. She goes home to the Chateau des Fleurs and tells her mother about the days as they go by.

Both stars are told to fix their teeth—Livvie prior to the first day of shooting, and Errol a couple of weeks into production. It is an interesting exercise to watch Flynn's teeth in various scenes, mostly straight and white, but once in a while discolored and broken. Over the years, he has acquired the habit of curling his lips over his teeth to hide them. He can't quite get used to his new choppers and has to be encouraged to show his now-pearly whites.

The studio is in his mouth and in his head—a head that is spinning, trying to memorize his lines, learning how to hit his marks and how to react to the dialogue of others. He must deal with lights everywhere, relentless, hot lights. And the sweat they produce, sopping sweat that drenches his costumes. The high-pitched Curtiz produces sweat as well, along with studio executives who watch from behind the lights. "I worked as hard as I knew how," says an earnest Flynn, who learns to keep his head buried in his script.[13] "We would sit very quietly in our canvas chairs, saying very little to each other," Livvie will remember years later.[14]

The shoot proceeds roughly in continuity, beginning in early August 1935, with a petrified Flynn, the guy who can talk his way out of any jam, finally meeting his match on a Warner Bros. soundstage under the direction of Michael Curtiz. Much footage is shot that later must be reshot because of the paralysis of the star.

The first meeting of Arabella Bishop and Peter Blood in the slave market, wherein she purchases him to spite her uncle, was shot on the old Prospect Avenue Vitagraph backlot on a blazing August day, but Wallis disliked the results and ordered a reshoot. Flynn failed to convey the coldness of a slave, and de Havilland displayed none of the impetuousness required of the moment. The reshoot was blocked with Flynn pulled away from the other prisoners so he and Livvie could play their introductory scene without dozens of extras close by.

Wallis watches the early dailies, notices terror in Errol Flynn's eyes and a tautness in his jaw, and pleads with Curtiz to ease up: "If you will work with the boy a little, and give him a little confidence, I know he can be twice as good as he is now, but the fellow looks like he is scared to death every time he goes into a scene. I don't know what the hell is the matter. When he has confidence and gets into a scene, he plays it charmingly."[15]

Flynn *is* listening to Curtiz and trying to get it right. "Errol was terribly ambitious," says de Havilland. "He wanted to be a success so badly and when we sat in that screening room to look at the first dailies, Mike ridiculed the footage unmercifully. And Errol did nothing, there was nothing he could do, not then when he was just starting, but I could feel the hurt for him on the other side of the room."[16]

De Havilland shows up 16 minutes into the film, and her Arabella is, at first, young, beautiful, classy, self-assured, headstrong, and unconventional. For the first few reels she helps to drive the plot, purchasing Peter Blood as her personal property presumably because she identifies with the gentleman slave—she too is a prisoner on the island; she observes Blood holding his ground against her uncle the authority figure, and it draws her attention and her interest.

The Warner Bros. publicity department received orders to sell the sex with these two. Errol and Livvie were posed in a variety of places, including on the lawn between the executive office building and the star dressing rooms. They barely knew each other, but minus the pressures of soundstage and sadistic director, the euphoria of their mutual infatuation is evident. (John McElwee Collection)

The courtroom scene wherein Blood and the others are sentenced to enslavement in the Americas is shot in the heat of a Los Angeles summer, with carbon arc lights beating down. Perspiration glistens on the foreheads of actors who are sweating faster than they can be blotted dry. The result is authentic; we believe that Peter Blood is arguing for his life and that the judge is a dying man. But Flynn is sweating for other reasons; he has no idea what he's doing.

The first two scenes played together by Flynn and de Havilland show the barest hint of chemistry between the characters, but none between the actors themselves. Their faces and eyes are tense, particularly in a garden scene, their second in the picture. Curtiz continues to drive them hard; they never feel that they can get their feet under them and grow into their characters.

Not far into production, Hal Wallis wonders what he has gotten himself into with Curtiz, who clearly loves the craft of making pictures, but likes to do it *his way*, and with a great deal of staginess. Wallis memos the director: "The stuff, generally, is good, but I feel that you are letting some of the people over-act. The worst offenders are Lionel Atwill, the man who is playing the governor, and now this new character who is playing the part of the Spaniard...who makes the speech about the men who have taken over the city.... You must hold these people down a little, or the thing is going to be ludicrous; they are over-acting and chewing scenery. Can't you see it on the set while they are doing it? Nobody is natural or real. Everybody is acting, and acting all over the place!"[17]

Pedro de Cordoba portrays the overblown Spaniard, and the scene in the governor's chamber is, to Wallis, typical of the downside of Curtiz: Giant shadows of Spanish soldiers splash against the far wall, a flaming candelabra lights the foreground and blinds all who dare look, and in the middle of it all, de Cordoba overacts.

In the dailies Wallis is especially displeased with his leading lady: "The little girl, de Havilland, is not as good as she has been in other pictures. She seems to have lost a naturalness...a sparkle.... She should be spontaneous, and bright, and light, and she has a sparkle in her eye, but in this picture, it doesn't seem to come out."[18] A day later Wallis is demanding retakes of the scene where Peter and Arabella meet in the slave market. Wallis tells Curtiz that "I will discuss the scene with you in detail before you shoot it" to assure that the director gets it right this time.[19]

Saddled with a novice star and co-star who are handled roughly by the director, Wallis is having kittens by early September. He memos his editor, George Amy, "I am very anxious to see some cut stuff on *Blood* just as soon as possible. When you get this note, leave word with [Walter] MacEwen how much stuff you have together now, and if I can look at it immediately after lunch today. Also leave word with him when I can see the sequence in the Slave Market cut."[20]

The memos fly fast and furious as Wallis tries to rein in his hard-driven friend Curtiz. The soft sell hasn't worked, so Wallis decides to become more aggressive.

Thanks to Arabella, Dr. Blood earns his way into favor on the island by curing the royal governor of gout. On the night the slaves are to escape, Blood is called to the governor's bedroom unexpectedly, which threatens to ruin the planned escape.

Terror on Stage 18: Livvie and Errol listen to direction from Mike Curtiz prior to shooting their second scene together. (John McElwee Collection)

On location at Laguna Beach, the audacious pirate Captain Levasseur (Basil Rathbone) menaces Arabella Bishop and Lord Willoughby (Henry Stephenson) with his horrific French accent, which veers from Charles Boyer to Bela Lugosi between one sentence and the next. Flynn, ever insecure and jealous of anyone paying too much attention to his would-be girlfriend, is bothered by the attention that Rathbone pays to de Havilland, which will continue two years later during production of *Robin Hood*.

Wallis is incensed when he sees the dailies and dictates a memo to Mike: "That scene in the bedroom, between Captain Blood and the governor, had one punch line in it; the line from Blood: 'I'll have you well by tonight, if I have to bleed you to death,' or something along these lines, anyhow. This is the one punch line to get over that Blood had to get out of there by midnight, even if he had to kill the governor, and instead of playing that in a close-up—a big head close-up—and getting over the reaction of Errol Flynn, and what he is trying to convey, and the crafty look in his eye, you play it in a long shot, so that you can get the composition of a candlestick and a wine bottle on a table in the foreground, which I don't give a damn about."[21]

Curtiz and his shadows. Curtiz and his candelabras. Curtiz and his foregrounds. All this art is getting in the way of the story!

Curtiz shoots the scene where the slaves come to America in the hold of a ship, and Wallis sees in the dailies that the hold looks like an airy apartment, roomy and scrupulously clean, with the slaves lounging about in comfort. "Why didn't you have more people in the interior of the hold on the slave ship?" writes Wallis to Curtiz. "When you moved in there, I understand that you had a lot of people out on the street, and that you let them go, and only picked out a small number for the slave ship. This should have been packed solid with people—there should have been a lot of people in there, to make the thing look uncomfortable and all of that—but instead, there were only a dozen or so men scattered around." Wallis orders the scene to be redone; when it is, he still won't be happy because the hold will continue to swallow the number of actors that Curtiz puts into it. Some of the scenes that Wallis complains about will remain in the picture because *everything* can't be reshot. He closes the memo with an exasperated, "I want you to write me a note and let me know why you do these things."[22]

On September 10 Wallis watches a scene between Livvie and veteran character actor Henry Stephenson in the hold of Blood's ship, then goes on the warpath about costume designer Dwight Franklin: "I don't want Dwight Franklin on the Curtiz set from now on. I raised hell with Mike today because he had a big, beautiful bowl of fruit right in the foreground on the boat going somewhere in the middle of the ocean, and the story I got is—that Franklin said it was perfectly all right because they put in at islands, or some such silly story. I thought Franklin was hired to make sketches and see that our costumes were done properly and to help wherever he could with suggestions on the construction of sets, and this is all I want him to do in the future. Will you please instruct him accordingly, and I don't want him to have any more contact with Curtiz."[23]

Then Wallis experiences motion sickness over Mike's innovative camera movements to simulate the rocking of the ship. "The movement of the camera going up and back only did one thing as far as I am concerned, and that was to make me dizzy and detract so much from the action that I don't know what the hell the people are talking about. I have told Mike to discontinue this in the future."[24]

Not all the dailies spell trouble. Wallis watches a lovely little scene one day, after Dr. Blood has become Pirate Blood, and at night his ship passes, from a distance, another ship, this one carrying Arabella to England. There is natural tension—will the pirate ship attack the passenger ship? Blood and his cronies consider the possibility but ultimately decide against it. "Sail on, little ship," says Flynn as Blood, looking through his spy glass. Arabella is awakened by the lookout's cry of a ship to starboard. She sits up in bed, beautifully backlit, and looks out her window at Blood's distant vessel. It is, for Curtiz, an especially quiet, subtle scene, nicely written, directed, and played.

From September 16 to 20, the crew moves to Laguna Beach to shoot the confrontation between pirate captains Blood and Levasseur on the Island of Virgen Magra, marking the beginning of Flynn's career as a cinematic swordsman. It is a difficult shoot, marked by bad weather, milky gray skies, audio challenges brought on by the pounding surf, and two actors—Errol Flynn and Basil Rathbone—who know nothing of fencing and yet must navigate sand, rocks, and seawater as their surfside duel unfolds. Curtiz brings in expert fencers to double the stars, causing Wallis to claw at the armrests over more offenses: "The dailies are coming in of the duel between Errol Flynn's double and the other double, and they don't look anything like the principals. The wigs are a different color, and they aren't dressed at all—they're all sticking out on the ends, they're not nicely taken care of—and, seemingly, when a double goes in to do a scene, the hair-dresser and everybody else must be looking out the window, or at the scenery, or something, because they certainly don't seem to make any effort to take care of the people...just because they are doubles."[25]

By this page of the script, de Havilland has been reduced to a five-foot-three cardboard standee, directed by Curtiz to display various degrees of curiosity, loathing, and knuckle-chewing fear. The wigs aren't the only problem

It's no day at the beach as all eyes at Laguna fix on Errol Flynn and Basil Rathbone (at center, in white shirts), including J. Carrol Naish, Ross Alexander, Henry Stephenson, and Olivia de Havilland (standing together at left) as Mike Curtiz (far right, in front of the man in the pith helmet) barks direction. The sky is a milky gray and the light is flat, necessitating a battery of carbon arcs. The pounding surf hisses into the boom microphone, forcing the actors to nearly shout their lines. (Robert Florczak Collection)

The last scene to be reshot was the sequence filmed near Palm Springs on November 10, 1935. In it Errol and Olivia dismount for a conversation that ends when Peter Blood steals a kiss from Arabella—the first onscreen smooch of Errol and Olivia. The real thing would have to wait a while. (John McElwee Collection)

with the Virgen Magra duel to the death. The fencing plays clumsily in *Captain Blood* if one considers the heights of science achieved only five years later in the furious, gymnastic duel to the death between this same Basil Rathbone and Tyrone Power in *The Mark of Zorro*.

But here at Laguna Rathbone and Flynn play it like kids in the backyard, with no technique and a lot of harmless clicking of blades. The real fencers would come in, bad wigs and all, and put on an exhibition, and then turn it back to the novices. Rathbone would boast that even though Flynn's characters could run him through according to the scripts, Rathbone is the real fencer and can take Flynn any time he wants. Well, maybe, but it sure doesn't show in the *Captain Blood* swordfight. (Christopher Lee would make the same boast after working with Flynn in the 1950s.)

Back in the studio they shoot for another month—for Wallis the chore of trying to rein in Curtiz is unrelenting. "I have talked to you about four thousand times," he writes on September 30, "until I am blue in the face, about the wardrobe in the picture." Under no circumstances is Flynn to be decked out in silk and lace. Well, that's exactly what Curtiz puts him in, in the scene where Blood directs the dividing of the loot. "I suppose that when he goes into the battle with the [French] at the finish, you'll probably be having him wear a high silk hat and spats."[26]

And then the memo to end all memos, sent this same day: "When you get this note I want you to stop shooting and come up and see me, and I want to find out once and for all why it is that you insist on doing things that I tell you not to do."[27]

Time heals all wounds, and Wallis will call Curtiz "my favorite director, then and always."[28] The final pictures always justify the decision to use the volatile Hungarian, but that doesn't mean Wallis finds it easy to use him.

Battle scenes are shot last and cut into stock footage left over from a number of silent pictures. The result is, somehow, a spectacular, visceral, thrilling climax to the picture, with Captain Blood's pirates out-dueling a squadron of French vessels in Port Royal Harbor. More and more during production, the front office orders up shots that showcase Errol Flynn. When they learn that he is a superb swimmer, a scene is written so that Flynn can slip into the water and steal a Spanish longboat. Since he is able to ride at the gallop on horseback, they want him to be seen doing it. When time comes for the final battle, Flynn swings from ship to ship, leading the attack. Despite the reservations of Curtiz, Flynn becomes a star thanks to these new scenes and reshoots of Curtiz setups that had favored the composition over the players in some cases. In the end Flynn wins, and so does the studio.

But what of de Havilland? Hal Wallis is unimpressed. The picture closes on Thursday, October 24, but on November 7, Wallis memos Harry Joe Brown: "Please get Casey Robinson immediately and have him re-write the end of the scene between Flynn and de Havilland that we shot at Palm Springs, retaining everything in the present scene but letting it end with Flynn kissing de Havilland and her slapping his face, and then a finish on the scene so that he can get on his horse and exit. Let's have this done as soon as possible so that we can shoot Monday."[29] The company travels back to Palm Springs for that last scene, with Blood rubbing his face after she has slapped it.

BLOOD: Your slave is grateful for all marks of favor.

ARABELLA: When you forget your slavery and go so far—

BLOOD: (interrupting, intensely) Now there you're mistaken. However far this slave may go, he won't forget. (brightens) It's a characteristic we Irish have in common with the elephants.

He leads his horse offscreen and is seen riding away as the camera moves in on her fretting reaction. *Cut! Print!*

Perhaps Curtiz is anxious to wrap, but his direction of this scene reveals his weakness with the human side of his stories and a lack of full coverage (shooting both wide shots and close-ups) that would also fuel Wallis's temper. Curtiz allows de Havilland to purse her lips when Flynn kisses her, almost frightened, as if she's being molested, and then her theatrical slap hits his shoulder and neck—she is afraid to slap Errol Flynn's face! Curtiz would have been wise to obtain full coverage, running through the scene once with a master shot (which he did), then a second time over de Havilland's shoulder and close on Flynn, and a third time close on de Havilland. Editors back at the studio expect full coverage, but Curtiz doesn't provide it for them. The practice he uses is called "editing in the camera," providing only the shots he wants, assuring that his vision will be maintained. Despite the Curtiz lack of coverage, the first hint of onscreen chemistry between 26-year-old Errol and 19-year-old Livvie is visible in the martini shot of the production, their last major scene together.

And so ends the first Flynn-de Havilland collaboration. They exit with an education-and-a-half in epic filmmaking, a strong bond forged under combat conditions, and feelings of bewilderment about the retakes—having no notion of the battles of the gods above them.

More than two weeks earlier, Wallis had written to the post-production department: "We have definitely scheduled *Captain Blood* for release in all theaters, with about 200 release dates, for Christmas week. This means that we must ship the picture around November 25, for they need at least a month to get out all of these prints, and to properly set this up, exploit it, etc."[30] Such were the times that with no computers, no high definition, no digital video files or non-linear editing systems, with manpower hand-splicing the cuts, Wallis gives his people two weeks to final-edit his two-hour film, including the process shots and many titles, and produce 200 copies for distribution around the country.

It is no coincidence that Warner places his editing booths right across the tennis court from the executive office building, visible from his window. He likes to keep his eyes on the editors to see who's working and who isn't, and they're all working hard in November 1935.

The bosses know now that the *Blood* experiment is going to work. They can feel it in their bones. Errol Flynn will be a star. The de Havilland girl is just another ingénue, but Flynn has what it takes.

Elaborate sessions for the still camera are part of the process, and Livvie doesn't mind posing with Errol; it's a quiet time away from the director and crew, and she and her prospective beau get to be safely romantic together. (John McElwee Collection)

THE LITTLEST PIRATE

Welcome to the world of the big boys, Livvie—the grown-up boys with visceral desires, financial and physical, who run Hollywood. And these boys believe that Olivia de Havilland is a dish best served raw. The publicity department, with J.L.'s blessing, wastes no time promoting the new ingénue, not yet of legal age, via a photo shoot that drags her out of her shell and places her in a satin blouse, miniskirt, stockings, and leather boots for dozens of poses, only a fraction of which are reproduced here. Discreetly airbrushed because Livvie's legs are a little heavier than the rest of her, the result is Arabella from the Bizarro World, a harlot who would become an integral part of the *Captain Blood* publicity push and be plastered in newspapers and theaters around the world. And do you suppose that Errol Flynn would lower himself to track down a full set at the first opportunity? You can count on it!

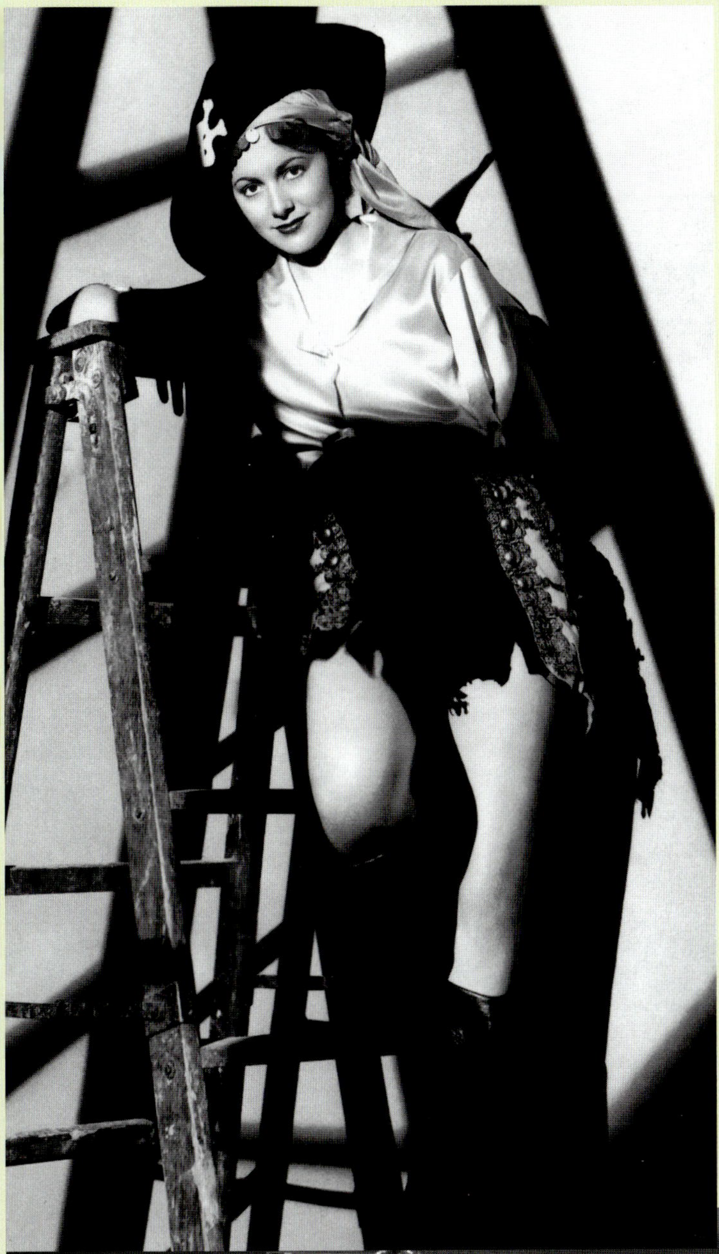
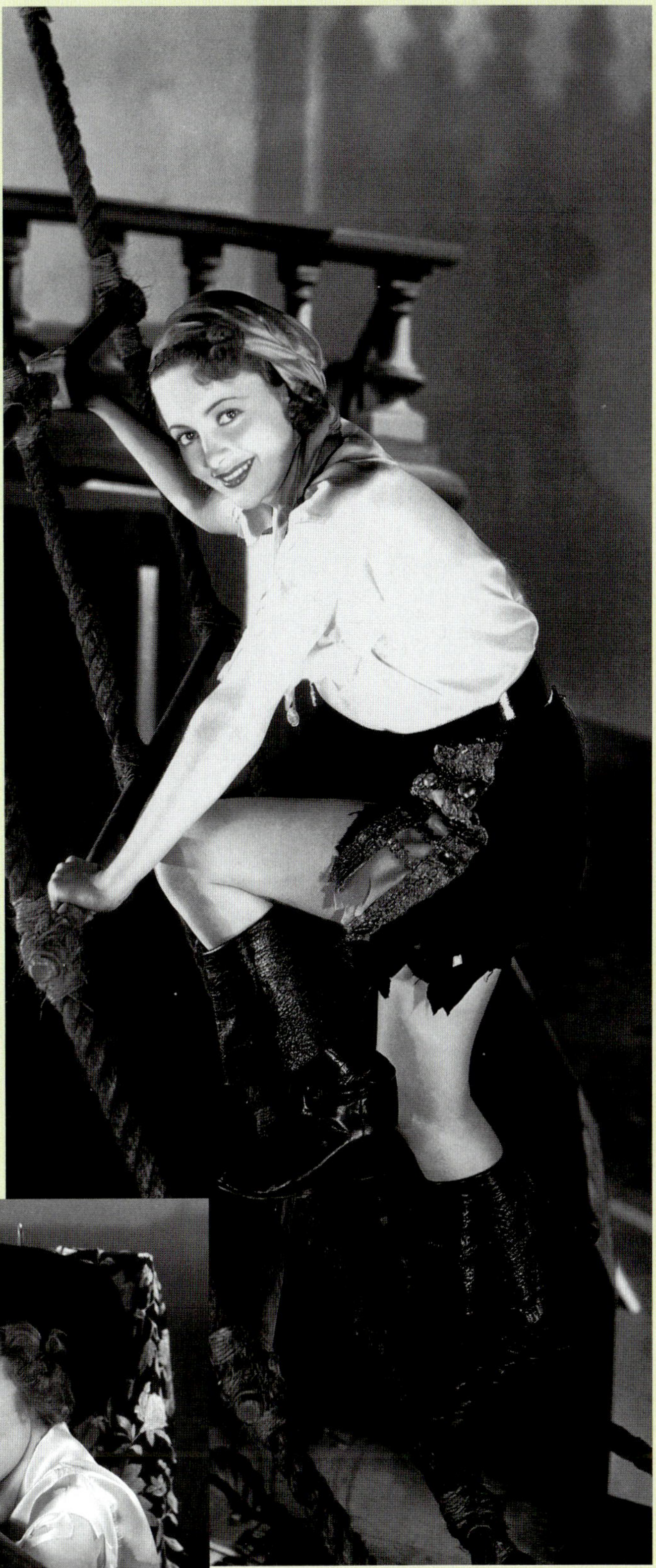
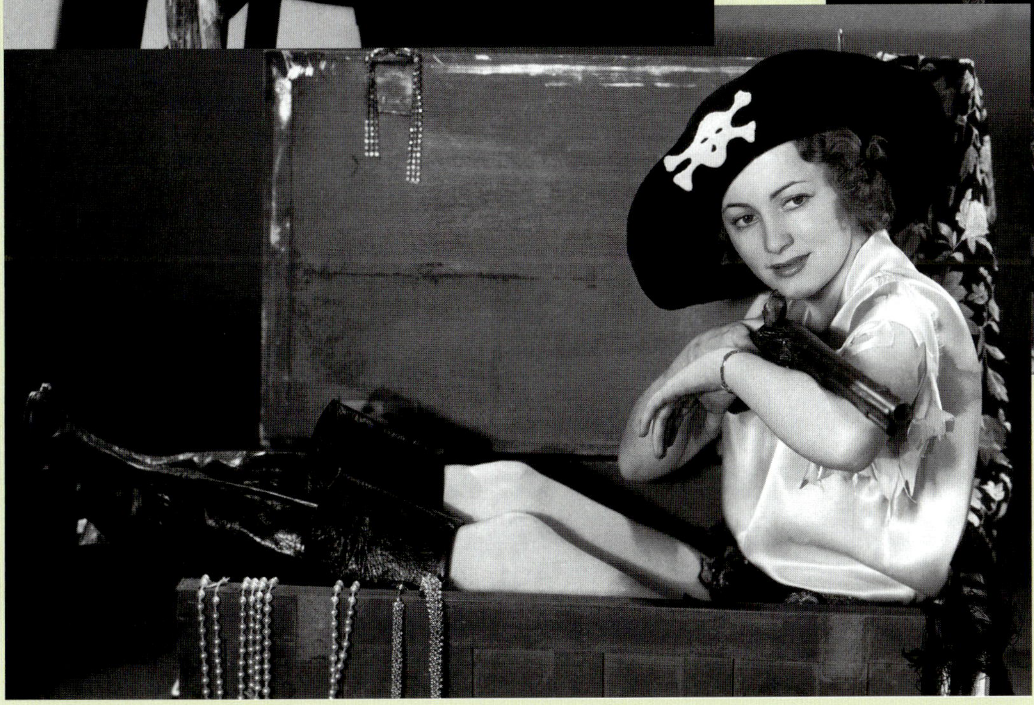

Their second feature together is remarkably different in look and feel from the first, considering that both are products of the same studio and director. The stagebound portions of *The Charge of the Light Brigade* feature lush, romantic backlighting of the principals. Unfortunately, the plot isn't as pretty as the pictures.

3 FLASHMAN AND THE LADY

"There were ominous crashes from below at every plunge. She pitched and heaved and rolled and tossed and the seas came green over the deck. Then suddenly all was calm. We had taken about five minutes to pass through Sydney Heads. The conflicting cross currents and heavy swell make an unexpected maelstrom which gives a small boat a quick but severe trouncing."[1]

Flynn writes in longhand, his mind racing back to his carefree, roustabout days in the South Pacific. Sometimes the writing comes easily, but usually it does not. He scans the Hollywood Hills from the Appian Way fortress above, with Los Angeles dead ahead in the distance and off to the right, the blue Pacific. He likes the place well enough. Motoring across Mulholland Drive and down the death spiral of Laurel Canyon, he leaves Burbank behind. At night he can look up at the blue-black velvet sky laced with stars and think back to similar nights at sea in the old days, and this helps him to write this novel to be called *Beam Ends* that is heavily influenced by his days sailing *Sirocco* in the South Pacific. Publishers are interested because he is Errol Flynn, star of motion pictures.

After his first starring picture nets a $1.462 million profit, people care what Errol Flynn has to say, and they pay attention to the fact that he labels himself a writer. A hundred times a day he thinks back to the premiere of *Captain Blood*, the popping of the flashbulbs, the carbon arcs piercing the night sky. He likes being a star. At the same time he doesn't miss the soundstages and the barked orders of that lousy Curtiz. Flynn hears from the studio that Curtiz won't be around on the next picture, which will be directed by Frank Borzage, just off of the Dick Powell-Ruby Keeler musicals and some Kay Francis pictures. If Flynn never experiences the ravings of Curtiz again, it will be too soon.

Life is awfully good for Errol Flynn these days. He lives in luxury with Damita, and she offers high-quality sex any time he wants it. Twenty-odd years later, when he is in the autumn of his life and has little good to say about Damita, Flynn will still allow that she is about the sexiest woman he had ever known and that she had taken him new places between the sheets—which is saying something. She also takes him other places, to the best social gatherings, to Carole Lombard's parties, and to the Ronald Colmans, and to Pickfair and San Simeon. The beautiful pair cavorts with other stars, turning heads wherever they go. Their reign as *the* Hollywood Couple won't last long, but they are making the most of it.

It will be Flynn biographer John Hammond Moore who first likens the young Errol to Harry Flashman, the blackhearted Victorian rogue of a series of adventure novels by George MacDonald Fraser, which had in turn been inspired by the same character as presented during adolescence in the 1857 Thomas Hughes novel, *Tom Brown's Schooldays*.

Says John Hammond Moore of the Flashman character as interpreted by Fraser: "Volume one proclaims Flashman to be bully, liar, womanizer, coward...yet irresistible. Errol Flynn was, to some extent, all of these—but there was an essential difference. He assumed each role with more style, grace, and charm than Harry Flashman could muster even in his balmiest days."[2] The similarities are rising to the surface now, after the release of *Captain Blood*, when Flynn

Hair and makeup tests are never fun for the talent. Here 19-year-old Livvie tries on her "older self" as the mistress of Napoleon in *Anthony Adverse*. Crew members are routinely misspelling her name, even after *Captain Blood*. (John McElwee Collection)

doesn't have to be so damn polite or work so damn hard, because he finds work to be loathsome, and he can enjoy his time away from his oppressors, namely the Boss and his henchman, Mike Curtiz.

So Flynn writes his book and wrestles with his hellcat in the sack—and bickers with her everywhere else—while Olivia de Havilland is immersed in a different kind of passionate opportunity. The film is *Anthony Adverse*, based on the immensely popular 1933 historical novel by Hervey Allen that had been written in brooding Victor Hugo style—noble child is orphaned and grows up poor, only to learn of his lineage later in life, meet his true love, part from her, suffer the torments of the damned, and then find her again years later—and learn that the love is doomed. Livvie is cast opposite popular 38-year-old leading man Fredric March, who is a 1932 Academy Award winner and yet no Errol Flynn when it comes to adventure pictures. In a role Flynn was born to play—virile young man with a chip on his shoulder—the middle-aged March stumbles along, while Livvie's role is truly minor. She will receive second billing, but show up only sporadically, at first to win Anthony's heart and then later to break it when he learns that she has become the mistress of Napoleon Bonaparte.

The role of a fallen woman forced by circumstances and loneliness into such a sordid life is ill-suited to a 19-year-old, and between the miscast hero and the miscast heroine, *Anthony Adverse* will not stand the test of time. It does, however, prove to be a splendid training ground for a young actress, working with seasoned screen actor March and director Mervyn LeRoy, veteran of *Little Caesar*, *I Am a Fugitive from a Chain Gang*, and *Gold Diggers of 1933*. LeRoy is an actor's director, and Olivia likes him. March is a lecherous wolf of the highest order, which she learns to appreciate not at all—another kind of training ground for a starlet.

Livvie is seen by the executives as a decent find at a decent price, but in her year in town she has learned that a leading lady in motion picture spectacles should expect to earn *more* than $200 a week. Soon after *Anthony Adverse* wraps, Wallis wires Warner: "Some weeks ago Olivia de Havilland contacted us, as you know, and talked about an adjustment. I think it would be a very wise move at this time to call her in and make an adjustment with her. A year of her contract is already passed, and if we wait too long it is going to be difficult to make a deal."[3]

J.L. proposes a set of numbers for de Havilland: $450 a week for the first year, bumped to 550 the second, then 850, 1,000, 1,400, 1,750, and finally 2,250. The Boss knows he's low balling, and if the kid goes for it, fine. If not, no harm done. It will be a typical star contract, with the talent working 40 weeks per year, with 12 weeks on unpaid layoff.

Then Livvie, who is indeed learning fast to protect her interests, pulls a surprise and hires professional actors' reps of the Ivan Kahn Agency as her mouthpiece. She had heard of Kahn from her first leading man, Joe E. Brown. On

March 28 Ivan Kahn rejects J.L.'s salary numbers and presents the studio with a counteroffer. She will agree to a five-year contract starting at $600, a six-year deal starting at $750, or a seven-year deal that starts at $1,000 a week and ends at $4,000 in the seventh year. Those are numbers that clear the sinuses of Jack Warner and Hal Wallis in an instant. The proposal reflects for the first time Livvie's regrets at signing her life away. If they take the most affordable of the offers, she won't just make more money. She'll also gain her freedom two years earlier.

Studio legal head R. J. Obringer presents J.L. with Kahn's salary proposal. The Boss is used to stealing the lunches of "movie stars" on these contracts, but now he realizes that dishy little de Havilland has a conniving head on those pretty shoulders. J.L. sits in his office, picks up a pencil, and scribbles a new set of numbers: 500 750 1000 1250 1500 2000 2500. Nice round numbers that he can live with because this kid is making the studio a fortune.

Ivan Kahn advises Livvie to take the deal. She is already learning hard truths about the picture business, including the truth about Errol Flynn pictures, in the bargain becoming a self-professed Hollywood snob. The view around town is that Flynn has no pedigree as an actor; therefore his pictures earn no respect from people in the know at Warner Bros. and elsewhere. One features writer says of the way Flynn had backed into pictures, "Flynn is far, far from the conventional actor. He has none of the mannerisms, ideas, ideals, aims, thoughts and looks of the average actor. He's an accident to the acting profession, pure and simple and Hollywood resents it."[4]

Flynn himself shows a growing lack of appreciation for the regimentation of his studio. He adopts a nonchalance

Lights can heat up the set ten degrees in five minutes, so they're killed for rehearsal as Luis Alberni stands on an apple box to deliver his lines to Fredric March and Olivia de Havilland during production of *Anthony Adverse*. Mervyn LeRoy slumps in his director's chair to watch; Director of Photography Tony Gaudio (in trademark driving cap) and crew look on gangster-like from the other side of the camera.

that J.L. finds alarming. "It's a job," says Flynn with a shrug. "First you get them and then you lose them."[5]

In the 1940s de Havilland will look back on this period and say with a sigh, "I most painfully grew up."[6]

By now she is already an unhappy human being, trapped in her own skin, having experienced *that* upbringing, not as herself but as G.M.'s vision of what she should be. Becoming an actress has taken her further away from any concept of *self*, and the public adulation that goes along with fame has spoiled her as well. For the next 10 years writers will say that she is a frantic bundle of energy, multi-faceted to be sure, charming as all get-out, and under it all, unhappy. Now she turns her unhappiness not on Flynn but on the properties developed for him.

De Havilland will say much later on the topic of her growing snobbery: "Those [Flynn] films didn't have much prestige on the lot. We had many very intellectual writers and they sat around at the writers' table [in the commissary] and they dominated the lot quite interestingly. Nobody who was in the Errol Flynn films had any prestige at all, but Paul Muni's films had prestige, all of Bette [Davis]'s films had prestige, and we were second-class citizens out there."[7]

Says Warner Bros. historian Rudy Behlmer, "*A Midsummer Night's Dream* would have been considered in 1935 a prestige picture. You're dealing with Shakespeare, and you're dealing with Max Reinhardt, who at that time was a big man on campus. *The Story of Louis Pasteur* and *The Life of Emile Zola* would have been considered prestige pictures because of the subject matter and social implications, and because of *Mr. Paul Muni* of course. He was billed as *Mr.* Paul Muni. *Tovarich* would have had prestige because it was sophisticated, continental in aspects, and had big stars like Claudette Colbert and Charles Boyer."[8] Flynn pictures aren't so encumbered with thought-provoking subject matter, sophistication, or social implications. They are escapist adventure, where Depression-rattled audiences are invited to shift their brains into idle and enjoy the show.

Someone—likely Ivan Kahn—has poisoned the well for Olivia de Havilland, and at the tender age of 19, her thrill at wearing grand costumes and being rescued by Flynn is gone. The adventure pictures are nothing; the prestige pictures are everything. Flynn is nothing; Muni and Davis are everything. How can you have a crush on someone whose pictures aren't important?

How can you *not* have a crush on Errol Flynn? The conflict confuses her because they still have so much in common, and they are still in this thing together.

Prestige or no, the Warner Bros. executive offices are alive with costume pictures. *Anthony Adverse* is moving right along, and J.L. has set his sights on Paramount's *Lives of a Bengal Lancer*, now in release to sensational reviews and outstanding business. Late in 1935 the production of *Lancer* had been the talk of the town, causing the Boss to run the picture over and over in his home. His people are told: *Gentlemen, this studio has to answer with something—what's it going to be?*

Boss, you know what would make a great picture? The charge of the Light Brigade.

Say…you're right; that would be something. We need to put Flynn in a big picture. That accent will work for the British Empire. I don't know, though—the Crimean War—who knows anything about that? Or gives a damn? Get me some research on the Crimean war. Let's think about this.

They come back with some collected material purchased from a newspaperman named Michel Jacoby, who had combed through historical records and knows the whole story.

One of the young studio writers, Rowland Leigh, is assigned to work with Jacoby on story development for a picture based on the Light Brigade. They begin by working backward: *OK, so we have this great climax, but the real story isn't a good one in terms of how and why the charge was made. The fact is that the British commanders had been brothers-in-law and hated each other and refused to communicate and disaster resulted. It's too confusing! It'll never play.*

Leigh and Jacoby construct a convoluted tale set, not in Crimea, but in India, a stage that has worked well for *Bengal Lancer*. The story involves two brothers of the British army, officers Geoffrey and Perry Vickers of the 27th Lancers, in love with the same girl, Elsa Campbell, daughter of a British commander. Geoffrey and Elsa are engaged, but she is secretly in love with younger brother Perry. The British Army is trying to negotiate with a local Indian chieftain, Surat Khan, and on a hunt for big cats, Geoffrey saves the life of Khan, who is about to be eaten by a leopard.

Horror at 3,700 feet: Flynn smiles bravely as stunt men move into position near cold, dusty Lone Pine, California. In the distance can be seen snow-capped mountains; snow would plague the five-day location shoot. (John McElwee Collection)

When the British are no longer willing to pay Surat Khan for his loyalty, he defects to the Russians, and soon overruns the 27th Garrison at Chukoti, massacring the soldiers there and the wives and children of the Lancers out on patrol, although Geoffrey and Elsa manage an escape thanks to Surat Khan, who evens the score for Vickers' earlier heroics. The Lancers are then transferred to the Crimea where war has broken out, and Khan also heads thataway, setting up the final confrontation. Upon learning that Khan is over the next hill, Geoffrey falsifies orders to make sure the Lancers attack Khan's position as retribution for the Chukoti massacre. But Geoff doesn't care that he is ruining his career, because he knows the charge is doomed and he will be dead in a couple of hours anyway. His desire to seek revenge on Khan has become an obsession. As a last chivalrous act, he makes sure that Perry does not participate in the attack so that he will be able to make a life with Elsa.

Hal Wallis sees Elsa as an Anita Louise role, but J.L. doesn't understand why anyone would be considered other than de Havilland, and Livvie is now available after completing *Anthony Adverse*. Warner wires Wallis: "We definitely want you to use Olivia de Havilland in *Charge of the Light Brigade* with Errol Flynn as we must have combination because *Brigade* follow-up picture to *Captain Blood* and intend to handle the campaign that way. This is in no way any reflection on Anita Louise, whom we all admire and to whom we look for big things, but because of the foregoing, we must insist on using de Havilland."[9]

It doesn't matter at all to J.L. that the relationship the audience will pay to see, featuring Errol Flynn and Olivia de Havilland, is already over at FADE IN! From Geoffrey and Elsa's meeting to courting to Geoff's asking the permission of Elsa's father, Colonel Campbell (bet that would have been a smashing scene) to the popping of the question

The front office's big idea: Livvie falls for Patric Knowles, the pipsqueak brother, instead of Errol Flynn as the gallant brother. *Sounds good! Let's go with that.* But nice costumes, slatted lighting, and romantic backgrounds can only go so far; he's *still* only Patric Knowles, and Flynn is still Flynn, and the whole thing makes no sense.

and the tearful, "Oh yes, Geoffrey! I'll marry you!" *Sorry, ladies and gentlemen. We didn't make that picture.* Livvie's character is in love with the wrong brother, and spurns Errol in the end, but once the fannies are in the seats, it doesn't matter who gets who, and the ad campaign will get the fannies in the seats. It will sell Errol Flynn and Olivia de Havilland cheek to cheek, and in formal portraits, and in all ways appearing to be one fine-looking British couple that will live happily ever after. Even if they don't.

For the role of Perry Vickers, Wallis chooses Patric Knowles, tall, thin leading man imported from England. For another key role, young Captain Randall, Flynn's best friend killed trying to bring reinforcements to Chukoti, Wallis chooses G.P. Huntley, Jr., a Boston native skilled at playing Brits. This decision draws an entreaty from the screenwriters, who memo Wallis: "This part was written with David Niven in mind.... Niven has just the right brand of flip comedy. He is also of a possible age to be a junior officer to Errol Flynn."[10]

Three short days prior to the start of production, Wallis makes the switch and borrows David Niven from the Samuel Goldwyn Company. Flynn is reacquainted with the acerbic Brit, whom he had met through Damita at the Garden of Allah, before *Captain Blood* had come along. Now Niven finds Flynn a changed man. "It all went straight to his head, and by the time I joined him in his second superproduction..., he was cordially disliked by most of his fellow workers—particularly by the extras."[11]

But it's no wonder Flynn is cranky. He finds out that Mike Curtiz is now slated to direct *Light Brigade*; that Mike had entreated his friend Hal Wallis for the job, and promised to be good, and Wallis had bought it! Off goes Borzage from the picture, and Flynn is stuck with a guy he considers to be a pompous, irritating maniac. After wardrobe fittings and the final casting selections, the company boards a Southern Pacific passenger train in Burbank and heads north to Lone Pine, where the rugged terrain will stand in for dry and dusty India. So begins a wretched location shoot for Errol Flynn in a land that boasts wickedly cold winters and the hottest temperature on record in North America: 134 degrees in 1913, at 3,700 feet above sea level, where the air is thin and fatigue sets in fast.

The company arrives in Lone Pine at 6 a.m. Monday, March 30, 1936, steps off the train, and reports to the set one hour later, after traveling all night, with the first shot at 9 a.m. J.L. runs a tight ship all right. Weather is bad that day, cold, with a dust storm followed by clouds and rain. And it gets worse—on the early morning of April 1, a fire breaks out in the restaurant across the street from their hotel, forcing the location crew out into the cold. The fire also destroys a garage next door that contains some production equipment. Of the hotel evacuation, says Hal Wallis: "Flynn ran out of his room with a blonde.... Damita raised hell when she saw the photograph in the paper."[12]

Remembers Flynn: "Afterward we were quartered poorly, and for the whole five months' period of the screen work, we froze. Warners spent a fortune on the picture, and it was a giant hit. But for much of that period of time we huddled around in the cold and the dust, with no facilities, waiting for the action and eating gruesome food."

In fact, the intrepid Flynn and his confederates spend six *days*, not several months, in Lone Pine, at the base of Mount Whitney, shivering in the howling cold and wearing glycerine spray to simulate sweat. A snowstorm hits as soon as they are prepared to shoot—snow that is visible in the mountains around the mounted lancers in several scenes in the final picture. Says Flynn: "The action of the picture was supposed to take place in India, in the sweating heat of India. Our costumes were thin, as they would have to be in India to absorb the heat. But this wasn't India. It was California, the cold time of year, and we were in an area and at a height where the cold was numbing.... A cold, piercing wind, not perhaps at the freezing point, but it blew through you—while the illusion was being given that this was blazing Indian heat."

He adds: "Meantime the hard-boiled Curtiz was bundled in about three topcoats, giving orders. As I was pretty green in pictures I didn't know enough to tell him to give me one of his coats, or to drop dead. He didn't care who hated him or for what."[13]

Upon the return to Burbank, unit manager Frank Mattison reports that all had gone well, considering the fire, and that there is only "minor friction," meaning that Flynn may not have known enough in the past to tell Curtiz to drop dead, but he is learning fast.[14]

At the studio, shooting proceeds at a fast and furious Curtiz pace. As with the sets in *Captain Blood*, Khan's palace fills a soundstage, towering high and sparse and unlived in. Instead of the visual treat of real belly dancers, silhouettes of belly dancers appear 50 feet high on the far wall, courtesy of the visionary Curtiz, and the floor is so polished that it's a wonder the cast isn't slipping and falling like Buster Keaton or Harold Lloyd. In the early scenes of *Light Brigade*, one thing stands out: Flynn owns the screen. He draws the eye in every frame, standing ramrod straight in a smashing, form-fitting uniform of the empire. In the nine months since *Captain Blood*, he had learned to underplay, which he would do the rest of his career. Here on the Warner soundstages in April 1936, the Flynn persona is born, dashing noble Flynn, a guy people want to know, a guy they can trust, a fellow who takes the worst news with shoulders squared and jaw set. Gone are the ill-fitting clothes and effeminate wig of Peter Blood. Gone is the theatricality of his performance and the pudgy face produced by the lavish meals of his early Hollywood days. Warner and Wallis have found a look for Errol Flynn, and they know it. "The mustache certainly looks good," J.L. memos to Wallis. "I am sure that the mustache is the thing for this picture."[15]

No small credit for Flynn's progress is due to the very man he despises—Mike Curtiz—for creating visionary worlds in which a larger-than-life young star can thrive.

Flynn is, in a sense, the product of Warner Bros. smoke and mirrors, because he is not the highly capable guy they make him out to be. On April 10, a few weeks into the production, Mattison writes the first of a hit parade of memos, strikingly similar in language and tone, that will follow Flynn's exploits at Warner Bros. for 16 years: "Company called at 7:00 a.m., with the first shot at 10. Two hours were spent lining up and rehearsing. We finished shooting at 6:05, owing to the late start because actors were not up on their lines and stumbling through all day."[16]

No one takes the time to understand that Flynn has a problem. To the front office, Flynn is a lazy bum, but in a more enlightened age, they would see that this fellow cannot muster the concentration to sit and memorize the lines of his script. He may appear to be a cultured man, widely read, but he is too easily distracted, and after a short time spent reading, literally minutes, the words make no sense to him. The self-discipline involved in memorization is an art lost on Errol Flynn. In the time it takes a typical actor to sit and memorize lines, Flynn's mind has pinballed to sev-

Oh, for pity's sake, Geoff, will you stop looking at her like that! She's as genuine as the wall of the set that you're standing behind! Here Flynn and de Havilland strike a pose that has nothing to do with the plot of this picture. Oh, yes it does. Elsa is dreaming of Geoff's little brother, Perry. Tramp! (John McElwee Collection)

half of Hollywood's dream couple, but in such a short time, Flynn has developed a nasty habit of looking right past her at other women and worse than that, girls—*young* girls not out of high school. Lili, with a memory like the elephants, keeps a long mental list of his transgressions. How he will pay for them down the line.

Then there are the *real* elephants needed for the picture, for the big game hunt in the first reel. The logical place to find them is Ringling Brothers, which is already on tour by the time the picture starts shooting. But they do find their elephants and venture out to Lake Sherwood, west of the Warner Ranch, to shoot the leopard hunt for the second sequence of the picture, in theory evoking the same kind of thrills produced in Frank Buck action pictures like *Wild Cargo* and *Fang and Claw*. But on the first day of the leopard hunt shoot involving three elephants, the leopard hired from a local zoo wants to play, behaving more like a frisky kitten than a man eater. Then one of the elephants decides to scratch its back by flopping over and wriggling—with Flynn almost crushed to death. There are also endless problems with the howdahs (those baskets rigged to the top of the elephants for people to ride in).

The safari shoot is abandoned after one day, and they decide to settle on the footage of Flynn and cast that they had captured. It's not much. As a result, plan B calls for rear-projection interiors with actors simulating the howdah experience, with Breezy Eason taking a second unit and the elephants back to Lake Sherwood in the middle of May. They shoot the grim and realistic moment when Vickers shoots a prowling leopard dead as it's about to maul Surat Khan. Of course, if the leopard had eaten Khan, the Light Brigade would still be alive today, but in the formula of the epic, irony rules, so the playful kitty must die, and Khan must live, and Vickers must regret the bully shot because it

eral topics, and usually ends up settling on the nearest pair of gorgeous legs, which are everywhere on the Warner lot! Amidst secretaries and typists, starlets and bit players, and especially the dancers, Flynn the leg man is in his glory, all day, every day. And the owners of the legs are, in most cases, eyeing him right back. And his highly volatile—hell, downright flammable—little French wife knows it.

Lili is *always* showing off her legs for her man, and for the press, and for anyone else from whom she can draw attention. She is out there, happy to offer herself up as one will cost many hundreds of British lives in the reels that follow, not only at Chukoti but in the Valley of Death.

On April 14 Livvie reports to Obringer's office to sign her new seven-year contract that abides by J.L.'s scribbled numbers. Suddenly, as she is about to start work on the new picture, the little girl from Saratoga is making $500 a week—and yet is still bound to Warner Bros. until 1942.

As Livvie signs, Wallis is at the director's throat again for lack of coverage. Curtiz had promised to no longer edit in the camera by shooting only selected scenes. Instead he had promised as a condition of being hired for *Light Brigade* that he would shoot full master shots and over-the-shoulder close-ups. But right away Wallis finds great gaps in the coverage.

"You are still doing some things which for the life of me I cannot understand," memos Wallis. "I don't know what it is. Are you trying to keep me in a state of turmoil, or just why do you do the things that you do?" Wallis cites chapter and verse the indiscretions in a scene, later deleted, between Flynn and Donald Crisp as Elsa's father. Curtiz shoots only portions of the scene in close-up, the implication being that he wants to control the final look of the picture and not leave it up to the editor. Wallis brings up the promise Curtiz had made to behave, "but I have had just one headache after another…. Every day that you have shot so far there has been something wrong."[17]

Livvie's first sequence is the Lancers' Ball in Calcutta, where she dances the Lancers' Quadrille with Flynn. The fellow she meets up with this day throws her for a loop. What happened to shy, introspective Errol? He's chatty with the other actors, and cracking wise. He smokes one cigarette after another, knowing that cigarette smoke bothers her. More than anything, he appears distracted, which she is not used to. The Flynn she knows seems to rivet his

Shooting in Lake Sherwood proves to be no picnic for Flynn and de Havilland, who spend hours a day in water up to the waist, or the neck, depending on the scene. The misery is real as Olivia and Errol, under the watchful eye of Mike Curtiz, head for shore. It is here that the vigilant Flynn amuses himself by putting a dead snake in Livvie's costume. (John McElwee Collection)

Flynn's best scene in the picture takes place with David Niven as Capt. Randall, who is about to attempt an escape from the besieged fort. Facing the prospect of imminent death, Randall turns serious on his friend Vickers and offers up a pocket watch. "You wouldn't mind giving this to my family," he says, "just in case." Geoff attempts to lighten the mood. "Looks like a pretty cheap one," he says. "Does it go?" Then he chastises Randall by saying, "You're an idiot." It's a quiet and touching vignette, and another scene lit through the slats of the blinds, this time to foreboding effect. (John McElwee Collection)

concentration on every task, but not the "new Errol." She can't know that this *is* the real Errol—the other had forced himself to concentrate to save his own skin.

A Hollywood reporter covers the day's shooting. Upon arrival on the soundstage, the writer searches for Flynn, explaining, "The quickest way to find Errol Flynn in a mixed crowd is to study the women. Consciously or unconsciously, they will be watching him." The writer claims to have found Flynn in 30 seconds in a room full of similarly dressed British officers just by following the eyes of the women on the set.

Flynn, uniform jacket unbuttoned, is spied sitting on a step and grousing to an extra how much he hates to dance in scenes like this. In rehearsal with Livvie, Errol cusses his way through. "But when the scene was shot," says the writer, "his face betrayed none of his rebellion of the previous moments." Flynn claims to be discontented to the writer and says, "I'm likely to decide to quit Hollywood any day."[18] He doesn't just state this case one time to one reporter; he says it to all the reporters, all the time.

On Saturday, May 9, 1936, the company goes on location at Lake Sherwood to shoot the Lohara River sequence wherein the prisoners of the Chukoti garrison, mostly women and children, are massacred in the river by Surat Khan's men. They work Saturday and Monday without Flynn to capture British subjects succumbing to a hail of gunfire. It is difficult work—an hour or more in the water at a time, during an uncommonly warm May. The hard-driving Curtiz is not only the enemy of Flynn, but of de Havilland as well.

"He was savage," she says. "Oh, he was a beast, a real beast."[19]

Flynn returns to work on Tuesday, May 12, and on this day pulls a prank on unsuspecting de Havilland that becomes legendary. "I had a brown dotted Swiss dress on," Livvie remembers. "It was beside that lake that this traumatic occasion occurred. It was very hot weather, and I used to go around just in the petticoat and the hoop skirt of this Victorian costume, because it was so hot. And one day [Curtiz] said to us all, '…you must get dressed for the scene that's coming up.' So I went in to this little canvas dressing room, and my pantalettes had been laid out on a cot. I picked up the pantalettes, and out slithered a long, dead snake, four feet long. So, I let out a shriek, and just lifted those hoop skirts and I rushed out, and I tore into that lake, right into the middle, where I thought I might be safe."

Flynn's admission: "I was sure I was in love with her." This had been the motivation for the prank.

"*He* was sure it was love," Livvie says, "and *I* didn't think it was anything of the kind."

He admits to his "very teasing ways—though I was really trying to display my affection."

She says, "He thought, somehow, that this message would get across to me. And you know—it didn't?"[20]

So there stands Livvie in the water, all brown eyes and teased. "She was terrified and she wept," he laments. "She knew very well who was responsible and it couldn't have endeared me to her."[21]

The fact that one of the world's most charming, attractive men would be reduced to such juvenile tactics with a younger woman little more than half his size is telling. Around de Havilland he is reverting to pure Flashman; in other words, a mean bully. Says Niven, "He suffered, I think, from a deep inferiority complex—he also bit his nails. Women loved him passionately, but he treated them like toys to be discarded without warning for new models, and for his men friends he really preferred those who would give him the least competition in any department."[22]

According to Livvie, Errol "picked his friends foolishly. They were wild, undisciplined, boisterous, reckless and most of them older than he was, and gave him a poor image of himself."[23]

Right now he is bored and frustrated, and every day on the set, de Havilland remains a closed book; a creature of depth and intelligence; a girl that recognizes Flynn's charm and seems to entice him so easily, to dangle herself like a shiny gem. She exudes quiet competence—something that Flynn's chaotic mind resents, and he cannot control her, not for a moment, and it eats at him, causing him to act out to get her attention, just as he used to act out with Mother, to get hers.

Flynn relishes the hunt, pursuing a woman until he claims her, a trophy for the ego. He has always been a trophy hunter, but this girl seven years his junior doesn't succumb! She plays by different rules than other women, and it begins to bring his demons to the surface. He is now so very *married* (to the point that his wedding ring is visible in key scenes), but he has figured Lili out: Lili sees herself as

Errol and Livvie play a grown-up scene and feel the magic for the first time. Geoff prepares his kit for the trip to the Crimea; Elsa tells him that he's the "finest man I've ever known." Even in a shaky plot, they play it perfectly. (John McElwee Collection)

Martini shot for *Light Brigade*: de Havilland and Flynn return to Lake Sherwood and she dons her brown polka dot dress one more time for this picturesque, backlit two-shot that finishes them both in the picture.

the center of the universe—not just hers and not just his, but everyone's. The sheer force of her ego is compelling—it reminds him of Mother and there is a dark *something* there, a something that keeps him coming back to Lili for years and decades—but he's just not up to how much *work* his wife is.

De Havilland finds herself drawn to powerful, older men; she always has been and always will be. Flynn is typecast there. She fancies men of depth, with an intellectual streak. Flynn could be said to fit that bill as well; she knows he is writing a book and also magazine articles for *Photoplay*. But time will tell that she likes her men a little bit tortured, a little bit autocratic, and Flynn hides that part of him behind a mask of devil-may-care fun and wicked ways. Not until six or seven years later will he wear his tortured soul for all to see, and by then, they will be quits. By then she won't want to have anything to do with him. He will be a pariah and a laughingstock at a time when she is fighting serious battles against serious men for all the marbles in Hollywood.

In the middle of Lake Sherwood, after the dead snake episode, one other incident almost proves a disaster as they shoot waist deep in water. "Mr. Flynn, the brute, tried to murder me when he saved me from a brutish savage," Livvie tells a reporter at the time. "He slashed at the man with his sword but it slipped and cut my face."[24]

Actually, it is more like a clonk on the head, and when Errol realizes what he's done, he panics and, as Livvie hangs on his arm in the water, he shouts, "Olivia! Look at me! Are you hurt?" She pulls free of him and snaps, "No, but I'm disgusted."[25]

For Livvie, especially after the soggy and bloody goings-on at Lake Sherwood, *Light Brigade* is a thankless picture. Her character, Elsa, is gloomy to the point of the audience wanting to smack her. She cracks not one genuine smile in all her screen time. She is in every scene either melancholy, tortured, or unhappy, and seems ready at all moments to blurt out, "Geoff, I'm a two-timing tramp!" She wrings her hands for the decision she must make, to follow her heart into a future with Perry while letting Geoffrey down as gently as possible *(Honey, are you nuts?)*. The cast is so earnest that when the picture is released, the audience follows along thinking, this has to start making sense soon, but it doesn't!

De Havilland knows by the time the film's in the can that she stinks in it. "I thought I was horrible in *Charge of the Light Brigade*," she will say upon the picture's release, "simply horrible. I was smug to the point of smotheration. My sister Joan and I went to the movies the other night. Joan hadn't seen *The Charge*. They ran a trailer of it and what Joan said about my brief and trailey appearance is not fit for publication."[26]

This type of ink doesn't win her fans in the publicity department, but young Livvie is proving to be a young firebrand who speaks her mind like a *man*.

Flynn fares much better in the picture, and plays a nice scene with Knowles, when Perry levels with Geoff about the carrying-on behind big brother's back. Geoff at first sympathizes with Perry for his feelings—until Perry states that Elsa is in love with him. Then Geoff reveals a darker side that will pay off in the crazy finale. He jabs at his brother with the bowl of his pipe and says, wild-eyed, "You lie! And lie and lie!" It's a fine scene by Flynn, showing a raw edge that must have existed in real life, some terrible wellspring of himself that he can tap into when needed.

But Flynn's finest moment in *Light Brigade* is a quiet scene in the besieged Chukoti fort, at night, when Captain Randall, played by David Niven, is about to go for help through enemy lines. He self-consciously gives his pocket watch to Geoff to send to the Randall family, "just in case." Despite the tension of the moment, the odds that Randall is about to die, Vickers examines the watch and says quietly, "Pretty cheap one. Does it go?" Randall gets a bit too sentimental as the scene unfolds and Geoff chides, "You're an idiot." These are lines that Flynn couldn't have played a year earlier, but now he captures the moment with ease. Such examples of Flynn's seminal underplaying, generated by an organic talent within him, reach out across the generations with the capacity to touch audiences even today.

Production moves from the soundstages to the backlot, where a swatch of Delhi, India, is recreated, and to Lasky Mesa, where the Chukoti Garrison is recreated at full size. At the end of June, Flynn delivers his pre-charge speech to fire up the 27th Lancers, and Wallis doesn't like the rushes for two reasons: Flynn is flat, and Curtiz has altered the dialogue again, which Wallis will not tolerate. "I want you to shoot over again the three-shot and the close-up of Errol Flynn…all the way through exactly as they were in the script. The reason they must be made over is that you have changed the whole idea of the scene, as well as the dialogue. Be sure that Flynn builds up his speech as he goes along, and delivers it with a lot of fire."[27]

The final, spectacular charge is shot in nearby Chatsworth, directed by Curtiz in jodhpurs and riding boots, barking orders in mangled English, driving stunt men to injury and horses to death but capturing spectacular shots, with riders filling the landscape even in wide shots—riders who are mowed down by a brutal artillery barrage.

Screaming ambulances take casualties away from the carnage. B-unit work in Sonora directed by Breezy Eason involves four or five dozen stunt men doing falls and close-up action, and between the two directors and the hundreds of others that help to create it, more than 70 years after its filming, the Light Brigade's destruction in the Valley of Death remains one of those sequences that leave the viewer to wonder, "How did they *do* that?"

Finally, after all the other cast members have been finished, Errol and Livvie convene at the studio for their final scene together, the kind of meaty moment actors dream of playing, and they attack it. Elsa is heartbroken, and yes, she loves Geoff, but it has evolved into a sisterly affection, admiration for his strength and his goodness. For Geoff the romance is real, deep, and passionate, but he must step aside for the common good, so that the woman he loves and his own kid brother can be happy. Elsa dissolves in tears and calls Geoff "the finest man I've ever known." In the process of playing this scene, they leave their comfort zones behind, and Errol Flynn and Olivia de Havilland go to a new place—they become a couple onscreen; a Hollywood love team. Unfortunately, they will go their separate ways now and make several pictures apart, except that offscreen, Livvie will show up at Errol's house, and they will date, and things will get interesting.

Flynn and stunt men storm the Russian lines in the final charge by the Light Brigade, shot in multiple locations with some scenes directed by Curtiz and some by B. Reeves Eason. Here Eason directs Flynn and a smaller contingent of stunt men at Sonora in the close shots. Flynn's double would have more safely made the mounted leap over the wall, but Errol preferred to do it himself. (Image courtesy of Hershenson/Allen Archive)

TODAY'S MENU: CHEESECAKE AND BEEFCAKE

From the beginning, Jack Warner sold his young stars as sex objects. He saw Olivia as "a fresh young beauty that would soon stir a lot of tired old muscles around the film town." Flynn was, said Warner, "one magnificent, sexy, animal package."

Even before starting de Havilland in *Captain Blood*, he was parading her in leather and a miniskirt, and for a year she was forced into one bathing suit photo session after another. Wanting to be taken seriously as an actress, lacking confidence in her 32-inch bust and pear shape, and fretting over every little weight gain, she detested the experience. Not long after signing a new contract in April 1936, she would *not* make herself available for posed swimsuit shots.

To play up the sex angle, in an early photo (opposite page), Livvie in a swimsuit is seen fawning over dreamy Errol, also in a swimsuit.

Errol Flynn was photographed in various stages of undress all his life, including a shot or two taken in locker-room showers, and paid it no mind. But in the end, it would be Flynn who became the sex object and struggled in vain to be considered something more.

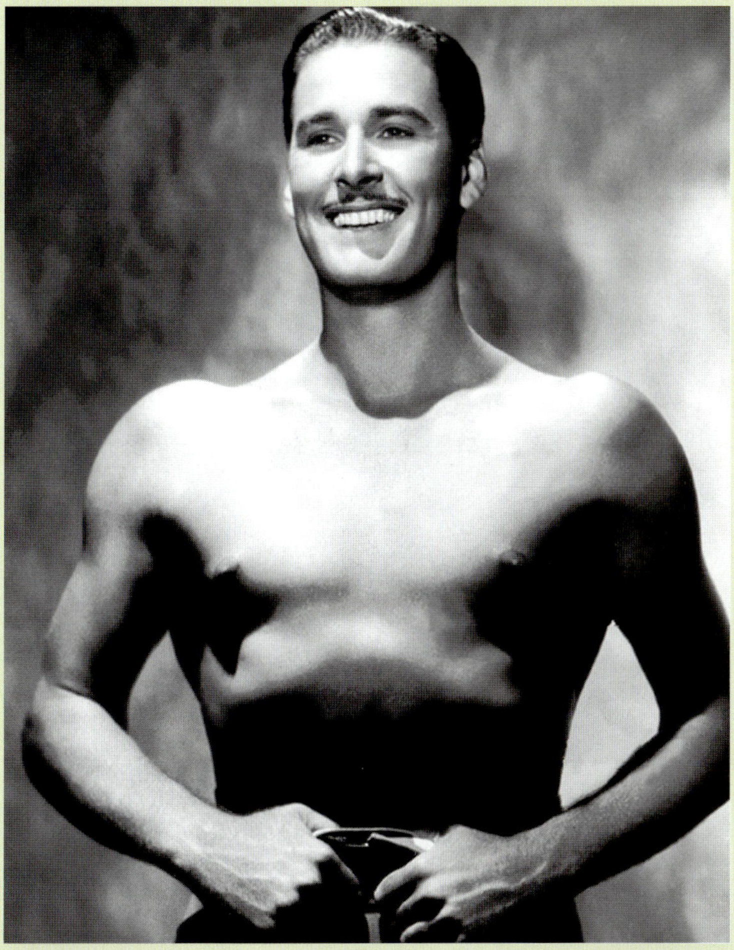
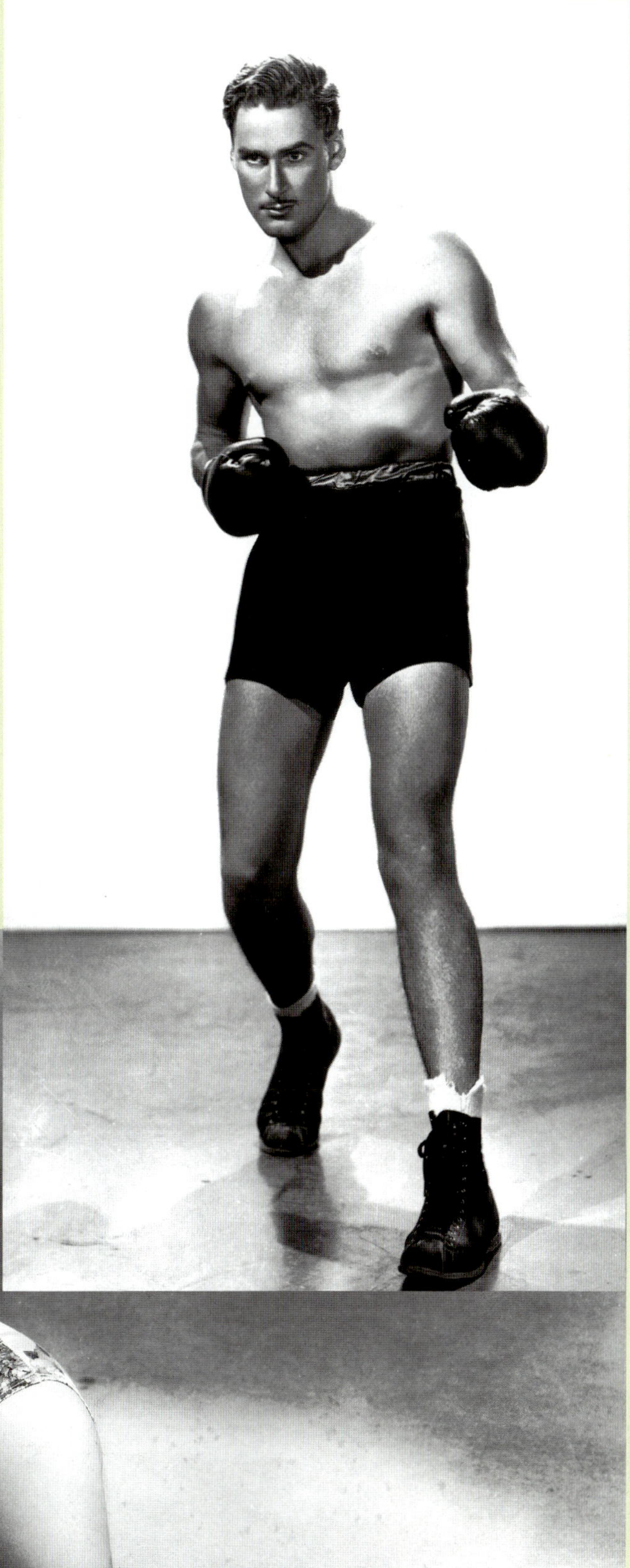
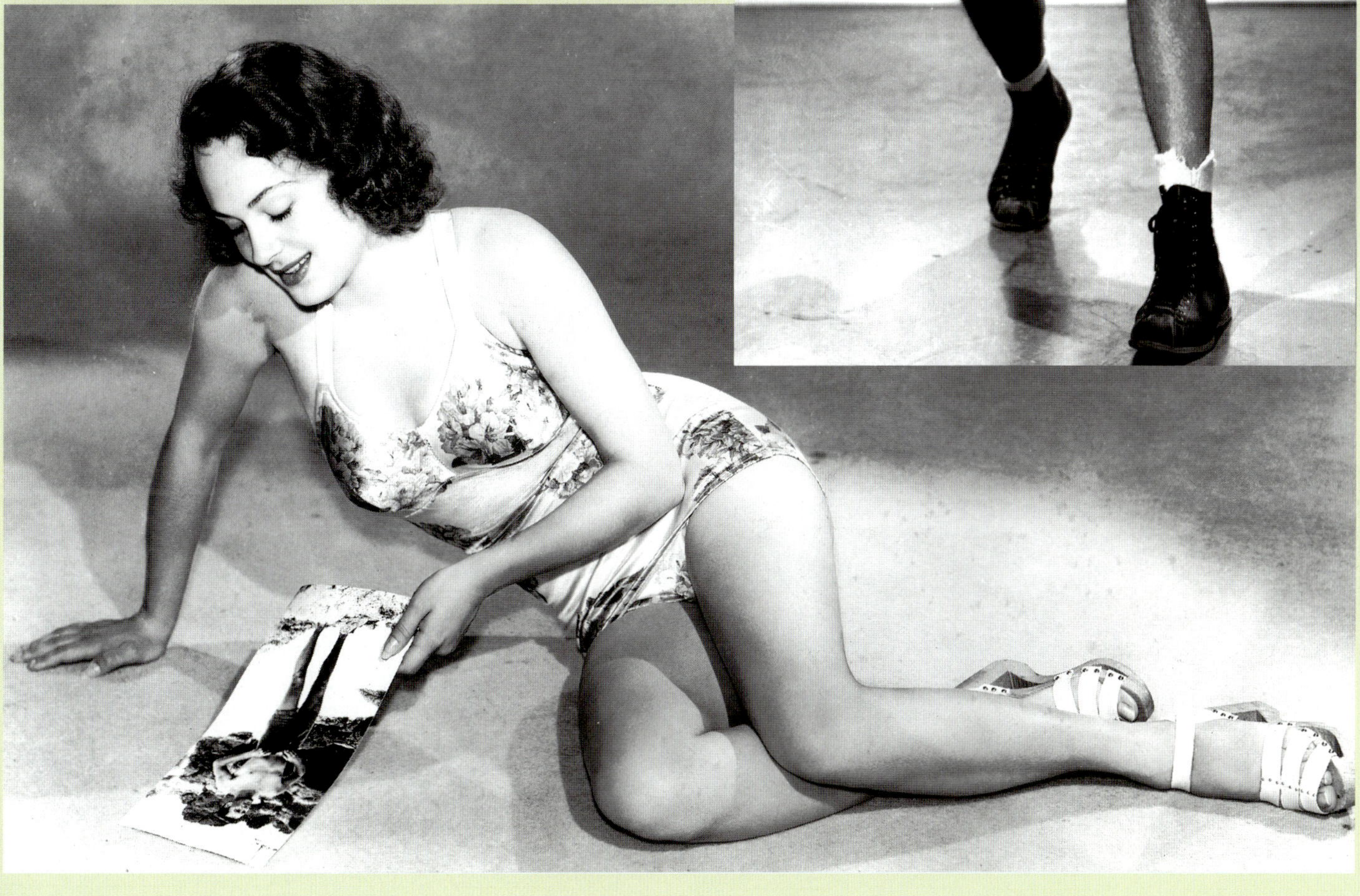

Whatever Jack Warner thought of Flynn and de Havilland personally, he continued to gamble on them professionally and in late summer 1937 committed to making the most expensive picture in Warner history up to this time, with these two in the leads. It would also be the most ambitious Hollywood production to date to use Technicolor, the pricey new process that called for special cameras using three strips of film for each shot. Errol ate up the attention; Livvie not so much.

4 THE BIG DANCE

By the time he completes his third starring picture, an economical, contemporary little drama called *Green Light*, based on the Lloyd C. Douglas novel of a noble young surgeon, and a fourth, an economical soap opera called *Another Dawn* with Kay Francis, a sexy older woman, Flynn is crawling out of his skin to be shed of Hollywood. Every time a reporter drifts near, Flynn buttonholes the poor soul and threatens to retire to the South Seas where Jack Warner and Hal Wallis can never make him report for a 7:00 a.m. call again. When Errol doesn't show up promptly at the studio, when he is 15 or 30 minutes late, the phone rings on Appian Way at once, or there is a knock at the door because the unit manager has ordered some flunky to race over Mulholland Drive to Laurel Canyon to find out where the hell Flynn is.

He must keep the option of retirement in his head, because he can't reconcile himself to living this life under the thumb of The Man, a bird in a gilded cage; nor can he go on serving as the escort of Miss Lili Damita, screen star, sexual tigress, and narcissist. Flynn is an addictive personality and, deep down, he knows it. He is hooked on the fame and he is hooked on the money, both courtesy of Warner Bros. But mostly he is hooked on the sex, to this point courtesy of Lili. But whenever he enjoys a free moment, at the studio or on the way there or on the way home, he slips it to the nearest girl, most of them young and leggy, the way he likes them, and all very, very willing.

So, in January 1937, instead of fleeing to the South Seas, Flynn accepts the devil's pay to make a quick appearance in another costume picture, Mark Twain's *The Prince and the Pauper*, because Hal Wallis doesn't believe that this vehicle, starring a couple of teenaged twins along with veteran character actor Claude Rains, can stand on its own. Flynn scores a quick 25 grand for the part and now, with the Flynn name front and center, *Beam Ends* hits bookstores and newsstands in the second half of February, and Flynn cashes in big. The book sells well, and earns him a reputation as a serious artist on screen and in print.

Errol had tried his hand at writing in the South Seas. "Before I became an actor," he says, "I nearly died of starvation trying to sell my stories.... Sometimes I ask myself why I bludgeon myself into spending late night hours at my desk. I've never been able to give myself a satisfactory answer. I've just *got* to write, that's all."[1]

Flynn biographer Thomas McNulty will say, "…under different circumstances he might have become a celebrated writer-adventurer such as William Beebe and Thor Heyerdahl whose books are a testament to the adventurer's spirit."[2]

But Errol Flynn is neither. Rather than planning more books or taking any kind of strategic view of his careers—cinematic and literary—Flynn decides to go delinquent and stage a getaway from Hollywood with the worst possible choice of companion. Doc Erben is in town, and they make plans at the Brown Derby on Friday, February 19, to go on a grand transcontinental adventure. The ultimate goal: the Civil War in Spain, a right-wing conspiracy by army generals to overthrow the Loyalist republican government. Erben says that they can have some fun there, and Flynn respects the good doctor and his ideas. A nice war sounds like just the tonic for a fellow under the thumb of a scheming boss in Burbank (and a shrill wife on Appian Way).

Of course Lili will not go. Flynn finds her to be a strangely vulnerable creature, so terribly insecure and self-involved. "What I regarded as erotic love-making in those days came as natural to her as the proverbial duck taking to water," says Flynn. "But the purely animal, ferocious woman-tiger can pall on you after a while. You get bewildered. What else is there? What about good talk? ...A serious discussion bored the hell out of Tiger Lil, as I came to call her (but behind her back)."[3] Damita is a creature of spontaneity and instinct—she is the beast to which he has chained himself. Flynn feels sympathy for her because she tries to make a go of it, and yet Erben is urging Flynn to escape, to be a man and go off to see the war. In what is a small world, Erben knows Damita, having worked as a physician on two of her movie sets in Europe more than a decade earlier.

The Boss gets wind of Flynn's hair-brained scheme and tells his star to *stay home*. J.L. wants to put Flynn in a new version of *Robin Hood*. It will be a big picture, the biggest of the year, and it will be in Technicolor.

"It was a big deal to shoot in Technicolor," says Rudy Behlmer. "Technicolor brought in the cameras in the morning and brought their own people in, and took the cameras away at night. So it wasn't like you just decided to shoot in color and loaded different film in the camera. That didn't happen until Eastman Color in 1951."[4] This is all a grand investment, especially considering that only two years earlier, nobody outside of the South Seas had paid any attention to a guy named Errol Flynn. Now he will be the focus of the costume picture to end them all. *So if that imbecile goes over to Spain and gets himself killed, I'll—*

Too late; Flynn and his pal Erben are already packed and gone.

So begins a cross-country Mad, Mad World chase from L.A. to Chicago to New York City, with Damita on the trail of Flynn and Erben. They all meet up for a time in Manhattan, but the boys catch the *Queen Mary* and sail away. While Errol kicks around London, Erben is off to various points east, and ultimately to Berlin for nefarious consultations with the Third Reich, for whom he is a cut-rate spy. Erben doesn't make Errol aware of any of these goings on, and the friends reconnect in Paris, where Lili, "a ball of intuition" according to Errol, has tracked her husband down again and blisters him with invective. It is what Erben describes as a "big quarrel."[5] Once the storm passes, photographs show them convivial enough on the streets, although Flynn says, "there was a running argument" during their stay in Paris, which makes these days like any other days of their marriage.

They linger in the City of Lights for a while, including a long night in a lesbian bar, with Lili dancing intimately with another woman and Flynn drunk and feisty, leading to a beating at the hands

A photographer shoots Errol and Lili at the Paris train station, then infuriates her by asking, "And what is the lady's name?" (Robert Florczak Collection)

of the gendarmes—or that, at least, is the version of the story in the first edition of *My Wicked, Wicked Ways*. Later editions will be scrubbed of this incident at the insistence of Damita's lawyer.

When Erben's attempts to secure a visa are denied, he goes off looking for a way into Spain. Errol and Lili travel by taxi to a train station where a news photographer takes a series of photos "of self and Damita," Flynn writes in his diary, "then infuriates that lady by asking in French, 'And what is the lady's name?'"[6] The fiercely proud, profoundly insecure Damita is not prepared to be less popular than her husband in *her own country*.

They board a train heading south toward the Spanish border. "Very nearly boarded the wrong one going in the opposite direction," he writes, "due to the usual last-minute frenzied rush always necessary when Damita is along." The next day they arrive in the city of Perpignan, just above the Spanish border, where Erben shows up, having somehow made arrangements to enter Spain. "Mysterious," Flynn comments thoughtfully in his diary.[7]

Errol and Lili part company here. The plan all along has been to escape Damita, yes, but when she asks to go along, he refuses to expose her to a war zone. Even Flynn has a streak of the gentleman in there somewhere—not to mention that she would only slow him down.

He and the Doc hop a train to Barcelona, with Erben mooching the cost of the ticket off his movie-star friend. The two of them rollick through war-torn Spain in a series of well-documented adventures, with Flynn often pondering the irony of various situations. One reporter states that Flynn had told him in Paris: "I've got a million dollars which I've raised among the friends of Loyalist Spain in Hollywood. I'm going to Madrid and we're going to build a hospital and buy ambulances for the Loyalists."[8] This obvious lie, probably fabricated by Erben, puppetmaster of the entire scenario, makes sure that the pair will be well treated throughout their stay in Spain.

They travel to the fringes of the fighting, sometimes incredulous, sometimes uncaring. But sometimes Flynn

Errol Flynn and Dr. Hermann F. Erben seem mighty pleased with themselves aboard the Queen Mary *headed to Europe in February 1937. And why not? They had just ditched Lili in the States. (Copyright by Josef Fegerl, Seb. Kneipp-Gasse 1/13, A-1020 Wien)*

records horrific moments that touch him. "Am absolutely sick at the dishes of blood and puss everywhere. One little boy of about six—leg amputated below knee after his town was bombed three weeks ago. They are dressing his stump. He is crying 'Madre! Madre! Madre!' Erben took picture. Horrible."[9]

When a Cockney soldier-of-fortune reports being shot through the testicles, Flynn asks urgently, "Did it damage them?" The soldier says he doesn't know. "Good luck," says Flynn. "Anything you want?"[10] He can relate to this particular injury.

Flynn complains bitterly to his diary about the inactivity of a doctor who watches some patients die, and sees gangrene set in for others, and refuses to treat them. Something about protocol and not wanting to interfere with the care of other doctors when Flynn sees it as a lack of skills and a fear to operate.

In Catalonia they stay at a hostel full of soldiers. He writes at the time, "This pub—shithouse is impossible to enter so great a stink… Am feverish with very sore throat and have only one thin blanket—lucky have flannel trousers and overcoat to sleep in. Desultory firing in distance—am getting used to it. Am sure Don Quixote stayed in this inn—it's so old. Rat holes in room corners—walls all crumbling away."[11]

Flynn labels himself a journalist and will use his diary as the basis for articles about the war for newspapers and

Errol claims in *My Wicked, Wicked Ways* that he hates Lili at this time and their marriage is at an end, but he has been in Spain less than a week when he tries to wire Lili, NEED BATH TERRIBLY ALSO A ROMP. But the censor reviewing the message thinks that "romp" is a code word to the Fascists and won't allow it. Flynn tries to explain that romp is a code word for sex.[12] *I want to go to bed with my wife!* he bellows to deaf ears, and the telegram is never sent. But the fact that he wants to send it at all means that the marriage lives on.

The next evening, Erben wants to take "night shots" with his camera at the front. Flynn goes along and later describes a distant cannon shot that whines closer and closer and explodes on the far side of a brick wall nearby, the concussion knocking them flat. He hears "the sickening sound of shrapnel smacking up against the brick with a sound like fifty eggs cracking on a footpath."[13] And then all goes black.

Five thousand miles away in Hollywood, young Olivia de Havilland, not yet 21 and still living with Mother, now on quiet Nella Vista Street in the Los Feliz district, continues to make pictures and live the agreeable life of an ingénue. She is cast in *Call It a Day* with Ian Hunter and Anita Louise, *The Great Garrick* with Brian Aherne, and *It's Love I'm After* with studio queen Bette Davis, British sensation Leslie Howard, and *Light Brigade* co-star Patric Knowles. Finally, Livvie feels that she has achieved the ultimate: being cast in a Bette Davis picture! She is happy to be free of work on the Flynns and on her way to becoming a star who rates her own prestige scripts and directors.

Imagine Livvie's shock when the bombshell fired all the way in Madrid finally hits Hollywood. FLYNN GRAVELY WOUNDED AT THE SPANISH FRONT! The same Flynn who has been her secret crush. She doesn't understand how this could have happened—why is he over there in the first place?

Warner Bros. reels—J.L. is mortified. *A million-dollar investment down the drain! I told that idiot to stay away from the mess in Spain!*

While Flynn is off adventuring, de Havilland grinds out picture after picture... and quietly grows up. Here she appears in *The Great Garrick* with Brian Aherne, who will be seen squiring her around town. Before long Aherne will marry Joanie in one of many instances where the younger sister goes after what belongs to the older sister.

magazines back home. Erben's motives remain nefarious from the first to the last—he is, it is revealed much later, acting on behalf of Nazi Germany. For Errol, it is a difficult time—his marriage is dissolving, glimpses of human suffering and corruption are all around him, including the brazen lie about the million dollars in aid. Spain turns out to be less of a frolic than Errol has expected, and his conscience will not escape unscathed.

Lili issues a statement of concern from England, hoping that Flynn's handsome face hasn't been marred.

Meanwhile, back in Spain, Errol finds himself horizontal, but alive. Not unlike George Washington, who in 1755 had written that reports of his death had been exaggerated (a quote later appropriated by Mark Twain), Flynn will write, "I AM quite dead. I am quite a bit surprised about it, too…. For three weeks I've had to argue with people—trying to prove that I'm not some new kind of zombie."[14]

He has awakened on a cot in a makeshift hospital, and the Loyalists pooh-pooh his injury as "the merest of scratches." Flynn protests: "Scratch indeed! It was my head and it hurt like hell!" He will suffer headaches for weeks afterward.[15]

That same night Flynn and Erben skip the country, having ridden the lucky streak of their million-dollar caper to the very last instant. Flynn returns to Hollywood minus Erben, and must run a gauntlet of Warner Bros. executives, from the Boss on down, who want a pound of his flesh or something comparable for risking their investment on a whim to go adventuring in Spain. Flynn finally gets his romp with Damita in the new, lush, and remote St. Pierre Road house she has found in Bel Air. Appian Way had become too crowded, too popular, too known. Now they can make love and war in relative seclusion, although right across the street is Hollywood gossip columnist Hedda Hopper, whom Errol charms into not reporting the shrieks of ecstacy—or rage—coming from the Flynn home. She swoons when Errol cuffs her chin and calls her "Hedsie."[16]

Back in civilization, Flynn enjoys seeing his new book on display in stores and newsstands. He sets pen to paper at once for an article entitled *What Really Happened to Me in Spain*, for *Photoplay* magazine. A year earlier he had been contracted to write a series for *Photoplay* with the theme, Young Man About Hollywood, and forwards the finished piece on Spain three weeks after returning home. And it is time for him to face the music and report to the studio for his next picture. He has been lobbying for something more challenging than another stiff-upper-lip drama, which is almost all that he has played. He had enjoyed the lighter moments of *Pauper*, when he could interact playfully with the young kids, and pitches the idea of doing some sort of comedy. *The Perfect Specimen*, a story by Samuel Hopkins Adams, who had written the Academy Award-winning *It Happened One Night*, is bought specifically for Flynn to satisfy his urge for comedy, while also playing on his good looks, physique, and reputation. Flynn is to play a perfectly ingenuous and reclusive millionaire who, thanks to the intervention of a young woman who is curious about him, learns of the world and, naturally, falls in love. Joan Blondell plays the girl, and the two will remain friendly for the rest of his life.

On the second anniversary of their elopement and Arizona wedding, while *The Perfect Specimen* is still in production, Damita invites two dozen well-wishers to a reception, for which Flynn is an hour late. She suspects the worst, that he has rendezvoused with some admirer, and when he finally arrives, she whacks him in the head with a champagne bottle. Blinded by rage, he balls his fist and decks her. Both end up in the hospital, and the 20-stitch

Flynn, always with notepaper and pencil in photos taken by Erben, surveys bomb damage in Madrid. (Copyright by Josef Fegerl, Seb. Kneipp-Gasse 1/13, A-1020 Wien)

THE CORONATION BALL

The coronation ball for King George VI at the Ambassador Hotel begins at 12:01 a.m. on May 12, 1937, and is the social event of the spring. Livvie is driven to Flynn's home on North Linden Drive in Beverly Hills for supper. She is the date of David Niven and Flynn escorts Mrs. Lewis Milestone.

After the dinner, the group proceeds crosstown to the Ambassador. Right: The elegant foursome enter the Ambassador—Mrs. Milestone with Flynn, and Niven with de Havilland. Says Livvie of Errol: "Suddenly, he takes my arm and David Niven takes somebody else's arm, and I...get the picture."[17] In other words, it's the ol' Flynn double-cross, and she's now on a date with a very married man. Below: Errol clowns around to the delight of all.

Above: The Cocoanut Grove nightclub in the Ambassador Hotel was a hangout of the stars. The Cocoanut Grove rose to fame in the Roaring Twenties as a hangout for gin-swilling movie stars and up-and-comers. Joan Crawford danced in Charleston contests here, which led to her fabled career in pictures. After the 1968 assassination of Robert Kennedy in the Ambassador, the hotel and its nightclub declined steadily, until the property held more value without a hulking landmark astride it. Despite its historical significance, the Ambassador Hotel, site of Errol and Olivia's big dance, was torn down in 2006. The nightclub in its heyday was faithfully recreated in the 2004 Leonardo DiCaprio hit, *The Aviator*, which includes a cameo appearance by a brawling Errol Flynn (as portrayed by miscast Englishman Jude Law).

Above right: Basil Rathbone the space invader crowds Livvie, who doesn't seem to mind, with Niven and Nigel Bruce nearby and Flynn in the shadows.

Right: After the ball, says de Havilland, "we went downstairs to the Cocoanut Grove. One photographer got that picture. We danced to *Sweet Leilanni*."[18]

Errol Flynn's bachelor pad at 601 North Linden Drive in Beverly Hills as it looked at the time he lived there. It was in this house that Livvie dined on roast beef and Yorkshire pudding with Flynn and Niven on the evening of May 11, 1937. By the end of the year Lili was back in the picture, and Errol invited her to move in with him on what became their marital last stand.

gash on Flynn's forehead threatens his career. The fact that Damita goes for the face now hints at the growing enmity between them, and Flynn has had enough. He will say, "I knew that if I stayed any longer with Lili it could be that I would have to kill her or get killed."[19]

He hears that Rosalind Russell has a place for rent over in Beverly Hills on North Linden Drive. Nice neighborhood, centrally located. He knows that based on logistics alone this hotspot could become babe central. It is now that David Niven receives a phone call. "Let's move in together, sport," Flynn says. "I can't take that dame's self-centered stupidity for another day."[20] As soon as the bachelors are under the same roof, they conspire to land the big game that Flynn has been hunting since summer 1935, using the coronation of George VI in the plan.

From North Linden, Niven calls Olivia de Havilland at Nella Vista. *Hello, Olivia? David Niven. How are you? Listen, there's going to be a coronation ball on the night of the eleventh at the Ambassador. I was wondering if you would accompany me. Errol? Yes, Errol's going. In fact, Errol has invited me to bring my date for supper at the house, and... You would? Splendid! What's that? You've never been to Errol's house? Yes, that would be something, wouldn't it? I'll ring you again with more details, all right? Fine, Olivia, fine. Talk to you soon. Bye-bye.*

Of course Flynn is listening in, and giggling, through the length of the conversation. The depth of Flynn's feelings are revealed by his actions the evening of the ball, which is to say, he's a man who intends to score.

Hearing reports of Flynn's death in Spain have only fueled Livvie's feelings for him. It will be the first time she has seen him in all these months. For this important evening, dining in the home of Errol Flynn, and attending a ball in celebration of the coronation of King George VI, Livvie dresses in a white, empire-waisted gown with flower accents and a fur coat. She says of her evening on North Linden, "I went over there, you know—to dine. And there was Errol in white tie and tails, sitting at the head of the table. We had roast beef and Yorkshire pudding. It was all terribly dignified and English, and lively at the same time. I thought he was simply stunning in this role as host under his own roof."

After supping on North Linden, Niven and de Havilland proceed with Flynn southeast to Wilshire Boulevard to the Ambassador Hotel for the ball, which is attended by the British film community—Basil and Ouida Rathbone, the Nigel Bruces, Brian Aherne, Cary Grant, and dozens of other stars and dignitaries. "Now, he's separated, but he's not divorced," is the caveat Livvie uses to set up what happens next. As they walk into the hotel ballroom, Livvie says: "Suddenly, he takes my arm and David Niven takes somebody else's arm, and I suddenly get the picture." The career-minded Olivia de Havilland is appalled. "I thought, 'This is going to be a scandal. It's going to be something awful.'" And yet, Flynn is separated, and Livvie is there with him, both of them in formal attire. It's almost as if they're on a Michael Curtiz set with other beautiful people. Suddenly she is on a de facto date with Errol Flynn. She calls him "very attentive and charming" throughout the evening, which is Flynn's M.O. when on the chase.

Livvie enjoys the experience of being with Flynn, while admitting that the need for discretion remains at the forefront. "I sort of tried to avoid all those 50,000 photographers that were always present. Then afterwards, we went downstairs to the Cocoanut Grove. One photographer got that picture. We danced to *Sweet Leilanni*."[21]

Flynn has to figure that tonight will be the night that he finally seals the deal with Livvie, and so he brings out the big guns. He tells her that his marriage to Lili is over. He confesses to Olivia, *I love you, darling. I want to marry you.*

54

Perhaps he means it all, because the shy, quiet, brown-eyed beauty is so very different from any female he has ever known and twice as intoxicating.

Despite spending two full years in Hollywood, Olivia is just young enough and still naive enough to be thinking, *Errol loves me, and soon we will be able to be together*. In the meantime, de Havilland remains far too sober, serious, and in control to throw caution to the wind. "I suppose I regret that now," she will say in the 1980s. "I was inclined to.... Maybe if it were today I might, but you kept those things very much to yourself then. But I was deeply affected by him. It was impossible for me not to be."[22]

She will end the evening on a sobering note: "I said, we really mustn't see each other again until you've straightened out your situation with Lili."[23] Flynn is horribly entangled with Damita, despite his assertions to the contrary; he knows it, and while Olivia is young and in love, she's also far too canny to believe Damita is history.

Rumors are ignited this night that will smolder forever, but de Havilland is a working girl and about to start her next assignment for Curtiz, *Gold Is Where You Find It*, the second Warner Bros. Technicolor picture. She will shoot on location south of San Bernardino in farm country as Flynn remains idle and waits to begin *Robin Hood*, a project that continues to be stalled in story development. Week after week Hal Wallis remains unsatisfied with the scripts he is forwarded by Norman Reilly Raine, the latest in a series of writers. The dialogue isn't right, the scenarios aren't right, the characters aren't right.

Finally Wallis sees the script come together: England in 1191 is a country in crisis. King Richard the Lionheart has gone crusading, placing the country in the hands of a regent, Longchamps, but Richard's scheming brother, Prince John, seizes power and, aided by his right-hand man, Sir Guy of Gisbourne, launches a reign of terror on the Saxons that includes not only high taxation but also murder, rape, hangings, pillaging, and other nasty business.

Sir Robin of Locksley is a Saxon noble who decides to fight the oppressors. He takes to Sherwood Forest and recruits a stout band of freedom fighters, including his own squire, Will of Gamwell, quarterstaff ace Little John, swordsman Friar Tuck, and scores of others who follow Robin's lead to steal from the rich to care for the poor.

Robin's first action is to crash a feast held at Nottingham Castle for high-ranking Normans. Here he meets Prince John and Saxon-hating Lady Marian Fitzwalter, King Richard's ward. When John announces that he has replaced Longchamps, Robin calls John a traitor and a fight ensues. Robin Hood proves to be pretty much hell on wheels by breaking the place up, killing many, and escaping to the forest. His freedom fighters then launch a counteroffensive against the Normans, and capture a treasure caravan that nets Sir Guy, the Sheriff of Nottingham, and Marian, who now gets a crash course in Norman-Saxon politics and learns that Robin's not half bad. Robin releases his prisoners, and John responds to the Saxon moves by holding an archery tournament that draws marksman Robin out of hiding. Robin is captured and sentenced to be hanged, but the smitten Marian helps Robin's men plan a successful escape for the boss. Marian's antics cause John to sentence her to death for treason. He also

With the picture still in pre-production, Flynn studies the latest version of the script. (John McElwee Collection)

Livvie's wardrobe test for *The Adventures of Robin Hood* in October 1937 takes place on the set for a picture being shot on Stage 15. Livvie certainly couldn't beef about the costuming. Her gowns created by Milo Anderson had an estimated value of $10,000.

plans to assassinate Richard, now known to be back in England. With Richard dead, Prince John will claim the throne. But Much the miller's son, one of Robin's men, intercepts the assassin. It is up to Robin and King Richard to infiltrate Nottingham Castle prior to the coronation and defeat the forces of Prince John. In the climactic battle royal, Robin kills Guy, Richard arrests John, and Robin asks for, and receives, permission to marry his lady love.

As of mid-August, with production to launch in a month and Flynn in wardrobe and makeup tests and rehearsing with sword, quarterstaff, and bow and arrow on Stage 1, the casting of Maid Marian and every other player remains a subject of debate. Hal Wallis never automatically pencils in de Havilland opposite Flynn. Wallis's first inclination is to use Anita Louise, who is the same breed as de Havilland, an ingénue, one in a stable, no more, no less. Livvie's work rarely impresses Wallis, and again he pitches Louise for the Marian role. But the Boss looks not only at the production side but at box office, and Flynn with de Havilland plays better than Flynn with anybody else. He and Wallis had tried Anita Louise with Flynn in the medical drama *Green Light*, released a few months past with moderate success. J.L. believes that if de Havilland had been billed with Flynn, returns would have been better.

After September 15 no more discussion of Anita Louise for Maid Marian takes place, and it is proclaimed that Livvie will do it. The only problem is the schedule. Rain in the normally arid San Joaquin Plains has delayed location work on *Gold Is Where You Find It*—bad news because of the cost of the Technicolor cameras. De Havilland can't begin *Robin Hood* until she finishes *Gold*. And rainy locations make production manager Tenny Wright question all the location work scheduled for *Robin Hood* in the municipally owned Bidwell Park in Chico, California, in the northern Sacramento Valley. It is a long way—450 miles—for a caravan of trucks, buses, production crew, equipment, and players to go to get stuck in the rain, "and the rains generally set in around the first of October," notes Wright.[24] He wonders if they can shoot some of the forest scenes at Lake Sherwood west of Burbank and some in the studio to save time, expense, and potential delays.

Directing *Robin Hood* will be 53-year-old William Keighley, veteran of slam-bang Warner gangster pictures

An unretouched portrait of 21-year-old Olivia de Havilland with only lip rouge and mascara for makeup. A tough upbringing in the home of G.M. Fontaine and the grind of the picture business are visible in her face. (John McElwee Collection)

HOW NOT TO AVOID COLDS AND FLU

The first two weeks of production on *The Adventures of Robin Hood* on location in Bidwell Park featured extended periods of rain. When the sun shone—and Technicolor cameras required *lots* of sun—cast and crew spent their time in or near Big Chico Creek, and the October chill and dampness, combined with a legion of film folk in close quarters who were used to the sun and high temperatures of L.A., led to a flu epidemic that cut down scores of inhabitants of Warner City, including most of the stars of the picture. Script girl Flora Pam was rushed to Enloe Hospital with a severe cold and sore throat and then sent home to Los Angeles to recuperate.

More than 70 years later, noted artist and illustrator Robert Florczak journeyed to Bidwell Park to indulge his hobby of Errol Flynn scholarship by finding and documenting the key *Robin Hood* shooting locations in the park as they look today.

"I don't think anyone has attempted anything like this, said Florczak. "I scoured that whole area over three days. I covered about 15 miles on foot, including walking the entire stream, right down the center. And that water was *cold*. I had under my arm a ton of written research, screen grabs that I had done, and production photos from the archives."

He found the park to be a vastly changed place: "Many of the imposing oaks, if still existing at all, had long lost huge branches, making identification next to impossible; entire areas of forest were either covered in thick vines or lacked identifiable vines from 1937; and the creek itself had changed enough along its banks to dampen my overly optimistic enthusiasm."

Dye used to make the forest a more vibrant green in three-strip Technicolor also made it difficult to identify "medieval" sites.

After a long search, Florczak finally identified the location of the quarterstaff duel between Alan Hale and Errol Flynn. "In the film still of Robin jousting with Little John, I noticed a curious, curved sycamore tree with two distinct trunks on the left bank of the stream in the distance. Upon close inspection of the area, I discovered a dead sycamore with the same markings as the trunk in the movie still, along with the remnant of the secondary trunk just behind it that had broken off as well."

Of the spot of the quarterstaff fight, Florczak found important production details in the Warner Bros. Archives.

After being knocked into the creek, a stunt he handled himself, "Flynn asked for a heating system to be put in the stream because when he'd fall in, it was freezing." Florczak also discovered that "the stream was so noisy that the production guys had to put burlap flaps over the rocks to minimize the sound of the babbling water."

Top: Three screen captures show Errol Flynn dueling his way across Big Chico Creek, including the spot where he jumps onto Eugene Pallette's back. The photo at bottom is the same spot today as viewed through the lens of Robert Florczak.

Florczak was back at home in Southern California analyzing the stills he had taken before he realized he had found the exact spot of Robin Hood's duel with Friar Tuck. At this location, a wide-mouthed portion of Big Chico Creek known as Hooker Pool, Eugene Pallette contracted a cold that knocked him out of action for days and also stumbled in the river carrying Errol Flynn on his back and broke a finger. Says Florczak, "As a result of that, when they started filming again, they formed some sort of guide wire across the stream above him, with a wire down to him, to hold him upright so he wouldn't slip."

The epic location shoot for *The Adventures of Robin Hood* was the news event of 1937 in Northern California. More than 100,000 people from as far away as Oregon and Nevada watched the filming from a respectful distance, and hundreds of local inhabitants were employed as nonspeaking extras, including some of the "poor wretches" sheltered in Robin Hood's camp, the people that Robin took Marian to see so that she would understand the cruelty of the Norman oppressors.

When asked what evidence remained today in Chico, California, of the great location shoot of one of the enduring classic motion pictures of all time, Robert Florczak said, "There's nothing, and that's sad. It would be really nice if they had markers, you know, 'On this spot they filmed the duel with Friar Tuck,' but there's nothing. You'd never know anything ever happened there at all."[25]

Upon first reading the draft script, director William Keighley suggested adding a major sequence to the front end of the picture—a jousting tournament. Here Flynn and Basil Rathbone test costumes for the jousting sequence on the backlot. Rathbone would not wear a pageboy in the picture; Flynn would. (Robert Florczak Collection)

G Men with James Cagney and *Bullets or Ballots* with Eddie Robinson. Warner and Wallis give *Robin Hood* to Keighley for three reasons: he brings exciting pacing to his action pictures; he directed *God's Country and the Woman* in Technicolor, so he knows the cameras and their requirements; and he directed Flynn in *The Prince and the Pauper*, and successfully so. Flynn had renewed his complaints about Curtiz after finishing *The Perfect Specimen*, and Wallis worries that Errol might feel compelled to leave Hollywood for the South Seas in the middle of the highest-budget production in the history of Warner Bros. No way will they create that sort of situation, or give Flynn that much power, so *Robin Hood* will be a Keighley job and not a Curtiz job.

Keighley has *ideas* right off the bat—and *ideas* are the domain of the highly paid writers who have been toiling for months on the script. The grandest of these is the idea to open the picture with a bang—a jousting tournament to establish the story, the characters, and the conflict between the ruling Normans and oppressed Saxons, with Sir Robin jousting his arch-nemesis, Sir Guy of Gisbourne. All this malarkey out of left field causes screenwriter Raine to grouse that Keighley is lousing up the picture. "The jousting tournament," says Raine to Wallis, "if done with the magnificence Mr. Keighley sees, will have the disastrous effect of putting the climax of the picture at the beginning, and I'll be goddamned if that is good construction dramatically in fiction, stage or screen."[26]

Except it isn't malarkey. An examination of the September 4, 1937 "final script" proves Keighley to be right: the jousting tournament would provide sweeping spectacle right out of the gate on a scale never before seen. It would also establish the enmity between Sir Robin and Sir Guy, and introduce a smoldering conflict between Robin and Lady Marian.

As written in the September 4 script, Robin approaches the royal box of Prince John and company in chain mail after he has unseated Sir Guy in a joust.

ROBIN: (cheerfully) Lucky for Sir Guy my lance was tipped with a cronell, sire, else Nottingham would need a new lord… (bows to Marian) …and my lady a new master!

MARIAN: (angrily) If that's some of your Saxon wit…

ROBIN: (grins) You don't like it?

MARIAN: (snaps) And I don't like Saxons!

ROBIN: (shrugs, smiling) That's because you don't know us. We've some remarkable qualities…for instance, the art of servility, which we've been forced to learn (bows to Prince John) in good King Richard's absence.

The group listens aghast.

ROBIN: (continues cheerfully) You really should study us, my lady. We're easy to find. Just look under the heel of any Norman boot!

MARIAN: (to Prince John) Why, he speaks treason!

ROBIN: (bows) Fluently!

This conversation is broken up by a messenger from France to announce that Richard has been captured in Vienna by Leopold of Austria and held prisoner in the castle of Durenstein. Several pages of Norman atrocities

60

against the Saxons follow—some really nasty stuff that never would have passed the censors. The last of these involves a poor old Saxon peasant killed by the Sheriff of Nottingham. Robin lifts the body across his saddle and rides to Nottingham Castle, where Norman officials are having a great feast, and the Sheriff is recounting how he had tried to collect taxes that day and been accosted by 100 giant Saxon men, whom he had to fight off single-handedly. Into the midst of the revelry rides Robin astride his horse. With great tumult he pushes his way to the royal table and dumps the peasant's body practically onto the plate of Prince John.

ROBIN: (cool insolence) Well, your royal highness, aren't you going to bid welcome to your guest?

PRINCE JOHN: (strangled) How dare you!

ROBIN: (addressing corpse) This is the good, the noble Prince John. Have you a greeting? (looks at Prince John and shrugs) He's made speechless by the honor you do him. (to corpse) Aren't you hungry? (to Prince John; shakes his head) It seems he's already stuffed belly-full, with Norman kindness.

PRINCE JOHN: Who is he? What do you mean?

ROBIN: (smoothly) He's the (acid irony) great giant of a man who had the impudence to address (jerks his chin at cowering High Sheriff) that fat windbag yonder, and got this (gestures at corpse's shattered head) for his pains.

Wallis knows that the morbid confrontation, should it somehow pass the censors, will break new ground in more adult adventure entertainment the way that Warner Bros. had brought gangsters to the screen in earthy fashion.

Juxtaposed with it is another sequence by torchlight wherein Robin's newly formed band of outlaws undergo christening in the forest by being dunked in a cask of ale by Friar Tuck, after which they are given outlaw names. Thus Robin of Locksley becomes Robin 'Hood,' the man-mountain John Little becomes 'Little John,' Will of Gamwell becomes 'Will Scarlett,' and so on.

Flynn's reaction is delight because of the growing lavishness of his new starring vehicle. He has *arrived* as a superstar, and wields enough clout to keep Curtiz off the picture. And he is making ground with Livvie, now confirmed to be his Marian. Freelancer Basil Rathbone is signed to portray Sir Guy, which doesn't thrill Flynn because the limey bastard fancies Livvie, no question of it, and touches her when he can and fawns over her. Errol had seen it at Laguna in '35 and at the Coronation Ball.

The cast rounds out—when Flynn's pal David Niven is found to be unavailable to portray Sir Robin's squire, Will of Gamwell, a second pal, Patric Knowles, is called for the role; another pal, Alan Hale, portrays Little John; gravel-voiced Gene Pallette signs as Friar Tuck; and Melville Cooper portrays the Sheriff of Nottingham.

On September 23 a memo circulates from Wallis to the production and publicity departments: the official title of the picture will be *The Adventures of Robin Hood*. Don't go calling this thing *Robin Hood* or else—except that for the next four months, Hal Wallis will continually call it *Robin Hood* in all his memos.

A scene shot in Bidwell Park and later deleted shows an adoring Marian watching Robin of Locksley as he gives comfort to wounded Saxons in a makeshift hospital. This was among the first scenes shot upon Livvie's arrival. In fact she is only in partial makeup at the time that stills were taken.

61

Suddenly, *The Adventures of Robin Hood* moves from the theoretical to the very real. On Saturday, September 25, Flynn, Hale, Knowles, and Pallette rehearse their opening routines on Stage 1. First will be the meeting of Robin and Little John with quarterstaffs on a stout log; second will be the meeting of Robin and Friar Tuck with swords. The goal is to hit the ground running on location and knock off the first sequences with speed and efficiency.

Later that day the entire production departs for Chico by train, arriving at 9:30 the morning of Sunday, September 26, where nine production trucks are waiting. The day is spent unloading people, equipment, costumes, and props, and moving into the hotel. Flynn and a schnauzer named Arno, who is closer to the actor than any human, land at Richardson Springs Resort tucked in mountains eight miles north of the shooting location. One of Arno's more peculiar habits is to stick his muzzle in the crotches of pretty girls, which Flynn finds quite an icebreaker.

As Errol settles in at Richardson Springs and idly thumbs through the script, unit manager Al Alleborn's production team establishes a tent city in Chico's lower Bidwell Park. Warner City, as it will soon be called, includes a police and fire department, two doctors, a butcher shop, tailor shop, restaurants, soft drink stands, a beauty parlor, and a theater to run the dailies.

As seen in *The Adventures of Robin Hood*, Bidwell Park will give the impression of being a wild, medieval place. In reality, civilization surrounds this modest stand of trees, which is a strip of terrain running from Chico in the southwest to the Sierra Nevadas to the northeast, a long, thin tract of 2,500 acres donated to the city by the widow of city founder John Bidwell. Thousands of onlookers from as far away as Oregon and Nevada converge daily to catch a glimpse of Flynn and his actor cohorts and watch the four Technicolor motion picture cameras that are pushed, pulled, and cajoled from location to location around the rugged terrain of the park.

Long before such a thing as the Weather Channel, Bill Keighley and his production crew learn harsh realities presented by northern California's climate, as September is

Shooting progresses slowly after days of rain as Alan Hale and Errol Flynn stand on a makeshift platform and recite their dialogue with the camera shooting over Flynn's shoulder to obtain Hale's close-ups. Director William Keighley sits just out of frame. Under the forest canopy, a big light focuses on Hale, and reflectors offer fill. Light was always a problem for the Technicolor cameras. (John McElwee Collection)

Above: In October 1937 Lili Damita is on the comeback trail and poses with her famous husband for Warner Bros. publicity stills on one of the massive prop boulders brought in for the Bidwell Park shoot. They are laughing over the fact that photographic evidence will now prove that their marriage is indeed on the rocks. (John McElwee Collection) Right: This photo and others from the shoot appeared in fan magazines around the world.

about to give way to October, by stepping outside and peering up at the sky. Technicolor cameras require abundant light, which means sunshine and plenty of it, and there is no sunshine on Monday, September 27. Al Alleborn reports to Tenny Wright: "Company did not shoot today due to cloudy weather and lack of sunshine. Started and worked Errol Flynn, Alan Hale, and Patric Knowles, and rehearsed Eugene Pallette. Company rehearsed EXT WOODS—bridge and stream." One day into William Keighley's production, the company is one day behind schedule.[27]

On Tuesday, September 28, the sun appears for three hours, from 11:15 to 2:30, and Keighley rolls on the meeting of Robin of Locksley and Alan Hale as Little John on a log bridge over Big Chico Creek. "Give way, little man!" urges Robin to the giant across the way.

"Only to a better man than m'self!" says Little John.

"Let him pass, Robin," urges Patric Knowles as Will Scarlett. "It's much too warm to brawl with such a windbag!" Again and again they run through it, from various angles. And at 2:30 they lose the sun, and that's that. Tenny Wright's concerns about the weather, expressed weeks earlier, are proving to be real and justified.

The next day is also lost to dark skies. On the 30th they shoot all day, and start staging the meticulously choreographed quarterstaff fight on the log bridge, but it won't be shot fast, that's for sure. Then rain hits on October 1 and 2 and suddenly the company is three days behind schedule.

Al Alleborn is sure by now that Keighley is taking too much time to shoot the picture. When the clouds part and the sun appears, they need to charge ahead like the Rough Riders, not hem and haw and lose precious minutes looking at the light and tweaking the shots and the set dressing.

Into the first week Hal Wallis realizes he is going to have to cut budget because of the expense of keeping 400 people housed and fed for weeks of location work, in addition to props and wardrobe and horses and equipment, especially the Technicolor cameras.

After watching the first of the developed film that makes it back to Burbank, Wallis wires Keighley on October 6: "I don't want to start worrying you or ride or crowd you, but while the first three days' dailies are gorgeous and just the last word, at the same time it has taken three days to shoot the meeting between Robin and Little John and it was not yet complete at the end of three days' work. I don't have to tell you that at this rate we will be on location until it snows."[28]

It seems to be, quite unexpectedly, that the veteran director is treating his lavish Technicolor production like dad's new car. He's afraid to drive it above 20 mph for fear of getting a scratch on the shiny fenders. Wallis hadn't counted on this turn of events, so he needs to figure a way to contain costs and snap Keighley to attention. Then it hits him and he memos Heinz Blanke: *Kill the jousting tournament and go back to the old version of the script where all the key exposition plays out in the banquet hall.*

Olivia de Havilland, Basil Rathbone, Melville Cooper, and Errol Flynn share a scene shot in Bidwell Park in late October 1937. Flynn liked Rathbone generally, as long as he wasn't pawing Livvie.

Just like that, Wallis gets his scriptwriter off his back, saves a hundred grand, plus several days on location, and sends a warning to Keighley to get it moving or things may grow unpleasant.

Not far away from Wallis's office, on Stage 15, Olivia de Havilland shows up to test wardrobe for the first time. Livvie is in a tough spot this time. She has to admit that *Robin Hood* is a prestige picture—she will be seen in the grandest Technicolor spectacle ever! But she is reduced to the consort of Flynn yet again, this time in a fantastic piece of medieval nonsense with her part written so vaguely that there is nothing to hold on to; nothing at all. She knows she is better than *Gold Is Where You Find It*, and better than *Robin Hood*. No one else in the front office sees it, or they wouldn't keep doing this to her!

Livvie tells a reporter, "I have felt, quite often, that I'd like to quit.... But whether I will ever have the courage, the initiative, the gumption to leave of my own free will is another matter."[29]

Up north, by the time Keighley reads the Wallis telegram, he is already back at Bidwell Park shooting the swordfight between Robin and Friar Tuck. Keighley may have lost three days to rain and gloom, but he won't lose any more now that the weather has improved. He gets great performances out of Flynn and Pallette—all the work on Stage 1 to prep with swords has been worth it. The action is fast and athletic, even for fireplug Pallette, with crisp comedic touches. When Wallis sees this footage, he will be shouting with joy.

Unfortunately, Pallette breaks a finger, and all that time in the water gives him germs that settle in his chest. It is a dark omen—within 24 hours the cast, used to drier, warmer climes, is decimated by the same virus. Alan Hale, Patric Knowles, and many crew members drop. Script girl Flora Pam lands in the hospital.

On October 9 footage is shot of Much the miller's son, played by Herbert Mundin, being rescued by Will Scarlett and taken to Robin to warn of the plot to kill King Richard. That same day, Ian Hunter and the British contingent arrive to portray Richard and his knights. On the 10th and 11th they shoot the arrival of Richard in Robin Hood's camp,

No wonder Lili was having kittens! The storybook couple is in a storybook setting, and Livvie sports a form-fitting gown that accentuates her curves. But Damita needn't have worried, because those crazy kids, Livvie and Errol, each try to outdo the other with frostiness after their big date. (Robert Florczak Collection)

and the counterplot to save the throne. Basil Rathbone arrives on location for his exteriors just in time for the rains to descend once more; three days of heavy downpours keep the company under cover, killing time.

And now, who should show up but Damita, eight trunks in tow, doing her best Marlene Dietrich, in a blazing effort to be seen by the press as she wraps her feline self around dear hubby. She knows that without Flynn, no shafts from the spotlight would hit Damita at all. Lili has also heard the rumors about Errol and Olivia—all

Lili knew enough to find the backlight, even when posing for a snapshot, as she watches her husband portray Robin Hood in the "wilds" of a chilly October Bidwell Park. Motivated by the imminent arrival of Olivia de Havilland in Chico, Lili has no problem braving October winds or frost to watch over her man.

Hollywood has, and Lili will not give him up without a fight—so here at Richardson Springs, Damita makes her stand; she will be highly visible when de Havilland arrives. Flynn doesn't mind that Lili is around; it's boring during the rainy days, and the romps are sensational, and Damita is on her best behavior.

But Lili is disconcerted to learn of two new Flynn passions: first, he has taken up hunting, courtesy of new pal Howard Hill, the champion archer doing the trick shots for Robin Hood. In the mountaintops above Richardson Springs, Hill bags a bobcat with one high-tension kill shot—and gives the prize to Flynn for publicity purposes.

FLYNN, ROBIN HOOD STAR, KILLS WILDCAT WITH ARROW screams a banner headline above the masthead of the Chico *Enterprise* on October 18, 1937.

Flynn's other new love is flying, courtesy of pal Pat Knowles, who takes Flynn joyriding in a Piper Cub out of Chico Municipal Airport. At once Flynn decides that flying is for him and tells Knowles that he wants to solo. "It took 12 hours of dual instruction to solo," says Knowles later. "Flynn made it in four."[30]

Errol's antics in the cockpit continue in off hours as cast members work straight through from October 16 to 21 on shots in Robin's camp—anything they don't need de Havilland for. This is no problem for Flynn and Knowles since the airport is only a couple of miles north of location.

Dorothy Jordan, Livvie's double, arrives on the 21st for long shots of the treasure caravan, and Livvie herself pulls into Chico aboard the Southern Pacific at one in the afternoon on the 22nd. A mob awaits her at the train station, but by advanced signal the train stops a few hundred yards down the track, where Knowles, dressed as Will Scarlett, greets her along with Al Alleborn, the location manager, two publicity men, and dozens of suddenly curious locals. Livvie and her luggage are loaded into a car and sped to the Hotel Oaks, while the mob at the train station waits for a Hollywood star who will never arrive.

Livvie's luggage is dumped at the hotel, and the lady is taken straight away to Warner City, where she steps into the largest base camp she has ever seen, a town of tents at the edge of a stand of trees, and it's chilly, and there are extras everywhere. In the distance she can see prop men spraying the dingy autumnal foliage with vivid green vegetable dye. Lunchtime is wrapping up, and box lunches are everywhere, 230 of them. Livvie hurries into costume to sit at a banquet table in the forest with Flynn, where they catch up briefly in this first meeting since the Coronation Ball.

After a very short hour's work in the afternoon, she retires for the day, and her car takes her into sleepy Chico to the Hotel Oaks. She has already learned she will not be staying at the posh digs where Flynn and Rathbone are sequestered, and she knows this is because of the rumors about her and Flynn—and Damita is here as well. That's a crazy little woman, that Lili Damita.

At just about the time that de Havilland reaches her hotel, Pat Knowles stands by an airplane hanger where he is shown an urgent telegram sent by Wallis to Al Alleborn: "Just learned that Flynn and Knowles are doing some flying up there from local airport in rented plane. Absolutely insist that Flynn, Knowles, and all other members of company stop this immediately. We are investing close to two million dollars in production and these foolhardy stunts must be stopped. Wallis."[31]

Knowles says, "I asked the 'old boy' [Flynn] what we should do about the threat and he laughed loud and long." Flynn's response to the long arm of the law is to hide their car in the hangar, out of sight. "Then the snoopers won't know whether we are here or not," he tells Knowles, and the Piper Cub hijinks continue.[32]

The next day the company begins shooting the forest banquet scene in earnest. Here Maid Marian resists the friendly overtures of Robin at first, then slowly thaws. Livvie tries to interpret the part but there's nothing there for her; it's the typical male view of a haughty heroine who needs a hero to barge in and tame her. Her frustration becomes obvious at once in the first de Havilland film footage to reach Burbank. Wallis fires off a telegram to Keighley: "Latest dailies continuation exterior banquet scene excellent. However, not so happy with de Havilland's interpretation of part. She seems to have gone elegant on us and her reading of lines is reminiscent of the leading lady in high school plays. Please watch her carefully in balance of scenes. Wallis."[33]

Location candids and home movie footage taken at the time reveal a somber, withdrawn Livvie. As they sit there for hours, Rathbone, one of those space invaders, is always right in her mug, fawning over her as usual, pawing her at every opportunity. Rathbone of the deep voice and the high British culture. No matter that he's nearly 25 years older than Livvie; when Rathbone turns on the masculine charm, he becomes competition, and Flynn hates competition. The hunt intensifies, and Flynn doesn't even care that Damita is close by for Livvie's first day on the set. For Flynn, this becomes a matter of principle.

Day after day they shoot the sequence in Sherwood where Robin slowly warms up Marian, first at the banquet table, then on a quiet walk and dialogue fest in the forest. Some of the Saxon "poor people" used in the Robin-Marian walk and talk are Chico folk, part of the publicity push to involve the locals and build homespun buzz.

But by now things are not going Flynn's way in his wooing of Livvie, which is obvious on film because he commits an offense with a message. He knows that she will understand this message because Errol knows how sensitive Livvie is to being upstaged—so sensitive that sometimes she sees it when it isn't really there.

During their walk, Robin lists the atrocities of the Normans against poor Saxon peasants. Marian is hearing information about her own Norman people that is new and shocking, leading to growth of character, so it becomes vital to the story that we see her acquire a glimmer of understanding of the situation. Right now, the focus must be on de Havilland. Flynn knows this very well—he has read the script, and he is a veteran of six Warner Bros. A pictures. But rather than let Livvie have the scene as written, he fiddles with a twig in his right hand.

Says actor Andrew Parks, son of Columbia 1940s star Larry Parks (Oscar-nominated for *The Jolson Story*) and MGM starlet Betty Garrett, "In a classic sense, upstaging is when one actor faces the audience and forces the other actor to turn his back on the audience. Actors are aware,

As the air turns colder late in October 1937, Olivia de Havilland sits next to dialogue director Colin Campbell and thumbs through a book about Robin Hood to be used for publicity photos. The book rests on top of her script as she tries to cram for upcoming scenes. A thoroughly disinterested Errol Flynn waits for director Keighley's call. At this time Flynn was not removing his hat because of ongoing problems with the styling of his wig. Errol sent Hal Wallis a sketch and detailed instructions on the look he wanted. (Robert Florczak Collection)

Errol Flynn made the newspapers when he took up flying while on location at Chico. Lili (seen with Errol above) loved the idea because it would make their glamorous life even more so. Word quickly reached Burbank, and Hal Wallis attempted to stop the daredevil antics of Flynn and licensed pilot Patric Knowles long distance, which only made Flynn want to outwit "the snoopers." After four hours of instruction, Flynn competed with Knowles (below left) to see who could perform the craziest stunts. The pair stopped only occasionally to make a picture about Robin Hood.

'Oh my God, I'm upstaging you!' and you don't want to do that. But…it can also mean *stealing focus*…, moving on someone else's lines is a big one. Apparently Yul Brynner wasn't fond of Steve McQueen, because when doing *The Magnificent Seven*, McQueen liked to have very little dialogue, but he would do *stuff*; he would fidget around. It wasn't obvious, but it led members of the audience to think, 'Ooh, he's interesting—I'm going to look at *him*!'"

Livvie's definition of scene stealing is broad—Andrew Parks doesn't consider Flynn's actions to meet the definition of scene stealing; nor does Rudy Behlmer. But Olivia *does*, and says of this time period, "Flynn had become so selfish…, did unbelievable things he didn't have to stoop to…."[34] And this is one of those things, upstaging her in a key scene.

De Havilland never addresses the *Robin Hood* incident, but in 1974 she will speak of another, similar episode involving Ralph Richardson in the 1949 film, *The Heiress*, that shows how much she loathes the practice of upstaging. Of Richardson: "He was a wicked, very selfish man. There's a very old-fashioned expletive, which I'll delete—SOB are the initials—but he really is a devil, an unnecessarily selfish artist to work with. I was in a constant stage of outrage over his slick, British tricks." Later in the same interview she says: "Oh, those gloves. I had to play some agonizing scenes, and it was imperative that I had the audience's attention and the proper place for the audience's attention was on Catherine, not on those wretched gloves. That sort of thing, ridiculous kind of upstaging…"[35]

In Bidwell Park, the incident with Flynn does nothing but reinforce her unhappiness with these roles, playing comic book characters and having scenes wrestled away from her, not by a Paul Muni or even a Leslie Howard, but by Errol Flynn, who is behaving as only he can.

Damita knows exactly what her husband is about: "He loves to annoy people in childish ways. He knows their weak points and plays on them."[36]

The foolishness in the air continues as well, as Flynn continues to fly that damn Piper Cub despite the studio's edicts. Knowles writes of the deciding incident in the affair: "We hid the car in the back of the hangar while Flynn… fooled [around] all over the sky, showing off. Nothing really dangerous, just hammer stalls, tight turns and wing overs. After only four hours dual he was a veritable Rickenbacker.

"He didn't say a word as he climbed out of the cockpit and I got in. He simply leered at me with a let's-see-what-you-can-do look. Well, I did everything but fly through the hangar doors." Knowles is determined to outdo and impress his friend. After Patric Knowles lands the plane, his smug grin fades as Al Alleborn and a Civil Aeronautics rep lift his flying license. And where is his pal during the pinch? "Why, in the car having forty winks, old son," said Flynn. "I started to learn my lines for tomorrow and simply dozed off."[37] In true Errol Flynn fashion, when the going gets tough, the daredevil is nowhere to be found.

Hal Wallis isn't the number-two man at Warner Bros. for nothing. Wallis knows that he can't go to Flynn because Flynn is a dangerous radical. Knowles, on the other hand, is the weak link, because Knowles will be keenly interested in future Warner Bros. paychecks. It is Knowles who will fix the situation. After the Civil Aeronautics man confiscates Pat's flying license, Alleborn hands Will of Gamwell a telegram that reads: "Dear Pat: Have had reports about your joyriding in planes up there and requested Alleborn to ask you to please discontinue doing so. In spite of this, understand you are continuing flying. Have always tried to be cooperative and accede to various requests from you from time to time. Am asking you now to please cut out this flying, at least until picture is finished."[38] In other words: *Keep flying and you're fired.*

Above: Maid Marian feels the agony of the tortured Saxon refugees—and Livvie the pain of co-star and would-be boyfriend Errol stealing the scene from her by playing with a twig for the length of a dolly move. Below: De Havilland is caught in a relaxed moment sitting before one of the targets at Busch Gardens in Pasadena and chatting with two extras during production of the archery tournament. Watch out for flying arrows, Livvie! (John McElwee Collection)

69

The onscreen lovers wait for lighting adjustments with always-busy dialogue director Colin Campbell on the William Keighley balcony scene shoot. (John McElwee Collection)

Thus end the flying adventures of Errol Flynn and Patric Knowles, leaving only the production of *The Adventures of Robin Hood*. Film stock flows back to Hal Wallis endlessly. The day after he has quelled the Piper Cub uprising, Wallis wires Keighley with genuine enthusiasm: "The meeting of Robin and King Richard, the arrival of Knowles with news of Gisbourne's trip through forest all excellent. Color beautiful and action seemed to have more tempo and more spirit than other earlier sequences. Much better this way of course and know you will try to keep all action moving fast, people bright, rapid delivery of dialogue, and picking up cues et cetera, as we all know picture needs this."[39]

By October 28 they are so far behind schedule because of the weather that Keighley dispatches Breezy Eason to capture second-unit footage. October is turning to November, calling for more green touch-ups for the foliage. Eason shoots wide on the Norman caravan—the pieces leading up to Robin's capture of Sir Guy's treasure train. These days, Livvie's double in the long shots rides a golden palomino stallion, a movie rookie named Golden Cloud, hand chosen because this horse is smart and gentle. History will know Golden Cloud as Trigger, the steed of cowboy star Roy Rogers.

Wallis looks at the shots of a hundred extras and horses and wagons moving through the forest, and the frustration with the directing team mounts: "I don't think he used good judgment in his setups," Wallis memos to supervising producer Heinz Blanke. "Practically all of the shots are almost straight on to the approaching line of men and you never get the effect of a huge entourage moving through the forest.... It seems criminal that they should go up there and shoot all of this stuff, and waste that much money."[40]

With Hal Wallis in this frame of mind, Keighley is happy to wrap in Chico after six long weeks and return to home base. Flynn packs his suitcase, Damita packs her trunks, Livvie packs her dampened ambitions, and the company returns to Burbank in fair weather on November 8, 1937, having shot spectacular exteriors and thousands of feet of film, really flavorful stuff in rich, three-strip Technicolor for an epic look.

The cast minus Flynn shoot some interiors on Stage 2 in Burbank on Friday, November 12, but Keighley is now focusing on the archery tournament about to shoot at Busch Gardens 20 miles to the east in Pasadena, in the direction of the stars' hangout, the race track at Santa Anita. Keighley is 10 days behind schedule—the front office keeps reminding him—and he dare not lose any more days to bad weather. Ten busloads of players and crew drive out to Pasadena on Monday, November 15, to kick off the archery tournament on two days with wall-to-wall sun. The setting is established with cheering extras, and the golden arrow makes its heraldic entrance on a satin pillow. On the 17th and 18th they are back on Stage 1 for the scene where Maid Marian overhears the plot by Prince John, Sir Guy, and the Sheriff to assassinate Richard, who is known to be back in England.

Reporter Mary Parkes interviews Livvie at the end of a shoot day at Busch Gardens. The star changes clothes and hops into her roadster to meet the reporter, and, when questioned about settling down and getting married—a topic on the mind of every stringer who interviews her—Livvie gives the standard answer, that she's in no rush to marry. She then veers onto another course: "I just don't feel real," she says. "I don't feel *me*. I have gained many identities and sort of lost my own." She will revisit themes like this through much of her life; not knowing who she really is; getting mixed up between the characters in the script and the flesh-and-blood person underneath.[41]

The archery tournament is completed in six days, and on November 25 de Havilland and Una O'Connor shoot the long scene, later heavily edited, wherein Bess the maid leads Marian to admit that she is in love with Robin. Flynn is held this day, and while studying the scene in Marian's chambers, forwards some notes to associate producer Henry Blanke—some changes he'd like to see. One particular passage of dialogue will be impossible for him (Robin's

The styling of the wig, beard, and shirt suggest that this still represents the William Keighley version of the love scene between Robin and Marian, the version in which Olivia de Havilland admits to blowing the takes of their kisses so she could cocktease Errol Flynn—payback for stringing her along.

thought, well, I'm going to torture Errol Flynn.... And so we had one kissing scene, which I looked forward to with great delight. I remember I blew every take, at least six in a row, maybe seven, maybe eight, and we had to kiss all over again. And Errol Flynn got really rather uncomfortable, and he had, if I may say so, a little trouble with his tights."[42]

It is their only kiss in the picture, after Robin has jumped to the floor from the windowsill and pulled her to him. Livvie will lay several open-mouthed kisses on Errol in their subsequent pictures; kisses quite unlike the tight-lipped stage buss of the day. Often Livvie and Errol will nearly step on each other's lines to get to the open-mouthed kiss, which fuels the image of a couple as hot for each other offscreen as they are on.

"The love scenes were marvelous!" she says later. "I couldn't wait to get to them..., especially when I had to kiss Errol Flynn."[43] But right now, Livvie feels jilted, and teases Flynn out of anger and not any notion of romance. Her message: *Here's what you're missing, big boy.*

Olivia de Havilland isn't the only unhappy member of the Warner Bros. family as shooting progresses on the medieval epic. By the end of November, Wallis experiences growing apprehension that Keighley's *Robin Hood* is lacking the scope and sass of the Curtiz *Captain Blood*. True, Keighley brings a dimensionality of character to his productions that Curtiz lacks, but the grand setups just aren't there. Keighley's spectacle just isn't spectacular enough for the world's first three-strip Technicolor adventure picture, and is Wallis willing to gamble that his director will pick up the pace and create a successful finished product? On the other hand, what's the alternative? If the answer is firing

On Stage 1, a prop man, looking to Curtiz for approval, points to the spot where a spear will pierce Flynn's chair as the star contemplates the scene to come. After the spear punches through, he will tip the chair back and roll out of it to commence a melee in the Great Hall of Nottingham Castle. (Robert Florczak Collection)

banter with Marian and Bess in her chamber), and he cuts it by about two thirds. He also lays on more charm with the Bess character than originally written. Per the script, the Robin-Marian love scene is played on a divan, but he doesn't want to be sitting there all legs and tights. He wants to be standing. Blanke notes the changes and Wallis approves them, and on Friday and Saturday, November 26 and 27, Flynn and de Havilland shoot their balcony love scene, with Keighley at the helm, on Stage 4.

Almost 70 years later, in 2005, Livvie will add new perspective to the shooting of this scene when she reveals that she had turned Flynn's own desires against him. At the time that the balcony scene is shot, six months have passed since the Coronation Ball, and Damita is famously, almost desperately, back in the picture. At Chico de Havilland had seen this, had seen what appeared to be Flynn's delight to have his wife around again, even though he had professed his love for Livvie. Now she decides to turn the tables: "I

Keighley and replacing him with Curtiz, what impression will this make around town? What impact will the move have on Flynn? Errol is behaving beautifully for his hand-chosen director and creating a character that Wallis admits is "good-humored, uninhibited, and athletic."[44]

Wallis consults with Warner. Given the facts, the move has to be made to assure box office, no matter that Flynn and, yes, de Havilland too, despise Michael Curtiz. Warner's take: *We're in charge here, not them.*

Wallis knows the foibles of his friend Curtiz now better than he did in 1935. Yes, Mike frets over composition; yes, he edits in the camera and only shoots the angles he wants the editor to use rather than providing full coverage. And yes, he drives the talent hard. But with most of the exteriors out of the way, and the meaty interiors ahead—starting with the Great Hall banquet scene that establishes the conflict between Robin, Prince John, and Sir Guy—Curtiz will supply some badly needed passion to the set.

Flynn and de Havilland can endure a hard month with Curtiz after spending two easy months with Keighley. If they complain, Wallis will tell them, "That's show business!"

Also out will be director of photography Tony Gaudio, if only because Curtiz will want his own trusted DP, Sol Polito, to be with him on a job of this magnitude. The bloodless coup takes place at midweek, on Wednesday, December 1, 1937. Curtiz and Polito are in; Keighley and Gaudio are out. Mike starts with the feast in the Great Hall, for which Polito devises a 36-second crane shot that rakes across and down the entire set skimming a flaming torch and then three live falcons, past the ensemble supplying music, finally ending on a dog (often the Saxons are called "dogs") gnawing on the remainder of a cooked animal carcass. It's classic Curtiz-Polito stuff, from the foreground objects to the movement of cooks turning a pig on a spit to no fewer than eight busy servants serving dozens of ravenous diners, while a knight toasts Prince John and the cast members stand for the toast, each raising a goblet—all in the same shot!

This is what Curtiz brings to the picture. Keighley had been straight ahead, unpretentious, often elevating his players to a level of warmth and humor that Curtiz might not have realized—qualities that will help this version of *Robin Hood* to stand the test of time. But now Mike will do the heavy lifting, the darker stuff.

Eventually, *Robin Hood* will be known as a Curtiz picture, even though Keighley directed about half of it, including most exteriors in Sherwood Forest, the capture of the caravan, and all of the archery tournament. Wallis makes a list of retakes he wants to see done by Curtiz to match the new energy level, including some exteriors, making it even more difficult to distinguish how much of the picture belongs to the first director and how much to the second.

The banquet sequence and Robin's battle with Sir Guy's knights, culminating in Robin's escape from the cas-

Lunchtime is suddenly lived in the fast lane at the studio, because replacement director Mike Curtiz demands that his actors forego half of their midday break to keep production running smoothly. At the Warner Bros. commissary, Flynn enjoys a moment away from shooting the Great Hall action sequence on Stage 1 and shares a laugh with former co-star Margaret Lindsay. Melville Cooper, the Sheriff of Nottingham, toys with his glass uncomfortably, aware that Curtiz will have a fit if they don't get back to the set soon. (John McElwee Collection)

73

Flynn, looking to be none too happy, straddles a rickety stepladder and glares at director Mike Curtiz, who sits on a higher stepladder, during the second reshoot of the balcony love scene between Robin and Marian. Tempers are understandably short all around during the last round of retakes to be shot during the arduous production. (Robert Florczak Collection)

tle, are shot over six highly aerobic days, with Flynn's performance bristling—he must be sharp because he is playing before a hundred people on Stage 1, and before one pair of discriminating Hungarian eyes.

As the year winds down, with the picture 15 days behind schedule, Curtiz keeps up his frenetic pace, and Wallis's list of retakes is passed along. Al Alleborn's report for December 7 says: "Mr. Blanke is going to discuss with Mr. Wallis and the writers necessary scenes that have to be retaken and added scenes as well to build up sequences that were shot by Mr. Keighley before Mr. Curtiz took the picture over. As soon as he gives these scenes we will make out the necessary schedule for the additional shots needed."[45]

But Flynn will turn into a pumpkin the moment 1937 becomes 1938—his contract calls for eight weeks off at the start of the year so he can go sail his new black-hulled schooner, *Sirocco*. If anybody can accomplish the goal of finishing Flynn in 20 days, it's Curtiz—if an antagonized Robin Hood doesn't finish the director first with a sword or, worse, walk off the picture.

From December 15 to 18 the company shoots the hanging of Robin Hood on the backlot's Dijon Street, and then retakes are shot in the Great Hall on December 20. The list of retakes is long, and there are still original shots to make—it's clear that Flynn will not be finished before the end of the year. The ramifications are severe, as Alleborn notes: "Each day that we use him will run into quite a bit so far as Flynn is concerned with his next year's work in pictures in which he will appear." In other words, he is guaranteed 12 weeks off a year, the first eight of which will occur in January and February, cutting down the amount of work he can do, and, potentially, the number of pictures he can make. Not to mention the fact that they will be paying him $6,000 per week if he reports for work on January 2.[46]

And he *does* report for work in the new year to reshoot the love scene once again, and enjoys a hefty payday, although candids show he doesn't enjoy the experience one bit; nor does Livvie. "Oh, Curtiz…was a tyrant," she will say later. "He was abusive, he was cruel. Oh, he was just a villain but I guess he was pretty good. We didn't believe it then, but he clearly was."[47]

The world will never know what Keighley's love scene looked like, although history suggests it might have been superior to the Curtiz version, because the actors trusted Keighley, and he had earned better performances from them in the quiet scenes than they would now give Curtiz. And there would have been the electricity produced by Livvie as she teases Errol through retake after retake. "You know that the Keighley version had to be different from the Curtiz version," says *Errol Flynn Slept Here* co-author Michael Mazzone. "I have to guess that it was softer, maybe even erotic, compared to the Curtiz scene. It's such a shame that this earlier footage is gone."[48] The version surviving today shows actors who know their lines but recite them in a rush, almost as if wanting to be done with the scene.

Curtiz chooses to capture the scene as a tight two-shot, with no over-the-shoulder coverage. In typical fashion, Mike cuts in the camera—only providing the editor with one set of shots that must be assembled the way Curtiz sees the scene playing out. But in doing so, he paints himself into a corner and when Wallis orders additional close-ups, the stars have already been shot in the focal length of a close-up and their faces are too close to the camera for over-the-shoulder shots. Instead, the stars are each captured addressing the camera instead of each other. In 50 years, these odd close-ups, one each of Robin and Marian, will draw chuckles in retrospective movie houses because they are self-conscious and don't fit in the sequence of the love scene. Solving the problem of close-ups this way serves as testimony to the fact that the Curtiz method of editing in the camera doesn't work—at least not on a Wallis picture.

On January 8 Flynn and Knowles shoot the Robin of Locksley establishing shot at Calabasas as Robin and Will ride into frame and jump a log, which cuts into Flynn's first close-up of the finished picture. On January 10 major retakes involving a legion of extras for the archery tournament are shot at Midwick Country Club near Pasadena. Then on January 12 Errol and Livvie meet at Calabasas for a much-discussed new ending for the picture, called a "tag," with Robin on horseback and Marian sitting across his lap, described in notes as the scene "where Flynn and de Havilland ride off in the hills." They appear to be gloriously happy and beautifully photographed in a shot that will be used in trailers promoting the picture, but not in the picture itself. After more retakes, Flynn finally finishes *The Adventures of Robin Hood* on Friday, January 14, 1938, having earned two more weeks' pay than planned, and he can begin his long-awaited vacation at sea.

The picture will premiere in four months, and Olivia, who never feels affinity for the character of Maid Marian, not on the first day and not on the last, won't run the risk of going to see it. "I never saw *Robin Hood* when it came out," she will say later. "There is…an ambivalence and at that time I was sort of afraid to see it. You know, you are always afraid of not being any good, terrified of it."[49]

Flynn experiences no such fear of the picture, which goes on to return a $2 million profit. He does see *Robin Hood*, and loves it, and orders a print in 16mm for himself from the lab, as he does with all his pictures, and for the rest of his life he will sit in the dark and marvel at Errol Flynn, Movie Star, in his grandest role ever, with his grandest girl ever, and as the years pass, it will become an ever-more bittersweet two hours to be washed down with ever-greater quantities of vodka.

Flynn and de Havilland mounted a horse to shoot an alternate ending in the rolling hills of Calabasas, but Hal Wallis decided he liked the original ending better, in which Robin and Marian exit the picture arm in arm and the doors of the Great Hall close behind them. And so the unsettled pair wrapped production of *The Adventures of Robin Hood*—a picture she would avoid seeing for more than 20 years because she had no faith it would be any good.

They should have been having the time of their lives, but Flynn's insecurity and de Havilland's growing discontent made *Four's a Crowd* an unhappy production and the least profitable of the eight pictures they made together. (John McElwee Collection)

5 THE SURE THING

Beginning in the dark, depressed year of 1934 with the unexpected success of an afterthought romantic comedy from little Columbia Pictures called *It Happened One Night*, America discovers a taste for funny business that is absurdist and a touch surreal—almost, but not quite, Daliesque, like the Marx Brothers. Critics dub it "screwball comedy," and three studios work at perfecting it—MGM, through a series of pictures starring Jean Harlow, Clark Gable, William Powell, Spencer Tracy, and others, and RKO and Columbia, both of which recycle Cary Grant, Katharine Hepburn, and Irene Dunne in picture after zany picture.

Nobody much thinks the Brothers Warner are very funny. The Burbank studio has made a reputation on mugs and bullets; the "working man's studio" is built on a mountain of gangster bodies, not Vaudevillian jokes. But J.L. thinks he *is* funny. No, J.L. thinks he's hilarious and makes a habit of telling jokes very badly, and because he is Jack L. Warner, nobody tells him how unfunny he really is. Instead he hears, *Yeah, that's a hot one, Boss!* But J.L. sees in *Daily Variety* that there's money in screwball, and since everybody else is making comedies, then dammit, Warner Bros. will make comedies too!

Hal Wallis understands that the studio isn't necessarily very funny and ensures that the story will be just what the public wants by optioning *All Rights Reserved* from Wallace Sullivan, who had been responsible for conceiving the story line for the smash hit *Libeled Lady* with Harlow, Powell, Loy, and Tracy. In fact, *All Rights Reserved* is the same story line as *Libeled Lady*, with only the most minor of alterations to keep MGM from dragging Warner Bros. to court.

To doubly assure success, Wallis gives the Sullivan story to Casey Robinson, a studio writer working his way up through the ranks, from a Flynn action script, *Captain Blood*, all the way up to a Davis vehicle, *It's Love I'm After*. Robinson is such a fast-tracker, in fact, that he's penciled in for a couple of new Davis projects as well.

The Sullivan story as fleshed out by Robinson is: The *News-Herald*, a big city paper, has been in a downward spiral since managing editor Robert Lansford left over differences with publisher Patterson Buckley. Now the *News-Herald* is closing its doors, while Lansford has gone on to a career as a slick PR man who sabotages and then rescues the reputations of filthy capitalists. Lansford sets his sights on John P. Dillingwell, eccentric and hated millionaire, who wants nothing to do with Lansford. Dillingwell's granddaughter Lorri happens to be dating Lansford's nemesis Buckley. When Lansford hears this, he schemes to meet Lorri and get to Dillingwell through the back door. But the cranky millionaire sees Lansford for the skunk that he is and calls out the dogs, who chase the PR menace off his property. Humiliated but undeterred, the cunning Lansford asks Buckley for his old job back as managing editor at the paper so he can launch a smear campaign against Dillingwell—who must then come to Lansford to save the millionaire's ruined reputation. Along the way, Lansford romances Lorri behind the back of hapless Buckley, while reporter Jean Christy is in love with Robert from afar. After much hijinks, Robert and Lorri and Pat and Jean end up at the justice of the peace, realize they are marrying the wrong people, and switch partners at the last minute.

David Niven snapped this photo of Flynn and an ardent admirer aboard *Sirocco* in 1938. Honeys always found their way on board anytime Errol could shake himself free of Lili. (Photo Courtesy of the Academy of Motion Picture Arts and Sciences)

With the script written, thoughts about casting begin while *The Adventures of Robin Hood* is on location at Chico fighting the rains and the flu. As of October 1937, the thinking is that freelancer Fredric March would portray the unscrupulous Robert Lansford. March is a J.L. favorite and hot off the successful screwball *Nothing Sacred* with comedy queen Carole Lombard. The original plan has March leading a Warner Bros. cast that includes Miriam Hopkins as Jean Christy, Pat O'Brien as Patterson Buckley, and Joan Blondell as Lorri Dillingwell. But timing goes haywire and Fredric March, off shooting *The Buccaneer* for Paramount, is unavailable, which throws a monkey wrench in the works and sets off a scramble to find funny people to populate the funny script. Lombard had been on the Warner lot during the *Robin Hood* production cycle making a screwball called *Fools for Scandal*, and there was talk of putting her on contract, but *Fools* will bomb upon release and nothing comes of a Lombard-Warner Bros. pact.

Put-upon swashbuckler Errol Flynn has been crying to get out of the tights and down off the horse, and the project he pitches to Warner and Wallis is Cyrano de Bergerac. J.L. thinks to himself: *Only Flynn would have the balls to go after a part with comedy and gut-wrenching tragedy and tender romance. The only parts of it that Flynn could possibly handle are the costumes and the swordplay.* J.L. knows that Cyrano calls for more of an actor than Errol Flynn dreams of being.

The truth is that Flynn doesn't particularly like himself. He will say at the end of his life, "I have been tired of this face for a long time."[1] But it's not the face he dislikes. Oh, no. The face works. He will own all his pictures in 16mm and watch them endlessly and marvel at the face. Happy, sad, brave, sorry, boyish, impudent, lustful, but mostly brave, the face scores every time. But the soul—the soul is ugly, Flynn suspects, and the soul suits Cyrano's deformity. What Flynn fails to understand is that Cyrano's face is ugly but his soul is divine—that's the point of the Rostand work. Flynn sees only the opportunity to put a rubber nose on the face and become something grotesque.

Warner and Wallis know better than that, so they will put Flynn in a comedy, and, of course, Livvie has to go where Flynn goes to assure box office. Livvie is a case unto herself. Far from the "always a lady" image that evolves in the 1970s and beyond, a few years into the picture business, de Havilland has picked up a rough side in her long days and weeks on soundstages. She has evolved into something of a minor-league Lombard, she the dean of the epithet, a trait that helps her fit in with the male-dominated production crews. Lombard knows that if you want the guys to make you look good—light you right and make you up right and shoot you right—you have to get in good with them. Perhaps this is Livvie's intention as well. Says Hollywood historian John McElwee of the Warner Bros. blooper reels of the '30s and '40s: "One clip finds Olivia blowing a line with Paul Henreid as they're shooting *Devotion*. 'Son-of-a-bitch!' she exclaims, giving each syllable the benefit of her precise, measured delivery. She really stole my heart with that one."[2]

Errol's friend Steve Hayes would be a guest at the Flynn home. "I was looking at pictures from *Robin Hood*," Hayes remembers, "and I was saying, 'Oh my God, de Havilland! What a pure creature!' and Flynn laughed and said, 'Have you ever met her?' I said no. He said, 'You will; I'll introduce you to her.... But beware; it's like talking to a sailor. She can really give it to you.'" Hayes, a Hollywood bit player and writer, says of the ribald Livvie: "I was always stunned because she and her sister, Joan Fontaine—both of them seemed so refined but they had as bad a mouth as Ava Gardner. I was on a movie over at Fox and she was in the commissary in costume for *My Cousin Rachel*. I overheard her, 'That so-and-so.' I thought, 'Boy, Errol was right!'"[3]

But Hollywood will do that. It's a town populated by ambitious businessmen, by course tradesmen on the soundstages, and by a galaxy of stars—many, if not most, coming from rough backgrounds, and all expert at *not* being or sometimes even knowing themselves, including Olivia, who will say later, "...it is very hard for me to tell who I am, because I really don't know."[4]

So, here are all these people, good looking or they wouldn't be on the screen, adept at putting on facades, and turned loose in the area running from Santa Monica and Pacific Palisades to the west to Glendale and Pasadena to the east, and that exotic area becomes an island controlled by the studios who control the stars. The studios also con-

At least the extras are having fun. Olivia de Havilland sits at left, with Patric Knowles next to her. A standing Rosalind Russell gazes at Errol Flynn. All four stars are coming off illness, and de Havilland is throwing tantrums. But the Flynn-de Havilland scenes have some sizzle.

trol the columnists, meaning that only good things are written about the stars, and scandals involving sex, drugs, and the occasional death are covered up at every turn. In future interviews, Olivia will speak of the glamour of old Hollywood, and how sheltered she is during the 1930s, but how sheltered can she be in such an environment? Jean Harlow at MGM and Carole Lombard at Paramount religiously shun underwear in their pictures. Joan Crawford often beds her directors and leading men to control them. Closer to home, Kay Francis (of de Havilland's own studio, Warner Bros.) keeps a running diary that rates her nights spent "fucking" directors and stars and casually mentions the abortions she endures to remain active on the screen.[5] Fredric March and Errol Flynn are known as sexual predators who bag anything in a skirt anyplace that's handy. And Jimmy Stewart, a man soon to be dating Livvie, is renowned for speaking softly but carrying a big stick. So yes, the stars glitter at the big Sunset Strip trio of Trocadero, Ciro's, and Club Mocambo, but later in the evening, an earthy, sexual atmosphere pervades, and anything and everything goes.

In this world, Olivia de Havilland comes of age. Already she has spoken frankly with Flynn and told him they can have no future until the situation with Lili is resolved. Already she has cockteased him on the set of *Robin Hood*. Now she is feeling her oats about the scripts being forwarded. Livvie is sick of being rescue fodder for Errol Flynn, where she literally has nothing to do but pray to heaven to be saved from the villain by the brave hero, which only differs from Pearl White being tied to railroad tracks by the fact that now pictures have sound.

Warner and Wallis find themselves in the unenviable position of creating stars like Flynn and de Havilland and then watching these kids turn what the front office believes to be evil when, in truth, anybody is lucky to be getting a regular paycheck these days.

Once J.L. had the stars where he wanted them. Now, as *Robin Hood* comes together in post-production and the front office understands what a hit this might be, suddenly the stars have some power of their own. Now the bosses have to think ahead and find ways to capitalize on the new blockbuster. Long term, Flynn and de Havilland have to be put in more costume pictures. But for now, the thinking is to find a quick vehicle and stick them in front of the camera. J.L. need look no further than *All Rights Reserved*. He can put the kids in modern dress, on modern sets, and let them go at it in a comedy—at a fraction of the cost of making a costume picture. And he can get both Flynn and de Havilland off his back because both are sick of the costume pictures and both want a change.

To direct this comedy, Warner wants Eddie Goulding, and then he wants Bill Keighley. The third and final choice is Bill Dieterle, who has worked with the entire Warner Bros. company, from Davis (*Satan Met a Lady*) to Muni (*The Story of Louis Pasteur* and *The Life of Emile Zola*) to de Havilland (*A Midsummer Night's Dream*) to Flynn (*Another Dawn*). Dieterle is a guy who sees the depth in a picture and handles the comedic and the grotesque with equal ease. His claim to fame: he wears white gloves on the set, possibly to make his hand gestures more visible against the lights. Even though he's a tough director, Flynn finds him tolerable compared to Curtiz—and every Dieterle picture is a success.

Flynn has been promised two months off after the completion of the grueling *Robin Hood*, for which he worked nine weeks with Keighley

Oh my! I've discovered MEN! By the time of the Flynn-de Havilland screwball comedy, the starlet had come of age. Here in an *All Rights Reserved* still shoot, she contemplates being a Livvie sandwich between suave Flynn and mugging Knowles. (John McElwee Collection)

and six more with Curtiz. Flynn would label *Light Brigade* his toughest production because of the stint in the cold at Lone Pine, then all the sloshing around Lake Sherwood, and the dusty final charge. But it would be difficult to imagine anything as punishing as the siege of rainy, flu-infested weeks in Bidwell Park, the endless studio calls, the Busch Gardens and Calabasas gymnastics, and the exhausting Stage 1 swordfights of *Robin Hood*.

Warner and Wallis know that Flynn is not typecast as the Robert Lansford of *All Rights Reserved*. The part had been written for the cynical world-weariness of Fredric March or the brashness of Cagney. And Joan Blondell would make a dizzier dame for a picture like this than Livvie. But *All Rights Reserved* is ready to shoot, and Hal Wallis can have it in the can and cut and in the queue right after the hubbub of *Robin Hood* begins to subside.

Given that Flynn and de Havilland are *in* and March and Blondell are *out*, the roles of Patterson Buckley and Jean Christy are up in the air. Wallis considers requesting Ralph Bellamy on loan from Columbia; Joel McCrea is also considered. For Jean Christy, J.L. contemplates giving the part to Kay Francis, but she has become box office poison, and why would they want to wish *that* on their Flynn-de Havilland picture? J.L. wants somebody who can do comedy, so he borrows tall, square-shouldered, 30-year-old Rosalind Russell from MGM. Russell is proven in both comedy and drama. She can play it fast-talking and cynical, or quiet and tender.

For Buckley, the addle-headed newspaper publisher, they decide to stay in-house. Memos reveal that the brain trust is *settling* on Patric Knowles, who nobody thinks can do comedy. It will be make or break time for Knowles, who has tried the patience of the brass a little too much of late, starting with that nonsense with the airplane on location at Chico and continuing through episodes of lateness on the set. Flynn has been a bad influence on his friend, and Wallis is about ready to cut Knowles loose.

All Rights Reserved is thrown together so quickly as a Flynn-de Havilland vehicle that the stars are alerted of the impending picture while still decompressing from *Robin Hood*. They must report to work at the beginning of February for Bill Dieterle. Flynn is vacationing in New York: *What? I'm supposed to be off until March 15!*

Comedy, they reply. *Romantic comedy with de Havilland for Dieterle. No tights, no horse—so pipe down and get in here!*

Flynn has enjoyed working for Dieterle in the past and heads back to Hollywood with high hopes. But by the time he lands in Burbank, Dieterle is out and Curtiz is in. Mike's stock is very high now because he is seen as the savior of *Robin Hood*, the guy who injected vitality at a critical moment and salvaged the most expensive production of the year. Flynn knows that Curtiz wields the power now, and plays along because this is real screwball comedy. He arrives back in Burbank on February 3. The next day, the company begins shooting in Lansford's office with Flynn and supporting players. In this first scene, Flynn dictates a letter to two secretaries in a long bit of dialogue that would have been impossible for him to memorize given that he has just been introduced to the script—so he reads it out of a small notepad, as if remembering it from notes he had made in some coffee shop. It plays nicely, and gets around Flynn's not knowing his lines. In this early sequence that establishes Lansford's character, his luscious secretary Gertrude is played by Gloria Blondell, Joan's kid sister. At 22, Gloria is just Flynn's type—young, leggy, and ambitious, and it's not difficult to imagine Flynn suggesting Gloria for a role in the first week of shooting in exchange for a personal favor...or two.

Early on, Wallis sees the rushes and admonishes Curtiz for allowing Flynn to ad-lib. He writes crankily in a memo: "Tell Flynn to stop saying 'old boy, old chap, old fellow'—cut out all this English business. He's supposed to be a bright American man."[6] Wallis also nails Flynn for picking his own wardrobe. Wallis wails at Curtiz of Flynn: "He's a terrible dresser!"[7]

Production progresses through the week of February 7, but by the morning of Monday, February 14, Flynn and Knowles are ill, and by that afternoon de Havilland and Russell are down for the count as well. Colds and flu rip through 1930s soundstages as easily as they had infested Big Chico Creek, given the long hours and close quarters of actors and crews. *All Rights Reserved* goes dark for two days, but it seems that Livvie's mind has been dark since she first learned of her participation in this latest bit of fluff. She is irritable on the set and doesn't know her lines, so Tenny Wright gives her a talking-to, which doesn't help.

Burned out as she is and forced to enact the manic-depressive Lorri day after day, Livvie is missing her morning calls. And Curtiz is unsympathetic.

She will say later: "He was caustic, critical; he was furious when you took an hour for lunch. You didn't take an hour for lunch with him, you took forty-five minutes."[8]

Hal Wallis notes that Curtiz would never stop and have lunch himself, so why should anyone else? "He paced the floor while everyone was off the soundstage," says Wallis, "thinking about what he was going to do when they got back. If an actor blew a line later, he would scream, 'You lunch bum!'"[9]

"You would have to take off your costume," says Livvie, "and then you would have to go and eat something and then you would have to come back and get your make-up fixed, then you'd have to put on your costume and they were usually complicated, and you'd have to be ready for work. If instead of being 10 minutes ahead of time, you were ready on the dot, he was enraged and sulked all afternoon."[10] Less than two weeks into production, Curtiz instructs unit manager Lou Baum to note in his production report that Flynn is 25 minutes late returning from lunch.

The writers craft a script rife with inside jokes that hit home for Errol and Livvie, and it's presumed that audiences in Iowa City will laugh as well. On location at Chico de Havilland had told a reporter, "The careers of many movie stars are much more theatrical than the pictures they play in, but even if their actual lives could be worked into a story, the public would not believe it."[11]

The writers target Flynn's ego. In the opening sequence, after he has dismissed his secretaries, Lansford is visited by Jean Christy in his office. There Lansford presumes to know Jean's "type" and ventures opinions about her love life (but he's way off base). She says, mockingly, "Mr. Lansford, you're wonderful." And he replies, deadpan, "Miss Christy, I'm incredible." He pauses and adds,

Warner and Wallis brought in veteran comedy slugger Walter Connolly to work with de Havilland and Flynn. Connolly had supported Jean Harlow, William Powell, and Myrna Loy in *Libeled Lady* two years earlier, and Carole Lombard and Fredric March in *Nothing Sacred* a few months past. The front office knew early on that their screwball comedy needed all the help it could get.

Audiences in Iowa City didn't know what to make of Errol Flynn in top hat and tails, so the sometimes-clever Flynn–de Havilland screwball comedy that finally became known as *Four's a Crowd* never had much of a chance and squeaked into the black by only $15,000 to become the least profitable of the seven features that starred the couple as a team. (Image courtesy of Hershenson/Allen Archive)

"There are some things I don't know much about, but I have a knowledge of women that few men possess."

The scene is funniest inside the walls of the studio, where Flynn is known to have "gone Hollywood," and where his assumptions about women are well known. Flynn makes eye contact or lays on the charm and renders women horizontal often in seconds, so there's no arguing that Errol has knowledge of women. Just not as much as he thinks he does. Later in the script Pat Knowles as a frustrated Buckley sums up Errol Flynn by saying, "I may not have Lansford's fascinating nature or diabolical physical gifts, but neither am I a wolf," which sums up the king of swashbucklers well and draws a big laugh because of it.

The writers don't spare de Havilland either. In her first scene in the picture, she tells Pat Buckley on the phone, "Oh, Moses in the bulrushes, I'm bored! Bored? I'm ossified!" Robinson and co-writer Sig Herzig pay homage to Livvie's growing distaste for the Flynn pictures that are "beneath her"—the growing ossification of her career—and her entreaties to Warner and Wallis to step her up to the prestige pictures. Instead, she is stuck in another routine picture, propping up Errol, getting one minute of screen time to his three, earning a fifth of what he earns.

It speaks to a growing awareness on her part; she's aware now that what's good for him can also be good for her. She's aware also that Flynn's not the only one dying to

Livvie is 21 now, and a woman...who has grown up in Hollywood. As a result, her language has grown salty and she's become one heck of a kisser, as seen in an open-mouthed clinch with Flynn during production of...whatever it's called. The scene is recreated here later by the still photographer.

can't hurt to show Errol in his natural habitat, but a week into production Wallis kills the tennis scenes, depriving audiences of a look at the "Killer" in his tennis prime and at de Havilland in a tennis skirt. That's OK, because Wallis doesn't think that Livvie has the legs for short outfits anyway, like the one she's to wear in her bedroom scene with Flynn. "The dress is too short for her," he grouses to costume designer Orry-Kelly. "She can't wear dresses that short." Says Wallis, "The outfit looks indecent, if you get what I mean. I don't object to it being sexy; as a matter of fact, I would like to see it that way, but this somehow or other has an indecent appearance about it."[12] In the sequence as shot and printed, Livvie wears a full, long-sleeved robe that covers her from chin to ankles. The modest frock will be necessary to pass the censors, especially because of the very unusual (for the 1930s) kiss between Flynn and de Havilland in the picture.

Kisses these days are very stage-bound affairs. Lips are closed; it can be a long kiss but it's still a buss for the camera. But this particular day, on Stage 3, the scene calls for Robert to shush Lorri by kissing her, so Errol catches Livvie with her mouth open, and she keeps it that way and gives a sultry moan as well for a kiss that no one knows quite how to categorize.

get under her skirt, and it's time to start dating men who can move her career along. Men like Brian Aherne, her co-star in *The Great Garrick*. Livvie is seen around town with Aherne—it's not thought to be serious, but this is a new Livvie, still living with her mother and now sister Joanie on Nella Vista, and venturing out on the town on her own, with virile male escorts.

Other touches in the Robinson-Herzig script reflect the lives of the stars. They write in a tennis sequence for Flynn, then the darling of the West Side Tennis Club in Culver City and the acknowledged beast of the Hollywood courts. It

The new Livvie will tell reporters that she loves kissing, ever since her first experience with Peter at age 16. "I liked it then, and I still like it," she proclaims.

In this same scene in the bedroom, Grandpa Dillingwell knocks on Lorri's door and Robert is inside. Lorri sends Robert out to the balcony where Flynn (actually, his double, Don Turner) does a none-too-graceful reprise of *Robin Hood*'s balcony hang-from-the-vines; indeed, he hangs on for dear life. When intercut with Flynn, the shot produces a genuine laugh. So it goes in *All Rights Reserved*, with the writers and director making each other guffaw, assuming that the American heartland will laugh as well.

For the role of the hated, dyspeptic Grandpa Dillingwell, Warner and Wallis enlist pricey character actor Walter Connolly, veteran of *It Happened One Night* at Columbia, *Libeled Lady* at MGM, and full-blown screwball hit *Nothing Sacred* for Selznick. Connolly here reprises his *Libeled Lady* role of cynical, money-grubbing father to a beautiful young socialite. Then it had been Myrna Loy; now, since Livvie is a decade younger, father becomes grandfather. Connolly can play it straight or turn on a dime and become the put-upon victim. He sets up star players for success—Flynn and de Havilland need the help—which makes Connolly well worth his two grand a week. Also on hand is Melville Cooper as Dillingwell's stiff-upper-lip butler, Bingham. After his Technicolor turn as the Sheriff of Nottingham in *The Adventures of Robin Hood*, Cooper takes his demotion to butler well, and delivers the truest comedic performance in the picture.

As production continues, there is no real title for the new comedy. Warner and Wallis know as early as December 9, 1937, that *All Rights Reserved* is already owned and not available. On January 29, 1938, executive story editor Walter MacEwen suggests "Let's Get Together" to Warner and Wallis—his memo is returned the next day with "NO" scrawled across it.

Four days later, MacEwen sends another memo to Warner and Wallis that says, "Babbling in my sleep after going over 4 million titles—how about "Can't We Be Friends?" MacEwen receives the memo back. Handwritten across it in pencil are the words, "No—Sorry—about your sleep."

Five days later, "How about, 'A Fine Romance.'" The handwriting across the memo, in pencil, is the same. "No—don't like. JLW." MacEwen is fed up. He sends one more memo that urges J.L. to just go buy the title *All Rights Reserved* and be done with it. A handwritten response in pencil reads, "I don't like."

Naming the new Flynn comedy becomes the *cause célèbre* of the entire studio. It gets so bad that Wallis turns to Bob Taplinger in the publicity department, and Tap spends nights at the keyboard doing free association. He sends back an earnest list of a dozen titles that includes "The Two-Time Four," "About Faces," and, significantly, "Four's a Party." Wallis seizes on that one, and they go back to work.

Sleepless, ulcer-ridden Walter MacEwen has an hallucination a few days later; a title that plays off Taplinger's has possibilities and might end the stalemate. A search reveals that no one owns it. On February 16, 12 days into shooting, a memo routed to all departments reads, "The title of production #203 has been officially changed from ALL RIGHTS RESERVED to FOUR'S A CROWD."

Finally, the picture has a title along with a group of recalcitrant stars. Only Rosalind Russell remains a pro—the Warner Bros. players are too busy resisting Curtiz and grousing about the front office to have much fun in a picture that should have been a blast. Flynn shows up late; Livvie walks off the set when she feels the day should be over; Knowles behaves as if he's a star.

The company limps into a location stint at Busch Gardens for exteriors of the Dillingwell estate. Weather shuts down production for days, but finally Mike gets the action of Flynn in top hat and tails running away from Dillingwell's pack of dogs, and Flynn romances both Livvie and Roz at the pool—the scenes that should have taken place on a tennis court. They are finally shot at the pool at the Lakeside Country Club.

On March 24, 1938, Flynn and de Havilland are finished on *Four's a Crowd*, 11 days behind schedule but $12,000 under budget. Flynn has entered his prime as a Warner Bros. star and expresses displeasure about his life at every turn. Livvie is about to embark on her darkest time as an actress and suddenly ascend to the height of fame. *Four's a Crowd* ends their association as studio players who are plugged into productions by the front office and feel a close camaraderie as a result. They have been up to this time, despite it all, the two kids with a lot in common who had come up together in *Captain Blood* and matured in *Light Brigade*. But when Livvie and Errol next step onto a soundstage together in 11 months, they will hardly know each other, and neither will quite figure out why they were ever in love in the first place.

Troubled times are ahead for de Havilland and Flynn, both of whom are forced to adjust to life as adults, and superstars, and make some tough career decisions. (John McElwee Collection)

6 GONE HOLLYWOOD

Margaret Mitchell's *Gone With the Wind* becomes a sensation in Hollywood soon after its May 1936 release. First seen as a thousand-page woman's novel for the picnic basket or the front porch, it soon becomes much more. In a Depression, where all seems hopeless; in an era where women have started to see themselves as more than housewives; at a time when technology and urban sprawl threaten to wipe away gentle memories of pastoral life, *Gone with the Wind* whips into a cyclone the likes of which have never been seen anywhere before. It had seemed to Macmillan and Co. that 10,000 copies would suffice for a first run, until the Book-of-the-Month Club picks it up, calling for a print run of 40,000 more. Pretty soon, 3,700 copies of *Gone With the Wind* are selling every day, and not long after that, the book will touch the life of Errol Flynn and reroute that of Olivia de Havilland.

In the month of its release, the tale of the Old South is mailed to Warner Bros. and the other studios with an ungodly asking price of $100,000. J.L. doesn't read the book; he has people read it for him. He receives a briefing and thinks that, yeah, there might be a picture here, and the only person at the studio to play the heroine, Scarlett O'Hara, is tough-as-nails Bette Davis. But Warner and Wallis had already thought of Bette for another tale of the Antebellum South, a story called *Jezebel* that they had picked up in 1935. Walter MacEwen had written to Hal Wallis back then that *Jezebel* "would provide a good role for Bette Davis, who could play the spots off the part of a little bitch of an aristocratic Southern Girl."[1] And Scarlett O'Hara of *Gone With the Wind* is all of that and more.

J.L. is disinclined to spend a hundred grand on a property that would cost three or four million to produce when the studio already owns a tale of the Old South with Bette Davis's name on it. Besides, the Civil War doesn't sell—everyone knows that based on the release of King Vidor's *So Red the Rose* by Paramount at Christmas of '35. Margaret Sullavan and Randolph Scott had failed to draw crowds then—why should Warner Bros. stick its neck out and buy Mitchell's novel now? *Nope, pass.*

J.L. would later express his regret for making the mistake of not buying the book back when he could have had it "for a mere $50,000." But in May 1936 he doesn't know that's the price. He has only heard $100,000 quoted, and he knows that the head of cash-strapped Universal had said to his script reader in reference to *Gone With the Wind*: "I told you no costume pictures." Nobody is about to pay this king's ransom for a woman's story. In J.L.'s world, you spend a hundred grand making a picture; you don't spend it to buy the rights to make one.

What he doesn't know is that producer David O. Selznick is being egged on by his New York rep, Kay Brown, and his business partner, Jock Whitney, until he's worn down and lucks into a deal to buy the book for the $50,000 that Warner will quote in his autobiography in the mid-1960s. If *Gone With the Wind* is lightning, then it's Selznick, and not Warner or Zanuck or any of the moguls, who captures it in a bottle. And once Selznick owns it, he begins to understand the enormity of what he's done and consider the black magic it will take to convert 1,000 densely packed pages for the screen, considering that this is a

87

period in American history that the movie-going public finds distasteful to look upon.

Says Carole Sampeck, Clark Gable expert, curator of the Carole Lombard Archive, and native Atlantan: "Mitchell was renowned as an Atlanta historian as well as a delightful storyteller. She put incredible research into dates, battles, social mores, and even the weather of a particular day and place. Her characters were too numerous for any normal cinema event to contain. However, the novel exploded into such immediate popularity that the slightest deviation from the story line, characters, and details when translated for the screen would have been viewed as rank heresy by the legion of devoted readers."[2]

Faced with such a challenge, Selznick starts pragmatically by trying to cast his would-be epic. His company has an obligation to Ronald Colman for one more picture so obviously Colman will play Rhett Butler. It becomes a simple matter then of casting Scarlett O'Hara. "Might try someone like [Miriam] Hopkins or [Tallulah] Bankhead," Selznick cables to Kay Brown.[3]

No sooner does he settle on Colman than he *unsettles* on him. The suave leading man will turn 46 on February 9, and that's up there for a vital action figure like Rhett. And Colman comes off as way too fatherly and moral to have an Atlanta prostitute for a lover, as Rhett does in the book. Besides, as soon as American readers start devouring the novel, they envision MGM screen sensation Clark Gable as Captain Butler. BUT Gable is MGM property, and Selznick is determined that GWTW will be an independent Selznick Picture. If Gable is involved, then Louis B. Mayer, boss of Metro and not coincidentally David Selznick's father-in-law, will horn in on the picture, and all independence will be lost. As soon as Gable sees the tide of popular opinion coming in on this topic, he begins to backpedal as fast as he can. "I like to pick my spots," says Gable, "and now found myself trapped by a series of circumstances over which I had no control."[4]

Says historian Sampeck, "He was leery of attempting a characterization which was so firmly set in the public's imagination, feeling his acting abilities would fall seriously short and his adulation would turn to scorn."[5]

On January 4, 1937, David Selznick writes a memo to Daniel O'Shea, his right-hand man: "One of our strongest possibilities for the lead in *GWTW* is Errol Flynn. Myron [Selznick—David's brother and Errol's agent] is going to determine from Warner Bros. whether they would give us a picture a year with Flynn, if we gave him this lead. Please follow him up on this."[6]

"Selznick floated a trial Flynn balloon," says Carole Sampeck, "when it was appearing that Gable simply would not do the film."[7]

No one expects to hear David throw Flynn's name around, but Selznick has just seen *The Charge of the Light Brigade* and is shocked at the progress of Flynn as an actor. *Boy, does this kid have screen presence!* Selznick justifiably sees versatility, testosterone, rakishness, obsession, and heroism in the performance. It suddenly seems that he could do a lot worse; in Selznick's eyes, Flynn is a legitimate option.

"With Flynn, we're not talking about somebody who was *just* a new, good-looking leading man," says Rudy Behlmer, editor of *Memo from David O. Selznick*, "but also somebody who had made a major impression…, an up-and-coming major actor on the scene who could play all kinds of things, and he would have been a logical choice, early on, to do *Gone With the Wind*."[8]

"Flynn, in my opinion, could have pulled off the dashing qualities of Rhett Butler," says Sampeck, "but it would have been a very different film. The Flynn onscreen persona was a bit different from the Gable image—a bit darker, perhaps, more elusive. These qualities would have suited Rhett Butler quite well."[9]

"I think he probably could have done it," says Behlmer of Flynn in the role, "and he probably would have been pretty good. It's a vision that's hard to contemplate now… because we're so entrenched with Clark Gable as Rhett Butler.[10]

As *Gone With the Wind* takes shape over the next year, Flynn will show his range in a variety of pictures. With the guidance of a strong director, which Flynn clearly needs, he *can* act. And for *GWTW*, Selznick has already signed George Cukor, who has directed *A Bill of Divorcement, Dinner at Eight, Romeo and Juliet, Camille,* and many other A pictures working with most of the top actors in town, from Garbo to the Barrymores. Cukor classifies as an elegant director and a refined man—which is why he has never been invited to hang out at gritty Warner Bros.

Reacting to the query from Myron Selznick about Errol Flynn's availability, Jack Warner asks his brother Harry Warner and also Hal Wallis, *How much can we get if we loan Flynn out?* And, *Do we really want to loan out our hottest new star for a picture that could become the stinker of all time?* To Myron, J.L. simply asks, *What's in it for us?*

Selznick is hearing a lot of cryptic answers around town as he shops for Rhett Butler, Scarlett O'Hara, Melanie Hamilton, and Ashley Wilkes. A few months after he begins to think about Errol as Rhett, a deal will surface that involves Flynn and Bette Davis starring as Rhett and Scarlett on loan from Warner Bros. in exchange for WB distribution of the picture and 25 percent of the profits.

Warner will say in 1964 that this deal had been Selznick's idea. Selznick states to Ed Sullivan on September 20, 1938: "Warner Brothers offered me Errol Flynn for Butler and Bette Davis for Scarlett if I would release the picture through Warners—and this would have been an easy way out of my [casting] dilemma."[11] Following the theory that the contemporary quote is the accurate one, J.L. probably initiates the deal, and there's no telling what Flynn thinks of it, except that, as noted, Flynn has gone as bigheaded as one can go, and the attention that accompanies the role of Rhett Butler in a highly anticipated film would suit him fine. And if the picture doesn't work out in the end, there is always Plan B: retire to the South Seas.

But J.L.'s deal is take it or leave it, and when Selznick fails to accept, Warner doesn't follow up. Instead, he does what he usually does—he takes it personally that Selznick doesn't want to play ball and spends the next two years pouting and passive-aggressively fussing and feuding with Selznick on issues related to *Gone With the Wind*.

The Boss's favorite for every top role to come along, Fredric March (right), assumes a piratical pose in *The Buccaneer*, with, from left, Anthony Quinn, Fred Kohler, Akim Tamiroff, and a surly band of bit players. The DeMille epic of the War of 1812 would be a top money earner for Paramount. If he traded in his flintlock pistol for a six-shooter, March would already resemble Wyatt Earp, black hat and all.

89

Late in 1937, the new Warner Bros. melodrama, *Jezebel*, starring Bette Davis, is in the can, and J.L. directs Bob Taplinger's publicity department to consciously ride the popularity of Margaret Mitchell's novel by promoting *Jezebel* as a story of the romantic Old South, which is bound to burn up Selznick. When *Jezebel* premieres on March 7, 1938, both J.L. and Selznick attend, and David is none too pleased with the story parallels. He tells Warner so in sharp tones after the screening, and follows up with a memo to J.L. the next day: "Reiterating what I told you last night, I think it would be a very great pity indeed from your own standpoint, for so distinguished and costly a picture as *Jezebel* should be damned as an imitation by the millions of readers, and lovers, of *GWTW*. And I am fearful that this is what may happen due to a few completely unnecessary bits. The picture throughout is permeated with characterizations, attitudes and scenes which unfortunately resemble *GWTW* regardless of whether or not they were in the original material."[12]

J.L. sits back in triumph at having beaten Selznick into theaters by a year and a half with an Old South tale. *Jezebel*, a big hit and an economical picture to make in relation to *GWTW*, will earn Bette Davis an Academy Award as Best Actress and Fay Bainter one as Best Supporting Actress, not to mention nominations for Best Picture, Ernest Haller's cinematography, and the musical score of Max Steiner.

As Warner Bros. mixes it up with Selznick, there is another costume picture in the works, a property called *Dodge City*, which first appears on studio radar with *The Adventures of Robin Hood* in post-production. On February 1, 1938, J.L. fires off a memo to Walter MacEwen, full of enthusiasm: "This Wyatt Earp is a great character. Can you proceed with this story and use Earp, inasmuch as he is public domain and at the same time avoid *Frontier Marshal*, which you stated Paramount owns?"[13]

So begins the long and tortuous development of *Dodge City* as a Warner A-caliber western, starring Fredric March as Wyatt Earp—just as he had been penciled in for seemingly every other Warner Bros. top-of-the-bill picture on the drawing boards for the past five years. In the early days of development of *Dodge City*, no one bothers to mention who should play the girl—in these action pictures, does it really matter anyway as long as she's got some sex appeal?

Fredric March is now 41 and has just been nominated for his second Oscar for playing the washed-up actor Norman Maine in Selznick's *A Star Is Born*. As J.L.'s memo about Wyatt Earp works its way through the system, another Fredric March picture for Cecil B. DeMille, *The Buccaneer*, hits theaters. In it, he portrays a larger-than-life French pirate, Jean Lafitte, who saves the United States at the Battle of New Orleans in the War of 1812 and even manages some prominent flag-waving for an isolationist nation observing dark European skies. Freelancer March is *box office*, and the Boss knows he'll make a sensational Earp.

A great deal of internal communication flows through the studio about Paramount owning the Earp story *Frontier Marshal*; J.L. claims that Wyatt Earp is a public domain character—anybody can make a movie about him without asking permission. Unfortunately, early in the game, *Dodge City* loses its would-be star, Fredric March, who signs a profit-sharing deal with independent producer Walter Wanger and takes himself out of the running.

Just about now, Warner Bros. receives a letter from Wyatt Earp's decades-long companion and common-law widow (Earp had died less than 10 years earlier, in 1929). In it, she warns the studio against making a movie about her late husband without permission—and, of course, compensation. And since J.L. isn't about to let some old broad strong-arm him for a payoff, he now finds himself without a star and without a main character.

The writers start again and develop a script with all the flavor of rip-roarin' cow town Dodge City and the Old West—and none of the Earps to weigh it down. Instead they create a generic hero, a fella named Hatton, and a generic villain, an hombre named Surrett, and a generic philly by the name of Abbie. In fact, the front office will never harbor any illusions that Harvard Classics are being written with the westerns, whether A or B caliber. The next year, after *Dodge City* has been released, supervisor Robert Lord will write to associate producer Mark Hellinger in regard to the story description for a new project called *Nevada*. "Dear Mark," Lord begins. "Your story line is about as good (perhaps a little better) than the basic story line of *Dodge City* and *Union Pacific*. That is to say: 'It stinks and they stank.' To be quite realistic, the basic story line of most westerns, including the successful ones, is prone to be somewhat feeble-minded. Why not—since they cater to the lowest common denominator of our mass audience?"[14]

Warner Bros. executives are running a factory; instead of stamping out Buicks, they're crafting pictures and they're doing it on a schedule. Right now, without a star in place, development of *Dodge City* is about to fall behind. On July 7, 1938, Robert Lord writes to Hal Wallis, "I have not gone insane, but I should like to suggest that we make an attempt to get Gary Cooper for *Dodge City*."[15] Cooper toils at Paramount Pictures in the heart of Hollywood, and his schedule just about now is pretty light; he's at work on a comedy called *Bluebeard's Eighth Wife* with Claudette Colbert and David Niven, but hasn't firmed up anything after that. So Warner and Wallis kick around the idea of Cooper as Hatton, but this goes nowhere.

A month later, Robert Lord sends a memo to Wallis suggesting James Cagney, the studio problem child—a fine actor who keeps bucking the front office for more money and better parts and gets put on suspension for it. This last time, he actually left to go make pictures at ramshackle Grand National, and a couple of real stinkers resulted. Cagney has just recently slunk back and his new picture, *Boy Meets Girl* with Pat O'Brien, is set to release that month. But Cagney faces a backlog of scripts and is already working on another picture, *Angels with Dirty Faces*, with Pat O'Brien and Humphrey Bogart and will move straight into a western of his own, *The Oklahoma Kid*.

Warner and Wallis have no star for their western, and it's the middle of August and there's a blockbuster western in development at Fox starring Tyrone Power as Jesse James and another picture about the laying of railroads over at Paramount directed by DeMille and starring Barbara Stanwyck and Joel McCrea. Walter Wanger is cooking up something of his own at United Artists by the name of *Stagecoach* starring that kid from the B pictures, John Wayne. It's the time of the western, and J.L. doesn't intend to be last in line, so the brain trust gets to thinkin' and there's no record of who says it first but there's the inevitable, "What about Flynn?"

What's that? Flynn? In a western?! So far, Errol Flynn has saved the empire of King William and Queen Mary, and gone to glory with the Light Brigade, and saved young Prince Edward, and then King Richard, and right now he's in the studio finishing up *The Dawn Patrol* as a boozing, combat-ace captain of the Royal Flying Corps. The common thread of all of them? *England!* Somehow the Tasmanian Aussie is as spit-and-polish British Empire as Hollywood can produce. He wears the uniform like a son-of-a-bitch and even salutes like he means it!

Wallis gives it to the writers to figure out, and they come back with: *There's a back story, see? He's…, he's a soldier of fortune. Yeah, that's it. He's a*

Olivia had co-starred with suave Brian Aherne in *The Great Garrick*. Just her type, tall, older, and an intellectual, he became her first beau in Hollywood. It may have been Aherne who led Livvie to believe that she should aim for prestige pictures and avoid the Flynn vehicles. Joan Fontaine would do Livvie one better and *marry* Aherne, whom she will describe as an arrogant cold fish. The antagonism of the sisters was fueled by the fact that one married the ex-boyfriend of the other. (John McElwee Collection)

91

soldier of fortune, and he's fought all over. Hell, he's even fought in the Civil War. We can tie it to GWTW! He fought for the Old South, and now he's kicking around out west. The writers change a few lines in the script and send it upstairs, and late in August, Lord doesn't hate what he's reading and forwards the script for *Dodge City* to Flynn on North Linden. Errol will never know that he is the fourth and last choice to play Wade Hatton.

Flynn forces his way through page by page and grows nauseous. He calls his agent, Noll Gurney at the Myron Selznick Agency. On September 1, 1938, Gurney sends a letter to the Boss on Flynn's behalf. The letter brims with understatement: "He [Flynn]," says Gurney to Warner, "is a little dubious about his ability to play a part that is so essentially American—or accentuated as he puts it—but Bob Lord is so enthusiastic about Errol for this part, and I know you are too, that I feel if we have a talk together it will give Errol some confidence. Bob thought perhaps we had better wait a day or two, maybe until next Tuesday, as the work on *Dawn Patrol* is pretty heavy going at the moment and it might be best if Errol concentrate on the job at hand for a little while longer. However, when and if I am needed I will come over."[16]

Two days later, *Four's a Crowd* hits theaters and does well enough in the big cities but falls flat in the sticks; the confusing plot and loud soundtrack help to sink Flynn and de Havilland as comic actors. And audiences can't figure out what to make of Flynn in contemporary dress, even though he looks comfortable in a modern story (his first in a year), and Livvie looks good with Errol, as she always does. In fact, it seems as if Livvie is everywhere—with Flynn in *Four's a Crowd*; with Dick Powell in the screwball *Hard to Get* on November 5; with John Payne in the service picture, *Wings of the Navy*, three months after that. In fact, de Havilland has just completed three pictures in six months, and she's a broken-down wreck as a result, clearly exhausted. Through her doctor, she begs for a break in the schedule.

J.L. knows it's risky to put Flynn in a western, but the trend, even with *Four's a Crowd*, is that casting de Havilland opposite Flynn guarantees breakeven or better. There is talk of Jane Bryan or Priscilla Lane as the female lead, but they're lightweights. *If we're giving them Errol, we're giving them Olivia. To the blazes with her exhaustion; it's not as if she's out there digging ditches—I made that girl a star, and she's taking a grand a week out of my pocket!*

Always, everywhere, at all hours, as business goes on in Hollywood, gossip swirls in all the studios and in all the restaurants and on every street corner about Selznick's epic-in-the-making, *Gone With the Wind*. The studio bosses, bitter rivals and yet comrades in arms, share a morbid fascination with the driven Selznick, who pops uppers to keep himself going and may well kill himself before he shoots a single foot of film.

Studio boss Hal Wallis pays a rare visit to Errol Flynn on the set of *The Dawn Patrol* as onscreen nemesis and de Havilland worshipper Basil Rathbone looks on. Wallis has shown up to lobby a skeptical Flynn that a foreigner can make a plausible western hero in the new super-project, *Dodge City*.

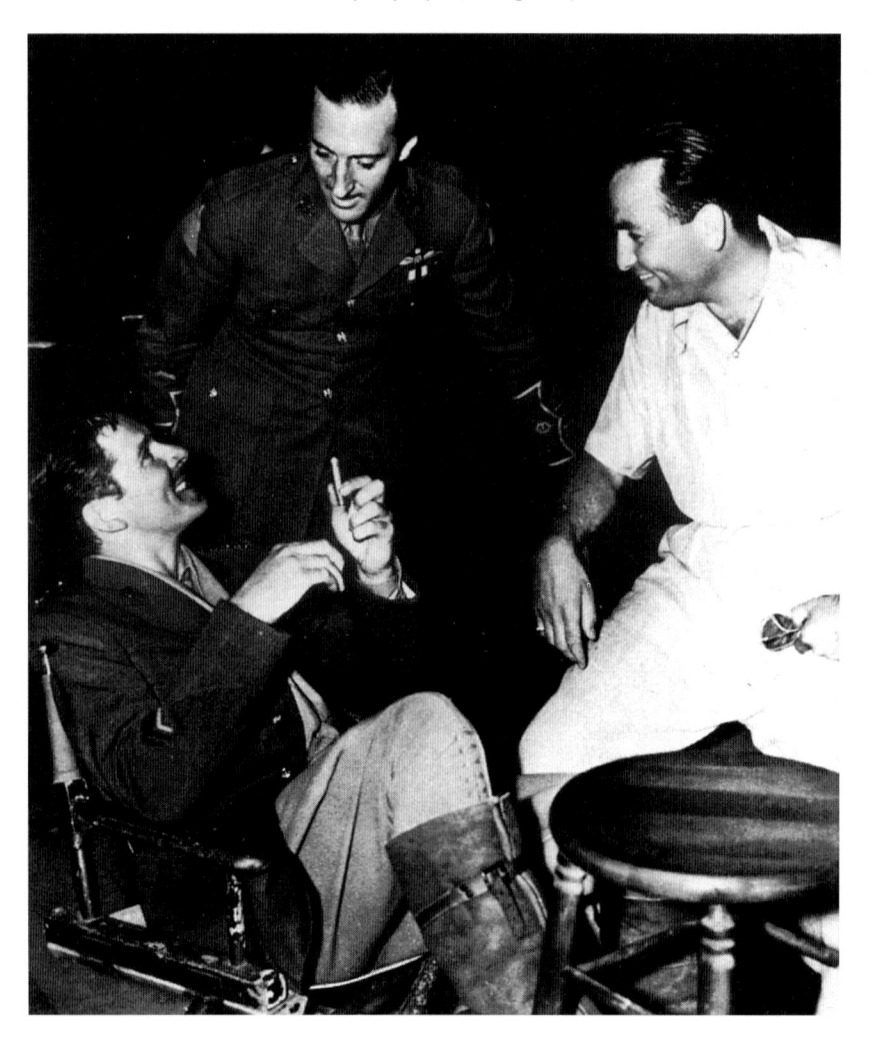

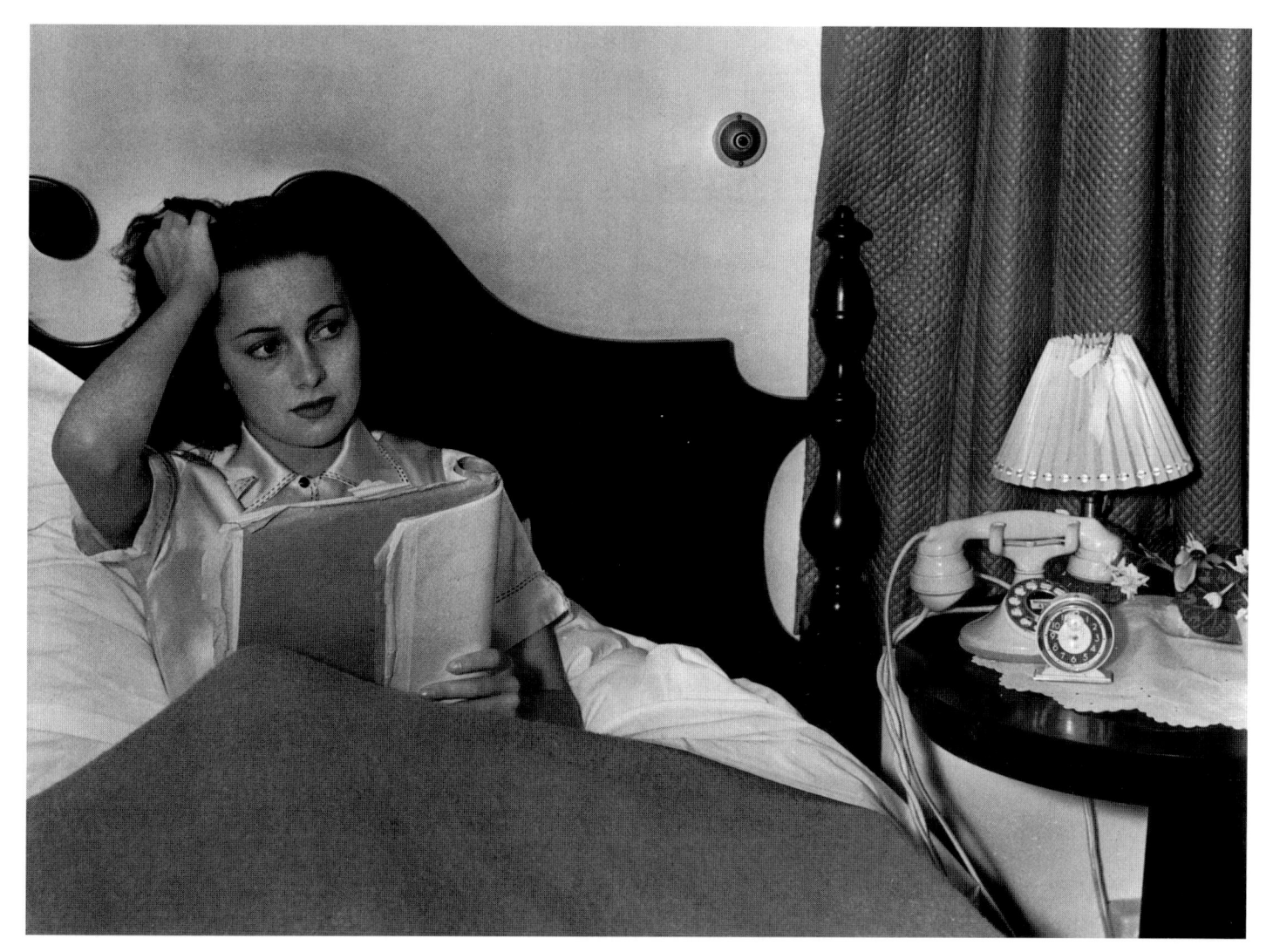

Olivia de Havilland spent as much time in her bed at the Nella Vista house as possible and considered sleeping as important to her health as exercise. The nervous breakdown she experienced over J.L.'s refusal to loan her out for *Gone With the Wind*, combined with the stress of her assignment to *Dodge City*, drove Livvie to this bed for weeks. (John McElwee Collection)

By now Selznick is desperate to cast his picture and start shooting, so desperate that he accepts father-in-law Louis B. Mayer's offer to infuse the production with $1.25 million in cash—half the estimated production cost—and provide Gable as Rhett Butler, in exchange for releasing the picture through MGM and taking 50 percent of the profit. Finally he has a Rhett, and it's not Errol Flynn, but at the same time Selznick has no Scarlett, Melanie, or Ashley.

By this time, Olivia de Havilland is Selznick's first choice for Melanie, the third best role in the picture. He writes to Dan O'Shea on November 18, 1938: "Certainly I would give anything if we had Olivia de Havilland under contract to us so that we could cast her as Melanie." He also mentions another Warner player: "I hear sensational things about Ann Sheridan and think we should check doubly to make sure we are not passing up a girl who many people think is slated for great stardom." A little later in the same memo he says: "Warners have so far definitely refused to consider letting us have de Havilland for Melanie, but I think they might be persuaded."[17]

Selznick makes quiet overtures to Livvie, who is sick of imprisonment at Warner Bros.—not to mention sick *from* imprisonment at Warner Bros. She says that of course she'd be interested, but she knows that J.L. will not loan her out. He has never loaned out either Flynn or de Havilland; why would he start now?

George Cukor calls her one evening at Nella Vista and asks her to do something "highly illegal"—namely, sneak over to Selznick International and read some lines as Melanie. Both know that if she is caught doing this, she will

Frequently mentioned by David O. Selznick in casting for *Gone With the Wind* are three Warner Bros. players: Olivia de Havilland for Melanie Hamilton, Errol Flynn for Rhett Butler, and Ann Sheridan for Belle Watling. Meanwhile, back at the ranch, Errol pursues both women, and finds that Annie is a lot more even-keeled than Livvie. Sheridan, like Ida Lupino, is a Flynn bedmate who becomes a lifelong friend and confidant. (John McElwee Collection)

be in breach of contract, and Selznick International will be vulnerable to significant legal action as well.

Livvie considers her options. She has spent almost four years under contract to Warner Brothers. She is a star who is written up almost every month in one or more of the fan magazines. She has heard that her three big Flynn pictures alone have netted nearly $6 million in profit. Just three pictures! She has achieved fame and some element of success, but the work—she's getting nothing out of the work anymore. Not that she had for a long time. Not since the beginning. It's been four very long and mostly unhappy years working at Mr. Jack L. Warner's studio. Now here is an opportunity for something grand. Maybe this picture will be great and maybe it won't, but the simple fact of the matter is that important, respected men in the motion picture industry are risking a lot because they believe in the talent of Olivia de Havilland. They are perhaps risking millions because they believe in her, which is a vote of confidence that she hasn't enjoyed from Jack Warner or Hal Wallis in years.

Livvie has never been and will never be indecisive. When she believes in a course of action, she moves at once, which is why she backs her car out of the garage and makes the long evening drive from Los Feliz to Culver City to meet with George Cukor. On a cavernous soundstage, Cukor observes her reading for Melanie and calls David Selznick over, and Livvie reads Melanie again for the main man. Cukor and de Havilland follow Selznick home. Prior to making a final decision, Selznick quietly looks at the screen tests of the other final candidates for the part of Melanie Hamilton, screening each one with Livvie watching. He is silent a few moments, and then tells de Havilland and Cukor that inquiries will be made to Warner Bros.

Cut to the next day at the Warner executive offices, where a red-faced J.L. paces his office, wondering what the hell has gone on to make David Selznick suddenly want to cast Olivia de Havilland in his picture *without a screen test*. He stops pacing: *Or did he test her? No, David wouldn't do that. We'd sue him for a half a million in a second if he tried that.* J.L. knows one thing: He has no intention of lending out de Havilland for *Selznick's Folly—this pipe dream of his to make a picture that can't be made*. There can be no doubt in the Boss's mind now: de Havilland is following in the footsteps of Davis and Cagney, just like they all do, turning traitor on the company that made them famous. Livvie's tantrums and now this—whatever conspiracy is going on—prove it. What would she be like once she leaves the lot and works over on MGM's side of town? She will never be satisfied with her place at Warner Bros. again, but she'd still have five years to go on her contract!

J. L. has a gut feeling that Livvie has stabbed him in the back by, one way or another, going around him to Selznick. Disloyalty is one thing Warner will not abide, and his hasty assessment of the situation, uncanny in its way, shapes his opinion of de Havilland for the rest of his life. Despite his later claims that he had always been fond of Olivia de Havilland, the truth is that he despises her. And despite her later claims that she had always liked him personally, she loathes the man. The condition isn't temporary for either of them. It's for the long haul.

J.L. is also a practical guy, and it's impractical to despise one of his players who is less than three years into a seven-year deal. He can't reveal his loathing to Livvie. He would never give her that kind of satisfaction. Instead, since he is stuck with her, he will settle the score over time, and collect interest.

In this poisoned environment, Livvie approaches the Boss about *Gone With the Wind* in his second-floor office as he sits behind his imposing black desk. She recalls saying that it would mean a great deal to her if he would make this loanout to Selznick.

With his usual gale-force charm, J.L. says, "Oh, you don't want to play Melanie. Scarlett's the only part."

"I don't give a darn about Scarlett, I want to play Melanie. I just love her enough to play her."

"You don't want to be in that picture," says Warner. "It's going to be the biggest bust in town.

"I don't care if it *is* the biggest bust in town, I want to be in the picture. Can't you lend me? Won't you lend me out?"

"You'll go out there and you'll come back and you'll be difficult."

She tells him, "I won't be difficult, I promise you. I give you my word of honor that I won't be difficult."[18]

She leaves Warner's office with no encouragement at all. Instead J.L. assigns her to a western with Flynn! A *western*! With *Flynn*!

She is just about to report for costume tests on *Dodge City* when she goes to lunch with a journalist. Halfway through, she will say later, she "just started to cry. I didn't know why, but I couldn't stop." The journalist gets Livvie back to Nella Vista, where de Havilland remains for days, "simply crying. I went to bed and I wasn't going to get out of it." A neurologist friend cares for her. "He came ten times and I cried every time he came, out of relief. I couldn't wait for him to come back."

She's less than halfway into a long-term deal that she never wanted to sign, appearing in pictures she doesn't want to make. Her weight is down to 100 pounds soaking wet. The doctor convinces her to create a schedule for each day—when to get up, what to eat, when to eat.

"He made me an extremely simple program," she says, "so I had something to live for and I did exactly that, let a day go by, then two days, then two weeks."[19] She feels cut off from the two most important men in her life—Jack Warner and Flynn the cruel practical joker and upstager.

At about this time, Hollywood beat writer Dan Camp says of Flynn: "Errol hasn't ever gotten over being 15 years old" and calls him "an overgrown brat." *The Adventures of*

In the script, Lee Irving tries to kill Wade's pal Rusty, forcing Wade to shoot Lee dead. But on location, Mike Curtiz revises the script so that Wade only wounds Lee, and stampeding cattle kill him. The change infuriates Hal Wallis because it makes Abbie appear unreasonable in hating Wade and weakens an already shaky plot. (John McElwee Collection)

Early in production of *Dodge City*, east of Modesto, California, Flynn waits for his call. As always, best friend Arno is nearby. (Photo below from the Josef Fegerl Collection)

Robin Hood has twisted a man already warped by his narcissistic mother and withdrawn, intellectual father. The guy who had once turned jewel thief was now pulling in three grand a week legitimately and, at every turn, people worshipped him.

In the interview with Dan Camp, Flynn labels himself as "lazy" and says that "acting is a hell of an easy way to make a living." Camp asks Flynn if he's happy. "I don't think I am," Errol Flynn sighs. He thinks a moment and allows, "I don't really know whether I am or not."[20] And with that, Flynn sums up Flynn. He can find happy moments on *Sirocco* or on a tennis court or nailing a girl. In fact the late 1930s are the best years of his life and he spends them on the edge, stunt-flying planes, water skiing in Mexico, and driving too fast through the Hollywood canyons. But bookending these years are many unhappy, bewildered, angry, and bitter years—proof that depression is Flynn's companion his whole life. Even now, as the calendar flips over to the most glorious year of all for the movies, 1939, Flynn honestly can't say if he's happy or not as he takes in an astronomical 120 grand a year!

This is the guy that nervous-breakdown plagued Olivia de Havilland meets face-to-face on November 10, 1938, for the first day of shooting on *Dodge City*, after a taxing 280-mile train ride north into the San Joaquin Valley not far from Modesto. Curtiz is in charge yet again, and Hollywood's supply of Technicolor cameras has been rounded up once more. In typical, unplanned fashion Flynn has ruined the first two days of shooting by showing up with a sprained ankle courtesy of a fall on the *Sirocco*. He can't get his swollen foot in his boot, which limits Curtiz to shooting close-ups the first day. By the second day

Flynn can't work at all and is flat on his back with his foot up and ankle packed in ice.

Errol is in knots just about now over Lili. Time has told that he can't live with her and he can't live without her. He seems to be hooked on the adrenaline of the sex and the fighting and the making up the same way he would be hooked on morphine 20 years later. Damita is a tough, exciting, unpredictable, passionate dame. Infuriating as hell and as intoxicating as they come.

Of Errol and the prospect of a Flynn-de Havilland life together, Livvie recalls, "I said he had to resolve things with Lili first. But you know, he never did. I think he was in deep thrall to her in some way."[21] Yes, Flynn is hooked on the rush, and now begins to understand that de Havilland won't be a replacement to Damita in this category. She's too introverted, too vulnerable, too career oriented. Livvie knows what he's about and has seen him duck out of sight with script girls and bit players for a quick blow job or screw. It's just what he does, but Livvie would expect—no, she would *demand*—fidelity, and when he inevitably failed to deliver it, she wouldn't whack him with a champagne bottle; those big brown eyes would go all cloudy and cut him in two.

The sex is important, and he knows that Livvie is a dynamite kisser; he's experienced it, but he also suspects that she isn't the roll in the hay that Lili is or that a hundred other girls he's known are. Talk around the studio is that Livvie is frigid. He doesn't believe it; he's pretty damn sure she's not, but *what if*.

Then there is Livvie's sudden distaste for his pictures, which leaves him confused and angry. On one level he understands: this is her career, and she's only young once, and she has to look out for herself against the front office. They all do. But he also knows that if it weren't for the Flynn pictures, she wouldn't be anywhere. She might have been dropped by now as just another pretty face.

And in the next moment he recalls what a gorgeous creature she is. He thinks about the way she can look at him; he recalls the sight of her reading on the set, or sketching him, or cussing like a stunt man, or sneaking up on Arno and barking and raising him through the roof. Errol never quite knows what Olivia is thinking. And sometimes he suspects that what she's thinking is wicked!

All these thoughts pinball through Flynn's ADHD brain day and night because he is now facing de Havilland again for the first time in almost a year.

On the third day of production on *Dodge City*, Errol is back in the saddle, and Curtiz begins to shoot the cattle drive and covered wagon exteriors. In the script, Abbie Irving and her brother, Lee, are journeying west by wagon train to the home of their aunt and uncle in *Dodge City*. Wade Hatton is boss of the cattle drive to which the wagon train has attached itself for protection from Indians. Along the way, boy meets girl—Wade meets Abbie—and they establish their relationship through sassy exchanges that reveal growing affection. Abbie's brother Lee, played by William Lundigan, is a hothead and constant drunk (back story: they are orphans). Plot point one in the script has Lee drunk and taking potshots at Wade Hatton's sidekick, played by Alan Hale. Hatton is forced to draw on Lee Irving and kill him to save the sidekick's life, accounting for boy losing girl: Abbie loathes Wade for killing Lee.

On location Mike Curtiz doesn't think the scene plays as written and he re-envisions it so that Flynn only wounds Lee in the leg. Lee crumples to the ground, but the gunplay causes a cattle stampede that tramples Lee to death. It's a subtle difference—dead is dead—but the *cattle* kill Lee, not Wade Hatton, and the mechanism driving the story forward is all but disabled by the director's change while on location.

After the stampeding cattle finish running over Lee, Abbie and Wade rush over to the squished body and Abbie proclaims, "You killed him!" The audience can only think, *Wait a minute—we're eyewitnesses, and that's not true at all. Wade did not kill Lee.*

Says film historian John McElwee: "Abbie takes an unreasonable position with regard to Hatton after the death of Lee, her brother. The audience isn't really with her in this position because it's made plain that it's not Hatton's fault that the brother is dead; Hatton was forced to defend himself. She saw the whole thing, and now she's hating the hero for no good reason, so it makes the audience less patient with her."[22]

In this case Curtiz really burns his friend Hal Wallis, who sees the dailies and fires a hot memo off to Robert Lord wanting to know what is going on and who is violat-

Above: *Dodge City* begins production in the San Joaquin Valley of north-central California as director Michael Curtiz shoots the scene where Wade woos and wins Abbie. Errol understands that Olivia is facing some tough times because she's up for a part in *Gone With the Wind*, and Jack Warner isn't cooperating. But Flynn is fighting his own demons, and instead of siding with Livvie, he feels compelled to steal scenes. Below: The stars dismount and play the love scene between Wade and Abbie on the hillside. Far from the intimate two-shot depicted in the picture, the stars are surrounded by crew members—not only the director (Mike Curtiz, lying on the ground) but also production, camera, lighting, audio, script, wardrobe, and Technicolor people. As the stars recite their dialogue, Flynn can't help himself—he grabs a blade of grass and toys with it. With the crew so close by, with time equalling money, and with Flynn in control, Livvie has no choice but to ignore the move and play the scene. (Josef Fegerl Collection)

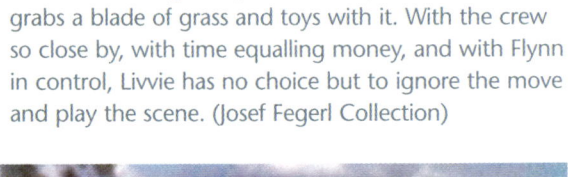

98

ing the approved script. "I am just curious to know," Wallis grumbles to Lord, "if Mike is starting to reconstruct the story on location." Wallis has been in this position before—too often. Mike had been on good behavior during *Robin Hood* production; now he's up to his old tricks again.

Meanwhile, de Havilland's weight continues to plummet and next to six-foot-two Flynn she's barely visible. It seems as if any old Santa Ana breeze will blow her clear to Nevada. From the first moment, Livvie seems genuinely unhappy as Abbie, dipping an oaken bucket into the San Joaquin River and carrying water to her wagon. In fact, she is in such a weakened condition that she is filmed filling the bucket at the river, but carries it empty up the slope to the wagon. As she climbs the hill, with the camera at the riverbank shooting upward at de Havilland in the foreground and Flynn mounted on horseback at the top of the hill, they begin a key scene.

WADE: Be sure to boil that water before you drink it!

ABBIE: (calls back) I'll wager that two minutes after you were born, you were telling the doctor what to do!

WADE: Think so? (dismounts) I'm sorry, Miss Irving. You know, it's really no fun playing boss, but someone's got to say what's to be done, haven't they? You know, out here, a trail boss has sometimes even got to take the law into his own hands.

ABBIE: (mocking) Oh yes, pioneering I believe you call it, don't you?

WADE: That's right. You don't seem to be enjoying it much.

ABBIE: (incredulous) Enjoying it?

Her question to Flynn is the cue to begin a walk-and-talk covered by dolly, which they execute in a single take. She carries the bucket and he leads his horse, reins in his hand.

ABBIE: Can anyone enjoy being jolted along week in and week out, through a nightmare of heat and dust, with sand in your teeth, and sand in your eyes, and sand in your hair?

A subtle move to the audience but a powerful one to de Havilland—Flynn upstages her by twirling the reins of his horse during her key line. It is the intersection of Flynn's insecurity and his cruel sense of humor; he has found Livvie's weak point and plays on it. (Robert Florczak Collection)

WADE: Faith now, if you didn't like sand, maybe you shouldn't have left home.

ABBIE: (quieter) I wouldn't have, but we didn't have much choice after Father died.

As she recites this line, Abbie is the focus of the action. She is revealing the personal pain that has forced her onto the frontier and, by inference, forced her brother to take up drinking. What does Flynn do with Livvie's moment? As soon as her face darkens, at the instant she internalizes the death of her father and prepares to deliver the line, he twirls the reins of his horse as they walk along, just as he had played with a twig as Robin Hood on a similar walk-and-talk in Bidwell Park.

De Havilland believes she knows what he's doing. "He'd steal my scenes," she says. "And I couldn't understand why he treated me that way, because I knew he was quite fond of me. I'm sure of that."[23]

Flynn is tall, broad-shouldered, and photogenic, dressed in a buckskin shirt that shows a bit of his bare chest, a six-gun at his side, a horse obediently following behind. In short, he already owns the frame, and yet he chooses Livvie's meatiest line in the picture to twirl the reins of his horse. Whether Errol does it intuitively, or has

Aw heck, now I have to look for a new job! thinks death-soaked Abbie after her boss is murdered. *Aw heck, I'm the worst sheriff in the west!* thinks Wade after, under his very nose, good-guy newspaper editor Joe Clemens is shot in the back. Henry Travers as Dr. Irving leans over the body. This scene would be rethought because Hal Wallis believed it was too stagy to have Frank McHugh as Joe highly visible in the frame. When the scene was retaken, Joe's body would be found on the floor and remain largely out of view.

been put up to it by master scene stealer Alan Hale, the move has much less to do with her than it does with the demons in his head. Livvie is always in control, and Livvie is in demand—Selznick wants her. But Lili knows Errol better than anyone, and Lili had nailed it: *He loves to annoy people in childish ways. He knows their weak points and plays on them.* On the prairie of central California, Errol certainly does annoy Olivia.

On November 22 they jump periods and shoot a love scene from past the midpoint of the story arc when the death of another character in Dodge forces Flynn to become the sheriff and clean up the town, which also deflects boy and girl back onto parallel romantic tracks.

Wade and Abbie ride into frame on top of a California ridge with a big shade tree in the foreground. He recites a line of dialogue, and then they dismount. With great assurance, his ankle now healed, he jumps down off his horse; she carefully climbs down, her face hidden for a moment by her mount. As they begin another dolly walk-and-talk, he owns the frame once again, and with thumbs in his gunbelt, he makes no attempt to take the scene—not right away. She relaxes into a sitting position on the hillside and he does the same.

When the editor cuts into a closer two-shot, there's a continuity problem: Flynn suddenly holds a blade of grass and waves it about as he recites his remaining lines; he had improvised and picked the innocent little prop in repeated takes sitting on the ground—and the audience is riveted. The blade of grass is a foot long in theaters—and there sits de Havilland, powerless to react. Neither Curtiz nor the script girl notices the continuity problem in the field, and editor George Amy can do nothing with the footage when it reaches the studio but cut what he's been given.

Down the road, Errol Flynn will aptly name his autobiography—he is a wicked, wicked fellow.

Flynn's cronies, the crew that Livvie had called "undisciplined" and "reckless," are key to putting Errol up to these stunts—Alan Hale, Big Boy Williams, Buster Wiles—they know all the tricks. But Flynn goes along gleefully. Hale is a veteran of more than 182 pictures going back to before the *Titanic* had gone down, and Flynn credits Hale with being the consummate scene stealer. This wild bunch has no love for de Havilland, the star who sometimes acts like a star, which makes them wild and not at all gallant.

Livvie's pallor for this scene is various shades of gray, with liberally applied makeup covering it, particularly heavy rouge on her cheeks, pancake to cover the deep, dark circles under her eyes, and peach-colored lipstick to warm her up. Her eyelashes are false and her hairdress girlish, with tresses hanging about her face to take attention away from the lack of color. At a close look, this is not a well woman.

The love scene shot on Tuesday, November 22, is a beauty, with a big, dramatic sky behind the characters, some of it vividly Technicolor blue and some of it heavy gray clouds, as Wade and Abbie convey to the audience that they are in love. When he speaks of kissing her, she says, "You wouldn't dare," and demurely heads back for the horses. After they are both mounted, he steals a kiss anyway. He is, after all, Errol Flynn. They ride off into a San Joaquin sunset in what will go on to become a signature moment for the screen couple—scored by Max Steiner.

The company prepares to head back to Burbank after fair weather and none of the lengthy delays that had plagued *Robin Hood*'s Bidwell Park shoot. Movie mogul and flying ace Howard Hughes, a new Flynn acquaintance thanks to the well-publicized antics at Chico airport, sends a plane to rush Errol back to Hollywood for a party. The incident will have ramifications for Livvie down the line. She has already had enough of *Dodge City*. She will say later, "The film had nothing to offer me and I was bored, so bored. Boredom beyond description!"[24]

She is only a month past the meltdown that had reduced her to a fetal position in bed, and she has been forced into a film she doesn't believe in and sent on a difficult location shoot. But that's not the crux of it. J.L. has smacked her down; he has dared to say no to her opportunity in *Gone With the Wind*. "I was in such a depressed state that I could hardly remember the lines," she says of making *Dodge City*. "I really mean it. It was an awful experience."[25]

Even in the love scene just completed, her eyes are sometimes vacant, and her reactions to Flynn's charming love talk lack conviction.

Nobody in Hollywood had more reason to appear smug and self-satisfied than Howard Hughes, who cut a broad swath of broads in 1930s Hollywood. Here he dines with a beaming Ginger Rogers, his on-and-off girlfriend for five years—until, that is, he discovered Olivia de Havilland ripening on the vine.

Although the stars have been directed by the still photographer to play it stoic, this pose sums up their mood during production. She doesn't want to be there, and he knows it.

But Flynn's association with Howard Hughes takes an unexpected turn. After a gossip column erroneously hints that Hughes had sent a plane to Modesto to bring *de Havilland* back to Hollywood, not Flynn, Howard phones her at Nella Vista. "I read in the paper that you and I are engaged to be married," says the nasally tenor Hughes. "I thought we should at least look at each other before we do something so permanent."[26]

The 32-year-old Hughes and 21-year-old de Havilland begin an involvement that sees them huddling in leatherbound booths at the Victor Hugo and Brown Derby and motoring to airfields where he gives her flying lessons. Howard is another one who fits Livvie's bill: a tall, older man with a commanding presence. She says, "In a whole community where the men every day played heroes on the screen and didn't do anything heroic in life, here was this man who was a real hero. And that impressed me very much."[27]

Hughes is a notorious collector of women, beautiful women, the cream of Hollywood, all at his whim because he *is* Howard Hughes, aviator and, significantly, *movie producer*. He mows starlets down compulsively, showing up at every party seemingly with a different girl, and woos them late in the night in the cockpit of his plane, where he is most comfortable and they will be wowed to be taking to the air with Hell's angel himself.

The 2004 biopic *The Aviator* will depict a close, exclusive relationship between Hughes and Katharine Hepburn, but this is a composite of Hughes and many actresses in town. He reveals to them a quiet, stoic, wounded, tortured soul and invites them to mother him, and in this way he builds his collection. Once he conquers, he adds to his black book and moves on—to Olivia de Havilland, and she promotes the relationship not only because he is a hero but also because he is connected in the business, and connections can't hurt as she struggles to break the bonds of the Flynn vehicles in favor of better parts. And right now she is all about that part in *Gone With the Wind*.

Says Hollywood historian John McElwee, "There was this contrast between Warners and Metro in terms of women hooking up with men who could help them careerwise. At Metro most of the top actresses would attach themselves to powerful executives and producers within the company who would advance their careers; like Thalberg did with Norma Shearer. That became the model of such a thing. Harlow went for Paul Bern. Another MGM executive, Benny Thau, had Greer Garson as his mistress, which Scott Eyman covers in *Lion of Hollywood*."

About Warner Bros. says McElwee, "I don't get that sense of actresses aligning with executives, but the principle is the same. If Olivia de Havilland is involved with an actor, that's not going to be very useful to her, except maybe in terms of publicity. But Howard Hughes might be different because he *could* be helpful to her. I have to assume that any relationship she was in at this time was somehow tied to her career."[28]

But being connected to Howard Hughes isn't for schoolgirls. Livvie dates Hughes knowing that he's a rogue both in the air and on the ground. Everyone knows Howard is what they call "fast," just as his girlfriend Ginger Rogers is known around town as a hot number. Rumor also has it that they are engaged. Granted, Hughes seems to pop the big question nearly as often as he pops a champagne cork, but Livvie allows herself at this difficult period to be wined and dined and put in the middle of a genuine triangular situation.

In 1943 the Chicago *Tribune* sends reporter Marcia Winn to Hollywood for an exposé. Winn writes of rampant sex and corruption in the movie capital, and the changes in people who become involved in the picture business. "Once here," writes Winn, "sense of values changes overnight, and slowly, but inevitably, the human degradation that is Hollywood sets in."[29]

Says McElwee of de Havilland, "If Howard Hughes didn't have her, it's just because he didn't want her, and why in the world would he *not* want Olivia de Havilland? That's the whole point of squiring her around town—to score. So you figure he had her. Howard Hughes had anything or anybody he wanted."[30]

Olivia had said a year earlier, "It's my soul I'm worried about. I have gained the whole world...and there are advantages, of course.... I love my independence so much that I don't really believe I could get along without it now." She goes on, "I feel that we lead a very selfish existence. We all do when we are screen stars, because we must. Everything is done for us. We are spoiled grown-up children."[31]

Obsessed with the need to land Melanie and now allied with Hughes, Livvie makes a professional move—perhaps at Howard's urging—that changes the course of her career and her life. "I was desperate," she says later. "I had to do something. I had to do *something!*"[32]

The course she chooses "really was not correct," she admits, "but I did it."[33] The move she makes now shows the guts and determination of a woman ahead of her time, playing for keeps in a man's world. She places a call to Ann Boyer Alvarado Warner, wife of the Boss, to invite her to lunch at the Brown Derby on Wilshire Boulevard in Beverly Hills. Here Jack's bride of four years (and a woman that J.L. *can't* control) listens to the tale of Olivia de Havilland, whose monologue must have gone something like: *I've given everything I have to Warner Bros. Everything. My time, my talent, even my health. Now I need the studio to give me something. David Selznick wants to put me in* Gone With the Wind, *the biggest project ever. The Flynn pictures are fine and they make money, but I'd like to do something else too. But Jack*

Ann Sheridan could play it glammed up or plain and simple, which is why Flynn was fond of the dame called "Annie," "Clara Lou," and the "Oomph Girl." The Flynn-Sheridan sexual adventure may have begun on the caravan to Kansas in the spring if 1939, and they would remain friends for two decades.

By the time she sat for portraits at the end of the production cycle for *Dodge City*, Livvie was already portraying Melanie Hamilton. Although she was drained by the turmoil of matching wits with J.L. and enduring the physical demands of *Dodge City*, she gathered herself for the ordeal ahead with David O. Selznick. (Robert Florczak Collection)

won't loan me to Selznick. There's no good reason he won't. He says it'll go to my head. He says once I work for Selznick, I won't want to come back, but, Mrs. Warner, how can I let this opportunity go by? Why should I? David wants me. Me! That means I've earned this shot, doesn't it? David has seen my work, and he thinks I'll make the perfect Melanie. George Cukor thinks so too, and he's a very great director. Why do these men believe in me, but Jack doesn't? Doesn't Jack understand that this will reflect very well on Warner Bros.? One of his players will be a principal in a very important picture.*

The woman-to-woman talk has the desired effect. Ann Warner offers to fix the problem.

As J.L. will remember later, "Olivia, who had a brain like a computer concealed behind those fawnlike brown eyes…simply went to my wife, Ann, and they joined forces in a plot to change my mind." Ann is the dark, sexy number for whom Warner had left his first wife, and she is capable of turning him inside out. He relates the ensuing conversation: "'I hear that Selznick wants Livvie in *Gone With the Wind*,' Ann said. 'Can you possibly imagine anyone else in that role? And think of the prestige for Warners. After all, you discovered her, and made her into a star.'"[34]

Livvie's end-around play wins the battle easily enough, and she will indeed be loaned to Selznick International to portray Melanie Hamilton in *Gone With the Wind*, but not until January 12, 1939, the day after *Dodge City* wraps.

Selznick International will pay de Havilland's salary of $1,000 per week, and her work must be completed by May 4, 1939. In exchange for this loanout, Selznick will trade the rights to James Stewart to Warner Bros. for one picture, which, in turn, will cause trouble between Errol and Livvie down the line.

Dodge City interiors begin in Burbank—in the home of Dr. and Mrs. Irving, Abbie's uncle and aunt. In the scenes played there, Abbie has to be cold to Wade, the man who has killed her brother (sort of), and she needn't reach far for the motivation to play cold with nasty Mr. Flynn. In the scene, Dr. Irving (played by Henry Travers—seven years later the angel Clarence in *It's a Wonderful Life*), accepts Wade's account of Lee Irving's death. Wade then attempts to offer his condolences to Mrs. Irving, who snubs him, and on his way out of the house, Hatton meets up with Abbie, dressed in a mourning outfit.

WADE: Miss Irving. I'll not be troubling you with any further apologies, but I would like you to know that if ever I can be of any service to you, I should be only too happy.

ABBIE: Thank you. The only way you can be of service to me is to keep out of my sight.

The stark, gaunt appearance of Olivia de Havilland lends credibility to the scene she plays as the grieving sister. No amount of pancake can hide the baggage she's carrying around under her eyes. Thanks to Curtiz and his script rewrite up near Modesto, however, Livvie's character comes across not as grief stricken but merely bitchy.

In other circumstances, Livvie might have enjoyed the experience of making *Dodge City* because in the guise of a shoot-'em-up, screenwriter Bob Buckner used the script to tackle legitimate social issues, among them gun control, voting, taxation, the power of the press, and women's rights. At the center of much of it is Livvie's character, Abbie Irving.

Abbie tries her hand at teaching Sunday school until the death-by-formula of little Harry Cole (some charming waif always dies in Warner dramas to spur the hero to action). Harry is among a wagonful of children in Abbie's care for a picnic when he's dragged to death by a team of runaway horses spooked by a gun battle in the street. So much for Abbie's teaching career. As Wade becomes the sheriff to squelch the kind of violence that cost little Harry his life, Abbie goes to work at the newspaper office, and pretty soon proves that she is the town's bad-luck charm by getting her boss killed by the enemies of truth and justice. But before newspaperman Joe Clemens (Frank McHugh) is iced by the delightfully evil Yancy (Victor Jory), Wade and Abbie run into each other in the newspaper office and play a clever, lively scene that turns around their relationship.

WADE: What are you doing here?

ABBIE: (ruffled) Well, obviously I'm working.

He pooh-poohs the idea of a woman taking a job.

ABBIE: Well, what's wrong with my working here?

WADE: It's undignified; it's unladylike. More than that; you ought to be home, doing needlework; things like that.

ABBIE: Sewing buttons on for some man, I suppose.

WADE: Buttons come off; someone's got to sew them on.

ABBIE: That's a fine career for an intelligent woman!

Taking *Gone With the Wind* out of the equation, what would Livvie have thought of the *Dodge City* experience? She overlooks the fact that the role of Abbie Irving provides her with the strongest, most vital character of her career to date. She is the ingénue, yes, but she is also a catalyst in the plot line; Abbie's actions set in motion events that resolve the story. Intrepid reporters Joe Clemens and Abbie Irving get the goods on bad guy Jeff Surrett for the murder of good guy Matt Cole. It's not the brightest move to confront Surrett with this information in his own office, because pretty soon Joe ends up dead and Abbie—the only witness against Surrett—is forced to leave town for her own protection, riding on the same train as Yancy, now in custody. But for three reels of the picture, Abbie is out front in the action, a far cry from passive, hand-wringing Elsa of *Light Brigade*, or storybook Maid Marian. It's easy to see this in retrospect, with so much Hollywood history having rattled through the projector, but in November 1938 Olivia de Havilland is just 22 years old, a pampered movie star and a self-professed snob now trapped in an Errol Flynn western.

Hal Wallis is trapped too, at the hand of his close friend Mike Curtiz. Wallis has watched his Technicolor horse-opera progress from location to the studio. He realizes that he's wasted one of his bright young stars, Ann Sheridan, on the thankless role of Ruby, the hard-hearted songstress of the Gay Lady Saloon and girlfriend of Jeff Surrett. She only gets a few lines in the picture, and the dailies show that Curtiz has only captured Sheridan in long shots. Wallis fires off a memo to supervisor Robert Lord: "I hope Curtiz has close-ups and full figure shots of Ann Sheridan when she's singing and dancing up on the stage. We should by all means have these. I haven't seen much of her in the picture, except in long shots, and she is rather decorative in her outfit and we should use it."[35] So Curtiz puts her back onstage and shoots medium shots and close-ups of her song-and-dance routines.

The practicality of Wallis and artistry of Curtiz will somehow find balance here and for a few more years to come, hitting a crescendo with the production of *Casablanca* in 1942. In the case of *Dodge City*, both Wallis and Curtiz brainstorm last-minute ways to bolster the weak script.

Wade has two comic-relief sidekicks, Rusty and Tex, played by Flynn's pals Alan Hale and Big Boy Williams. In one of those devices that seems to prove Lord right ("the script stinks"), Rusty swears the pledge and ventures into a den of old teetotalers called the Pure Prairie League. There, as a barroom brawl unfolds next door, Rusty testifies to his past evil ways as an embiber, and one of the crones makes a pass at him. Wallis watches the footage and fires off a memo to Lord: "I saw the first dailies in the Prairie League meeting, and they are a little disappointing. The whole sequence seems very forced and unfunny to me, and I only hope that it will cut up better than it looked. The one saving factor is that we have cuts outside and we can leave in as much or as little of this as we please, but the whole scene seemed phony to me."[36] An entire day is lost trying to coax lines out of poor Cora Witherspoon, the elderly actress playing the head bitty. "We should have been out of this set yesterday," gripes unit manager Frank Mattison.[37]

Then there's the bar fight: the signature tussle of 100 extras in the Gay Lady Saloon that will be used as stock footage for the next 50 years. It is the fight that refuses to end. Curtiz begins shooting it on December 21 and continues on the 22nd. On Christmas Eve he's still shooting it. Santa comes and goes and Mike is still shooting. On goes the bloody struggle, angle upon angle, stunt man upon stunt man, bottles and chairs and tables smashing with equal ease. Finally on December 27 Wallis writes to Lord: "I hope that Mike is through shooting the fight in the Gay Lady Saloon. We have enough film already for two or three fights, and if he isn't through with everything by now, I want it stopped today."[38]

Ah, the problems of an executive producer. Worst of all, Wallis is absolutely tortured by the last 20 pages of the script. The climax takes place on the train out of Dodge, with Abbie fleeing the Surrett gang, and Hatton and Rusty in the baggage car guarding Yancy. But Surrett's boys take over the train and attempt to spring Yancy, resulting in a gun battle that touches off a fire in the baggage car, and, of course, Abbie walks into the middle of the gunfight and is taken hostage. To make script matters more problematic, Yancy and his accomplices escape from the train by jumping onto horses galloping beside the mail car. Wallis thinks the story and the staging are implausible, because there is nothing logical about the bad guys riding alongside the train long enough to be picked off one by one when it makes so much more sense to ride *the other way*. But Wallis can't offer up a better alternative and sends Curtiz back out to Modesto to shoot the climax on the Sierra Railroad running east out of Oakdale.

The last scene of the picture also troubles Wallis when he watches the dailies: after the fire in the mail car, and after the gun battle and the deaths of Surrett and Yancy, Wade and Abbie return to the passenger car—singed from the fire and breathless from the gunfight, but both very much alive. They start their usual byplay, at which point Rusty says, "If you're gonna bicker, you might as well get married," and it just so happens there's a preacher right on the train!

Of this scene, Wallis writes to Curtiz: "I am sure it will not work out. It is flat, and not important enough for the picture, and I don't want to end the picture on that phony laugh of Olivia de Havilland's."[39]

The entire last reel of *Dodge City* is going to be the death of Hal Wallis! So he orders Buckner to write something different, which results in the scene that ends the film, shot on the last day of production, January 18, 1939.

DISSOLVE TO DODGE CITY, a day or two after the gunfight on the train. Wade, Rusty, and Tex are offered the opportunity to go clean up another murderous town, Virginia City, Nevada. Wade says he can't do such a thing to his bride, to place her back in harm's way, and the boys are depressed that their town-tamin' days are over. Then Abbie, who has overheard the conversation, walks in and delivers the last line in the picture, "When do we leave for Virginia City?" and the boys whoop it up. It is a strange, unsatisfactory ending because Abbie is clearly not enthused about reliving the experience just passed, which has seen the deaths of her brother, boss, and a cute little kid—not to mention that she is sacrificing her own happiness for that of her thrill-seeking husband.

The original *Dodge City* ending: Abbie and Wade get hitched moments after Wade shoots all the bad guys off their horses from the moving fire train. Hal Wallis doesn't just dislike this finish to the picture, he hates it.

The contrived last shot of the picture shows Wade driving a covered wagon on the journey to Virginia City, with Abbie snuggled next to him. Wallis and Curtiz paint a pretty picture—the stars riding off into the sunset in Technicolor, but in truth, there *is* no ending to *Dodge City*. Nothing that makes sense, anyway.

Compounding the problem of the finish of the picture is a bout of bronchitis that has laid de Havilland flat. A week away from closing out production, Frank Mattison begs Lilian to let her daughter ride over the hill to the studio to work. Livvie does report in for duty, but Mattison says of Livvie in his daily report to Wallis, "I talked with her in Makeup this morning and she is really sick. As you can tell by looking at her, she has no color whatever."[40]

Livvie describes a surreal experience amidst this medical drama. On December 31, 1938, Jack and Ann Warner throw an annual New Year's Eve party at their 12-acre Beverly Hills estate. De Havilland is expected to attend along with all the Warner Bros. players and the production team. Livvie and Jimmy Stewart had made plans to go, but she is laid low by this bout of bronchitis. At 10:30 Howard Hughes calls Nella Vista and says he will swing by to take her to Warner's. She tries to protest, but Howard is half deaf and telephone conversations are problematic. When it's clear that Hughes is on his way, she throws on her gown and off she goes. Arriving on the arm of the millionaire flier at the Warner estate, she finds Stewart there stag. She recalls, "Jimmy came up a little put out and took the other arm. We sat down at the bar and Errol Flynn started serving me drinks. I was 22, with three of the most attractive men in the world around me. I don't know how my reputation survived."[41]

The nine-week ordeal featuring spats between leading lady and studio boss, and between the executive producer and the director of the picture—not to mention casting problems, script problems, illnesses, and injuries—finally ends. J.L. pressures editor George Amy to get the thing cut and out, and the Boss watches the edit suites buzz with activity below his office window. By the beginning of March, the film is dumped in the lap of the Technicolor processing lab, which adds a second shift to get prints out by April 1.

As written in the final script, Wade and Abbie get hitched on the fire train taking them back to Dodge, but Hal Wallis hated the way this scene played in the dailies, especially Livvie's "phony laugh." So the new final sequence has Wade and his pals off to fight crime in Virginia City, Nevada, with Abbie (who has seen everybody she ever cared about killed before her eyes) apparently happy to go off to new adventures. Here Wade and Abbie gaze westward into a Technicolor sunset in the picture's revised payoff shot. Unit manager Frank Mattison reported that Livvie had no color in her face due to deepening illness, so makeup hides this fact, and the fur hood helps to soften her emaciated features.

What's the rush to get cans of film to the hinterlands? J.L. hears that Paramount's blockbuster, *Union Pacific*, is going to premiere in Omaha in May, and that C.B. DeMille and his cast are about to travel to Nebraska from Hollywood aboard a special train.

J.L. decides to skunk Paramount by staging the premiere of *his* western in the picture's namesake, Dodge City, Kansas, on three screens April 1, five weeks ahead of the *Union Pacific* event, which will lead to some classic Flynnanigans and no small amount of intrigue, not to mention the apparent kidnapping of Melanie Hamilton Wilkes.

TWO WEDDINGS AND A FUNERAL

Charlie Einfeld, Director of Publicity and Advertising at Warner Bros., seized upon the Paramount idea of dispatching a trainful of movie stars to America's heartland, and thus was born the Dodge City Special, 14 cars in all, which carried the cast of *Dodge City* to America's heartland. Bob Taplinger, head of the publicity department, made a deal with the Santa Fe Railroad, which underwrote part of the trip in exchange for a little something down the road—Warner Bros. promised to name an upcoming picture "Santa Fe," and the railroad would get its name on billboards across the nation. The Warner publicity department rounded up 200 reporters and photographers, along with *Dodge City* players Flynn, de Havilland, Ann Sheridan, Frank McHugh, Alan Hale, and Big Boy Williams; Warner contract players Humphrey Bogart, Jane Wyman, Priscilla Lane, Rosemary Lane, and Wayne Morris; and freelance players Hoot Gibson, Buck Jones, Jean Parker, Gloria Dickson, Allan Jones, and "Slapsy Maxie" Rosenblum for the train ride. Warner would send only lower-paid talent, although Flynn's new black horse, Onyx, did make the trip, along with a dozen studio security men and four prostitutes brought along to *try* to keep the stars off the starlets.

But a funny thing happened on the way to departure. Twentieth Century-Fox staged a last-minute junket of its own to San Francisco to promote *The Story of Alexander Graham Bell* starring Don Ameche and Alice Faye, robbing some of the newspapermen from the Dodge City trip. Hollywood superstars Clark Gable and Carole Lombard used the double diversion of the junkets to elope to Arizona for a quick wedding.

"Once performers caught the public interest with the intensity that Gable and Lombard together generated," said historian Carole Sampeck, "the popular press demanded new story angles, different photos of the pair, always more, more, more. Clark and Carole, discreetly living together at her home, dealt continuously with the intrusion of reporters camped outside their gate..., although the studios dictated that the pair's status as living 'in sin' not be glorified. Once Gable's wife Ria announced that she was going to Nevada to divorce her husband, members of the press knew that this could be the scoop of their careers.... So they watched, and eagerly waited."[42]

The elopement skunked the journalists about to depart on trains heading in different directions and also columnists Hedda Hopper and Louella Parsons.

On Thursday, March 30, 1939, the Dodge City Special pulled out of Los Angeles with the first of four California stops made at Pasadena. There Olivia de Havilland was pulled from the train by special arrangement between Jack Warner and David Selznick, who was by now making *Gone With the Wind*, with

Moments before the Dodge City Special pulled out of Los Angeles, Errol and Livvie posed for this photo. An hour later, after the photo op with Flynn, she exited the train in Pasadena. (John McElwee Collection)

Livvie a vital part of his cast. Selznick was well into production by now and de Havilland was working every day. Selznick simply could not permit Olivia to participate in this gaudy hinterland spectacle with the stakes so very high.

Conservative estimates placed the crowd greeting the train in Dodge City on April 1 at 150,000, making for a mob that threatened to crush the visiting stars. A mile-long parade snaked its way through town, headed by a brass band and the governors of three states, with Flynn riding Onyx and waving his hat, followed by the other stars on horseback or in touring cars. Five nationwide radio broadcasts chronicled the festivities.

Hours later, a morose-going-on-funereal Big Boy Williams was found dead—dead *drunk*, that is—among the graves of Boot Hill, and a posse of his pals coaxed him oh-so-gently back to the train so as not to enrage the beast that Big Boy could become.

The trip home proved eventful. The battling Bogarts went at it after Bogey was caught eyeing up a starlet by wife Mayo Methot, who spiked him in the head with a high-heeled shoe and produced a gusher.

Said Jimmy Starr, one of the reporters in attendance, "When Hollywoodites go on a romp, it can mean a quick romp in the hay..., each person not necessarily in his or her own room."[43] Starr noted that, aside from the starlets, Flynn laid one of the pay-for-play babes in a barber chair in the club car.

Livvie's absence also gave the lone wolf time to get acquainted with Ann Sheridan, unattached and bawdy Warner starlet. Their liaison seemed to have been brief, but set off rumors of impending marriage that lasted for almost a decade.

Above: Errol Flynn is the center of attention as the Warner Bros. train reaches Dodge City, Kansas, on the night of March 31, 1939. Flynn addresses the press while Humphrey Bogart stands to Flynn's left with pipe in his teeth, and to his left, Mayo Methot is partially visible. Below: As the premiere takes place in America's heartland, a press conference is held at Clark Gable's ranch in Encino, California. Here an exhausted but gleeful Carole Lombard poses with her new husband and her mother Bessie. The royal elopement of the Queen of Comedy and the King of Hollywood had been made possible by the diversion of not one but two premiere junkets heading in different directions.

Two miserable stars, de Havilland and Flynn, play their only scene together in the picture about the knight and the lady, or the lady and the knight, or Elizabeth and Essex, or Essex and Elizabeth, or... (John McElwee Collection)

7 DYSFUNCTION JUNCTION

The instant that *Dodge City* wraps on January 12, 1939, Errol skips town for Acapulco, leaving thoughts of Mike Curtiz and *Gone With the Wind* behind. Two days later Olivia scrapes herself off a sick bed and reports to Selznick International Pictures in Culver City to watch Vivien Leigh sign on the dotted line, ending an agonizing 2.5-year search for Scarlett O'Hara. The signing takes place in David Selznick's office beside Selznick International headquarters—the Mt. Vernon knockoff seen at the head of Selznick pictures. The photo of Leigh seated beside her new boss and happily signing her name, with de Havilland over her one shoulder and Leslie Howard (who finally agrees to portray Ashley Wilkes) over her other, sends a shock wave across the entertainment world. *Gone With the Wind* is finally moving forward, although Clark Gable—Captain Rhett Butler by conscription—is absent for the festivities.

David Selznick's instructions to Livvie this day: Eat!

For all involved, the hard work begins in 48 hours, on Monday the 16th with wardrobe, hair, and makeup tests. Leigh and de Havilland rehearse with director George Cukor, who is a genteel and compassionate director—the antithesis of Mike Curtiz. Says de Havilland of Cukor: "All actors respond to his keenness and enthusiasm and the sharpness of his images and oh, he's thrilling, really thrilling to work with."[1]

All get a crash course in Southern diction, colloquialisms, manners, and comportment. Shooting of Scarlett with the Tarleton brothers, the first scene in the picture, kicks off actual production on Thursday, January 26, but the shots printed here will be discarded and the scene redone later, and redone again after that. Cukor shoots other sequences with Scarlett and her family, and always Selznick is on the set, hovering, analyzing what's being done, how, and *how fast*. Then he hurries back to look at film the instant it's processed…, and he's disappointed that the Technicolor shots don't look as vibrant as those captured by the same cameras for *The Adventures of Robin Hood*.

On Wednesday, February 1, after two weeks of coaching and rehearsal with Cukor, de Havilland hits the soundstage at the Atlanta Bazaar, with Scarlett and Melanie in mourning after the death of Charles Hamilton in the war. Here Gable also appears for the first time, making his hero's entrance to the applause of the assembled guests. It takes days to shoot the complex dance numbers and family dynamics of the Hamiltons. Gable is quiet and withdrawn on the soundstage through these early days. He has no friends here; this isn't an MGM picture, and he's no fan of George Cukor.

Next Leigh and de Havilland jump ahead in the script and shoot the birth of Melanie's baby with Butterfly McQueen. Cukor envisions the delivery as a dramatic silhouette, a la Curtiz, and the sequence comes off well despite the fact that the actors haven't settled into character yet, without interpersonal relationships established, and without a script to anchor them in the story—the script is still written only in patches.

Cukor then moves to the sequence where Rhett Butler spirits Scarlett, Melanie, Prissy, and the baby out of war-torn Atlanta. For these scenes, in which Melanie has been

111

worn ragged by childbirth, Livvie can certainly recall her emotional breakdown of three months earlier, with its physical ramifications, as she allows Clark Gable to scoop up her limp form and carry her off.

Cukor moves on to a couple of other sequences before he is suddenly, unceremoniously sacked by David Selznick in a move that would have been thought impossible because of the close friendship of the two men. Hollywood reels at the news. But Selznick, with uppers coursing through his body, is ravenous for dailies to look at, and after two weeks of shooting, the picture is already a week behind schedule.

Leigh and de Havilland are on the set when they hear the news that their mentor Cukor has been dismissed. Says Livvie, "We immediately left the set and we went to see David Selznick. We spent three hours in his office beseeching him. We cried, we pulled out our handkerchiefs…, and you should have seen the poor man."[2]

"Selznick refused to reconsider," writes film historian Ronald Haver, despite what Livvie describes as "two women in black beseeching him." Selznick's reply: "I have learned that nothing matters except the final picture."[3]

Heady stuff: Livvie's first shot for Selznick is the bazaar scene with the King himself, Clark Gable. Here the uncomfortable widow Scarlett (Vivien Leigh) and Melanie Hamilton Wilkes are befriended by the gallant Captain Butler. Leigh and de Havilland would be wearing their black mourning outfits when they assailed David O. Selznick over the firing of George Cukor.

The production goes dark for a week, and then another. Livvie retreats to Nella Vista and waits for the other shoe to drop—who will come in and direct *Gone With the Wind*? Her darkest fear: Mike Curtiz. He had stepped in to light a fire under a big-budget Technicolor production once already; who's to say he won't be brought in again? She knows from the grapevine that Mike has just directed *Sons of Liberty*, a two-reel Technicolor short subject at Warner Bros.—right before the color cameras had been forwarded to Selznick. And now he's available.

But Selznick needn't reach all the way to Burbank for a director. Just down the road a ways from Selznick International is MGM. As Cukor has been gently massaging performances out of Vivien Leigh and Olivia de Havilland, no-nonsense Victor Fleming has been directing flying monkeys, a green-skinned witch, a high-strung girl, and what seem like a thousand disagreeable midgets. Fleming has about had it with *The Wizard of Oz*, his nerves are frayed, and he's within two weeks of the martini shot and vacation…until the phone rings and it's Louis Mayer on the other end of the line.

Vic, I've got a tough job, and you're the guy to do it.

L.B., I'm on a tough job.

For a fiftieth birthday present, burned-out Victor Fleming is appointed to take over the helm of a ship off course, *Gone With the Wind*. This is the same Vic Fleming who had helped to create Gable's persona, directing the dimpled one in *Red Dust*, *The White Sister*, and *Test Pilot*. He is probably Gable's best friend, as a matter of fact. And Gable is the King of Hollywood and not a man to go friendless on any soundstage. Suddenly, silently, Gable strikes, and a Gable Man now runs the show.

Neither Livvie nor Vivien has worked with Vic Fleming, so they go in search of the inside story on the guy.

His talk is pretty coarse.

The handsomest man in Hollywood.

Quite the charmer—he sleeps with his leading ladies.

He'll bring out the woman in you.

After working with the heavenly Cukor, Leigh and de Havilland can't imagine the likes of Vic Fleming and don't *want* the woman brought out in them. Not Fleming's way, anyhow. This is, after all, the Old South; a gentler time.

Selznick gives Fleming the script. Fleming looks it over. "David," he growls, "your script is no fuckin' good."[4] Selznick panics and calls for screenwriter Ben Hecht to punch it up. Hecht is a veteran of big MGM pictures, not to mention the John Barrymore-Carole Lombard gem *Twentieth Century*, and another Lombard hit, *Nothing Sacred*, for Selznick. Hecht is a tough Chicagoan, cynical, funny, and the best typewriter-for-hire in the business. Hecht is well aware that a dozen writers have already been sucked dry by this script. *I'll give you two weeks, no more,* he warns his new boss.

Selznick wants Fleming to read the book and help Hecht to reinterpret the script. *I'm not reading the book,* Fleming grouses. Hecht hasn't read the book either, and there's no time for him to kick back and peruse the thousand pages now. Instead, Selznick and Fleming act the script out for Hecht, who bangs away on the typewriter, fixing as he goes. The exercise goes on almost around the clock. On the fifth day, a vein ruptures in Fleming's eye. Then Selznick collapses in exhaustion. According to Ronald Haver, "Hecht contributed…the all-important ability to cut through the dense underbrush of numerous rewrites, clearing away the clutter of the minor characters' digressions and loquacity that strangled the main plot line."[5]

"For instance," says Gable historian Carole Sampeck, "there is not one battle scene in the film, whereas Mitchell went into carefully crafted descriptions of campaigns, and even delved into the personalities of the Confederacy's military leaders. At times characters had to be combined, as was the case with Ashley's vanishing youngest sister, Honey. Honey's lines and loves (but very little of her giggly, girlish persona) were transferred to the film's only Wilkes female, Ashley's sister India.... Two of Scarlett's three children were jettisoned; they were not instrumental to the plot in any way other than to show Scarlett's utter selfishness and lack of mothering skills. This effectively made her daughter with Rhett Butler, Bonnie, and her ultimate tragedy, that much more moving in the film."[6]

Dapper Victor Fleming sits with Vivien Leigh on the backlot. Some in cast and crew like his no-nonsense approach; others call him a bastard and hate his foul language on the set.

Hecht makes it through his two weeks and Selznick offers him more money to stay on. Hecht replies that "there isn't enough money in the world for this kind of suicide work."[7]

But now Selznick has a script, finally, and a hard-charging director with clear vision (except for the ruptured vein in his eye).

Twenty miles to the northeast, J.L. is also following a costume-picture agenda, and Warner and Wallis are developing *Elizabeth the Queen* as a prestige picture with Bette Davis in mind as Queen Elizabeth I. The front office intends to change the title to *The Knight and the Lady* to make it clear to audiences that this is, at heart, a love story between the aging queen and a reckless and dashing nobleman. Granted, it's a tempestuous and unhappy love story, but a love story just the same, like *Camille*, but with beheadings. The trick is to land a big-name leading man to justify the title change that puts the Knight before the Lady. In other words, they need to bring in an actor even more powerful than Bette Davis.

The story concerns lonely, aging Queen Elizabeth I of England, surrounded by Sir Francis Bacon, Sir Walter Raleigh, and other treacherous courtiers. The queen's favorite is Robert Devereux, the Earl of Essex, a charming young rogue who adores her despite the age difference and the million and one obstacles that would keep them apart. A conspiracy hatched by Raleigh's crowd and involving Lady Penelope Gray puts Essex at odds with Elizabeth, and after a disastrous campaign fighting the Irish rebels of the Earl of Tyrone, Essex marches on London to seize the throne. Elizabeth makes an empty promise that if he disbands his army they will share power, but once the army is gone, she arrests Essex and condemns him to the block, unless he asks for his life to be spared—which in effect signifies that she has broken his spirit. Penelope, who is also in love with Essex, makes a last-minute appeal for his life, but Elizabeth and Essex remain at loggerheads and he goes to his death.

Davis feels a great amount of ownership of the Queen Elizabeth project and sees it as her answer to the recently completed historical epic, *Juarez*. She considers herself, and correctly so, as the *grande dame* of Warner Bros. leading ladies—her opposite number on the male side is *Mr.* Paul Muni. Since Muni had just acted up a storm in *Juarez*, with tremendous support from Davis as Empress Carlotta, it is now her turn to be the center of all the historical fuss.

A March 13 memo lists all players up for Robert Devereux, the Earl of Essex, and what a roster it is—there are perennial favorites like Ronald Colman, Brian Aherne, and of course Fredric March, all of whom are a little *up there* to project boyish charm; there are younger leading men like Douglas Fairbanks Jr., Cary Grant, Laurence Olivier, Ray Milland, and Joel McCrea; there are two new kids if the desire is to cast against type—Henry Fonda and Vincent Price; and there's the 800-pound gorilla in any Warner Bros. casting room, Errol Flynn.

In case for some reason Bette Davis doesn't make the picture, there are other queens in Hollywood, and Wallis's list includes Margaret Sullavan, Barbara Stanwyck, Miriam Hopkins, Norma Shearer, Irene Dunne, Helen Hayes, Katharine Hepburn, and Tallulah Bankhead.

For Penelope Gray, scheming lady-in-waiting to the queen and the would-be other woman in the love story, actresses of many types and age groups are considered—contract players like Margaret Lindsay, Ida Lupino, and consistent also-ran Anita Louise, as well as a long freelance list that includes Virginia Bruce, Gail Patrick, and Gale Sondergaard. Actually, Sondergaard is the perfect choice, given the dark hues and the scheming of the part. Even Margot Grahame, who had been a star at Warner Bros.-Teddington when Flynn made his first screen appearance there in 1934, receives consideration as Penelope. Back then Flynn had been earning extra's pay. Now he is a five-grand-a-week star, and Margot Grahame is on her way out.

Davis actively lobbies for Olivier as her leading man—Olivier, who had portrayed heroic Michael Ingolby in 1937's *Fire Over England*, another tale of the court of Elizabeth. Granted, Olivier doesn't have much of a name in the States, but he is classically trained and—

You're what? You're giving it to Flynn? Oh dear God.

Davis knows what Flynn is about, having worked with him the year before in a melodrama called *The Sisters*. She doesn't doubt his screen presence or his looks or his charm. She has seen all three. But he's, well, he's Errol Flynn, a personality who makes those juvenile action pictures. In no way can Flynn carry off the script's sassy and exacting dialogue, which is being punched up by two of the studio's best writers, Norman Reilly Raine and Aeneas MacKenzie.

But forces larger than Miss Bette Davis are at work. J.L. has just decided to make *The Knight and the Lady* in color. This color thing is tricky, and the studio can't just release any picture in color, their contract with Technicolor notwithstanding. They've tried making Technicolor pictures five times, and three have lost money. Setups are tougher in Technicolor, and a Technicolor consultant is always around on the set. And time is money. *The Adventures of Robin Hood* had been one of the two to turn a profit, despite its long production cycle, and *The Knight and the Lady* provides another opportunity to use color for a historical picture where bright costumes and personalities will light up the screen.

Given that this picture will be done in color, no matter how much J.L. likes Fredric March or knows that Ronald Colman or the Limey kid Olivier would be perfect, there's only one guy for a color historical picture, and it's Errol. J.L. has got to keep his star working and in front of the public, and Flynn has been away getting sunburned on his boat for almost four months. He is due to make his public reemergence at the *Dodge City* premiere on April 1 in Kansas. It is just possible that with *Dodge City*, Flynn's popularity will hit a new high.

It's going to be Flynn, Bette. Get used to it.

Just now, on March 30, the Dodge City Special chugs out of Los Angeles and travels all of 20 miles northeast to Pasadena. There Livvie, who has just been photographed with a smiling Flynn, is spirited off the train as part of a compromise between J.L. and David O. to keep the newly arrived-at peace. Livvie gives the *appearance* of going along and then quietly departs the caravan with no official announcement made that she's not part of the festivities. Livvie's not complaining since she has finally engineered herself the role of a lifetime. She has recently said, "I always resented dependence, even when I was a youngster. I love my independence so much that I don't really believe I could get along without it now."[8]

Unfortunately, when Livvie stays in Hollywood and doesn't travel to Kansas with the cast of *Dodge City*, she is top of mind with the front office, just as pre-production meetings are taking place for *The Knight and the Lady*. During briefings by Bob Lord on the progress of casting, J.L. takes notice of this Penelope part. He asks a lot of questions, as he gazes out his window at the edit booths and star bungalows laid out across the way, about how de Havilland is doing on the Selznick picture, about their production schedule, and particularly he is curious about when she will finish over there. Wallis and producer Robert Lord inquire why.

Because I want to make sure that Livvie is available to play this Penelope character, that's why.

Hal Wallis points out that it would be unusual to demote a top player like de Havilland, now so highly visi-

J.L. could do the math easy enough; of all the actors available to portray Essex, Flynn played British best of all, Flynn was a hot commodity, Flynn could wear the costume, and Flynn needed to keep working. (John McElwee Collection)

115

There are plenty of lesser-name actresses who could portray Lady Penelope, but the Boss insists on Livvie, to teach her a lesson. Here, on May 5, 1939, on a day off from *Gone With the Wind*, she visits J.L. Hell and poses in costume at Warner Bros. She is doing important work over at Selznick International, and now, back in Burbank, she is reduced to, quite literally, window dressing. (John McElwee Collection)

ble, to what will be seen as a minor part. But the Boss says nothing; he merely stares out the window.

Of course Livvie doesn't know any of this right away. She is still distraught at the replacement of Cukor. Over a romantic dinner, she talks with Howard Hughes: "I told him how anguished I was by this change. I was sure that I couldn't relate, that the characterization would escape me with anyone else on the set… and Vivien had the same terror, too." Hughes thinks a moment. He has grown up in the business—prior to directing an epic of his own, *Hell's Angels*, he had apprenticed under directors James Cruze and Lewis Milestone, and worked with Frank Lloyd and Howard Hawks as well. Hughes knows all the key people in town. He tells de Havilland that Cukor and Fleming are the same talent. They are artists—they may even be geniuses at the craft of filmmaking. Vic just isn't as genteel about it. She credits Hughes for allowing her "to start to work with Victor Fleming with a positive and receptive viewpoint."[9]

Production of *Gone With the Wind* begins again with a vengeance. Fleming rips through the early scenes, Scarlett's first sighting of Rhett, the parlor encounter, the Twelve Oaks barbecue, and the declaration of war. Still seeking more of a *Robin Hood* deep-saturation look, Selznick brings in Ernie Haller from Warner Bros. as cinematographer. Haller had photographed several de Havilland pictures, beginning with *Captain Blood*.

As shooting progresses, it is Fleming who keeps Livvie's attention, and draws from her a strong performance. In her long career, she will never meet up with more of a ruggedly individualistic director than Vic Fleming. But one person's individualist is another's nightmare.

"I thought he was a *bastard*," says Selznick's assistant, Marcella Rabwyn. "I found him to be obnoxious in many ways, but I certainly could recognize his talent; he was a very very strong macho man." On the other hand, Rabwyn has to admit, "He revitalized the whole theme of *Gone With the Wind*. Suddenly things began to happen. The girls don't realize that…the film has spirit and tempo." Or as Ann Rutherford says of Fleming's ability to call "print" on the first or second take: "He had marvelous command."[10]

De Havilland will later say, "It's almost sexual, really, between the woman and the director. It is the most intimate kind of collaboration. It's exquisite and it's sexual without being physiological, and it's a unique experience."[11]

In a sense she "cheats" on this new sexual collaborator, director Victor Fleming. Whenever she feels stuck with the Melanie character, she steals off to secret consultations with George Cukor—Livvie doesn't know it at the time, but Leigh is following the same practice, meeting secretly with her ex-director to better interpret Margaret Mitchell's complex heroine, Scarlett O'Hara.

On the other hand, de Havilland will credit Fleming, not Cukor, with the success of her interpretation of Melanie. Fleming's first scene directing her is the opening of the Twelve Oaks barbecue. In rehearsal Melanie greets Scarlett with social superficiality—the kind of playing that Wallis endlessly criticizes de Havilland for—and, says Livvie, "Victor then drew me aside and said just this: 'Whatever Melanie says, she means.' Thus he gave me not only the key to playing the scene but also the key to Melanie's whole character."[12]

De Havilland knows her career is at stake and proceeds to handle the fluid situation with seasoned professionalism. J.L. makes no attempt to take the high road; he is already anticipating how Livvie will react when she learns of the assignment to support Flynn and Davis. Of course the names of Flynn and de Havilland on the marquee guarantee box office, even if Livvie's name will be *under* the title for a change. After *The Adventures of Robin Hood* and *Dodge City*, the public expects to see them together in Technicolor pictures, and the public will *get* them together. Sort of.

This is such a small part, J.L. is reminded. Only one scene between Essex and Penelope.

Miss de Havilland is supporting Gable and Leigh in Selznick's prestige picture; she can very well come back here and support Flynn and Davis in my prestige picture.

Livvie gets word through Robert Lord that she is being assigned the role of Lady Penelope Gray in *The Knight and the Lady*. It is a kick in the gut. It is a knife in the back that Warner would actually do this to her, but she knows it's the price she must pay for going around him. Her response is measured: *I don't see how I can do it. There's still so much to shoot at Selznick's*. She calls Hal Wallis and gently presses that there is a conflict in the schedules and she can't see it working out. She rattles off the names of others who would be fine for Penelope. But Wallis isn't calling this shot; the Boss is.

On March 20, 1939, Wallis asks Steve Trilling, Warner casting director, to find out from Selznick's when they're due to finish de Havilland on *Gone With the Wind*. Trilling makes inquiries and memos back that Selznick expects to finish Olivia in late April. Wallis then memos Lord, "Olivia will be available for Penelope—figure on her for it."[13]

Warner calls de Havilland, ostensibly to chat, in reality to gloat. He assures her that Selznick will make her available to portray Lady Penelope. End of story.

The script for the Davis-Flynn picture is messengered over, and Livvie reads it and sees just how small her part is. Small and unimportant. The kicked-in-the-gut feeling returns. There's another message as well: Lady Penelope is a traitor to the Queen and to Essex, which is just how J.L. now views Olivia.

She knows that Warner has her boxed in. She makes the best of it that she can. First, she devises another scene to be played between Penelope and another character, Margaret Radcliffe, that helps to explain Penelope's otherwise strange motivations. Olivia also asks Wallis and Lord that she not be given any dialogue on the new picture until she's done with retakes at Selznick's. They listen to her reasoning: "As you know it is impossible to perform two decided and difficult characters at the same time," she explains, so their problem is to work out the schedules to avoid conflicts.[14] They all pretend to listen, but she gets nothing in writing.

Is J.L. an ogre for his approach to the de Havilland situation? His points are valid: He knows there's money in teaming Livvie with Errol in the costume pictures, and contrary to the inclination of the contract players, the idea is NOT to make life comfortable for them but rather to make money. And as much as Livvie will say that *Gone With the Wind* is big-time Hollywood, Warner believes the role of Melanie is one-dimensional. Even Abbie Irving in *Dodge City* shows more growth than Melanie does. At least Abbie has to overcome the death of her brother at Wade's hand, and the death of little Harry Cole, and of Joe her newspaper boss. Melanie's too stable and lives in a rose-colored world; who the hell can sympathize with that?

Production of *Gone With the Wind* plods into April, with Belle Watling's scenes postponed because no one has been cast in the role. On April 10 Steve Trilling memos Jack Warner and Hal Wallis: "David O. Selznick Productions would like to borrow Ann Sheridan for the part of 'Belle Watling' in *Gone With the Wind*. I was advised that the part actually works only about ten days but was spread over three to four weeks. Are we at all interested—before I go to the trouble of getting a script to find out how important the part really is. So far as billing is concerned, only the stars, Gable, Leigh, Howard, and de Havilland have been guaranteed billing so we could probably demand fifth billing."[15]

Warner sees little reason to lend another of his players to the Selznick enterprise, bitter as he is over the de Havilland situation. And although Annie Sheridan would make an earthy madam and mistress of Rhett Butler, at the last minute Selznick realizes that she's young enough and sexy enough to serve as competition to Scarlett, which is not the idea of the character at all. He opts instead for a woman a dozen years Annie's senior, freelancer Ona Munson, for the worldly wise Ms. Watling.

Sheridan isn't the only one drawing interest around town; other studios are suddenly wanting to borrow Livvie, and J.L. has to consider that maybe having de Havilland appearing in *Gone With the Wind* isn't all bad. On April 19 Warner Bros. loans her to Samuel Goldwyn Productions for the leading feminine role in *Raffles*, to start in July, and three days later RKO expresses interest in borrowing her for the role of Ann Rutledge in *Abraham Lincoln in Illinois*, to start in August.

At the end of April, Livvie tackles the death of Melanie Wilkes, shot out of order since it involves all four leads, and Selznick must finish her up by May 4 per the loanout contract with Warner Bros. Fleming approaches the death scene warily, with good reason. Directors get attached to characters. Particularly male directors with female characters. The characters become real for all involved, cast and crew. Losing one produces real grief, and just as the stars internalize their death scenes, directors internalize them as well. The experience of Melanie's death has Fleming near the breaking point, and on the afternoon of April 27 he collapses and is driven off the lot. Selznick has been worrying that Fleming is too worn down to make it through the remainder of the production.

Shooting the death of Melanie on April 27 proves to be more than Victor Fleming can bear, and he succumbs to exhaustion.

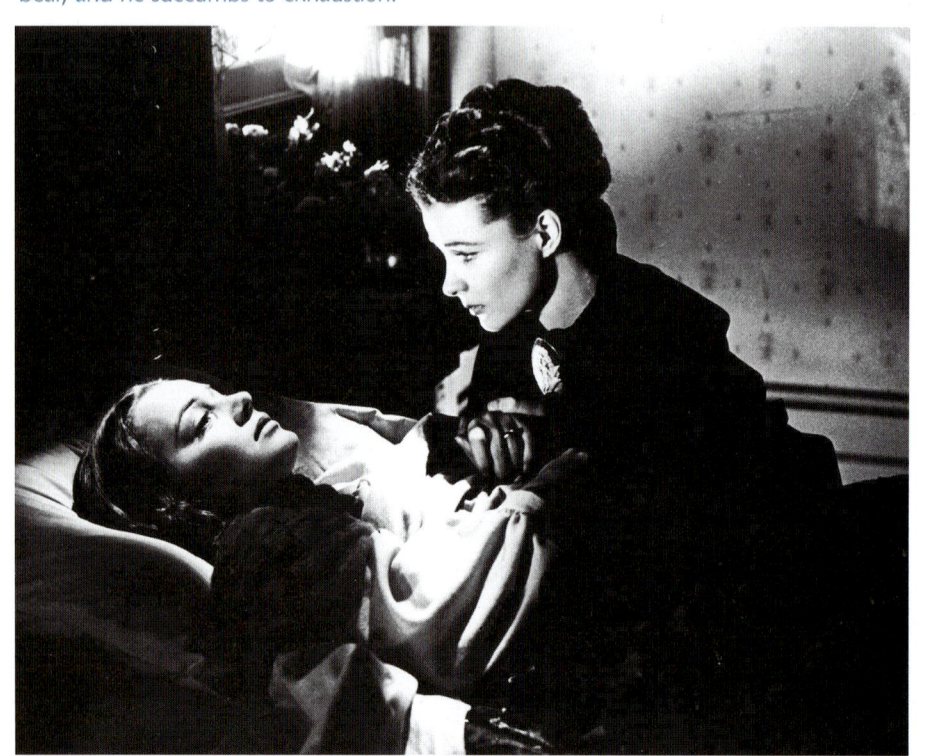

MGM director Sam Wood steps up to the plate, and by now Leigh and de Havilland know the drill, thanks to the wisdom of Howard Hughes: whether refined or coarse, it's pretty much the same talent with this caliber of director. Wood shoots Scarlett and Ashley at the lumber mill, and Scarlett turning drapes into a gown, and the powerful carriage scene wherein Melanie thanks Belle for her kindness and, more than that, treats her as an equal. Then Scarlett shoots a dirty Yankee in the face and Melanie, weakened from childbirth, helps to clean up the mess, and on it goes.

At the same time, at Warner Bros., they're testing Queen Elizabeth's wigs and makeup on Bette Davis's double, with disastrous results that call into question the entire premise of the picture: aging Elizabeth and dashing Robert Devereux, 2nd Earl of Essex, are in love, but history and politics come between them. In fact, Elizabeth was about 67 years old when she had entertained Essex, an ambitious, charming 35-year-old rascal of no great military skill. In her twilight years, the Queen apparently relished the attentions of the young Earl. Whatever existed between them probably wasn't the kind of passionate love that Maxwell Anderson and the Warner writers now envision, and presenting it that way could be seen as a little…creepy.

Bette Davis wants to go the whole nine yards with her presentation, including shaving back her hairline at the forehead a good inch and fitting it with a wig to simulate Elizabeth's baldness. Technicolor testing of Miss Davis's double, who runs through a scene with young contract player Dennis Morgan as Essex, results in a reel that Hal Wallis watches, apparently chewing on his knuckle all the while at this poor creature who, with a shaved hairline and eyebrows, dead-gray pallor, and orange fright-wig, looks like something out of Universal Horror. "I am a little worried about the effect of that bald, shaved, high forehead when we get it on Davis," Hal Wallis writes to Robert Lord in understatement. "I know that this is correct and all of that, but I am afraid we are going to have to take some little license in order that our character won't be laughable and ruin the entire drama of the situation."[16]

A week later test number two on Bette's double sends Wallis scampering to write Lord another memo about the work of makeup guru Perc Westmore: "I don't like that greenish tint that he is giving to the face makeup, with the eyes narrowing down to slits…; we don't want to make Davis up as a female Frankenstein…; we have a story that we are going to try and make into a great love story, and

Flynn, seen on the lead horse at left center, kicks off production of *The Lady and the Knight* on Stage 11 as Essex and his army march through bogs on their campaign against the Robin Hood-like Earl of Tyrone.

this is not going to be possible if we try to do it with Flynn, as handsome as he looks in his clothes, in love with an ugly woman."[17]

Westmore's third try is closer, but color tests of the Queen's makeup against Flynn's are not kind—suntanned, outdoorsy Flynn as Essex and pasty, balding Davis as Elizabeth still look like two different species. J.L., Wallis, Curtiz, Westmore, assistant director Sherry Shourds, and unit manager Frank Mattison all look at the film of the third makeup test. Rather than lighten Flynn, they decide to darken Elizabeth, but all begin to worry at how anyone is ever going to believe that someone who looks like Essex would ever have anything to do with someone who looks like Davis.

And just then, Bette Davis gets *really* ugly. Her letter to J.L. on April 28 begins: "I have been trying for some weeks to get an answer from you concerning the title of my next picture. I felt confident that you would of your own volition change it, considering the fact the play from which it is taken was bought for me and was called *Elizabeth the Queen*. I have found out today you are not changing it. You of course must have realized my interest in the title change concerned the billing." J.L. skims on down…first billing, yadda yadda yadda…give the man first billing, blah blah blah. "You force me to refuse to make the picture unless the billing is mine."[18] It's easy to imagine J.L. giving himself an Edgar Kennedy face wash.

J.L. is now besieged on two fronts, by what he sees as egomaniacal drama queen Davis and her egomaniacal lady-in-waiting de Havilland. And that damn fool Flynn hasn't even been heard from yet!

A little more than a week later, J.L. receives a letter from the Warner Bros. sales manager for New York, Gradwell Sears, who grouses about "a serious problem," namely, the title of this new picture. Sears was alarmed by reading in Louella Parsons' gossip column "that you are trying to get the title *Elizabeth and Essex* in place of *The Knight and the Lady*. I implore you not to make this change. *The Knight and the Lady* with Flynn and Davis indicates a romantic swashbuckling sort of thing, while *Elizabeth and Essex*, except to the classes, indicates something entirely different."[19]

Now it's class warfare in addition to the sane against the crazy and the good-looking versus the ugly. But the Boss has no qualms about rolling over and giving Davis the

Tension mounts on Stage 7 as a tense Flynn takes direction from Mike Curtiz while Bette Davis looks on. The experience will be so vivid for Flynn that 20 years later, even with a booze-soaked brain, he can describe it in detail in his autobiography. (John McElwee Collection)

title she wants—Davis makes a whole lot of money for the studio, and she'll do it again with this picture, and J.L. will call it whatever he wants to call it.

The day after Sears' memo, J.L. calls Bette and weighs in about the title. This picture will either be called *The Lady and the Knight* or *Elizabeth and Essex*—either way, the billing is hers. Flynn will have to be happy in the knowledge that he takes home a grand more a week than Davis does, even if she's the one making the *important* pictures.

Fifteen miles closer to the ocean, over at Selznick International, production is moving at a brisk pace, but the number of scenes remaining to be shot is vast—the equivalent of a feature film yet to go. Selznick realizes he can't finish de Havilland's scenes by the agreed-upon May 4, so he asks Warner Bros. through R.J. Obringer in Legal for an extension; Selznick chooses not to go to J.L. personally. Obringer sends it up to Wallis, who at first says there can be no extension because Livvie is set to start in a new picture, *The Lady and the Knight*, on May 1. But Wallis knows he can't force de Havilland to leave Selznick with an incomplete film. In an April 28 memo, a solicitous Hal Wallis says: "Possibly if they can have de Havilland come over here during the next couple of weeks if she has a few days off to get her wardrobe, tests, etc., we will permit her to remain with them until we actually need her for photography."[20]

In the meantime, Vic Fleming returns from his breakdown, but so many scenes are written on Selznick's matrix that Sam Wood stays on to direct a B unit while Fleming works with the A unit. It is a grim, desolate part of the story—after the war, the barren landscape, a civil war brewing between Rhett and Scarlett as husband and wife.

On a day off from Selznick, May 5, Livvie reports to Warner Bros. for a wild wardrobe test, but won't be on the call sheet for at least another 10 days or more. She has to admit that Warner and Wallis are being humane with David Selznick, letting him keep her long enough to finish his high-pressure epic. But it's torture driving into Warner Bros. even if her costumes are lovely; she'll *look* wonderful, but after breaking through in *Gone With the Wind*, the demotion in *The Lady and the Knight* is going to be highly visible; she knows it will be the talk of the town.

Livvie still has her earlier request of Wallis and Lord on her mind: She is so intensely involved with the Melanie character, about to shoot tough scenes with Gable, that she can't read lines for Penelope until she's closed out as Melanie. She doesn't hear back from Wallis but knows he's a pro; he will understand and advise Curtiz accordingly.

Flynn has his own cross to bear. He opens the production on Monday, May 15, in the Irish bogs created on Stage 11, battling the Earl of Tyrone, played by Alan Hale. After sizing up the challenges of this first sequence to be shot, unit manager Frank Mattison memos Tenny Wright that he will print two takes of several scenes because they're using glycerin smoke to represent the fog-enshrouded bogs, and it's difficult to match its density from shot to shot. It's easier to print multiple takes than to go back later and try to recreate the shots using more smoke.

Flynn is barely into day one before he has trouble with his lines. He starts out on horseback, with his trusted lieutenants. His dismal army marches through a dark marsh, and he is prompted by a line from one of his lieutenants, Robert Warwick as Mountjoy: "Our losses are growing serious, M'Lord."

Flynn's line is a tough one: "Losses I expect, and can understand. It's this forever going on and on after a retreating enemy; over these fever bogs, getting further and further from our base. One bold, swift advance now and we'd have Tyrone in a trap. How can we advance lacking arms, ammunition, necessities even?" It's a mouthful to start the picture, on a moving horse, with mounted actors in motion beside and behind him—and with no one to play against. Frank Mattison informs Tenny Wright in a memo: "Mr. Flynn had considerable difficulty with his lines as you will notice that the OK'd takes were numbers 5 or 6."[21]

As champion archer Howard Hill mops up on Stage 11, portraying an Irish sharpshooter who picks off Essex's men with arrows in the back, work is progressing at a fever's pace on the palace set on Stage 7. And that's where Flynn is headed for his first horrific confrontation with Davis, which he describes in vivid detail in *My Wicked, Wicked Ways*. It is two weeks past Bette's victory in the billing wars, and they are to play a long scene together, Essex back from Cadiz, where he has had misfortune with the Spanish fleet. He confronts her on the throne, and they exchange a great amount of dialogue, and then he spins on his heel and turns his back on her to walk away, and she angrily calls after him. In the first take, with camera rolling and what Flynn describes hyperbolically as 600 extras watching, Davis approaches him and says her line, "You day-uh turn your back on Elizabeth of England? You day-uh?" And she slaps him. Except it isn't a stage slap. "I felt as if I had been hit by a railroad locomotive," says Flynn. "She had lifted one of her hands, heavy with those Elizabethan rings, and Joe Louis himself couldn't give a right hook better than Bette hooked me with. My jaw went out."

He describes going to her dressing room and appealing to her to take it easy. Davis states she can only do it one way. They go back and forth, and at length Flynn promises that if he's slugged again, he's going to hit back.

"What the hell are you talking about?" Davis demands. "Just—what—I—said!"

He leaves knowing that "If she hit me, and I knew she was going to, I would have to whack her and drop her."

They play the scene again, and posterity records the results. Davis and Flynn exchange their exquisite dialogue, and he spins on his heel, and she rises from the throne and walks to him. In the New Millennium, with today's technology, there exist superb remastered 35mm shots, looking past Flynn and focusing on Davis, and plainly visible is the welt on Flynn's cheek from the earlier run-through.

"You day-uh turn your back on Elizabeth of England? You day-uh?" And reaches back her hand to slap him. "I braced myself for this hit," says Flynn. But at the fateful moment, he says, "She did it in the most beautifully technical way. Her hand came just delicately to the side of my nose, missing by a fraction of an inch. I don't even believe she touched me, but I could feel the wind go by my face, and it looked technically perfect." Flynn scores a point, tying Bette at one all.[22]

But the confrontations on the throne-room set are not over. Livvie has arrived on Stage 7 and climbs into costume for her first scene in the picture as Lady Penelope, which amounts to nothing more than wide-eyed reaction shots to the goings-on between the Queen and Lord Essex (the man Penelope loves) and the slap of him in front of the assembled court. Livvie's mood is dark; she describes the experience as "torture for me…leaving this wonderful atmosphere at Selznick for a very different atmosphere…at Warner Bros."[23]

As they're lining up the talent, not 600 as Flynn had estimated but a lot of people, upwards of 50 in costume and a like number on the crew, Frank Mattison mentions to Livvie that she will also be needed to shoot a scene that evening. She asks if the scene will require dialogue, because she has made an agreement with Mr. Wallis and Mr. Lord that she will not be asked to change character from Melanie to Lady Penelope before she finishes *Gone With the Wind*. Mattison shrugs—says he hasn't heard about any such agreement—just knows he needs her on the set on Stage 3 at 5:00, knowing her lines and ready to go.

At 5:00, Livvie reports to Stage 3 for the scene with Nanette Fabray. By 5:30 they're ready to rehearse, at which point Michael Curtiz settles into his director's chair. *Let's get this over with.*

Nausea washes over her. *Mike, I'm not going to play this scene today. It's dialogue, and I have an agreement with Wallis and Lord not to do any dialogue until I'm finished at Selznick's.*

Curtiz is unmoved. *This scene was your idea, to give you more screen time, and we went along with it.*

Yes, but I can't do it now.

He stares her down a moment and then says something along the lines of: *Jack knew you'd pull this shit, and I'm here to tell you, play the damn scene.*

She will admit decades later, "I lost my cool, which was not like me, and which is unforgivable."[24]

Mattison reports to Tenny Wright, "She talked so loud and fussed so that Mr. Curtiz gave me the high-sign to take her off the set, which I did, and walked her out into the alley still in the discussion as to what she would and would not do."[25]

Despite her iron will and her resolve to outlast J.L., Livvie storms off to her dressing room in bejeweled Elizabethan regalia with Mattison giving chase.

In private now, on what passes for home turf, she gathers herself and says she's given Wallis the names of other actresses who could play this part with no problem if scenes with dialogue have to be shot right away. Mattison challenges her: *Do you really want to be in this picture? Or are you trying to get out of it?*

Livvie looks him full in the face. She knows he's front office; it's his *job* to be front office, and what she says now will go into a report and make its way upstairs.

She says that, yes, she absolutely wants to play this part, but reiterates that she can't work in the character of Penelope until she finishes *Gone With the Wind*, as per the arrangement with Mr. Wallis and Mr. Lord.

Mattison quietly asks what's left to shoot at Selznick's, because they've only asked for her for a few scattered days. She tells him she doesn't know, exactly, but there are three big scenes coming up with Gable.

Mattison departs, and Livvie is alone in the quiet of her dressing room, looking at herself in the mirror. It has been a hell of a first day on *The Lady and the Knight*.

Almost two months later she will write a letter to J.L. and try to smooth everything over. She will say that it had been a misunderstanding, a "triviality," and she will absolve Curtiz of any blame, saying the whole thing was about her nervousness and a long day on the set. But de Havilland's gesture will not get her anywhere with Jack L. Warner, who neither forgives nor forgets.

Over at Selznick International, de Havilland and Fleming start the week of May 29 with Gable's most terrifying moment: the prospect of crying onscreen in the wake of Scarlett's miscarriage.

Says Gable expert Carole Sampeck of the King in his moment of crisis: "He had difficulty forgetting his father's words that acting was not quite a manly occupation. Any heavily emotional scene called for in a script would have given him the heebie-jeebies, as he felt strongly about doing anything onscreen that would make him appear anything less than thoroughly masculine."[26]

"He was embarrassed," says Livvie. "Embarrassed at the naked suffering of Rhett Butler. Embarrassed as a man, as an actor, and as Clark Gable. Victor tried to reassure him, and I shyly tried to do the same, for I knew so well how much encour-

Above: On a tortured walk up the stairs of the Butler home, Mammy describes the tragic and macabre goings on in the wake of Bonnie Blue's death. Accomplished in a single seamless take with the camera moving upward with the actresses, this gut-wrenching scene helps both de Havilland and Hattie McDaniel earn Academy Award nominations—and seals McDaniel's victory. Below: Olivia is suddenly responsible for helping the King of Hollywood, Clark Gable, through a scene in which he has to cry on camera. The none-too-confident Gable wants it to be shot both ways, with and without tears, and agrees afterward with Vic Fleming that it plays better *with* tears. Experiences like these mess with Livvie's head as her talents are stretched at one studio and dismissed at another.

123

This posed publicity photo seems to show romance between the characters, but in the script Essex sees Penelope as a foolish girl and dismisses her warning that there is treachery afoot. (John McElwee Collection)

agement could mean. Then the silent moment came, just before the final rehearsal, when we could feel that Gable had committed himself. And when the camera began to roll, we knew he had, for the tears came, and the humble grief and remorse and despair, and he was wonderful."[27]

With special-effects rain rolling down the backlit window, Olivia de Havilland shares the magic of a powerful screen moment with Clark Gable. She has never been tested like this at Warner Bros.; she feels that these experiences—the scene with Ona Munson in the carriage, the Gable-in-tears scene, her own death scene—validate her claim that she is being stifled by J.L. in Burbank.

Livvie shoots her final scene of principal photography at Selznick's on Friday, June 2, a reshoot of the meeting with Belle Watling on the steps of the church. She had been on the schedule for Monday June 5 as well, but Selznick gives up the fight with Warner Bros. over keeping her on. With ice in her veins, de Havilland makes the commute to Burbank. She completes scenes with Davis and with Henry Daniell, Donald Crisp, and other players. The entire time, she is enduring the silent treatment from the crew as ordered by J.L.

"Nobody speaks to me," she says. "The assistant director says, 'We are ready.' I don't think he even called me Miss de Havilland, just 'We are ready now.' And I would come out and nobody would say good morning to me, nobody said good evening, nobody said anything beyond what they had to say. Now that, I must tell you, is really difficult to go through. I realized what it was and I thought, 'Well, I'm going to survive this.'"[28]

For de Havilland, the tests of her strength keep coming. Her mother leaves Nella Vista to care for seriously ill G.M. Fontaine in Saratoga. "Two months after she was gone, Joan got married. My mother had, naturally, always taken the responsibility of our household and, in a way, of us. It was her home; we were her children; we behaved accordingly…. The household became my responsibility. I became my responsibility…. I was alone with myself for the first time in my life. And, at first, I was alone with a stranger. I was alone with a girl I didn't know at all. I had to come to terms with me. I had to find out what I was all about."[29]

But she is born to manage her home. "She is never happy unless all the rooms are practically filled with flowers, books and candy," says Hollywood stringer Michael Sheridan. "She is a telephone fiend, and can stay on the line for hours on end…. She is an aggressively independent young woman who likes to make her own rules, choose her own friends and live alone—and be allowed to love it."[30]

In this frame of mind, Livvie plays a scene with Flynn, their only scene of note in the picture. Essex has eyes only for the Queen; Penelope intercepts him on his way to the queen's chamber and says, "May I have one moment,

124

M'Lord?" She uses that moment to try to seduce him away. After the audience has spent an hour watching Flynn as Essex romancing the Universal Horror Queen, the sight of 22-year-old Lady Penelope of the low-cut gown is one for sore eyes, and yet even after 70 years, the silent treatment she has endured shows onscreen. She is detached as Penelope; she hits her marks by looking right at them. She recites her lines like a pro, but reveals nothing about her character. Lady Penelope has been weakly drawn, and Livvie is at a loss to color in the details and bring her to life. What's missing is a sympathetic director to show her the way.

In one of the picture's foreshadowing moments, Penelope warns Essex: "Oh, Robert, be careful! You anger her too much!" She tells Essex that if they were lovers, she would never curse him as the queen does. He laughs the Flynn laugh, cuffs her chin, and says, "But if we were lovers, you might. So thank your lucky stars we're not." Errol must sell the fact that he loves the queen and has no interest in the ravishing creature before him, and manages to pull this off. Penelope makes Essex promise that he'll be careful, and she steals a kiss from him. And that is that for Flynn and de Havilland onscreen in *The Lady and the Knight*.

In the day and a half it takes to shoot this scene, Errol doesn't toe the party line and give Livvie the silent treatment, but neither does he shower her with sympathy or offer a shoulder to cry on—as much as she is struggling in her attempts to better her career, he's struggling too and merely attempting to *survive*. For Flynn it is an ongoing nightmare working with Davis and Curtiz. He is forced to leave Olivia to her fate and worry about himself as the ordeal of *The Lady and the Knight* goes on.

Flynn's next sequence might as well take place on the rack, because it's torture: Essex returns to London from his defeat in Ireland bringing his army to storm the palace and seize power. Neither he nor Elizabeth knows that his defeat had been caused by a conspiracy among the Queen's ministers to intercept the letters of the lovers. Essex muscles his way into the throne room and confronts the queen. This

The beleaguered stars sometimes hit a nice rhythm together, but more often struggle to get through the densely packed dialogue.

sequence is shot on Stage 7 the week of June 5. It is a long, complex series of scenes—Elizabeth begins to suspect that members of her court have been disloyal. She dismisses everyone but Essex. Finally, "Cut! Print!" and they play another key scene. He reaffirms his love, despite having stormed the palace. She offers him a place at her side, but he wants power equal to hers. Essex demands to be king, with Elizabeth his queen. (The real-life Essex was of noble blood and would indeed have been recognized as king.)

On Wednesday, June 7, Frank Mattison reports: "Yesterday, what should have been a very excellent day, turned out to be a very poor one. Miss Davis was compelled to stop work at 5:00 PM, as she and Flynn had been working all day in a very difficult scene. Today, however, we should be able to get a good day, as they have rehearsed the scene throughout to the end."[31]

It takes all week to capture the 12 minutes between the two of them in the throne room, full of dramatic twists and turns. He puts his head against her breast and swoons; she plays with his hair. He swears his love, but then he stands and squares off against her, speaking frankly—*he* should be king. She promises emptily that they can rule together. He releases his army and turns control of the palace back to her guard. She places Essex under arrest, and he is led away to the Tower.

Two major Flynn-Davis sequences remain: a love scene in her chamber, and their last scene, in the tower, prior to his execution. Reports Mattison of the shooting on Saturday, June 10: "When we were discussing Monday and Tuesday's work with Miss Bette Davis, she flatly informed us that she positively would not and will not jump directly to the big love scene with Errol Flynn and then to the Tower scene with Mr. Flynn."[32]

Jumping periods is common in picture making because scenes with the same cast members are grouped together and shot one after another, wherever they fall in the script. But in this case, Bette Davis—or *Miss* Bette Davis, as Mattison calls her at all times in his memos, seemingly with unhidden dislike—makes sense in not wanting to jump from an intimate scene to the imminent death of the lover. The only reason that management wants to shoot it this way is because the scheduling will finish Henry Daniell and John Sutton in the picture. It is part of the tried-and-true formula—do the big shots with the whole company, then close out the freelancers, then shoot with a smaller company, close out more talent, until you are left with the leads finishing up. Instead, Davis proposes to shoot the remaining scenes in continuity—three major sequences—which will allow the Elizabeth-Essex relationship to deepen, mature, and darken naturally. The approach makes sense to Davis and to Flynn, and even Wallis and Warner realize that it might help the picture, so they carry Daniell for one more week at $1,500 and Sutton at $200. J.L. knows that spending a couple thousand on Davis's idea is chump change compared with the cost of seeing her walk off the picture.

Stills are all that remain from the scene Olivia de Havilland had requested to build up her part. Here Curtiz establishes the setting (with trademark foreground objects) as Penelope confides in Mistress Margaret, portrayed by Nanette Fabray. When de Havilland snaps under the pressure of the Boss and his boys and throws a second tantrum on this set, the scene is scrapped. (John McElwee Collection)

The same memo recapping June 10 also informs studio brass of what Mattison describes as "another display of temperament late Saturday afternoon from Miss de Havilland." These are hard times for Livvie, as the record indicates that rehearsal for her added scene with Nanette Fabray, the one that had been postponed when she didn't want to recite dialogue while still working on *Gone With the Wind*, is scheduled to *begin* at 5:15 p.m. on a Saturday. Livvie has continued to endure the silent treatment and must play the two pages of dialogue with Fabray well into Saturday evening. For her own preservation, De Havilland informs Frank Mattison that she will stop at 6:00.

Mike Curtiz jabs his finger in her direction. *You'll stay and finish this scene! If you make trouble, I promise you I'll cut it from the picture!*

De Havilland's only opportunity for a marquee scene is afforded when luscious Penelope, one heck of a departure from Melanie Hamilton, begs a tortured Queen Elizabeth to spare the life of Essex.

"Miss de Havilland expressed herself before the company," says Mattison in his report to Wright, "and Mr. Curtiz came right back, with the result that she made a display of hysterics before the company and it became necessary for me to dismiss the company at 6:15 without shooting this sequence." Mattison backs Curtiz in cutting the sequence and says that this action "will put Miss de Havilland in a proper frame of mind so that she will take direction and instruction hereafter."[33]

The nightmare is never-ending for Flynn as well, and he now begins to understand how unappealing a prospect it would have been to land the role of Rhett Butler. Essex is just too far out of Errol's comfort zone. Too much studying of too much dialogue; too much criticism from "Miss Bette Davis," as Flynn also will call Davis in his memoirs. Too much pressure from Curtiz and from Mattison, who feel intense pressure direct from J.L. to bring the picture in ahead of schedule to give it the ghost of a chance of making a profit, given the cost of Technicolor—setup times, film stock, and the cameras and consultants to run the things.

On June 13 Livvie reports to Stage 3 for her big confrontation scene, as Penelope and Mistress Margaret sing a rhyming song for the Queen, one that not so subtly lampoons the relationship of much-older Elizabeth and young Essex. The song proves to be problematic; says Mattison: "The words of the song are of the Elizabethan period and not easily understood, and it is the consensus of opinion that the lyrics should be pointed up more."[34] Robert Lord looks at the footage and orders a reshoot, which is executed on Saturday, June 17.

As they sing, the Queen beholds babelicious Penelope in her low-cut gown, 22 and scrumptious, then looks at her own aging visage in the mirror. The queen picks up her silver wine goblet and hurls it into the mirror.

She rants at Penelope, "So, you brazen wench, you defy me! You dare hold your queen up to ridicule? You forward hussy! You who can keep neither your eyes, nor your nose, nor your person where they belong!"

Unfortunately, when J.L. goes gunning for Olivia by casting her in this picture, he hurts the chances for success of a risky Warner Bros. enterprise. As constructed, there is no motivation for Penelope to risk her life by taunting the queen, but taunt she does. Her actions with the song beg for the scene that Olivia had requested—wherein she

127

Down the home stretch come the two stars, in a grueling sequence highlighted by brilliant, clever, and for Flynn nearly impossible dialogue to master.

explains her motivations to another character—but the Boss and his crew have gaslighted Livvie so she would break, and break she has, inevitably, proving the Boss right that she would come back from Selznick's and be difficult.

If jealousy drives Penelope to self-destructively bait the queen—jealousy because Essex loves the queen and not Penelope—it's not obvious, and the picture suffers for it. Later Penelope conspires with those who would break up Elizabeth and Essex, even though the bringing down of Essex could mean his execution, and finally she begs the queen for his life. In short, her character is all over the place, motivationally speaking. She simply makes no sense. Under normal circumstances, Wallis wouldn't allow this to happen, and Curtiz wouldn't have let his player flounder, no matter his personal feelings.

After Livvie has received the silent treatment from the brass and crew, and suffered from a lack of direction that has left her adrift in this role, experiencing the on-camera rage of Davis as Elizabeth only adds to de Havilland's torment at being involved in the production.

The next day the company shoots the breaking-of-the-mirrors scene. The queen hurls objects through the many mirrors in the privy chamber. Davis is not a pro baseball player, so she misses more mirrors than she hits, and between takes the set boys come in to repair dinged walls and splintered mirror frames. By the time Davis finishes these sequences, dressing down Lady Penelope and smashing mirrors, she has yelled herself raw and is out the next week with laryngitis. Flynn also claims illness, and the production is closed down until Monday, June 26, at which time Flynn and Davis head back into the meat grinder on a redressed Stage 7, now INT. QUEEN'S CHAMBER SUITE. Here, on long days that start at 9:00 and end at 6:00, with the only break being a half hour for lunch (or Curtiz will have a fit), the leads play their longest sequence—Essex returning from his ancestral home, Wonstead, to meet with the Queen. It is brilliantly written dialogue. They share their first kiss in the picture, but they are still jockeying for power within the relationship. After the kiss, she looks away from him.

QUEEN: (sighs) Isn't it strange how one man's kisses can grow to be like any other's?

ESSEX: (sighs; playing along) Yes, or one woman's to be like any other woman's.

QUEEN: Not mine for you!

ESSEX: Nor mine for you! You lying villain! You double-tongued deceiver! Curse you!

QUEEN: Curse you and double curse you!

ESSEX: You devil of brass!

QUEEN: Silver, darling, let me be a devil in silver. It reminds me of Raleigh.

ESSEX: Raleigh! Must you forever be thinking of him?

QUEEN: What else do you expect, when you prefer the ants and the squirrels of Wonstead to me? (walks away; sighs) What's today? Thursday? Come again when I'm in a better mood. Next Wednesday, say. Or any Wednesday, later in the summer. Any summer.

It is 14 pages of script, fiery, confrontational, clever, revealing. In the end, despite the agony of shooting it, they play the scene beautifully, and there is no hint of the running feud, except when they kiss. Quite unlike Livvie, who is in the habit of sighing into Flynn's open mouth during their kisses, Davis is thin-lipped, and on that first kiss turns her mouth away so that he kisses mostly her cheek.

Day after day they attack that infernal script. Of July 3 Mattison says, "We lost considerable time because of Mr. Flynn's continual blowing up in his lines. We made 20 TBD [to be determined] takes, all on account of Flynn. Mr. Curtiz dismissed him at 5:00 p.m. as it was absolutely impossible to accomplish any more than he had already done."[35]

During the killer schedule, Davis wires J.L.: "I have waited now since day picture started for title to be settled. I was promised it would not be *The Knight and the Lady*. The present title *The Lady and the Knight* as announced in paper and called such in fan magazines, I consider the same thing…. You have the choice of *Elizabeth and Essex*, *Elizabeth the Queen*, or *The Love of Elizabeth and Essex*."[36]

They break for July 4 and go back at it on July 5. Flynn continues to blow his lines; he has had it and just wants to retreat to *Sirocco*. The next day they finish with retakes on Stage 11—they end where they had started, with Flynn and Alan Hale in the bogs—and that is it. Seven weeks, $1.075 million, cast blowups, hard feelings all around, and still no official title for the picture.

A week after production closes out, J.L. settles on a title and writes to Gradwell Sears in New York: "Note, we have secured the right to use Elizabeth and Essex, and I have added the words, Private Lives of to it. We ran into a big snag in using *The Lady and the Knight*, which I could not overcome. Furthermore, in case we both do not know, you cannot call a Queen a lady."

Sears tries the new title out among the people in his sales force and practically has to duck for cover at the response. He doesn't want to push the matter, but writes back to the Boss: "The reaction to the title *The Private Lives of Elizabeth and Essex* is extremely bad. I am getting letters of protest from every part of the country and my own people tell me that wherever they go exhibitors are objecting to this title. They say it smacks of Alexander Korda and that in the South, Midwest and small towns particularly, it will be confused with an English picture, which as you know do very little business especially in small towns."[37]

J.L. is out of options and counts on the power of his stars to sell this picture, but with Bette Davis seen in publicity stills looking like a cross between Laughton-as-Quasimodo and Karloff-as-the-Monster; with Flynn not swinging from vines or skewering anybody with his sword, and in fact walking to his own execution just before fade out; with a title and stage-bound talkety-talk drama that turns off America's heartland; *The Private Lives of Elizabeth and Essex* sinks of its own considerable weight, despite Technicolor, Oscar-nominated art direction and cinematography, some brilliant dialogue, an inspired performance by Davis, a game attempt by Flynn, and one of Erich Wolfgang Korngold's best scores to date, which is also Oscar nominated. Warner Bros. records will still show a $550,000 profit for *Elizabeth and Essex* due to the swift production cycle—although it certainly didn't feel swift to anyone involved.

Warner Bros. is not shy to advertise Davis's "Frankenstein" makeup. Flynn holds a sword as if he will run someone through, but unfortunately does not. And there below the title is Olivia de Havilland. The strange production with the clunky title is packaged—strangely.

Olivia and Errol pose for a still at the Warner Calabasas Ranch. Livvie's strategy in dealing with J.L. has changed: she is accepting the Flynn pictures now as she bides her time to escape from the studio. Errol grows ever-more jealous of her relationships with men who are *not* Errol Flynn.

8 BORED TO DEATH

War, war, war—that's all that anyone is talking about. On September 1, 1939, Germany invades Poland and the European situation goes steadily downhill. The American Civil War is about to play out onscreen with the release of *Gone With the Wind*. The War of the Rebellion and romantic tales of the Old South are such a rage that Warner and Wallis build a Civil War angle into the new Flynn super-western, *Virginia City*. Flynn is busy with both love and war, cohabitating with Lili once again, this time on North Linden Drive, and churning out picture after picture, with *The Sea Hawk* following *Virginia City*.

Meanwhile, Olivia de Havilland and Jack Warner are engaged in a nasty, private little war of their own. After she finishes *Essex*, Livvie cools her heels—except for endless callbacks to Selznick International for retakes on *Gone With the Wind*; a day here, a day there, in July and August.

The cold war has grown extra chilly following Livvie's loanout to Samuel Goldwyn Pictures where she joins an all-British cast for the remake of *Raffles*, the dusty old 1930 gentleman-thief caper picture.

"Usually in those days remakes were dreadful things," she says later. "I knew it was going to be a disaster…, but I went ahead and I did it. I never said one word, keeping my promise to him."[1] Ronald Colman had made the previous version and it was a swell picture. The new one is directed by Sam Wood, now quite burned out after all those weeks on *Gone With the Wind*, and pairs Livvie with David Niven, a supporting player in his first leading role.

Warner will not ease up on Olivia de Havilland. "There were many facets of him," J.L.'s longtime mistress, Jackie Park, reveals, "wonderful sense of humor, very compassionate, very loving…, but also very, very, *very* cruel, I mean to the point that he could be loving, he could be cruel.… He could just turn on you, just like that."[2]

Hal Wallis knows that Warner's vendetta violates the policy that business is business. Wallis sees in Olivia de Havilland a contract player who, if they aren't careful, can hemorrhage insincerity on the screen. But she's a woman of talent, no question. Wallis does subscribe to the policy that no one contract player is bigger than Warner Bros., not Cagney, not Davis, and certainly not de Havilland. So it makes sense to Wallis when Livvie is cast in a remake of a remake at Warner Bros.—*Married, Pretty and Poor*.

Livvie takes one look at the script and sees another of the endless variations of boy-meets-girl, boy-loses-girl, boy-gets-girl Warner pictures that she has already made up to her eyeballs, not only with Flynn, but also with Cagney, Dick Powell, John Payne, and all the others going back to Joe E. Brown.

The only thing going for *Married, Pretty and Poor*: it had been written by Maxwell Anderson, which the Boss sees as a trademark of quality, despite the casting, despite the fact it will star rising player John Garfield and be directed by a rookie named Vincent Sherman, who has done one other picture—a rare attempt by Warner Bros. at horror, *The Return of Dr. X* with Humphrey Bogart. In Livvie's hypersensitive mind, there is no limit to the underappreciation shown by her home studio.

It is December 1939. David Selznick is working 20 hours a day, as he has for months, to get *Gone With the Wind* ready to premiere. He has sneak peeked it, massaged it, trimmed it, reshot it, second-guessed it, and come hell or high water his film will play December 12 for the Hollywood press, and then December 15 in Atlanta for the world premiere. Livvie is invited by Selznick to go to Atlanta along with the rest of the cast, and the Boss sends her a message that says, ostensibly, no, she may not attend the premiere of *Gone With the Wind* in Atlanta. She has a picture to make at the studio holding her contract. That studio is Warner Bros., and the picture is entitled *Married, Pretty and Poor*, and she should prepare accordingly.

Livvie's reaction is to be hurt deeply by his edict. Then fate intervenes. At high noon on December 12, the press corps of what Livvie calls "a bored and hostile Hollywood" troop into the Four Star Theatre on Wilshire Boulevard to see *Gone With the Wind*—a tough, cynical mob 750 strong and out for Selznick's blood.[3] They have been stockpiling adjectives and adverbs to use like tar and feathers. At long last, they are finally getting their chance to go on the hunt for David O. Selznick's elusive great white elephant with all guns a blazin'.

SHOCK CUT TO A LITTLE AFTER 4:00. The theatre doors swing open and out pours a spent mass of limp writer-flesh, drained from tears and applause. Telephone wires are hot with messages: the elephant lives! *Gone With the Wind* is a triumph! By 4:10 Warner and Wallis receive the news in Burbank. *Damn it! OK, so it's not a dud. Now what'll we do? Well, yeah, we have to let the girl go to Atlanta. If her stock goes up, we make money. Fine.* By 4:30 R.J. Obringer is cabling Olivia de Havilland: "It is our understanding that you proposed Friday December 15th to be present in Atlanta…; we have no objection…; advise it will be necessary for you to immediately return to Hollywood to report to our studio not later than Monday December 18 to commence wardrobe and other preparation necessary for the role you are to portray in one of our forthcoming pictures."[4]

The Atlanta premiere of *Gone With the Wind* goes to everyone's head. From the airport arrival to the parade down Peachtree Street before 300,000 to the national radio broadcasts to the euphoric screenings, everyone associated with the film is hailed as a hero. Livvie is in a group that includes Hollywood's royalty, Gable and Lombard, and Southern royalty, the elusive, painfully shy Margaret Mitchell, America's darling.

Says historian Carole Sampeck: "One would have thought that the South had finally won that blasted war! The stars of the film and their consorts were hailed as conquering heroes, cheered at every turn. The accolades from the press and public rained down upon them like blessings from heaven. They could do no wrong. Of course it was not widely publicized that the black performers in the film were excluded from the premiere festivities in Atlanta due to segregation policies in place at the time. The marvelous Hattie McDaniel did not get to witness her triumph in the film at its premiere in Georgia. Even when I was growing

De Havilland will claim that she meets James Stewart this very night, after he had been flown 3,000 miles to escort her to the New York City premiere of *Gone With the Wind*. BUT, rumors are already swirling by this night that the couple is headed to the altar. *H-H-Hold on there!* says Jimmy of the marriage talk, because he has wild oats to sow.

up there, and during my visits since, the events of those three days are imprinted on the memory of Atlanta like a boutonniere proudly worn on one's lapel every day, every moment."[5]

While still in Atlanta, Livvie reads in the New York Times, "Olivia de Havilland's Melanie is a gracious, dignified, tender gem of characterization."[6]

Then Selznick twists J.L.'s arm to extend her leave so she can attend the New York premiere, and the Boss says yes because by now every mention of the name of his contract player increases her value. Irene Selznick asks her dad, Louis B. Mayer, to send MGM contract player Jimmy Stewart to New York City to serve as Livvie's escort for the evening. De Havilland will claim later that the New York premiere is their first date.

However, Rosalind Russell had suggested to Livvie way back during production of *Four's a Crowd* that she might like Stewart, so they had been dating for quite a while by the time of the New York premiere; dating so ardently that rumors are already swirling that Stewart and de Havilland are about to wed.

In New York, says Livvie, "Jimmy met me at the airport in a rented limousine…. We didn't say much that night, but I could tell that he liked me. I certainly liked him. We started seeing one another regularly."[7]

She's turning into a sexy and mysterious woman these days, who strives to keep her private life as private as possible. She may be sensitive to the fact that she is now dating another serious beau of Ginger Rogers—the same girl Howard Hughes had been seeing prior to making a move on Livvie. The last thing she wants is a reputation around town as the wolf-in-Melanie-clothing who steals men from Rogers, who is generally beloved around town.

But then the real James Stewart is not quite the bumpkin he portrays onscreen; he merely displays his "aw shucks" Indiana, Pennsylvania innocence, flashes the blue eyes and shy smile, and waits for the babes to line up. In his brief four years in Hollywood, Jimmy has already served as the kept man of Metro queen Norma Shearer and the lover of legendary Marlene Dietrich, who had taken one look at him on the set of the western *Destry Rides Again* and proclaimed, "That's for me!" then practically molested him in his dressing room.[8] Livvie now has herself quite an experi-

Jimmy Stewart sure looks like a guy who's about to get lucky as he squires suspended contract player Olivia de Havilland around town. Here she chats with the queen herself, Miss Bette Davis. (Robert Florczak Collection)

enced boyfriend, with a reputation in heartland America as a swell fella, and a reputation within the confines of Hollywood as quite the lover.

Olivia de Havilland's time away from Hollywood, enjoying the "blessings of heaven," can't last forever, and the return to Hollywood proves to be quite a comedown. With her ears still ringing from the cheers and applause, she sits in her house and contemplates her career. She is sensitized to the scripts now, sensing a figurative bomb in every parcel messengered to her home by the studio. She calls her agent, and her agent calls the studio: No, Miss de Havilland will not appear in *Married, Pretty and Poor*.

This is not an easy call for her because she knows she is playing into J.L.'s hands. He had predicted that she would become difficult after appearing in *Gone With the Wind*, and he had tried to fulfill this prophesy by bullying her on the *Essex* set. He had gotten to her then despite Livvie's best efforts to hold out. But she had made it through that picture, and she had gotten through the loanout to Goldwyn for *Raffles*, one of the most uncomfortable experiences of her life—a loanout designed to make her just that: uncomfortable. She says, "I had nothing to do with that English scene. I had nothing to do with that style of film and I was nothing to that part the way it was written."[9]

Warner Bros. has lots of actresses under contract and these women are worked hard and treated decently. But Olivia de Havilland is different. She is the subject of a vendetta and explains her decision to stand up to the Boss as a matter of principle: "I cannot after that *[Gone With the Wind]* do something I don't believe in; I really cannot and I am not going to be penalized three times in a row."[10]

Ironically, the resulting John Garfield picture, renamed *Saturday's Children*, will be a success. "She should have done that one," says Hollywood historian John McElwee. "It got good reviews and it was a nice little sleeper. It could have helped her career after *Gone With the Wind*."[11]

At Nella Vista, an hour after she had called her agent, the phone begins to ring. She knows who it is; she doesn't answer. In the afternoon, there is a knock at the door. A telegram is handed to her: "Dear Olivia: Am surprised to think that you would entertain any idea of not playing in Maxwell Anderson's play. If you are objecting to any other member of the cast, this too surprises me. Perhaps I should not be surprised at all because your present attitude is my anticipated reward for permitting you to play in outside pictures. [I] am certainly amazed at your neglect and apparent refusal to answer the telephone calls of Mr. Wallis or myself. Please remember you are under contract to this company and accordingly I believe it would be good taste for you to answer our phone calls. Please telephone me immediately at the studio in order that I may personally hear your assurances that you are reporting to the studio tomorrow for work. Jack Warner"[12]

There it is. *Your present attitude is my anticipated reward for permitting you to play in outside pictures.* He has needled and needled her until he gets the response that allows him to be right.

The following morning, Obringer sends a quick memo to J.L.: "Our contract with Olivia de Havilland has been suspended as of this date for cause. Miss de Havilland, therefore, should not be requested to do any publicity work or otherwise render services, as this would result in her suspension being terminated. Should she, however, serve any notice that she is able, ready and willing to resume her services under the contract, please notify me at once, in order that I may take such steps as proper in this event."[13]

De Havilland stays on suspension into February and spends her time reading favorable press about *Gone With the Wind*. On February 9 she is put back on the payroll to read another script that has been sent over, something called *Flight Eight*, a strange story written by Jerry Wald about a grounded pilot and some stewardesses that "again I knew," says de Havilland, "was going to be a disaster and he [J.L.] was just going to capitalize cheaply, really cheaply, off *Gone With the Wind* instead of doing something responsible and intelligent with me in terms of the public."[14]

Back on suspension she continues to date Jimmy Stewart. One evening he calls on her

Olivia de Havilland's modest house near the top of Nella Vista off of Los Feliz Boulevard. She first resided here with Lillian and Joan, and then by herself, and finally with John Huston. Jimmy Stewart parked his new LaSalle on this spot, and watched it roll a hundred yards down the hill. And it was here that bad scripts and telegrams from an angry J.L. arrived often.

up at the top of Nella Vista in a new LaSalle convertible. "I made sure the hand brake was on," Stewart recalls, "because Olivia lived on the top of a steep hill. Then I went inside to get her. As we came out, the LaSalle started moving by itself." The car easily outdistances even the long strides of Stewart as it tears down Nella Vista toward Los Feliz, sideswiping parked cars, bowling over expensive shrubbery, and smacking against a telephone pole. "You certainly know how to entertain a date," she tells him.[15]

It will be one of the few smiles she will get these days. *Gone With the Wind* had been released before the end of 1939, making it eligible for the Academy Awards to be held February 29 at the Cocoanut Grove.

In the year of *The Wizard of Oz* and *Mr. Smith Goes to Washington* and *Wuthering Heights* and *Dark Victory* and *Of Mice and Men* and *Stagecoach*, *Gone With the Wind* is up in a number of categories, including Best Picture, Actor, Actress, Supporting Actress, Director, Screenplay, Cinematography, Art Direction, Sound Recording, Film Editing, Special Effects, and Original Score. Such is the level of technical achievement resulting from Selznick's gamble—and the project to which de Havilland has hitched her star.

Selznick hosts a private party for the cast and production team at his home, hours before the Academy Awards banquet. There he receives a phone call from an insider who breaks all the rules and reads off a list of that evening's winners. Conspicuous by their absence are the names Clark Gable and Olivia de Havilland. So Livvie travels with the group to the Cocoanut Grove knowing she will not receive a statuette.

It is an excruciating ride. She has been desperate for this honor; desperate to prove herself better than the opinion of Jack L. Warner; desperate to prove herself better than her little sister who has now gotten into pictures and started to see some success. She thinks back to that conversation

Errol's new co-star is more than the hero bargains for. Athletic, charismatic Ronald Reagan knocks Flynn, and de Havilland, for a loop. Soon, Livvie is hanging on Ronnie's every word, and Flynn is green with envy. (John McElwee Collection)

with Warner when she had pleaded to be allowed to do *Gone With the Wind*, and he had condescended to her and tried to tell her what was best, forcing her to go around him to Ann Warner—at a terrible price.

She is frustrated that Selznick and the Academy have categorized her not as a leading actress and a star of the picture, which would have placed her in direct competition with Vivien Leigh, but as a supporting actress, "down" with Hattie McDaniel, who had put only a fraction of the work into *Gone With the Wind* that Livvie had. "I never said a word when that happened," says de Havilland later, "but of course it was a crushing blow."

...And the award goes to...Miss Hattie McDaniel! "Oh, there was no God," says de Havilland of that evening. "He didn't exist. I ceased to believe in Him."[16] It would take a long time to get past this experience and to heal. Perhaps she has never gotten past it and never healed.

In this frame of mind, she remains on suspension for two more weeks, but knows she must make a picture to get her face in front of audiences as something other than Melanie Hamilton. She settles on a script that, while still a B picture, isn't terrible. She decides to make *My Love Came Back* with Jeffrey Lynn, the usual Warner Bros. breezy fare with the stock company—Eddie Albert playing a character named Dusty, married to Jane Wyman playing a character named Joy, all of them musicians starting a band.

After finishing *My Love Came Back*, Olivia is sent a Robert Buckner script, which she takes on the road with her to a Red Cross benefit in Houston, Texas. The script is called *Santa Fe Trail*, named to fulfill the deal with the Santa Fe Railroad that had gotten Warner Bros. the train to Kansas. Livvie can't make sense of the characters or motivations, but she sees that she would portray an elegant cowgirl opposite Errol Flynn. She also realizes that this is yet another Civil War-era production cashing in on *Gone With the Wind*, but the cowgirl, Kit Carson Halliday, has some interesting qualities, including a spiritual side, an assertiveness with the male leads, and a surprising amount of screen time for an action picture. She is assured that if she accepts the role, she will get her name above the title with Flynn. After all she has endured the past six months, *Raffles* followed by one bad Warner Bros. script after another, she grabs at the opportunity, and feels a new appreciation for Flynn and his action spectacles.

She says, "I realized that if I wasn't doing what I wanted to be doing, then I had to be in an attractive film that was a box office hit. When a Flynn film came along, I did it. You had to keep yourself alive with costumes, sets, etc. I knew attractiveness was necessary to keep the career alive. And I had to preserve the career until the contract was up."[17]

Until the contract was up. She is beginning to wonder if Warner's anger is ever going to expend itself. If not, her goal must be to make it to the end of her present seven-year contract, signed in 1936, that will run for three more long years. But she faces another problem, the same one faced by Cagney and Davis and all the other stars who take suspensions: added to the end of the contract is a time period equivalent to that needed to complete the film that the star refuses to make. *Married, Pretty and Poor* takes eight weeks to produce? Eight weeks are added to the end of her contract. *Flight Eight* (released as *Flight Angels*) takes nine weeks? Tack on nine more. As crazy as it sounds, Warner seems to be sending her scripts that he knows she will turn down just to keep her on hand longer, to prolong the agony as long as possible!

In case de Havilland refuses *Santa Fe Trail*, Brenda Marshall and Frances Farmer are other possible Kit Carson Hallidays, and another role is just now cast— George Armstrong Custer will be played by newcomer Dennis Morgan, who has been making his way up through the B's and recently completed one of the pictures Livvie had turned down, *Flight Angels*.

Custer will be Morgan's part for all of 12 days, until Wallis and Curtiz begin second-guessing the actor who will play against Flynn. This is to be the studio's Christmas western, an A picture with a big cast and nearly a million-dollar budget, and they like what they're seeing from young Ronald Reagan on his new picture now in editing, *Knute Rockne, All American*.

De Havilland and Flynn pose at Busch Gardens on the first day of shooting, in the same field where they had shot the archery tournament in *Robin Hood*, and where she had shot the Twelve Oaks barbecue in *Gone With the Wind*. (John McElwee Collection)

Dennis Morgan comes off the call sheet; Reagan is rushed a script and crams his lines because director Mike Curtiz is ready to shoot.

In his career to date, Flynn has rarely shared the spotlight with another hero. Onscreen the formula calls for Errol to lead a band of good guys, but it's clear that, in every plot of every picture, Errol Flynn is without peer. At most, he has shared screen heroics to this point with two Englishmen, Patric Knowles and David Niven, neither of whom comes close to outshining Flynn. Offscreen, Errol's friends are (not by coincidence) character actors and stunt men. Flynn simply doesn't like competition anywhere, so Ronald Reagan faces a problem when he begins production of *Santa Fe Trail*. Reagan calls Flynn "likable, with great charm, and yet he was convinced he lacked ability as an actor. As a result, he was conscious every minute of scenes favoring other actors and their position on the screen in relation to himself."[18]

According to the Boss's formula, a story as grim as the outbreak of the American Civil War requires humor. As a result, there is a great deal of good-natured byplay between Flynn and Reagan. However, when Hal Wallis sees this scene in the dailies, he says to Curtiz, "Will you please be careful when you shoot the retakes with de Havilland and have the girl try to get some sincerity, some feeling, some warmth, and some charm into the reading and the playing of her lines?"

This is part of the treatment—stars of Flynn's magnitude are always favored. They are positioned closest to the camera, lit optimally, and given the greatest number of, and the best, close-ups. But Flynn has learned over the years to be wary of how his old antagonist Curtiz presents him. In addition, Flynn will chafe at Reagan's sudden popularity, and although he likes the guy, Errol will make life occasionally hard for Reagan through the course of the picture.

The plot of *Santa Fe Trail* involves the approach of the Civil War as seen through the eyes of eight graduating classmates of the West Point class of 1854: Southerners Jeb Stuart (Flynn), James Longstreet, George Pickett, and John Bell Hood, and Northerners George A. Custer and Phillip Sheridan, plus two fictional Northern characters, Rader and Bob Halliday. The Hallidays, including Bob's sister Kit Carson Halliday, hail from Leavenworth, Kansas, where all the classmates are stationed after graduating from West Point. It is known as Bloody Kansas for the violent confrontations between pro-slavery interests and abolitionist John Brown and his band. The classmates are caught in the middle, and fight the fanatical Brown across Kansas, and then in the east, culminating in the takeover of the Harper's Ferry Arsenal and siege by the U.S. Army that results in Brown's capture and execution. Warner intends that this new picture will serve as the Northern prequel to Margaret Mitchell's Southern war story.

Robert Buckner's script calls for a large number of coincidences, but in point of fact only Jeb Stuart had actually graduated in 1854. The historical liberties taken by Buckner are substantial as he tries to manufacture irony. He banks on the notion that all these great names will bear some weight with the audience (at a time when American history is drummed into schoolchildren). All the historically based characters in the story go on to become great Civil War generals, and five of the six will square off at Gettysburg. But in presenting this highly fictional tale as history, the studio opens itself up to criticism, which it receives right away, before a foot of film is shot, from not only the West Point historian but also from an officer in the U.S. Cavalry. Both protest that the story contains gross historical inaccuracies throughout, from fade in to fade out.

Production of *Santa Fe Trail* commences on July 15 at Providencia Ranch. It is the first time Errol and Olivia have worked together in exactly a year. Flynn has made two pictures in that time, the western *Virginia City* and then *The Sea Hawk*, a lavish-appearing Elizabethan spectacle that had reused the *Essex* sets and costumes to great benefit. Errol still lives with Lili after having told Olivia three years earlier that the marriage was over. And Errol must have been reminded by the front office just how unhappy Livvie had been in the Flynn pictures. Piled onto his discontent with his onscreen love is her success in *Gone With the Wind*, a resulting Academy Award nomination, and her new relationship with Jimmy Stewart. She certainly doesn't date lightweights in the eligible bachelor department.

The environment isn't primed for peace and harmony as de Havilland reports to the familiar field at Busch Gardens in Pasadena, where the *Robin Hood* archery tournament had been shot. Here Flynn and the other young heroes, including Ronald Reagan, appear in their graduation ceremony from West Point, and the cast and crew proceed to spend weeks in boiling heat to capture the production's abundant exteriors at Providencia, Calabasas, and Lasky Mesa.

The Calabasas Ranch represents the Leavenworth freight yard managed by Kit Carson Halliday, with shooting there the week of July 22, in the height of an unbearable California summer. Aside from the weather, Hal Wallis finds de Havilland's performance equally unbearable and insincere. After watching the rushes he notes that her scenes with Henry O'Neill (portraying her father) will need to be retaken later on.

This location work is intense, both day and night work—so much so that second-unit director Breezy Eason becomes involved, and a week later Flynn is called to work the second shift to supplement his star shots taken earlier in the day. This means Flynn must report at 3:00 p.m. at Calabasas for exteriors, and this is a big problem, as Frank Mattison describes to Tenny Wright: "Mr. Flynn informed me he positively would not work both day and night, and

The jealousy of Flynn's character for Reagan's over de Havilland isn't all for show. Flynn feels it deeply, and acts accordingly, at the Warner Calabasas Ranch during the latter stages of production. As a result, Flynn is a no-show and de Havilland's performance in key scenes is, according to Hal Wallis, "as bad as I have seen in a long time." Soon, things will boil over.

138

insists he will go home at six o'clock tonight. I told him that I had this up once before and that I was under the impression Mr. Obringer had informed me that once we called him, we were entitled to eight (8) hours of his time continuously, if required.... Just to protect ourselves in case he does not stay tonight, Mr. Curtiz is re-arranging his schedule so that we can, if we have to, use a double for the scenes which will be made after dark tonight. Inasmuch as it may be necessary to work him both in the afternoon, and again at night, later again in this picture, I believe the above matter should be straightened out at once...."[19]

R.J. Obringer in Legal reads this memo and has a fit. He fires back to Tenny Wright: "The effect of this statement was, apparently, to give Flynn the idea that once he is called, he need work only 8 hours. There is no provision as to how long we are entitled to his services once he is called..., there is no limitation, other than a reasonable one, as to how long we are entitled to have Flynn work once he reports, and I would not give him any basis to claim that he is obligated to work only 8 hours. If Flynn refuses to stay on and do the night work, he would be in default under his contract, or you could sue him for damages, but I feel quite certain we would not want to pursue the former course, and hauling Flynn into court and suing him for damages may prove a little awkward."[20]

Well, maybe just a little.

On September 3 they shoot the tag of the picture, after the hanging of John Brown, when Jeb and Kit are married on the train—the ending dropped from *Dodge City* is now used in *Santa Fe Trail*. Hal Wallis watches the dailies and notifies Curtiz: "Will you please be careful when you shoot the retakes with de Havilland and have the girl try to get some sincerity, some feeling, some warmth, and some charm into the reading and the playing of her lines. I just saw the finish in the railroad train, and if it were not for the fact that it was a big set-up again with a lot of people, I would do this over, because for the last line in the picture, she certainly tosses it away without any feeling at all. There is no warmth in her voice or in anything she does in this last scene, and I'm damned if I know now how we can finish the picture on that."[21]

As production winds down, and day after day de Havilland is seen to be chummy with Ronnie Reagan, Flynn becomes convinced that they are having an affair, not behind his back but right in front of his face.

Livvie's take decades later will be far different. "Ronnie Reagan was a very sociable creature. Extroverted in the nicest way..., [he] was already interested in the Guild and would sit beside me on the set to chat about SAG and other things."[22] Who would know better about SAG than Olivia, given her suspensions and the forms and letters she has been forced to send to SAG or the studio.

Flynn sees their closeness and hushed conversations, and it eats at him all hours of the day: de Havilland and Reagan are rubbing Flynn's nose in their affair. She is more beautiful than ever, now 24 years old and worldly wise. Errol has spent time fretting over Brian Aherne, Howard Hughes, and Jimmy Stewart—in fact Stewart is making a picture on the Warner lot now and intruding on the *Santa Fe Trail* soundstages. And now Reagan is on Livvie too!

The night work and cast antagonisms draw to a head on the night of September 9 at Calabasas, during shooting of the last sequence with all the players, the "barbecue sequence" at Fort Leavenworth. Here a clairvoyant Native American woman, with Kit translating, foretells of the Civil War that will divide the classmates of '54. It is Livvie's last night of work. Curtiz lines up the six classmates, but Flynn (who can't remember *anything* at any other time, yet now can't forget the closeness of Livvie and Ronnie) sees them carrying on again and determines to get Livvie's attention. Flynn complains that the placement favors Reagan and suggests moving Ronnie behind Flynn's right shoulder. The group is repositioned, with Reagan in the background.

The future President never tires of telling how he gets back at Flynn: "During the rehearsal I realized that I wouldn't even be visible to the camera above the shoulders of the men in front of me. I figured that under the rules of the game I was entitled to protect myself, so as the rehearsal went on I kept quietly scraping a pile of loose earth together with my feet.... When the cameras rolled, I quietly stepped up on my newly created gopher mound. When the time came for my one line in the scene it dropped like the gentle rain from heaven on the heads of the men in front."[23]

By 3:15 a.m. Flynn's guts are in a knot. Suddenly, he says, and loudly, "Goodnight, boys, I'm going home." He storms off and returns to his tent to grab his things.

Livvie chases him into the tent and says, "Errol, can't you finish this one setup so we won't have to come out again tomorrow night?"

He looks at her coldly, perhaps thinking that Reagan has sent her, and says, "Why must you approach me on a personal basis?"

She is shocked at his tone. "If by personal you mean that this involves my comfort and convenience as well as that of a lot of other people, you're right. Otherwise, I don't know what you're talking about."[24] She storms off in one direction, returning to the shocked company, and he storms off in the other, toward his car and home.

"Bad-mannered, selfish son of a bitch!" she mutters.

Curtiz reports Flynn's behavior to Wallis, who calls J.L. The next morning, back in Burbank, the Boss reads Tenny Wright the riot act. *You're the studio manager and you can't maintain control of the actors on the set? How many people have we got out there at three in the morning? Sixty? Seventy-five? And you let Flynn pull a stunt like that? I want chapter and verse on every infraction, and we're going to submit the list to SAG and get back every cent we lost last night if we have to take it out of Flynn's hide!*

Tenny Wright fires off a memo to associate producer Robert Fellows: "I want you to immediately sit down and give me a full report on how Errol Flynn has behaved during this picture, his cooperation to calls, etc., and if he held you up at any time. I want this report on my desk not later than 6:00 PM tonight, as Mr. Warner wishes this. Needless to say, do not say anything to anybody about this note or this report. If you do not understand, come in and I will explain."[25]

Fellows responds at once and in detail: "Dear Tenny: In answer to your note regarding Flynn's attitude in *Santa Fe Trail*. I can only tell you that his behavior during the latter half of this picture, when he apparently for the first time read the script, has been one of continual complaint about his part. He precludes every statement with the fact that he is trying to do his best and then launches into a tirade against this picture and all the outdoor pictures that he has ever been in. He has refused, as you know, to accept a late afternoon call and work on into the night. Otherwise his attitude has been that of the typical star."[26]

The final setups at Calabasas are not picked up right away. Since they will not have access to Flynn on a day that follows a night shoot, they bring Livvie back to the Ranch to shoot retakes, directed by Breezy Eason. Flynn is not present, so supporting player Henry O'Neill reads Errol's lines for close-ups as he and Livvie stand in the street. The late night and her displeasure with Flynn's antics are visible in her face. The next night, Wednesday, September 11, Flynn is on the call sheet but fails to show up at the Ranch. Instead, Frank Mattison receives word that Flynn is down with "a severe case of nerves" and won't be able to work this night or the next. Mattison replies that they could do without Flynn tonight but it is "imperative that we have Mr. Flynn out at the Ranch tomorrow so we can finish up a big set—which was left there on account of him."[27]

Far from the happy cavalier seen on page 130, Flynn displays undisguised contempt for Mike Curtiz (left), who seems harmless enough at the moment and shares a laugh with Livvie during shooting at Calabasas in the high heat of summer. (Josef Fegerl Collection)

At noon on Thursday the 12th, Tenny Wright, Frank Mattison, and a studio doctor visit Flynn at 601 North Linden. Flynn agrees to report to Calabasas that night to complete the missing shots, and *does* show up, although he and Livvie are not speaking.

By now Wallis has seen the retakes just shot at the Ranch, and can't miss the face of a leading lady pushed to the breaking point. She is in a no-win situation and Wallis shows exasperation tinged with a bit of sympathy as he writes to Bob Fellows: "How can you expect to get any feeling into the scene? The girl is supposed to be playing a scene with a man that she's in love with, and you have Henry O'Neill reading the lines off-stage. De Havilland is very phony in the scenes, we still haven't got the naturalness or the charm or the warmth that they need, and they'll have to be done over again."

The other retake is the shot where Kit's father wagers on which boy Kit will choose—Stuart or Custer—as they ride off. Of this retake, Wallis says: "In the scene with O'Neill, I want her much more simple and with a far away look in her eye as though she's thinking about the boy, and lose that hard-boiled, wisecracking attitude entirely. It wants to be a sweet, tender scene. These two scenes are as bad as I have seen in a long time."[28] This is the hazard of giving dialogue scenes with the stars to a B-unit action director—especially scenes with a bitter leading lady.

Wallis wants two things: get de Havilland in here so we can tell her explicitly how to read the lines. And get Flynn back so she can look in the face of the boy she "loves" and recite her dialogue with some feeling. And Hal Wallis doesn't care to hear about the enmity between the stars. *You're professionals; just play the scene!*

On Friday and Saturday the 13th and 14th, the company works in three separate units to finish the picture: shooting the Harper's Ferry battle at Calabasas and Flynn-Reagan close-ups on the West Point drill grounds at Providencia; the Flynn-de Havilland freight yard close-up retakes and the de Havilland-O'Neill retake at Calabasas; and the Byron Haskin special fire effects work in the burning Shubel Morgan barn, with Flynn and freed slaves

A gleeful Flynn is given action scenes at the battle of Harper's Ferry at the last minute because, as written in the script, his character is trapped between the lines and a spectator in the climax of the picture. As rewritten, Flynn escapes the no-man's land and leads the charge that captures John Brown and his followers.

trapped by John Brown's men. For a man with the shakes, Flynn is a trouper through two tough days.

The battle at Harper's Ferry begins with Flynn as Jeb Stuart walking under flag of truce up to the arsenal occupied by Brown's armed band. Stuart demands that Brown surrender, but instead shooting breaks out, and Stuart is trapped in a ditch between the firing lines. Here he sits out the battle.

While setting up his shots, Curtiz notices the problem and has Frank Mattison report to Tenny Wright: "When the truce is refused he [Flynn] jumps behind the walls and stays there until the battle is over and, as Mr. Curtiz says, this is not very good for the hero. He therefore wants to add some close-up shots and give Mr. Flynn something to do during the fighting. It will require about 30 cavalrymen to back it up."[29] Curtiz handles this added footage so skillfully that, when edited into the sequence, Flynn's last-minute inserts give the impression that he is leading the final assault on the arsenal.

In the finished film, Jeb Stuart's capture of John Brown transitions directly to a sunrise hilltop setup with a gallows that is startlingly Calvary-like and reminiscent of every

141

Why is this future U.S. president smiling? Because he is upstaging the great Errol Flynn, that's why. President Reagan loved to tell of the night shoot when Flynn repositioned Reagan a little to the rear, and Reagan mounded up dirt and stood on it to be taller than Flynn. And here is the proof. Flynn was so disgusted by the time that stills of this scene were shot that he didn't even bother to put out his cigarette. Shortly thereafter, in a jealous rage, Flynn would storm off, leaving a stunned cast and crew in his wake. (John McElwee Collection)

crucifixion-of-Christ picture ever made. The religious overtones of Brown's character throughout, including the reciting of scripture, further complicate the message of the film. Brown climbs the steps to the gallows, and the assembled cast of the picture is present and struggling for their motivations about what they are witnessing. Are they happy to see Brown go after all the trouble he has caused? Do they believe that Brown is right in his beliefs but wrong in his actions? The nation has never quite reconciled itself to John Brown, and Flynn, de Havilland, and Reagan stand there like uncomfortable waxworks figures, relying on a Hungarian to figure it all out for them. Flynn in particular despises the way Stuart is portrayed here, and how the star is upstaged by the freelancer.

As written, with Brown on the gallows, Kit weeps.
STUART: "Don't, Kit. He was born for this."

KIT: "I'm not crying for him, Jeb. I see something else up there; something much more terrible than just one man."

Livvie gets to foreshadow the approaching Civil War, leaving Flynn to stand there lockjawed, and this is all the dialogue he gets, one line, at the key moment in the picture and a pivotal moment in American history. The remainder of the scene is played out as a Raymond Massey soliloquy in which he alludes to Jesus and the Crucifixion with, "Forgive them, for they know not what they do." Of course, Flynn blames Curtiz for this, no matter that Mike had ordered more shots for Errol in the battle so he could be seen at his man-of-action best.

Bad news keeps coming for Errol when he is informed of a new final scene for the picture. The old payoff scene, shot previously with Livvie's flat last line, doesn't work, so it's reshot without dialogue. In a change of pace abrupt enough to cause whiplash, the audience goes from a somber hanging with religious overtones to the wedding of Jeb and Kit. The camera dollies from close on hands playing an organ keyboard past bride and groom to Custer and his girlfriend and on back to the other cast members. This dolly move catches Errol and Livvie furious with each other in what they must believe is a rehearsal and not a take for print. They stand there stone-faced while directly behind, Reagan beams happily, as does contract player Suzanne Carnahan. Then more grim faces are revealed as the dolly moves to the back of the car. No one gets an opportunity to blow the last line because there isn't one. Instead, *Santa Fe Trail* ends with the stars exchanging their wedding kiss, which dissolves to a panoramic shot of the train chugging into the sunset and a fade to black. It is Wallis's way out of a bad situation. He doesn't want to bring everyone back for yet another retake, so he quickly closes out a miserable production.

The last exercise for the two stars takes place on Monday, September 16, when they report for a Scotty Welbourne still photo session in costume as Jeb and Kit. Flynn has gotten under Livvie's skin like a bad splinter, and she has certainly been under his for half a decade. At the end of the session, they walk out into the California heat in front of the portraiture studio and she turns to him.

"I'm bored to death with you, Errol, and I don't want to work with you again. *Nothing personal*, you understand," alluding to his comment about putting things on a personal basis. "I'm sure you feel the same way about me. It's bad for us to work together. Sooner or later it's bound to show up on the screen. I'm going to talk to Hal Wallis about it. But you have more influence than I do. Will you talk to Mr. Warner?"

"Glad to," he says with an empty smile. "And may I add that I agree with you?"[30]

And that is that. The dressing rooms are right across the street from the portraiture studio—he retires to his, and she to hers. Doors are slammed appropriately. The couple that America believes to be as married as their characters onscreen is splitting up. She's going to Wallis and he's going to Warner, and they end it this way, each happy to be done with the other, each sure they know exactly what is going on in the head of the other. In a studio as compact as Warner Bros., word spreads fast: *Have you heard? Livvie's feuding with Errol. They're never going to work together again.*

On September 16, 1940, the unhappy couple reports for stills duty, their last obligation on *Santa Fe Trail*. At the end of what will turn into the portrait sitting from hell, Livvie declares that she's bored to death with Errol. They agree to call it quits and retire to their respective dressing rooms. (Photo at left, Josef Fegerl Collection)

143

SAY IT WITH FLOWERS

In 1976 a de Havilland biographer wrote that Olivia was "always a lady" and "never sexy." Errol Flynn, Jimmy Stewart, and a million other red-blooded male admirers would heartily disagree. So would Warner Bros. still photographer Scotty Welbourne. In the summer of 1940, he proved that de Havilland was very sexy indeed by shooting her wearing flowers, and nothing else, in a series of very adult portraits that would inspire four magazine covers and help to reinvent the star as a sultry woman and neither Melanie Hamilton *nor* the girl who had been typecast as a virgin in *Captain Blood* and *The Adventures of Robin Hood*.

THE NEW AND BIGGER!
Silver Screen
January

10¢
15 Cents In Canada

Olivia de Havilland

CAN A GIRL REALLY BE MORAL IN HOLLYWOOD?
WHEN TOMORROW COMES FOR MICKEY ROONEY

Flynn and Raoul Walsh decide, on viewing the story arc of the Custers, that another scene is needed to deepen the romance. It is written as a balcony scene as young Lt. Custer climbs to the second story of the Bacon home to see his love, Libbie. It will be their last extended work together and one of their finest scenes. (John McElwee Collection)

9 LIFE IS FULL OF SURPRISES

For three months, Livvie tells everyone who will listen what a heel Flynn is, and now, in December, she must come face-to-face with him for the first time since the photo shoot. They will board a train together on Thursday, December 12, 1940, headed for another of those gaudy world premieres, this one for *Santa Fe Trail* on Friday, the 13th of December, in Santa Fe, New Mexico. Charlie Einfeld of Dodge City Special fame has been at work again, rounding up 250 stars and reporters and shipping them east—four days out, two-and-a-half days back. By now the stars don't protest these assignments. They are under contract; they are on the clock; they eat well (and on the studio); they get the opportunity to promote themselves; they have plenty of opportunities to bedhop; so of course they go. Sometimes it makes sense where they are going, and sometimes it doesn't. *Dodge City* and Kansas they could see; *Gone With the Wind*, Atlanta, sure. But anyone who knows the script of this new production realizes that the plot has nothing to do with New Mexico.

Einfeld has more logistics to consider than an invading army, what with another train heading for Santa Fe from the east with more stars, as well as whistlestops along the way, events on the ground in New Mexico, and national radio coverage throughout the trip. But there's method to the madness as Warner Bros. gets another train ride out of the deal—the Santa Fe Railroad will pick up 50 percent of the costs, so Einfeld now simply wants to make it into and out of town with no casualties.

Clackety-clack go Flynn (and his ever-present shadow, Arno), de Havilland, Rita Hayworth, etc., eastward from Pasadena, where they are serenaded by the 150-piece Rose Bowl Band and cheered by 28,000 local schoolchildren who enjoy a two-hour recess to see the stars.

Livvie has just completed *The Strawberry Blonde*, a comedy, with Cagney; Flynn has finished *Footsteps in the Dark* with Brenda Marshall. For Flynn, much has changed in three short months. Toward the end of October he had been with Lili, and as she moved toward him, naked, she was wearing what he describes as "a curious cat-eat-the-canary look. Her tongue was in her cheek—a favorite gesture of hers." She had asked him if he liked what he saw and, of course, he said he did. Then she announced, "Fleen, you think you've screwed every dame in Hollywood, but now I've screwed you. You will have a child!"[1]

What a sucker he had been. He should have known by the roundness of her curves and by her responsiveness. It is a brilliantly conceived and executed exit strategy, a very risky exit strategy, considering that Lili claims to have been born in 1904 but Flynn knows she is older than that, putting her age at right around 40—risky for bearing children. He believes, because of the *I've screwed you* remark, that she will have this kid and file for divorce on any number of grounds. And it will cost him. As he sits on the train to Santa Fe, he thinks back to the last time he had seen her. She is showing now; word will get around Hollywood fast.

Now I have screwed you! The words echo in his ears.

Of course everyone at the studio knows that Errol and Livvie are on the outs, thanks to her uncharacteristic gabbing about it. The Pasadena kickoff of the junket features lots of candids of the embarking stars, and through this ses-

147

sion Errol and Olivia keep their distance. What Livvie doesn't tell Errol right away: She's ill. She has the shakes and she's clammy and nauseous, but she feels duty-bound to make this trip.

The train makes its first whistlestop in Barstow, where Flynn, de Havilland, and the other stars appear before a delighted crowd. They begin to speak, and the sound system goes out. They ad-lib and make it through the brief appearance, and then back inside they settle breathlessly into one of the food-service cars.

They let out some relieved sighs and nervous giggles. She turns to him and sees sweat on his brow. What's this? Errol Flynn is uncomfortable before a crowd?

She says, "Is this you, or is this the other one?"

"Which other one?" he replies.

"The one who wouldn't finish one more scene at three in the morning."[2]

He admits to her that he had been jealous of Reagan. He had been a boor. He asks her forgiveness.

As the train sets in motion and they sit there, he lets her in on the secret about Lili and reveals that they have officially separated; that she is pregnant and will have this child, not out of love but out of revenge, and that they hate each other and there's no turning back this time. Olivia admits that she and Jimmy Stewart are off because she told him she wants to settle down and Jimmy had made it clear that he intends to play the field, and she tells Errol that it hurts her that she isn't good enough for Stewart.

Livvie also admits that she's feeling truly ill and figures it's something she had eaten earlier. She's got chills and Errol is courteous and concerned, and soon they are holding hands and huddling close to warm each other, these two lonely people out in the middle of nowhere. They talk about their battles with the Boss and how unhappy they are with their careers. She wants good scripts with good parts to play. He doesn't want to be typed as the costume hero anymore, and he's banking on this new detective picture to be the start of something different for him—a modern character with wit and charm, a guy he would actually *like* to play, a detective like Bill Powell plays. And he tells her how he had often thought while making *Footsteps in the Dark* that Livvie would have been perfect to play his wife, Rita, a part that was made for her, but he well knew that she meant what she had said about the two of them not working together anymore. How could they be believable as a couple like Nick and Nora Charles when they can't get along between takes?

Photographers snap remarkably candid photos of the conversation, each of them absorbed in the other. Errol Flynn and Olivia de Havilland have been photographed together hundreds of times during the course of five-and-a-half years, so now, the cameras and cameramen are invisible. They see only each other, two beautiful, young people, powerful people, alone in the desert. Such a history they share, a history that no one understands but the two of them, beginning with a hammy pirate picture, and now they're literally reaching the end of the trail in Santa Fe, New Mexico.

Finally, after the dead snake, the date-swap, the upstaging, the pouting, the other women, the other men, the night shoot, they understand each other.

Early on the tour, the train stops at Needles, California, for some ad-libbing fun. Here Flynn paws a giddy de Havilland. Actor Donald Crisp is beside them. (Robert Florczak Collection)

As the clock strikes 12 and Thursday, December 12, becomes Friday the 13th, de Havilland grows increasingly nauseated. The train's first-aid man is called and sits with her until the train pulls into Santa Fe at 2:30 p.m. for the kickoff of "Santa Fe Trail Days," which includes the arrival of the train from New York bearing John Brown himself, Raymond Massey. Flynn and the other Hollywood stars, minus Livvie, are welcomed on the steps of the governor's mansion. Charlie Einfeld can plan like nobody's business, but he can't control sudden illness, and he can't control the weather. A cold wave has gripped Santa Fe. Poor old May Robson, character actress, succumbs and follows Livvie to the emergency room.

After dark the stars are whisked to the edge of town where they stare up at a grotesque 80-foot-tall animated stick man called Tiococco, the "god of gloom," which de Havilland was to have torched to officially open Santa Fe Trail Days, but Flynn must do the honors instead before a crowd in the tens of thousands. The flames of burning Tiococco lick skyward to be seen for 40 miles. A fandango follows, at which the stars drink liberally before pairing off for the night.

Livvie's day is quite different. At the Santa Fe Hospital, she is diagnosed with appendicitis and rushed into surgery, and Einfeld must make arrangements to fly her back by charter to Burbank.

On Saturday morning, as Livvie's TWA charter departs, the

Above: Fans were used to seeing Errol give *the look* to Olivia, but always on the silver screen. Here he is gazing at her romantically in person in Needles. Below: Another view is more posed, more of a, "1, 2, 3, cheese!" moment. Livvie's secret of the evening, yet to be revealed: She feels truly ill. In fact, surgery is a day away. (Robert Florczak Collection)

WORTH A THOUSAND WORDS

The most revealing photographs taken of Flynn and de Havilland are snapped on Thursday, December 12, 1940, on the train bound for Santa Fe. In a public Needles, California, appearance, Errol paws Livvie, who in one moment seems at ease and the next self-conscious. Later, with the train headed east, the pair settles in for drinks and conversation. These people are used to physical closeness with each other, as confirmed by the ample body contact. Livvie will say at the time that when the floodgates open, they finally understand each other after all these years. These photos were scheduled to appear in *Screen Guide* magazine, but the spread will be killed. Says film historian John McElwee, "They really are very intense stills that for all the world suggest some kind of off-camera relationship." (Mike Mazzone Collection)

COVERED
WAGON
JULEP
PLAIN

HE
VERED
WAGO
JULEP
PLAIN
CIGARETTES

A mere 36 hours after huddling with Errol, Olivia (minus one appendix) is lugged off a TWA charter in Burbank, where she is met by sister Joanie and brother-in-law Brian Aherne. Livvie would begin her long convalescence in an L.A. hospital.

stars head to Santa Fe National Park for a couple hours of skiing, and Flynn cavorts in the snow with his replacement-Livvie, very friendly young Columbia player Rita Hayworth, and then retires to the lodge for rum-laced cavorting of a different kind.

The caravan returns to Santa Fe for a parade and crowds that reach 60,000 for the premiere at Santa Fe's grand, Southwestern-style Lensic Theatre on San Francisco Street, one of three theaters in town showing *Santa Fe Trail*. The stars—introduced by New Mexico Governor John Miles—appear onstage at all three packed houses.

On Sunday the trains quietly depart Santa Fe and head straight back to their points of origin, the budgets blown, and quite a few brain cells killed in promotion of Hollywood product.

Livvie emerges from major surgery to begin a long period of recuperation. On Friday, December 27, Roy Obringer informs her by letter that she has been assigned the role of Sue Mayberry in the new production, *Affectionately Yours*, with Dennis Morgan and the stock company. On Monday the 30th, agent Jimmie Townsend informs the studio that Miss de Havilland is incapacitated and cannot work; the doctor can verify this. J.L. calls her at once demanding to know if she is stalling again.

This will be a good picture with a solid cast and Lloyd Bacon directing, and I want you to make it!

She explains to him that she is bedridden and will remain so for at least another two weeks. The Boss hangs up the phone and calls Obringer to put de Havilland on suspension for physical incapacity. But J.L. is informed that they don't want to do this because she has just been sent another script to read called *The Gay Sisters*, the story of three prominent sisters who must save their Fifth Avenue home after the death of their father.

One week later, after reading said script, Olivia de Havilland refuses to make *The Gay Sisters*—at the end of her convalescence or anytime—because she sees it as another in a long line of weakly plotted stories. Her suspicions of J.L.'s intentions grow with every script sent to her to the point that she can't tell which are promising and which are garbage. Now she is put on layoff without pay "due to illness of artist."

When she finally sees a script that she likes, called *Hold Back the Dawn*, it's not for Warner Bros. but for Paramount, where she is sent on loanout. Weeks of inactivity and depression cause her weight to shoot up dramatically, from a customary 110 to 126. She will always be highly conscious of her weight, sensitive to every gain and criticism by Warner and Wallis that she needs to lose. But for the press she is nonchalant: "You would have thought the sky was falling," she tells a reporter. "Edith Head, the designer, had phoned that she was delighted to work with me because she knew my figure would be no problem. You should have seen her expression when I entered the fitting room."[3] For the production de Havilland squeezes into a girdle and complains that she can't breathe.

Over at Warner Bros. J.L. spats with Sam Goldwyn about who owns the rights to tell the story of "Boy General" George Armstrong Custer. The Boss has read the tea leaves and history SELLS! *Santa Fe Trail* is in the black by $1.48 million, in part, he believes, because of the Civil War tie-in and the name George Armstrong Custer. Now the Boss has a World War I story in production, *Sergeant York*, and he wants to keep the historical wave rolling. The new script is called *They Died with Their Boots On*, and perhaps Ronnie Reagan could play Custer—Reagan wants the part and thinks it natural that he should reprise his role from *Santa Fe Trail*.

That's one school of thought.

Or Dennis Morgan could do it. Morgan's a square-shouldered kid with nice presence. But, as always, Flynn is the man and Errol needs to keep working. His new picture, *Footsteps in the Dark*, has opened to decent reviews. The romantic mystery pairing him with Brenda Marshall follows the William Powell-Myrna Loy *Thin Man* formula. Flynn likes this kind of work, and when Flynn likes something he isn't such a royal pain. He actually shows up at (roughly) his call times and even tries to know his lines before stepping onto the soundstage.

Flynn wants to turn *Footsteps* into a series, and J.L. might agree—if the box office justifies it. Another new production, *The Constant Nymph*, could use Flynn's name, but the story of a composer and a girl's unrequited love doesn't instantly bring Flynn to mind. By March 7 the Boss has made up his mind and wires Wallis: "Reference *Constant Nymph* next Flynn picture make following *Died with Boots On* as Flynn in modern clothes just doesn't seem to go over. *Footsteps* doing pretty good but not important everywhere it has opened. It is under *No Time for Comedy* 20 to 25 percent; believe *Nymph* would be all right for him. Then again am bit frightened as seems they only want Flynn in outdoor productions we have been having him in. Think it over."[4]

Wallis knows that when J.L. speaks in such convoluted terms, the decision is already made. *Flynn as Custer: got it.*

In addition, the Boss wants Mike Curtiz assigned to the picture, and in mid-May Curtiz, producer Bob Fellows, and writers Wally Kline and Aneas MacKenzie go over the entire Custer script and agree in principle on the story arc and how the locations will play out. Flynn of course knows that he's facing another Curtiz picture. At the moment Errol is overseeing construction of his new home high in the Hollywood Hills on Mulholland Drive, and he is happy to remain up there to supervise the workmen and *not* report to the studio to start working with Curtiz again. Flynn has had it with Curtiz and will later claim that the last straw had been a confrontation at Calabasas during the production of *Santa Fe Trail*, but the pair has just finished working on a Technicolor service picture, *Dive Bomber*, so the incident probably occurred on a *Dive Bomber* location near San Diego, where Flynn's character at one point in the story

Flynn was ardent in his pursuit of non-swashbuckler roles and knew that *Footsteps in the Dark*, wherein his strait-laced investment counselor by day is a mystery novelist and crime solver by night, would be the perfect Flynn-de Havilland series. But with Livvie calling it quits, Brenda Marshall stood in. Unfortunately for Flynn, the series failed to materialize.

The real George and Elizabeth Custer. The script under development at Warner Bros. would capture the essence of their relationship, while managing to get almost all the facts wrong. (Photo restoration by Val Sloan)

goes driving along a dirt road. Of the moment in question, Flynn says, "I grabbed Mike by the throat and began strangling him. Two men tried to pry me off. They succeeded before I killed him."[5] De Havilland hears through the grapevine that "it was a lethal, lethal scene."[6]

It has become the talk of the studio, and few could fully blame Errol Flynn for turning on Curtiz. Reagan would call Mike "a kind, good-natured soul" off the set and "a ruthless tyrant" on it.[7]

Flynn's pictures are making lots of money, and Errol decides to take a stand once and for all and exercise a star's veto power over the assigned director. This can be a risky move since the staging of class-A adventure pictures by Michael Curtiz has made Flynn the superstar he is today. In fact, a Gallup survey shows Flynn to be number two in popularity behind only Clark Gable. Flynn understands the stakes at a gut level, which is why he has been loathe to dig in his heels since the success of *Robin Hood*. Until now. "I deemed it wiser not to work with this highly artistic gentleman who aroused my worst instincts," says Flynn.[8]

He has heard good things around the studio from Livvie, Annie Sheridan, and others about charismatic, one-eyed director Raoul Walsh, an Irishman who has made a string of A pictures for Warner Bros. beginning in 1939, most recently *High Sierra* with Bogart and *The Strawberry Blonde* with de Havilland and Cagney. Flynn learns that Walsh can handle action and also excels at working with talent on realizing scene and character. Most of all, Walsh runs a tight ship—but doesn't make ridiculous demands of his stars or force them to slave away on a half-hour lunch. Flynn tells Hal Wallis that he wishes *not* to work with Curtiz again, *ever*, and asks for Walsh. After 12 pictures in six years, all of them in the black, Flynn has earned the change and wins out in a bloodless coup.

So, with Flynn happy to have a hand-picked director, the logical next question should concern whether to invest in Technicolor since this will be a Civil War picture—with the *Gone With the Wind* money trail still very warm—and an A-caliber western with a spectacular battle at its conclusion.

But, says Rudy Behlmer, "There's a memo from Jack L. to Hal in 1939 where he's saying, 'These color films are awfully expensive.... Maybe we ought to scale back and prolong our commitment,' because they had to make commitments to Technicolor. So they had a falling out with Technicolor after *Elizabeth and Essex*.... Also the foreign market was going away because of the war, and you had the fact that *Virginia City* and *Santa Fe Trail* had done very well in black and white, whereas with *Dive Bomber*, the draw was aerial photography in 'glorious Technicolor,' with formation flying and things that had never been done in color. That was a very big deal at the time."[9]

All in all, shooting the Custer picture in black and white is safer and less expensive. Decision made.

By early June Livvie has completed *Hold Back the Dawn*, and Flynn has been closed out on *Dive Bomber* with Fred MacMurray. J.L. had taken MacMurray on loan from Paramount in exchange for de Havilland specifically to work with Flynn on this picture.

On June 10, 1941, Flynn and other potential players begin wardrobe and makeup tests for the Custer picture, with no one yet cast in the role of Beth—Elizabeth Bacon Custer—the love of our hero's life. Always the first thought has been to put de Havilland with Flynn, especially after the strong numbers for *Santa Fe Trail*, but as far as the Boss knows, Livvie would rather go on suspension, would rather *die*, than work on another Flynn job, especially an outdoor Flynn job.

Next best thing? Olivia de Havilland's sister, Joan Fontaine. J. L. can see the way the publicity department will spin it for the press: rival sisters fight over who gets to work with Errol Flynn. Fontaine is Selznick property, having been a sensation in *Rebecca*, an Academy Award winner for *Suspicion*, and now between assignments. Wallis sends Fontaine the script for *They Died with Their Boots On* through Danny O'Shea at Selznick International, and they wait. Fontaine is one of the hottest properties in Hollywood, and the trouble is, she knows it. On June 9 comes the inevitable response: *Miss Fontaine does not like the part. Dan O'Shea has also read the script and won't push the issue because it's not a dramatic enough role to warrant Miss Fontaine's participation.* In other words, this is not a prestige picture. Danny O'Shea states that this is "merely a straight lead any one of a number of girls could do."[10]

These snooty broads, thinks Warner. *It must be some foul-up in their blood!*

Undeterred, he looks inside his own studio for a Beth Custer because, of course, O'Shea is correct, and any number of girls can play this part. He and Wallis order tests for Flynn with contract players Priscilla Lane and Nancy Coleman to see what kind of chemistry might be generated. Both girls had been with Flynn on the *Santa Fe Trail* junket, where everybody got to know everybody. Twenty-eight-year-old Coleman is a dark-haired, sexy girl just off a John Garfield picture. She isn't a bad Beth opposite Flynn, and Priscilla Lane is, well, Priscilla Lane. Both are OK; neither will help the picture sell in Peoria.

Flynn has other things on his mind right now because he has just become a father. Sean Leslie Flynn had been born on the last day of May. It is an event that will shove an unwilling Errol a little closer toward responsibility, if not adulthood, and may prompt the last thing that J.L. expects to happen: Errol Flynn goes to the front office on the issue of his leading lady, with the message something like: *Why am I testing with these other girls? We all know this is Livvie's part and no one can play it like she can. I wouldn't blame her if she won't work with me again. I was rotten to her, I admit, but you guys were too, in spades. She deserves better. You know she's box office, so let's cut the games and try to get her in here, and for God's sake will you give her an ounce of respect?*

Joan Leslie may have been the queen of hearts, but she was also J.L.'s ace in the hole to be played the moment that Olivia de Havilland said no to the script for *They Died with Their Boots On*. Beautiful, talented, innocent, and 16, Leslie had been looking for opportunities to meet Flynn on the Warner lot and had no idea how close she would come to being his new love interest, onscreen and, inevitably, off.

Lenore Coffee made what she called a "lousy fortune" as one of Hollywood's first script doctors saving "sick pictures." She brought her considerable talent to the new Flynn-de Havilland script and infused the romantic scenes with a woman's sensibilities while also managing to write the man's part like a man. The result was another highly profitable picture for Errol and Olivia.

The Boss knows that Flynn is correct about one thing: put their names together above the title, and Flynn and de Havilland are box office. So the Boss assigns Olivia de Havilland to *They Died with Their Boots On* and orders a script to be sent over to Nella Vista. No matter what Flynn has to say on the matter, Warner sees this as a formality—of course she will say no and go back on suspension—so he develops a backup plan: as soon as Livvie turns down the role, they will test sixteen-and-a-half-year-old Joan Leslie for Beth and then, assuming she does well with Flynn, rush her into wardrobe.

Joan Leslie has just finished *Sergeant York*, and Warner and Wallis know she can play older than her years. J.L. thinks she is dynamite as Alvin York's sweetheart Gracie—as sensational a find as he has seen in a decade. But with Joan Leslie they will face a considerable headache, because chaperone or no chaperone (and Leslie *always* has one), the studio's wolf, Errol Flynn, will have this sweet kid for lunch. There is nothing they can do about that because he has tremendous power over the young ones. He has the knack to charm their panties off in mere moments.

And worst of all, Joan Leslie has been angling for an opportunity to meet Errol Flynn, whom she idolizes. For Jack Warner it could be the perfect storm.

Wallis wants a decision from de Havilland, who is out of town suffering from exhaustion and can do "nothing else but lie around all day and try to pick up some strength."[11] To force her hand, Wallis memos Steve Trilling to summon Livvie back to the studio for wardrobe tests. On Saturday, June 21, producer Bob Fellows says to Trilling: "If we do not get a definite okay from de Havilland on Monday, then we must be prepared to make a test on Tuesday of Joan Leslie for the part of Beth. This test should be ready to shoot and I presume you have sent Leslie the dialogue."[12]

On Monday the Boss manages to get de Havilland on the phone, which is never easy. After some extremely forced pleasantries, J.L. asks Olivia if she likes the script. She tells him it isn't bad, "but you know how Flynn and I feel about playing together."

Warner says, "Maybe you feel that way, but Flynn doesn't."

"What do you mean, Flynn doesn't?"

"He asked for you in this picture."

J.L. relates that Flynn says he wouldn't blame her for not wanting to work with him again and thinks the studio has been giving her a raw deal.[13]

In Livvie's mind, it's one thing to have a couple of drinks and snuggle on a train car out of town, but it's another thing for a star to go to bat on her behalf with the front office.

Oh my God. Errol Flynn has grown up!

She tells them that of course she will make *They Died with Their Boots On!*

Problem solved, except now Flynn is taking a powder. On the night of Sunday June 22nd, he calls Bob Fellows at home. "I need confirmation on when we're going to start shooting this picture."

Fellows says, "Your call is to be ready Wednesday morning [June 25] to shoot the exteriors at West Point. That'll be Busch Gardens."[14]

Flynn gets right to the point: *Look, will you tell Warner that it's very unfair for the studio to expect me to start another tough picture right after I just finished one? I'm going in tomorrow to talk about it, and that'll be in Jack's office.*

156

Well, I can see if Mr. Warner's available—

Oh, he'll be available. And then I'm leaving for New York tomorrow night.

I don't know anything about that. All I know is that we—

Plan on me to report to the studio a week from tomorrow, and we can start Boots *the day after that. G'night, Bob.*

Click.

So as of Monday, June 23, production of *They Died with Their Boots On* is delayed one week, from a Wednesday, June 25 start to a Wednesday, July 2 start. The Boss likes to work his stars to exhaustion and get the most product out of them as possible. When they bemoan the brutal conditions—hopping from one production to another—then he rips the spurs out of their flanks and lets them take a break. But J.L. keeps them on the move up to that very moment. As a result, the production of motion pictures depends on a highly volatile ingredient: motion picture stars.

In retrospect the audience will watch classic films and believe that a great deal of thought and planning has gone on when most often the production team is thinking: *We're flying by the seat of our pants here—I sure hope this works!* The Warner Bros. front office is tough, savvy, and can turn on a dime. If Errol Flynn wants Olivia de Havilland, and if Flynn needs to recharge his batteries in New York, Fellows and Wallis will turn their attention to getting de Havilland up to speed.

Wallis knows that the status of the production has been elevated by Livvie's presence, and he worries that the romantic aspects of the script are weak. He decides to send it to a script doctor, in this case Lenore Coffee, veteran 44-year-old playwright and screenwriter. He asks for Coffee to evaluate and punch up the dialogue between Beth and George "on the usual terms."

He and Fellows, with the Boss looking over their shoulders, also cast the remaining roles. They test G.P. Huntley, Jr. for the role of Cooke, one of Custer's officers, and Suzanne Carnahan, now renamed Susan Peters, for the role of Lydia Kirkpatrick, George Custer's older half-sister. They also look for an actress to portray Callie, Beth Bacon's maid. Now that they have confirmed de Havilland, Warner has a natural solution: he will reunite Livvie with her *Gone With the Wind* co-star, Hattie McDaniel, which is sure to boost box office.

J.L. has just been to Pomona for a boffo sneak preview of *Sergeant York* that has him "jumping with joy." He memos Wallis: "About Hattie McDaniel and [African American character actor] Willie Best going into *They Died with Their Boots On*, we positively want these two people in the picture. As you know from experience, we must have comedy in these big, outdoor pictures so don't let anyone talk you out of this. This was proved last night at the preview whenever George Tobias came on the screen and a thousand and one other ways too."[15]

No arguing with the boss, so in come McDaniel and Best, while Livvie reports for Monday, June 30 wardrobe tests on Stage 11, capturing Beth Bacon's first outfit, worn when she meets George on the West Point grounds. Two days later Wallis looks at film of the test and fires off a memo to costume designer Milo Anderson: "I am afraid you have gone overboard again on de Havilland's wardrobe change #1, the graduation outfit. It is much too elaborate, and you have so much stuff on the front of it that she looks pregnant. Let's cut off some of the doodads, and make the outfit look a little more believable."[16] Of course it doesn't help that Livvie also carries upwards of 20 more pounds on her frame than Hal Wallis is used to seeing. Her round face and softer look give her a new physical maturity that happens to be perfect for Elizabeth Bacon Custer.

As promised, Errol returns to the studio on Tuesday, July 1 for a dye job. His dark brown hair is lightened to dark blonde, and the next day production commences on Stage 14 capturing the first interiors of the picture: Custer is "assigned" to Major Taipe's quarters as an act of hazing by Cadet Corporal Sharp, played by Arthur Kennedy. The sequence is completed in two days.

On July 5 Wallis hears back from Lenore Coffee, who has read the script and done some research on the real George and Elizabeth Custer. Coffee sends a four-page letter detailing script inaccuracies—Phil Sheridan (later a famous Union general) was never commandant of West Point; Custer wasn't promoted by accident but rather for merit; Custer wasn't an alcoholic but rather a teetotaler all his life; and on and on. Coffee also points out that Elizabeth Bacon was never known as "Beth," but rather as "Libbie," and suggests that this change be made throughout the script. Wallis takes Coffee's historical research under advisement (which means NO, he won't alter the dynamics of the story for the sake of historical accuracy, but he orders the change to "Libbie") and asks Coffee to once-over the sequence wherein George and Libbie meet at West Point, which is to shoot in a couple days at Busch Gardens. Wallis tells her that he wants charm; he wants romance. With this direction in mind, Coffee rushes through the rewrite and fires off new dialogue to Fellows, who forwards rewritten pages, in the customary blue, to de Havilland and Flynn.

The final story line for *They Died with Their Boots On* is: Young Cadet George Armstrong Custer arrives at West Point as an ingenuous, enthusiastic, undisciplined youth from the wrong side of the tracks, who proceeds to set new records for poor grades and demerits, although he excels at all physical activities. At West Point, Custer's antagonist is Ned Sharp, an upperclassman who looks down on Custer and believes that rank should have privileges. At the outbreak of the Civil War, Custer, on punishment tour, is the last in his class to graduate. While walking guard duty, he meets Elizabeth Bacon, and it's love at first sight. But George must go to war and in Washington seeks an appointment to the U.S. Cavalry. His efforts are blocked by Major Romulus Taipe, who had formerly been the quartermaster at West Point and run up against Custer's antics. But in Washington, Custer is befriended by the commanding general of the army, Winfield Scott, and given an assignment. Through the course of the war, Custer becomes a hero and returns to his hometown of Monroe, Michigan, to marry Elizabeth Bacon. At war's end the size of the army is reduced, and Custer has no assignment until Libbie intervenes, and they head west to Fort Abraham Lincoln in the Dakota Territory, where Custer becomes a feared Indian fighter and leader of the Seventh Cavalry. The latter half of the picture involves the Custers' life on the Plains as a cav-

De Havilland and Flynn pose for a still on their first day reunited, July 9, 1941, once again at Busch Gardens in Pasadena. Seven hard months after the Santa Fe train ride, they are genuinely happy to be working together again. (John McElwee Collection)

alry colonel who attempts to make peace with Native American peoples led by Crazy Horse, but Taipe and Sharp hatch a scheme to encroach on Indian lands, which sets in motion events that culminate in Custer's death at the Little Big Horn. In the final scene of the picture, Libbie presents the plotters with her husband's "dying declaration" revealing the land scheme and smashing the Taipe and Sharp land-speculation enterprise, meaning that her soldier "won his last fight."

Every screen biography takes liberties with the life of the person portrayed. Characters are omitted or combined; timelines are compressed or rearranged; events are portrayed faithfully when possible, but more often than not simplified or fictionalized for the sake of drama. George M. Cohan never danced his way down the steps of the White House, nor did Houdini die onstage, and Custer didn't become a general by accident.

Clearly, Warner Bros. subscribes to Napoleon's belief, "What is history but fiction agreed upon?" The plot line conceived by Kline and MacKenzie, with able assistance from Fellows, Curtiz, Walsh, and Wallis, is *history* in the sense that it portrays George Armstrong Custer as a brash, brave, headstrong, and charismatic personality who participates in the Civil War, marries a woman named Libbie, and is defeated in a big battle with Plains Indians. In almost every other respect, it is bunk, and the front office knows it to be bunk.

In a telling episode that reveals the charm of the man and his enormous balls, J.L. claims that his movie faithfully adheres to the painting entitled *Custer's Last Fight* by Cassily Adams (with lithography by Otto Becker), commissioned by Budweiser Beer in 1888, as if this statement should put to rest any and all criticism of the biopic. The Adams/Becker painting, seen by just about everyone who has entered a barroom in the United States for the 50 years leading up to 1941, is known by scholars to be a hideous fraud in its depiction of heroic Custer and his heroic band fighting and dying as a cohesive, tightly packed force facing savage hordes.

The next Monday, on Stage 14 at the studio, they complete the sequence where George and Libbie meet. This is the modified version of the gown that Hal Wallis griped about to Milo Anderson as having too many "doodads" and making de Havilland look pregnant.

Warner and Wallis fail to realize—not that it matters to them, as long as the picture makes money—that Custer is the centerpiece of a very strong cult. In 1941, as today, Custer's legions, men mostly, know every detail of the man's life and are apt to distance themselves from a picture that strays so far from historical fact. But the production pushes forward with enthusiasm because the Napoleonic formula had worked for *Juarez* and *Santa Fe Trail*, and it is working for *Sergeant York*, and it will certainly work for *They Died with Their Boots On*.

Let's get this thing moving! We must shoot!

On July 7 Raoul Walsh, working at Busch Gardens with Flynn, Arthur Kennedy, and Joe Sawyer as Sgt. Doolittle, rolls on the opening scene of the picture, with Custer showing up at West Point as a cadet candidate, trailing hounds and a black servant. This had been the role intended for Willie Best, who has just been dropped, along with George's sister Lydia, to tighten the story. Now the servant becomes a one-shot comedic throwaway to reflect Custer's initial self-importance, showing his status by having a servant and hounds to go with his "comic opera uniform."

Flynn is back at Busch Gardens on July 8 while Olivia and Milo Anderson get Hal Wallis's sign off on wardrobe change number one in time for the gown to be rushed out to Pasadena for her first shot, the next day, July 9. Livvie reports after lunch, and soon she is gliding across the lawn to run into her young cadet on sentry duty. From the first instant of the first rehearsal, de Havilland is aglow, her renewed affection for Errol Flynn apparent to Walsh and captured for posterity.

"I hope you won't think me bold for addressing a stranger," she begins when she runs into Cadet Custer, silently walking punishment tour, "but I'm Elizabeth Bacon from Monroe, and I think I'm lost." Custer has just been dressed down by the officer of the day—still watching him—and is not allowed to speak. George marches silently away from Libbie, who says, "Oh, but I'm speaking to you!" She walks with him and recites breathless, dizzy lines until he stops and pivots as she prattles on, not realizing that he has turned and marched the other way. "You see, I took that path over there by the rose garden, and when I got in the middle of the rose garden, I turned to admire the view—" She turns and finds him gone. It's pure Lenore Coffee, the focus on the woman's mind-set, the flighty dialogue, the chatty nature of the one character playing off the mute straight man.

The whole while they're walking, as she recites her dialogue and Flynn marches at rigid attention, Livvie plays with her handkerchief to slyly rib him for so often upstaging her. She finds it especially funny because the script has him marching at stiff attention and *he can do nothing about it.*

The next week they move to the studio, to the commandant's home on Stage 14, so that George can chase Libbie down in a continuation of their sequence shot at Busch Gardens. Libbie is offended that George has ignored her; he explains that he had not been allowed to speak, and she softens. Then George says, "Do you think if I were to come strolling past your house around nine o'clock at night, you might just be sitting around on the veranda?" (In the final picture, this is the cue to start Max Steiner's haunting love theme.)

She considers his question and allows, "Life is full of surprises."

"And if I did find you sitting on the porch, perhaps you and I could go for a walk together."

She laughs. "We seem to have been walking ever since we met."

He laughs with her and then says with the earnestness of youth: "Well I can't imagine, ma'am, if I may say so, any pleasanter journey, ma'am, than walking through life with you beside me, ma'am." It takes her breath away, and when he says he must go, comes to attention, and salutes her, she gives a dazed salute in return.

Thanks to Wallis's wise move to send the script to Lenore Coffee, and thanks to the way that Walsh understands the characters and motivations, this first sequence and, in fact, all the de

Flynn is a happy guy as he shoots the Battle of Manassas sequence at Calabasas, but he won't be smiling for long. Smoke inhaled during production will land him in the hospital and force Raoul Walsh and cast to shoot around Flynn for weeks. He will later send the hospital bill to the studio, and J.L. will refuse to pay it. (John McElwee Collection)

Havilland-Flynn scenes, bristle with an intensity that is new to their association.

Says Warner Bros. historian Rudy Behlmer, "To me it's a better-written part for Olivia versus just being *the girl*."[17]

Production moves fast. On July 14, character actors Sidney Toler and George Barbier test for the important role of General Winfield Scott, which Barbier lands. But at lunchtime on the 16th, this order is countermanded, and the role is handed to Sydney Greenstreet, a portly, diabetic, Lunt-and-Fontaine stage actor from England who, at age 62, has just completed his first film, *The Maltese Falcon*, for upstart writer-director John Huston.

On July 16 Walsh shoots the barroom scene in Sullivan's Place on Stage 6, where Custer first hears the song *Garry Owen*, a scene completed on the 17th, and they move directly to an MOS [without sound] shot on Stage 12: George and Libbie walk beneath crossed sabers after their wedding ceremony. In this brief scene, the romance of the entire ceremony is captured—twice in a year and a half the couple has been married on camera, and it's a far more agreeable experience for both this second time around.

From July 19 to 21 they shoot the second George-Libbie meeting, at her home in Monroe, Michigan, recreated on Stage 12, which includes Hattie McDaniel's first work in the picture as Callie, and the first time that McDaniel and de Havilland have appeared together since the Academy Award fiasco of 1940, when McDaniel won the Oscar and Livvie did not. The night that there was no God.

For a couple of weeks the picture progresses in continuity. Sydney Greenstreet starts; they shoot his scenes with Flynn in the restaurant, and in his office, and at the War Department, and on the street. Lenore Coffee has more rewrites; the blue pages that come in on Wednesday the 29th call for more shooting on Stage 12 in the Bacon home.

From July 30 through August 1, Walsh shoots the Manassas action scenes at Calabasas. On July 30 the unit takes two casualties. First, a stirrup breaks and an extra sprains his back. Then Ralph Budlong, an expert rider, falls from his horse and is impaled on his saber, "with the result that it pierced his back through his side," reports Frank Mattison. His condition, says the report, is "very grave."[18] Buster Wiles will later credit Flynn, who witnessed the accident, for phoning the hospital every day to check on Budlong. However, this will be difficult because Flynn sails away on his boat early on Saturday, August 2 to Catalina Island for a *Life* magazine photo shoot. For scenic backgrounds in shots taken by photographer Peter Stackpole, Flynn brings along a hot brunette named Peggy Satterlee—who, it will turn out a year later, is not yet 16 years of age as they set sail but looks and acts much older.

Flynn reports for shooting on Monday August 4 and is handed more blue pages from Coffee that send the company back to Sullivan's Place for retakes on Stage 6 and to the Bacon study on Stage 12. But after three days at the Battle of Manassas, with Flynn inhaling the battle smoke of Calabasas, his tender sinuses are inflamed and his voice is shot. He lands in the hospital. De Havilland and McDaniel rush in to play the Coffee-rewritten scene where Libbie tells Callie that the Custers are going away from Monroe to the Dakotas. The next day the company works without Flynn again, as the Sharps plot with Taipe about a fake gold strike in the Black Hills. This same day Frank Mattison reports, "I understand this morning from Mr. Walsh that Mr. Budlong, the boy who has been in the hospital, passed away last night at 7:00 p.m."[19]

Says tough-as-nails Buster Wiles, who will pile up bonus pay for difficult stunts on *Boots*: "[Budlong's] passing was a somber reminder of lurking danger, unexpected, swift as lightning. I wonder how many guys have died making pictures. That day, I believe, I shed lightheartedness and eagerness in stunt-work."[20]

The passing of Ralph Budlong stays with the company through the remainder of the production, grounding everyone to the hazards of working in the pictures. And Flynn remains down as well, hospitalized with infected sinuses and running a fever, which prompts the Boss to write longhand to Tenny Wright on August 8 that Flynn "will probably have to remain in the hospital until Monday or Tuesday of next week, and he should not return to work immediately after leaving the hospital probably not before the end of the week. I want you and Fellows to get together with Walsh and start lining up some more stuff that you can do without him, as it looks as though we will not get him back before the end of next week."[21]

The company shoots as much as possible without Flynn, and Walsh moves on to Lasky Mesa to begin the Last

Stand "with the largest crowd we will have which will number 400 men," says Mattison. "As you know we had some difficulty getting the Indians for these scenes as I was here at the studio this morning at 6:00 a.m. and all the old-timers as they came through, who are regular-men, offered to take their stand as Indians, with the result we had sufficient Indians today as required." In all, more than 460 horses and a like number of riders are called, plus 100 animal handlers. A steel tower is erected at the Mesa to record high shots showing the strategic action of the Last Stand, and the company works for days, taking many casualties, none serious, reports Mattison, as Flynn convalesces.[22]

His first scene upon returning takes place on Monday, August 18 in the Committee Room in Washington on Stage 6, where the weakened Flynn struggles to capture Custer's appearance before Congress to charge the Sharps and Taipe with conspiracy for fraudulently claiming that gold had been discovered in the Black Hills. Mattison reports that Flynn "told me he was very weak, but he felt that a couple of days inside and he would be much better. I spoke to him about going out to the Ranch but he said to let him stay in at least until he got his strength back so that he could go out to the Ranch on the exterior. Consequently we will try and remain inside all of this week."[23]

They knock off important scenes in the studio, such as Custer's triumphal return to Monroe after the war, shot on a brutal August day with Olivia tortured by the hot costume that causes her to faint twice and Errol to tease her for being pregnant. In the script Custer is now a general and hero met at the train by Libbie's humbled father, hat in hand. But George only has eyes for Libbie. He rushes to her and they kiss passionately, and her father protests.

BACON: Aren't you forgetting yourself?

CUSTER: It's quite all right, Mr. Bacon. Everything's all right; very proper. You see, we're engaged.

BACON: (taken aback) Well…, splendid! Splendid!

LIBBIE: And we're going to be married.

CUSTER: Today! I brought my regimental chaplain, and General Sheridan himself is going to be best man. That is, of course, with your permission.

BACON: My permission? Well, now, of course, General. I shall be honored to give it. But you mustn't be

On August 27, Gene Lockhart and Hattie McDaniel are brought back to Stage 7 for a reshoot of the crossed-sabers wedding shot, with Flynn appearing less than healthy from the lingering lung infection contracted on location shooting Civil War battle scenes.

Above: An uncomfortable Errol, a radiant Livvie, and a laughing Raoul Walsh all seem to be in on *something*. Was this around the time that the Flynn-de Havilland relationship was finally consummated right there at the studio? (John McElwee Collection) Below: Small carbon arcs light the couple intimately as Walsh directs the scene discussed in the meeting above, as the Custers adjust to life after the Civil War.

too impetuous. After all, there's the announcement, the arrangements. If you get married today, you can't have any of these.

LIBBIE: But I shall have General George Armstrong Custer, and he is what I started out to get.

BACON: Libbie, it's positively unmaidenly!

LIBBIE: After today, that won't matter.

Both the braided Maid Marian and the well-heeled Elizabeth Bacon are virgins being courted by heroes, but Miss Bacon is poles apart from Miss Fitzwalter. Libbie is not quite so innocent and not at all passive. She has set her cap for Custer—she proclaims to her father on the day that George and Libbie meet that he is the man she will marry—and she proves it by landing him after four long years of courtship. After a run of bad luck on the Warner lot, de Havilland lucks into Lenore Coffee's rewrites—dialogue created *by* a woman *for* a woman, giving her character dimensionality she has never enjoyed at Warner Bros.

The three actors handle the scene adroitly, thanks to the insight of Raoul Walsh. Flynn is in his usual zone, playing it bold and wide-eyed at the same time; Lockhart is the perfect straight man, managing to be earnest, well meaning, and overmatched; and Livvie is all woman. She can see her wedding night dead ahead, and she is out to overwhelm her father and win the day.

De Havilland and Oscar rival McDaniel are reunited, less successfully this time, with the latter again playing Mammy in a Civil War picture.

That Thursday and Friday, the company moves to Stage 16 where they shoot the parting of Libbie and George as he rides off knowing of his "certain death," while she has similarly grim premonitions. After Flynn's hospital stay, his face is gaunt and angular, and the nighttime lighting of the bedroom accentuates these features. Backlighting on Errol and Livvie lends an ethereal element, and Walsh shoots an abundance of close-ups to capture subtleties that Curtiz would have missed. Walsh's work coaching the actors is also evident. Livvie's countenance reflects quiet resilience; Errol's eyes show a softness rarely seen in his work, and in his face, vulnerability, even fear, when he says his final "Goodbye" in a whisper, with their final kiss shot close, dreamily, to bring the moment home for the audience.

Fans wonder where the line is with these two—friends? lovers?—and the parting scene in *Boots* further obscures that line. Says de Havilland: "I did have this tremendous feeling of grief while we were shooting it [the parting scene]. I couldn't shake it and I didn't understand it; I felt lost. It was something that had never happened to me; it was a warning. A long, long time afterwards I was thinking about that phenomenon and I realized that it was a real farewell, because we never worked together again."[24]

Two years later she will tell columnist Sidney Skolsky that after making all these pictures with Flynn, it is only during the last one that they will be close. How close? FLASH FORWARD 36 years to 1977 and production of the sci-fi disaster picture about killer bees, *The Swarm*, at the Warner Bros. Studios in Burbank. Livvie and actor Michael Caine are strolling the lot—her former home studio, where she hasn't set foot in 35 years—and she tells Caine that back in the day, she had been known as the "Iron Virgin" after holding off Flynn's advances for so long. But, *for some reason*, according to Livvie, Errol had bet the crew a hundred dollars that they would "do it" before the end of the picture. Because de Havilland claims that she and Flynn are "friends" during the production of *Boots*, it can be assumed that it is while shooting this one that Flynn makes the bet.

Says Caine, "I was dying to ask her if Errol had *made it*, but Olivia struck me as being a very staid lady and would not, I thought, appreciate such a personal question." According to Caine, "Suddenly she halted and pointed to a certain spot in the hills that rise behind the studio. 'That's where Errol won his hundred dollars,' she said naughtily. I was quite shocked at this but just said, 'Oh, really?' being unable to think of anything else. 'Yes, really,' she replied with a wicked little smile and we strolled on back to the stage and the bees."[25]

De Havilland's statement to Flynn in 1937: "We really mustn't see each other again until you've straightened out your situation with Lili."

Well, the situation is straightened out. Flynn is free of encumberment, and so is Livvie; free to take a stroll with Errol at lunchtime. They would never have had such freedom on a Curtiz set, but now Raoul Walsh, the director whom Flynn refers to as "Uncle," is in charge, and the production is a relaxed one.

De Havilland's indiscretion in speaking of the rendezvous with Flynn is easy to understand: "Here's an actress on her old home lot where she had always been safe," says John McElwee. "They had a code in the old days, the stars. They kept each other's confidences, because they were all in it together. They saw each other through. Thirty years later, she thinks she's saying something in confidence to another actor on the lot. She never dreams it's going to get into print because, back in the day, it never would have."[26]

Suddenly other questions arise, such as the dark turn in their relationship in 1940 during production of *Santa Fe Trail*, when each got on the nerves of the other, almost as if their relationship had changed—perhaps from work friends to lovers? Such changes knock expectations out of whack, and in this case, the change would explain Flynn's intense jealousy of Reagan. And the intimacy of the Santa Fe junket photos makes a lot more sense if these two are lovers rather than merely work friends. The problem is, much to their credit, neither of them will ever betray the confidences of the other. Not in 1940 or 1941, and never thereafter.

Above: On the darkened soundstage, Errol takes Livvie's hand so she can walk a tightrope on the rails and keep her fashionable (but not period) pumps, and her hemline, from getting soiled. She doesn't rely on the wardrobe department for help with her friend close by, even though he has been so ill that his color has just been applied in Makeup. Below: A little later, the lights come up and Raoul Walsh shoots the arrival of hero Custer at the train station in Monroe, Michigan, for his wedding to Libbie. When she is chastised by her father (Gene Lockhart) for "unmaidenly" behavior, Livvie says, in a line that tests the Breen Office, "After today, that won't matter." What does matter: the costume is heavy and hot, and it's August in L.A., and it's all she can do to survive until a printed take is captured.

The downside of a Hollywood studio trying to recreate the famous Budweiser painting of Custer's Last Fight was that not enough stunt men could be recruited to fill the massive landscape. The production team ran out of cavalrymen, Indians, and horses. As if that weren't bad enough, the unit was forced to roll day after day with no Custer, as Errol Flynn continued to recuperate from various illnesses. B-units and reshoots were in order to finally give Flynn's last stand the action and sweep it needed in a Jack L. Warner production. In the end, the patchwork job worked (barely), and Flynn and company died neatly and bloodlessly, with their boots on. (John McElwee collection)

De Havilland will say after the publication of Michael Caine's book that she had been "stung by misquotes" and she claims that the conversation had concerned John Huston and not Flynn.[27] But the world hasn't been nearly as curious about Olivia and John as about Olivia and Errol; wouldn't Michael Caine know the difference?

After Errol's "lunch" with Livvie, there is much more picture to make, and they move on for retakes. More blue-page rewrites come in, this time at the insistence of Flynn, who goes to Walsh with an idea based on the success of the farewell scene. Flynn thinks that the farewell scene will be enhanced if they expand a short George-Libbie exchange yet to be shot into something resembling the *Robin Hood* balcony scene. So Coffee gets to work and sends in seven new blue pages. Flynn is eager at this point to give Livvie screen time with him, which he has never been before—more evidence of their closeness.

Fellows clips a note to the new pages and sends them to Wallis: "Dear Hal: Attached is a love scene that replaces blue page 50d. We won't get to this until Tuesday and therefore, I would like to have you read it. Walsh and Flynn both wanted this type of scene written." Wallis reads the scene and jots on the Fellows memo, "This is OK."[28]

The new scene plays at night during George's convalescence in Monroe, after his wounding in the war. Earlier in the day George has run afoul of Libbie's father (Gene Lockhart), so now our hero must climb to the balcony, where his love is imprisoned. Here he proposes marriage.

Tenny Wright reads the scene and grouses to Wallis: "Flynn enters the garden, crosses over to the front of the house and climbs up the balcony and de Havilland is waiting for him on the balcony, a la Romeo and Juliet. The camera moves up on a boom and we play the love scene up on the balcony."[29] But, *Oh, by the way, the house on Stage 12 has no balcony! And how much will it cost to build one? As you know, we intend to shoot this scene fast so that we can spring de Havilland out of the picture and into* The Male Animal.

Nobody denies the potential of the new scene, but two grand is two grand, and that's how much it will take to build the balcony, and Flynn is down sick again and at various doctors' offices, leaving the company with no leading man, which gains Livvie another couple of hastily constructed scenes so that Walsh can keep moving.

Three weeks of retakes and exteriors follow, with Flynn in and out. Finally, on September 19 the balcony is constructed on Stage 12, and Hattie McDaniel returns to provide comic relief as Callie helps Custer outwit Libbie's father—which necessitates bringing Gene Lockhart back again as well. The last major scene that Olivia will ever play with Errol is a romantic powerhouse as he ignores his physical frailty, climbs the balcony, and hurries into the waiting arms of his true love. Once again Raoul Walsh works magic with the pair and shoots them close and knocked out of focus for a dreamy black and white look, their embrace intimate, especially because Libbie's gown is low cut and revealing. Flynn idly caresses her bare arms as he holds her.

When George believes that Libbie's father is approaching, he vaults from the balcony into a nearby tree, a difficult

In a beautifully backlit scent, Libbie and George know he is about to ride to his death. Here, in the most effective Flynn-de Havilland screen moment, he stumbles on her diary and then tells her, "Walking through life with you, ma'am, has been a very gracious thing." Even 35 years later she will not be able to watch this scene to its conclusion. (Robert Florczak Collection)

From September 2 to 4, Flynn and de Havilland shoot on the mountain peak above Chatsworth. Above: The lung infection continues to bother Errol, but they enjoy each other's company. (Mike Mazzone Collection) Below: Flynn rehearses on a stepladder; he'll recite his dialogue on the wagon's footrail. Olivia and character actor Charlie Grapewin can be seen in the wagon. (John McElwee Collection)

stunt performed by Buster Wiles. Cut to Flynn settling into the tree and blowing a kiss to de Havilland on the balcony, which she returns. And except for retakes, that is that for the great Warner Bros. love team of the Golden Era. They exit this phase in their careers as beautiful people interacting with great charm in a wonderfully written and directed scene. It all works for Livvie and Errol, because of the script, their own maturity, and a feeling that this is the last time for them.

McDaniel finishes the scene with a corny confrontation involving a hoot-owl. Because of the Boss's mandate to infuse comedy into the picture, her work in *Boots* feels like a force-fit, whether she's reading fortunes in a teacup or telling Libbie not to get uppity. She is wedged into the part, producing equal parts laughter and embarrassment, but that's J.L.—he likes it all *BIG*.

That Thursday and Friday, Flynn and the remaining principals drive out to Lasky Mesa to capture the final list of action shots that will close out the picture: death scenes at the Little Big Horn for Arthur Kennedy, G.P. Huntley, and Charlie Grapewin, all dying in the arms of Flynn. And finally Errol as Colonel Custer, the last man standing, grabs a saber and on foot he faces hundreds of Indians riding at him on horseback. Thus, as September ends, Custer dies with his boots on in grand style, and the picture moves into post-production for a Christmas 1941 release.

As noted by biographer Tony Thomas of *Boots* and the Custers: "Since they play an ideally mated pair, it almost seems like a fantasy idealization of the marriage their fans might assume Flynn and Olivia would have had in real life."[30] Except, of course, that he was a rampant womanizer who couldn't have settled down with anyone, and she would ultimately smother him.

In the end, the relationship whipped up by the fertile mind and machine-gun typewriter of Lenore Coffee is wrapped inside an over-the-top action picture rife with historical inaccuracies. As a result, *Boots* won't stand the test of time as a historical biopic, and in the process of being seen as a second-tier film from the Golden Era, audiences will be robbed of the opportunity to watch the couple give strong performances and work truly *together* for the first time in years.

Reviews will savage Warner Bros. for rewriting history, but audiences don't care, and *They Died with Their Boots On* returns $1.5 million in profit. It is also, at its heart, a sweet romance, and as such, Tony Thomas notes: "In 1978, at a retrospective showing of some of her films in Los Angeles, Olivia de Havilland found it impossible to sit through the farewell scene of *Boots*. As it began she got up and walked into the lobby, and wept. It is easy to understand why."[31]

At the end of September 1941, Errol and Livvie go their separate ways and march on into the future assured of security and stardom, if not career satisfaction. But within a year, both will be fighting for their security and stardom in separate courtrooms. It is winner take all for each, as it turns out, and one "winner" will do all right, while the other "winner" will pay a horrible price, and suffer the torments of the damned, and never recover.

The last scene they will ever shoot together is, ironically enough, a reunion as Custer returns home from campaigning. It is shot September 22, 1941, a day of retakes to clean up problems from earlier printed scenes. They embrace and kiss, and then he sweeps her off her feet to carry her inside their home. She will say later that she sensed they would never make another picture. Knowing of her contract situation as he did, Flynn must have sensed the same thing, although he never said so for the record.

TWISTED SISTERS

They were founding brothers, and U.S. presidents, and they were bitter rivals—John Adams and Thomas Jefferson. For decades Adams and Jefferson remained antagonists and ideological adversaries, and even after they made peace with each other and began a warm correspondence in old age, the rivalry would go on to death, with each determined to outlive the other. The last words Adams spoke were, "Jefferson still survives." Adams could not know that Jefferson had passed on a few hours earlier. Fittingly, both men died on the 50th anniversary of the ratification of the Declaration of Independence, July 4, 1826.

The comparison may seem far-fetched between the brothers in revolution, Adams and Jefferson, and the sisters in Hollywood, de Havilland and Fontaine—the American founding fathers changed the course of human history, and how can actresses compare with such august accomplishment? But in both cases, two strong personalities stood on the world stage, in the same place at the same time, and battled each other. Both were revered through the course of their lives, and won great honors, and passed into an old age that spanned centuries, each holding the other in contempt.

Livvie claimed in an interview with Hedda Hopper in 1952 that the seeds of conflict went all the way back to infancy. Sickly Joanie got all the attention while Livvie was shoved out of the way. Then, growing up, Joanie developed a penchant to covet everything that belonged to her big sister, from her career to her boyfriend, Brian Aherne, whom Joan married.

In her memoir, *No Bed of Roses*, Joan painted herself as the victim of her husbands, mother, and particularly her sadistic big sister. Olivia, always an intense introvert, chose to disdain public displays that would in any way fuel a feud between the two.

Nothing unseemly happened between the two in public until after the Academy Awards ceremony in 1942, when Joan won Best Actress and Livvie did not. Throughout the Oscar ceremony, de Havilland maintained a supportive veneer, but afterward in a nightclub with beaus Jimmy Stewart and Burgess Meredith, a *Photoplay* magazine reporter observed that she "was so overcome at having lost she had to be supported to the door for fresh air."[32] The crux of it was, to quote Livvie: "Oh, my God, I've lost prestige with my own sister."[33]

That statuette of Joan's bothered Livvie, who had, after all, started years before little sister, learned the craft under Reinhardt, Mervyn LeRoy, James Whale, and yes, Curtiz, not to mention that she participated in the most

The sisters agreed to a 1942 Kodachrome photo shoot to show that there were no hard feelings over the recent Academy Awards.

intense, successful motion picture in history under the lash of Selznick, Cukor, and Fleming. She had worked with some of the finest screen actors of her day, including Cagney, O'Brien, and Gable. Despite all of that, her neophyte sister grabbed Oscar first.

The fragile peace between the siblings survived minor snits for a few more years. In 1946 Livvie married one-hit-wonder novelist Marcus Goodrich only to learn that he had been married four times before. Observed Joan, "It's too bad that Olivia's husband has had so many wives and only one book."

Livvie told Hopper, "This cut me to the heart. Under the circumstances I expected her to at least say something about being sorry it happened—or that she shouldn't have said it and was sorry it was printed."

For six years the sisters didn't speak, "…not," says Olivia, "until after I got a divorce. Then it seemed ridiculous to demand this apology after I'd separated from the man about whom the issue arose. She asked me to dinner and I accepted, and so we resumed diplomatic relations."[34]

By now it was the age of television, and film work for both sisters was drying up, particularly for Joan. Each survived hard economic times, sometimes by asking the other for help, but always the air was indeed one of "diplomatic relations," as if they were India and Pakistan rather than sisters born of the same parents.

To make ends meet, each booked speaking engagements, and each took to the stage. Actor Andrew Parks worked in a stage production of *The Lion in Winter* with Joan Fontaine in the mid-1980s in New Orleans. Parks remembers a gracious, sometimes imperious performer—and an incident in a diner to which the cast had retired during a break in rehearsals. As she passed a series of wall posters showing various animals,

After Olivia stepped off the stage holding her Academy Award presented for *To Each His Own,* Joan "went over to congratulate her.... She took one look at me, ignored my outstretched hand, clutched Oscar to her bosom, and wheeled away."[35] Still smarting over Joan's comments about husband Marcus Goodrich, Livvie was in no mood to share the moment. This 1947 incident became the most celebrated moment in "the feud."

including the kitten subtitled, *Hang in There*, Joan spied a photo of an orangutan. "Ah! Olivia!" she drolled with perfect timing. "Must be recent; looks touched," as in, touched up.[36]

As of 2010, one sister continues to live in Paris and the other in Carmel, California—although Olivia's daughter Gisele resides in nearby Malibu. By this time, there are no public utterances made by one about the other. A query by the author to Joan about Olivia was met on the telephone with, "If I were to talk about Olivia de Havilland, it would be like an atomic bomb going off."[37] Perhaps the feud is over and the two have, like Adams and Jefferson, found lasting peace out of the limelight. It would be a fitting end for two people born of the same DNA on the same assembly line—fierce individualists who were comfortable in the skin of fictional characters but not in their own, and who could never quite seem to bear looking at the other and seeing so much *self* so close by.

By 1957, the sadness reflected in Errol's eyes broke the hearts of those close to him, including Olivia. By this time he had been estranged from her for years. He had also been betrayed by his business manager and by his best friend, and no amount of vodka or narcotics could make the pain of living go away. Airbrushing attempts to hide the hunching of his back, one of many signs of ill health.

10 LOVERS IN EXILE

In the 1930s another Hollywood love team, Fred Astaire and Ginger Rogers, had made a series of highly profitable pictures for RKO and their ego battles dwarfed those of Errol and Olivia. There had never been any sort of love between the dancers. But after 10 years apart Fred and Ginger will revisit their partnership one last time in *The Barkleys of Broadway*, one of MGM's big hits of 1949.

There would be no such professional reunion for Errol and Olivia for reasons that the lovers will carry to the grave. In January 1942 they are very close—experiencing the personal and professional afterglow of *They Died with Their Boots On*. They are seen around town together, as reported in *Life* magazine and gossip columns. And then something happens, something devastating that neither of them will speak or write about. They quite simply drop out of each other's lives for 15 years, leaving no clues behind to aid future biographers. This part of their story remains a bitter mystery and perhaps one reason Livvie will not be able to face her autobiography.

After the completion of *Boots*, Flynn moves into his newly completed two-story California colonial on Mulholland Drive, and the house and grounds succeed in holding his attention better than any picture or dame ever could. The sprawling ranch is a showplace with banks of windows opening up the view of the San Fernando Valley to Flynn and houseguests. The downstairs walls are pickled pine; there is a gilt-ceilinged formal dining room with mirrored walls at one end of the structure, and a rustic den on the other. In the middle sits a 30-foot living room with two sets of french doors overlooking a pool, and beyond it, the San Fernando Valley. For a decade it will be *the* place to party in Hollywood.

Since Errol and Olivia are dating upon the house's completion, she will be one of its first guests, although she won't be shown the secrets of the place designed in by the owner. Errol has a secret viewing space installed behind the bar that looks in on the ladies bathroom through a two-way mirror. He also builds in other peepholes and secret passageways—the complex Flynn has built a complex castle.

The dating of Errol and Olivia doesn't not slow down her career. She's making one picture after another now, while Flynn vacations in and out of town. The events of December 7 hit everyone hard; nobody knows quite what to think after Pearl Harbor, except everybody knows that America is in a war. A big one.

Of course, Livvie has been at war for more than two years, but the scripts have been a little better of late. *Boots* is followed by *The Male Animal* with Henry Fonda, and then an important drama called *In This Our Life* that stars Bette Davis and co-stars George Brent and Dennis Morgan. Livvie isn't exactly winning her war, but she's fighting J.L. to a draw, and her determination pays off in decent scripts. The boss now faces a simple fact: Olivia de Havilland is a Warner Bros. property that will be devalued by inactivity. Since she will certainly reject any weak script sent her way, we had better send some strong work her way.

On the set of *In This Our Life*, de Havilland is introduced to a new Hollywood whiz kid, John Huston, who is tall, lean, and athletic like Flynn, but not classically handsome. As described by Livvie's *Gone With the Wind* co-star,

173

Evelyn Keyes, Huston is: "Not beautiful at all, if anything, almost ugly. Handsome eyes, though, brown, well spaced. Deep pouches underneath gave them a sad look. Generous mouth, good teeth. Weird posture. The long back curved forward, a bit hunched over. A really queer nose, flattened (he told me later) by a boxer's glove."[1]

Nonetheless, Livvie will say later, "There was a man, someone I felt very, very deeply about after my long-term crush on Errol Flynn."[2]

Thirty-five-year-old John Huston is the sensation of Warner Bros., having just directed a little detective picture that struck gold. "They didn't have any hopes for *The Maltese Falcon* whatsoever," says Rudy Behlmer. *Falcon* is a remake, which is usually bad news in Hollywood, and, says Behlmer, "The thinking was, 'OK, give Huston a break. It's not going to cost much and we'll see what happens,' and of course it became a major sleeper."[3]

John Huston has been just about everywhere and done just about everything, from writing for the newspapers in New York City to winning a boxing championship in California and serving in the Mexican cavalry. Ten years her senior and possessing a brilliant mind, Huston hits de Havilland like a thunderbolt on the set of *In This Our Life*. With Huston directing the picture, Miss Bette Davis its star, and de Havilland in support, the situation is volatile. Another complicating factor: John Huston is married—on his second wife, in fact. But Livvie had summed it up years earlier: "Somebody walks into your life, and before you know it, you are in love with him.... And it's blind."

Blind indeed, because Huston is a womanizer, drinker, and scoundrel. He is the smartest guy in any room—funny, acerbic, articulate, and opinionated—but the trouble is, he knows exactly how smart he is and talks down to people, especially the women in his life.

Despite her discerning mind, inner strength, and professional savvy, Olivia has a knack for falling for the wrong guy. Two of her men have been married and a third engaged. Only Jimmy Stewart has been marriage material for her, but he left her to sow wild oats.

Howard Koch, scriptwriter for *In This Our Life*, sees the sparks fly between Huston and de Havilland on the Warner soundstages: "She was not an easy pickup. And with John,

Grown-up Livvie sports a new 'do in pictures like *The Male Animal* and *In This Our Life*, and during the war she takes up smoking. She also has plenty of time to relax and read in 1943 and 1944, since no one in Hollywood will hire her.

it was partly the game: here was a beautiful woman, could he win her?"[4]

Huston shares this trait with Flynn: they challenge themselves to conquer the most difficult women. The chase is everything; the thrill is in the hunt, and the great question to be answered: *Can I possess this beautiful woman desired by men around the world?* With Flynn, Livvie had held out for years. With Huston she falls head over heels, and holds nothing back. She succumbs to the charms of Huston that make him a ladykiller: the brilliance of the mind, what Evelyn Keyes calls "a melted-caramel voice," and a commanding presence. "There was a mystery in the way he spoke," says Keyes, "a promise of something I had never experienced before."[5]

Margaret Tallichet Wyler, wife of director William Wyler and a member of Huston's social set, observes John and Livvie: "She was crazy about John. Women were crazy about John. And Olivia just always comes on very emotionally. It's typical of her character to come on at a very high pitch about almost everything."[6]

Livvie will later call Huston "the great love of my life" and "a man I wanted to marry."[7]

Says Huston, "Olivia wanted to get married, but it was just impossible for me to get married at that time."[8]

Well, yeah, being already married and all. Huston's not a big fan of marriage with so many *women* out there.

The Warner soundstages reverberate with the de Havilland-Huston romance. The director gives his new girlfriend great setups in *In This Our Life*, causing Bette Davis to spit nails when she realizes what's going on. Retakes are in order, but the finished picture bears the mark of a testosterone-infused director looking past the Warner superstar in favor of his sexy girlfriend.

At Christmas *Boots* opens, and the numbers are out of this world, causing J.L. to think about another Flynn-de Havilland teaming. Warner Bros. has just bought the rights to Edna Ferber's best-seller, *Saratoga Trunk*, a costume story with a strong female lead, Clio Dulaine. Leading ladies around town see the part of Clio as another Scarlett O'Hara, and all angle for the part.

After turning down so many Warner Bros. scripts of late, this is one that de Havilland salivates over. The Rhett character this time is Clint Maroon, a Texas gambler, and Flynn isn't that, exactly, but with a few rewrites, he could be. After all, a few years earlier, simple rewrites had justified Flynn as a cowboy in *Dodge City*.

The sudden Flynn-de Havilland estrangement now entangles Livvie's ambitions for *Saratoga Trunk*, because a January 22, 1942 screen test is set for Errol and Olivia to read Clint and Clio—the part Livvie is desperate to land. And on the 22nd, she is a no-show and remains at home on Nella Vista claiming exhaustion. She will later say that it broke her heart to lose this role—and yet she is the one who refuses to report for the test with Errol. If she makes *Saratoga Trunk* she will be that much closer to finishing her contract, so the situation with Errol—whatever has caused the slamming of the door between them—is doubly damaging to her.

On other Warner Bros. soundstages, Flynn begins *Forced Landing*, an unhappy production with Ronnie Reagan that exemplifies Flynn's life at this time. He has just returned from a trip to Washington, D.C., where he had pleaded to be taken into military service only to be classified 4-F due to various and mounting health problems, including an enlarged heart, multiple bouts of gonorrhea, recurrent malaria, and chronic lung infections that may or may not be tuberculosis. When a star the caliber of Errol Flynn—a friend of FDR—walks into the War Department and can't get satisfaction, the situation must be serious. And it is, and has to do with more than the bugs swimming around in his body. There is the little matter of Flynn's careless escapades in Spain and elsewhere, with his name tied in FBI files to that of Dr. Hermann Erben, who, the feds reveal, belongs to the Nazi Party. So to some in the FBI, Flynn is a security risk by association in addition to a 4-F.

Every day Flynn of the giant ego looks at himself in the mirror and sees a sham of a fellow staring back, a fellow suddenly paying quite a price for his hedonistic lifestyle. For serving in the slave trade, he is left with malaria; for remaining Erben's friend, he is labeled a security risk; for unprotected sexual encounters, he carries around genital warts; for smoking his Lucky Strikes and working in the action pictures, his lungs are shot.

He also suffers from a diseased soul, and that's really at the heart of it all. Underneath his madcap high living and yachts and convertibles and water skiing and trips to the

John Huston doesn't seem particularly happy to have Olivia hanging over his shoulder in this photo from 1942.

track and cockfighting and hanging out with the boys is a gray world of depression that he tries not to see, so he literally avoids looking in mirrors. He chooses to drink away his troubles and seeks validation in girls, *any* girls. He prefers young ones, and says for the record, "They can jump up and down and talk away and you don't have to listen to them like an older woman."[9] Inside he fumes: *Older women know how to trap you and screw you over for alimony.* Indeed, right after the orgasm—*his* orgasm—he kicks the young ones out without a word.

It's no wonder that his looks are starting to go. The decline is first visible onscreen in *They Died with Their Boots On*, with lines about his face and a hint of jowliness. All this is in a man just turned 32.

During production of *Boots*, Flynn had suffered the death of best friend Arno, the high-personality schnauzer. Arno had gone overboard from *Sirocco* and drowned, and the loss devastates Flynn, who had seen Arno as a charming, fearless kindred spirit. In a few years, Flynn's human best friend, playboy adventurer Fred McEvoy, will also drown, and these are losses that Errol will never get past.

Errol and Lili are through now as a couple, although they will never get over one another. She wins a divorce settlement that gouges him financially, and her parting shot in the newspapers: *He paid more attention to his yachts than me.* The deal gives her half interest in $150,000 worth of property, and $1,500 a month as long as Flynn is an A-picture star. Flynn refuses to give her any part of his 11.5-acre Mulholland Drive estate, so he must scrounge up the cash equivalent. In this way they will spend the rest of their lives, Errol owing but never having the cash to pay. They see each other in court and always talk about each other, the memories forever fresh, the bitterness right at hand. He will speak about Damita more than anyone in *My Wicked Wicked Ways,* and to age 90 Tiger Lil will complain about Flynn and live life through Errol's son Sean, who will die in the Vietnam War.

Without Tiger Lil, Flynn sits on top of the world at Mulholland Farm and attempts to write a new novel, with new girlfriend Mary Ann Hyde doing the typing. Hyde is an 18-year-old aspiring actress fresh from Beverly Hills High. Dark-haired and dark-eyed like de Havilland, Hyde's legs go on for miles, but he's not serious in the least about the relationship and cheats on the earnest young girl on a sometimes hourly basis.

In Errol's surly frame of mind, gossip about Livvie and her director-boyfriend reaches Flynn on the set of *Forced Landing*, and he seethes. Like Damita, Olivia de Havilland is not a girl he will get over easily.

In *Forced Landing*, a picture about an Allied bomber crew trapped behind enemy lines (renamed *Desperate Journey* prior to release), 4-F Flynn must for the first time pretend to be a hero when he cannot portray one in real life. Jimmy Stewart has gone off to be a pilot, the first of a parade of able-bodied Hollywood stars to go off and fight while Flynn stays home and slowly comes unglued.

The glue is also failing de Havilland, whose work in *Hold Back the Dawn*, the Paramount picture she had made prior to *Boots*, earns her a second Academy Award nomination. Neither this nor *Gone With the Wind* had been made at Warner Bros., fueling her conviction that opportunities for quality pictures can be found only outside her home studio. In March 1942, after completing *In This Our Life*, she turns down the comedy *George Washington Slept Here* and goes on

Above left: For weeks Errol pushes his way through crowds of often freakish onlookers as he suffers the indignity of a public trial at the Los Angeles Hall of Justice. Above right: Worst of all for Flynn is the airing of details of his sex life. Here Deputy District Attorney John Hopkins points to a diagram of the *Sirocco* and a particular porthole through which, according to Peggy Satterlee, Flynn had said they could better gaze at the moon. Below: After being acquitted, a haggard Flynn makes a statement to the press, but he feels that these Hollywood beat reporters have betrayed him by focusing on the lurid details of the case. From here on he will be wary of the press.

suspension yet again. She feels she can't judge any script these days and gives Huston a look at *The Princess O'Rourke*, a romantic-comedy script that Huston advises her to make. The studio romance rages on as he directs *Across the Pacific* with Humphrey Bogart and Mary Astor.

Now comes the Academy Award ceremony of 1942 at the Biltmore Hotel, a night of supreme awkwardness for Livvie on two counts: she is up for Best Actress against little sister Joanie, who had been a sensation in Alfred Hitchcock's *Suspicion*. Other contenders are Bette Davis, Greer Garson, and Barbara Stanwyck. Worse yet is the fact that John Huston and his wife Lesley sit across the way in the banquet-style setting, and Livvie must endure the indignity of being the "other woman" for the evening, watching from afar as Johnny dines with his wife.

Best Actress goes not to Livvie this evening but to Joanie, and an eyewitness, Fontaine herself, says that, "Olivia took the situation very graciously."[10] When Joan's name is read from the podium, Olivia stridently calls, "We've got it!" in a move designed to retain some semblance of control of a difficult moment.

This evening she gives a tough-as-nails performance for her peers—not letting them see her disappointment at losing the award to her neophyte sister. And she gives an equally convincing performance for Huston—not letting him see her annoyance at the fact that he sits with his wife.

On May 4, 1942, *Life* magazine releases an expose titled *Sister Act* that dives into the strange world of the de Havilland family and traces the sometimes sordid history of Walter de Havilland, G.M. Fontaine, Lilian, Olivia, Joan, and Joan's husband Brian Aherne, whom *Life* describes as "the man who looks like the man who smokes a pipe."

The article goes easy on Joan, the "brilliant" sister with a tested I.Q. of 160 and "an extraordinarily beautiful girl" who is capricious with her men. Olivia is painted as the older girl jealous of her sister's successful marriage and envious of the Academy Award statuette. Livvie's relationship with James Stewart is depicted as surreal because of her affectations and propensity for letting others horn in on dates. Nowhere in the in-depth character study of the sisters is John Huston mentioned, although Errol Flynn is listed among Olivia's suitors around town. In fact, the article's writer, Oliver O. Jenson, notes with some surprise that Livvie is gloomy and not prim and proper, and she doesn't travel with the "Puritan set."[11]

Since Huston is married, Livvie insists that he not be mentioned in the article, although their relationship is public knowledge in Hollywood. He has been a fixture at Nella Vista, and the two cohabitate for stretches at a time, something the studio would not have tolerated even a few years earlier. It had been an offense for which Flynn had paid the ultimate price in 1935—he had been forced to marry the woman with whom he was shacking up. Now it's Olivia de Havilland who is doing the deed, and with a married man.

But John won't be around much longer. He enlists in the Army Signal Corps, and Lt. John Huston is about to head off to the Aleutians to make a documentary for the war effort. He will be gone some time, and for Huston, the war zone is a relief. He likes certain things about life with high-octane Livvie—the sex, certainly, and having Olivia de Havilland as a rapt audience—but he is the opposite of a one-woman man, so heading into a war zone beats the oppression of a steady relationship. He has, after all, been successful on the hunt, and the hunt is the thing. Suddenly, with Huston shipping out in a few weeks, Livvie faces a dilemma when she is sent a script that isn't terrible. Soon she goes on suspension again to spend some final days with her man—her heart's in the right place but it's futile chasing John Huston, who leaves Nella Vista and moves on to many new loves in succession, returning to Livvie occasionally and causing her to carry a torch for three decades.

As bad as it is with Huston, she will thank her lucky stars that the flame for Flynn has been extinguished when she hears in September—as Huston is packing to leave town—that Errol has been charged with the statutory rape of an underage farm girl named Betty Hansen, and then a second girl, Peggy Satterlee. The headlines rip through Hollywood like a windswept California wildfire: ERROL FLYNN NABBED BY VICE SQUAD AT MOUNTAINTOP HOME! ERROL FLYNN DRAGGED TO HEADQUARTERS FOR QUESTIONING, FINGERPRINTING, MUG SHOTS!

A dream team assembles, and a very public trial drags on for weeks. Livvie reads the papers; Livvie sees photos of a gaunt, tortured Flynn in the courtroom. She is horrified that he has come to this; horrified, but not surprised. She has seen the selfishness, the self-destructive way of him.

How many jams has Flynn gotten himself into and out of? How many times has the studio quietly come to his rescue? But not now. Once, his wicked ways made him all the more attractive—that young, wild, impetuous, not-to-be-controlled fellow of the 1930s. She possessed a little streak of that wildness herself back then, but she has grown up and he has not. And what has perpetual adolescence brought him but disaster?

She also knows how alike are Flynn and Huston. Selfish, self-involved, brilliant men in their way. Utterly charming, intoxicating men that no woman will ever tame.

They share one more dark and potentially violent trait. Says one of John's lovers, Doris Lilly, "John had a thing about women that was very cruel. It wasn't that he used women. I mean, they used him as much as he used them. But I really believe that John didn't like women very much." Another friend sums up Huston in terms of self-loathing—which strongly resembles the self-loathing of Flynn—by saying of Huston's women, "The more you loved him, the less respect he had for you."[12]

John stirs Olivia to her very depths—and yet he's damaged goods, like Flynn, and a pathological womanizer, like Flynn. She says of Huston, "I watched him bring great destruction into the lives of other women."[13] And Olivia must wonder why she has been compelled to invest everything in Huston, only to watch him walk away, leaving her with nothing.

In February 1943 Flynn is acquitted of three counts of statutory rape after 13 hours of jury deliberation that visibly ages the actor as he sits it out. As with most Hollywood scandals, there is more to the case than meets the eye. J.L. himself is at the heart of Flynn's folly because there has been a secret system at work in Los Angeles that involves payoffs to the District Attorney's office from every studio to keep the antics of the stars quiet, from marijuana busts to the occasional wrongful death. But for whatever reason, in 1942, the Boss refuses to kick in, even though the D.A.'s office warns him that he had better *or else.* The or-else ends up being the indictment of Flynn. Reporter Marcia Winn of the Chicago *Tribune* first brings up the rottenness of the

Celebrations all over Hollywood mark the end of the World War, including a victory ball at Flynn's regular hangout, Club Mocambo, where he shows his comely 21-year-old wife Nora the menu. Errol had long ago claimed his own victory in the conquest of Nora, who had been, in the end, something of a pushover. By now their first child, Deirdre, has already been born.

Flynn accusations in a five-part series about the seamy underside of Hollywood that rubs nerves raw.[14]

Livvie agrees that Flynn's rape experience is about J.L. and not Flynn: "Jack Warner had not contributed.... Seeking to avenge this, they put the biggest moneymaker on the lot—subjected him to this degrading experience, and therefore got back at Jack Warner."[15]

In a literal sense, Flynn is a victim of crooked doings in the D.A.'s office, but Flynn is hardly an *innocent* victim. Prior to the rape trial, he had met a 19-year-old virgin, Blanca Rosa Welter, in Mexico, and smoothly seduced her on their first night together. In the wake of their orgasms, she had wept at the physical release just experienced. "He gave a chuckle and kissed me lightly," she will say later. "I felt in his manner a certain drawing away."[16] Flynn brings Welter to California and stashes her at Mulholland during the rape trial. Such high-risk behavior, squiring a teenaged girl around Hollywood and introducing her as his protégé at a time when his career is on the line for dalliances with teenaged girls, is surpassed only by his next move.

For sport, Flynn picks up the scent of new prey, an 18-year-old redhead working the cigarette stand at the Hall of Justice during his trial. He passes by her daily and can see only her flaming hair, blue eyes, and an exotic, pubescent face. "Finally I stopped and bought some cigarettes.... I craned my neck a bit over the counter, and saw that all was well. She had about a nineteen- or twenty-inch waist, hips to go with it, and slender ankles and wrists. All my life I have been partial to slender ankles."[17] Suddenly Blanca is on her way out. Under Flynn's tutelage, Blanca Welter becomes Linda Christian, after his ancestor Fletcher Christian, and leaves the bondage of Mulholland for a career as a socialite and actress.

Flynn barely remembers his Mexican now that he is chasing the girl at the cigarette counter. The seduction of Nora Eddington will be one of the most enjoyable of his life in terms of time and strategy. As a bonus, her dad works at the county sheriff's office, which raises the stakes for Flynn and makes the chase more exciting. He squires Nora around town, buys her jewelry, and then finally bags his 18-year-old, as with Blanca, at a moment of lowered resistance, after a pleasant evening together. But unlike Blanca, Nora loathes Errol for what he has done, which engages his guilt and remorse and draws him into a relationship that will last for six often-horrible years.

The two ships that once passed in the night, Errol and Olivia, move ever further apart. Flynn grows bitter, sadistic, and underneath it all, sad. Magazine writer Nancy Winslow Squire writes in 1943, "Despite his surface gaiety, there's something strange, withdrawn and lonely about the inner man."[18]

Errol affixes a jagged question mark onto his handkerchiefs, his stationery, and the pennant of his new yacht, *Zaca*. The question mark symbolizes his bewilderment over what the Errol Flynn brand has become. At the same time, Livvie changes addresses, leaving behind Nella Vista and its memories of Mother, Joanie, and John. She leases a new place off Coldwater Canyon in Beverly Hills, where there are few neighbors since a mountain juts up from her backyard. But soon she is on the move again, hopping from apartment to apartment and ending up in the West Hollywood hills.

Her constant wandering reflects a growing isolation as she battles Warner Bros. over the coldness of the Boss and the disrespect shown to her. The last straw is this new Warner picture, *The Animal Kingdom*, yet another remake of a story already covered in 1932. She protests when handed a partial script of only 20 pages—the rest is still being rewritten as production is scheduled to start! On March 24, 1943, Livvie goes on suspension rather than report for *The Animal Kingdom*, which will eventually be made with Ann Sheridan and released in 1946 as *One More Tomorrow*.

Livvie makes a picture on loan to RKO, *Government Girl*, and then remains inactive waiting for a decent script. When she refuses to report for a loanout from Warner Bros. to Columbia (then particularly down on its luck), J.L. suspends her again and informs de Havilland that 25 weeks have now been added to the end of her seven-year contract—the time she has spent on suspension for *Saturday's Children*, *Flight Angels*, *Affectionately Yours*, *The Gay Sisters*, *The Animal Kingdom*, and the rest.

Such extensions are at the heart of the studio system as it now exists. Livvie's seven-year contract signed in 1936 would have ended in May 1943 had she not gone on suspension. In theory she could bite the bullet and make *The Animal Kingdom* and anything else Warner Bros. wants and become a free agent in November, but she refuses to give an inch to J.L., and of course the Boss isn't budging either. It is their own personal Stalingrad; a test of wills and resources. J.L. always gets what he wants by charm or by muscle. Until, that is, he goes up against pint-sized Olivia de Havilland, a girl who *has* to win, even though she has no notion how she can.

"I'm stubborn," she tells a columnist. She also admits to a ferocious temper that makes her "ruthless."[19] After years of pushing back at the bully Boss, she is due a break, and she gets one. Livvie meets an attorney named Martin Gang. She says: "He told me that there was a seven-year law in California which forbade an employer from enforcing a contract against an employee for more than seven years. I asked to read it...; it seemed to mean calendar years...; he said that we would have to ask the court for a declaratory release, that is to say, an interpretation of that law as it applied to an actor's contract. Nobody had ever dared to do that before."[20]

Under Martin Gang's tutelage, agent Jimmie Townsend calls Roy Obringer's office at Warner Bros. on August 19, 1943, and states that Olivia's contract had expired three months earlier, in May. Olivia de Havilland, he proclaims, is now a free agent.

J.L. reacts Capone-like. "The Olivia de Havilland situation is a very serious matter," he memos his lieutenants, who snap to attention because it's clear that this time, the Boss is chewing razor blades. Warner states that her claims are "ridiculous."[21] Trial is set for November 5, 1943 in the matter of de Havilland v. Warner Bros.

Livvie takes the stand in Superior Court, grilled by studio attorneys. One in particular "was very ferocious with me," she says. "He kept saying, 'Isn't it true that you refused...?' and he got terribly melodramatic and violent—he was something." De Havilland holds her ground and does not give J.L. the satisfaction of reducing her to "just a fractious, irresponsible, spoiled movie actress."[22]

Livvie wins in Superior Court, and J.L.'s vengeance is swift. He orders his staff to generate a list of all motion picture studios in the country—more than 80 of them, large and small—and sends a personal letter to each requesting that they not hire Olivia de Havilland under any circumstances. The blacklisting works. Except for a few radio appearances, de Havilland disappears from Hollywood's radar screen.

In September 1944 an appellate court upholds the decision in favor of de Havilland and against Warner Bros. In February 1945 the State of California Supreme Court refuses to review the case, and the de Havilland Decision enters legal precedent, establishing limits for Hollywood actors in servitude to studios. "I freed the slaves," she says gleefully later. "I did. They said that, that I had freed the slaves."[23]

Olivia de Havilland has prevailed by employing that self-acknowledged ruthless and stubborn streak. She will do what she wants, when and *how* she wants. But fighting Warner Bros. costs her dearly. She pays enormous sums in legal fees. More important, she loses a chunk of her career as a youthful leading lady during three of Hollywood's last good years—war years when entertainment is badly needed and movie theaters rake in cash. At the time that she begins to work again, television is already on the horizon.

Errol now hears a new term, *in like Flynn*, which means that a guy has scored with a girl. Errol likes fun as much as

In the 1930s Flynn had been a student of the "sweet science." Here David Niven photographs his friend mixing it up in the backyard of the Linden Drive house with a sparring partner. In the mid-1940s Errol will use his fists often, with his most protracted bout against John Huston—a fight inspired by Olivia de Havilland. (Photo Courtesy of the Academy of Motion Picture Arts and Sciences)

the next fellow, but this new slogan is created at his expense. People are laughing at him, not with him.

So Flynn had ended up in court and de Havilland had ended up there. The *de Havilland Decision* and *in like Flynn* are terms that enter the American lexicon and plot the positions of ex-lovers heading in opposite directions.

Livvie steams ahead with a purpose. Flynn is adrift in his work, in his social life, and in his isolated homestead where he sits at night, pistol in hand, and contemplates scattering his brains all over the nicely papered walls of his spacious bedroom. He hears *in like Flynn* everywhere; he sees the sneers of the masses, guys at bars, reporters. He clams up. He won't talk to the press.

Livvie observes in retrospect, "His self-esteem was… profoundly affected—wounded…by that trial because he became a figure of fun, which he had never been before."[24] His drinking increases, causing him to get nasty in a hurry, so that when somebody gives him *the look*, he starts swinging. The chip on his shoulder soon outsizes his ego, and the handsomeness melts off his face, through the horrible marriage to Nora that produces daughters Deirdre and Rory, through a series of good and bad pictures at Warner Bros., and through experimentation with cocaine, heroin, and morphine.

The fact that a world war continues to rage doesn't help Flynn's opinion of himself. Huston had gone to the Aleutians to make his documentary, and then churns out more pictures for the folks to view at home. Flynn can only fight the war on a soundstage, in pictures like *Edge of Darkness*, *Uncertain Glory*, and *Objective, Burma!* He feels like a fraud and a coward and a bum for not being able to do what Huston can do, and it's no mere coincidence that Flynn heads to the Aleutians with the USO in November 1943 for six weeks of Vaudeville-style touring, or that Olivia de Havilland will follow to the Aleutians a few months later on another USO tour to see the boys at the front. The Aleutians become a fashionable place to go see the war without really seeing the war. The Japs had bombed and invaded this far-flung American possession in 1942, but since then, since Midway in the South Pacific, the resources of the enemy have been pulled away, and Alaska is no longer in the Japanese game plan. U.S. troops still have to guard it, and these troops need entertaining, so the stars endure a long plane ride and keep their names in the headlines touring for the war effort, far from the exploding shells and carnage of the European and Pacific theaters. Flynn needs to go to the Aleutians to prove to himself that he's as good as Huston. Livvie needs to go because she pines away for John even though he's a rogue and a relationship killer. She also needs to keep busy during the prolonged blacklisting from the picture business.

In 1944 Jack Warner quietly loses Hal Wallis as his right-hand man; Hal Wallis had been responsible almost single-handedly for directing the directors who coaxed performances from Flynn and de Havilland in all their pictures together. Wallis had gotten Flynn past weak delivery and self-consciousness and de Havilland past bouts of insincerity and overacting. When Wallis goes independent, the loss is of such magnitude that J.L. never recovers.

Why does Wallis walk away from his home studio? He leaves because of a magnificent, willful show of disrespect by the Boss during the Academy Award ceremony of 1943 when *Casablanca* is announced as winner of Best Picture. "I stood up to accept," says Wallis, "when Jack ran to the

Rumors of impending marriage dog Livvie and her boyfriend of 1944 and '45, Major Joe McKeon, but the bachelorette still can't quite settle down—maybe because Joe isn't a bad enough boy.

stage ahead of me and took the award with a broad, flashing smile and a look of great self-satisfaction. I couldn't believe it was happening. *Casablanca* had been my creation; Jack had absolutely nothing to do with it. As the audience gasped, I tried to get out of the row of seats and into the aisle, but the entire Warner family sat blocking me. I had no alternative but to sit down again, humiliated and furious."[25] Wallis had observed Warner's disrespect of Olivia for years; Wallis will fight in his own way, as she had done.

De Havilland heads deep into the Pacific for her next USO tour, this time to Fiji, where she entertains 3,000 servicemen her first day on the ground. On the second day she contracts a fever and in hours is cut down by viral pneumonia. She spends six weeks in a Fiji hospital among the wounded, and then returns to Hollywood to spend weeks more in bed with a recurrence.

By now she has begun a hot-and-heavy romance with Major Joseph McKeon of the Army Air Corps that seems destined for the altar because, report the fan magazines, "they're always together." These same reporters call McKeon "sincere, thoughtful, and full of integrity," godlike qualities to be sure but not necessarily the bad-boy spice that Livvie needs to see in the mix. McKeon will be shot down over Germany in 1944 and survive his own *Forced Landing*/*Desperate Journey* to be reunited, scarred and limping, with his Hollywood girlfriend in 1945, and *still* Livvie won't agree to settle down and get married.

In February 1945, after spending 18 months away from soundstages and garnering two preliminary victories in court, Livvie is offered the lead in a Paramount Pictures romantic comedy, *The Well-Groomed Bride*, after Paulette Goddard withdraws due to pregnancy. The state Supreme Court has not ruled on her case, so Livvie accepts the Paramount offer sight unseen because of the studio's courage in bucking Jack Warner. But once she reads the script she understands that it's far worse than stories she had read at Warner Bros. Ray Milland is trapped with Livvie in this bit of fluff about the last bottle of champagne in San Francisco, which wraps at the end of March 1945.

A month later, de Havilland's two most fascinating former lovers, Errol and Johnny, go toe-to-toe over the lady, and Livvie is nowhere near the encounter. The date is April 29, 1945, and the place is a David Selznick party. Errol is with Nora and Huston is stag when they meet face-to-face. "I remember we had drinks in our hands," says Huston. Of course each holds a drink; both are drinkers. Both are half in the bag, and both are mean drunks.

Flynn has been waiting a long time for an opportunity with Huston after carrying a chip on his shoulder over the fallout with Livvie and her choice of men, and he has spent a long time preparing the line he will deliver now. It is a line neither Flynn nor Huston will ever repeat, but he delivers it coldly and matter-of-factly, and it probably has something to do with who was sleeping with who and when. Whatever it is, Huston reaches the flash point at once.

"That's a lie!" he rants. "Even if it weren't a lie, only a sonofabitch would repeat it."[26]

Flynn's pithy comeback: "Go fuck yourself."[27]

Huston may be in the bag, but he's wise enough not to damage the home of David O. Selznick. Flynn demurs as well; anywhere else he would already have taken his shot, with breakage likely. They head outside unnoticed, "down to the bottom of the garden—just the two of us," says Huston. "No one knew we'd left the party."

Huston had been an amateur prizefighter, while Flynn hadn't just boxed in his pictures *The Perfect Specimen* and *Gentleman Jim*; he had been a student of the sweet science, studying under welterweight-boxing-champion-turned-Warner-Bros.-grip Mushy Callahan. Neither Errol nor John will go quietly this night.

On a gravel driveway, Flynn's first punch drives Huston to his elbows and knees. Even an Errol Flynn in decline is a worthy opponent. "I was up right away," says Huston, "and I was down again right away; and each time I landed on my elbows. Beginning some months later, and continuing for a period of years, little slivers of bone came out of my right elbow."

Huston describes the fight as the equivalent of John Wayne and Victor McLaglen in *The Quiet Man*, except for the epithets thrown along with the punches. "…'motherfucker' was not a term of endearment," says Huston.

These men, twin souls full of misplaced anger and self-loathing, are fighting themselves as much as each other. Huston will cite with admiration Flynn's sense of honor in the fight. "When I was first knocked down, I rolled, expecting Errol to come at me with his boots. He didn't. He stepped back and waited for me to get up, which I thought rather sporting of him."[28]

Finally they are discovered, and a crowd forms. Selznick is furious, which sobers up the combatants fast—Hollywood people, even drunk and bloody Hollywood people, don't want David O. Selznick to be furious at them. Errol and John realize from the blood and torn clothes just how much damage they have done to each other and, potentially, to their reputations and careers. Flynn lands in one hospital with broken ribs; Huston in another with a broken nose and contusions. The next morning, sober and concerned, Flynn calls Huston to check on him and their conversation reveals a sudden bond produced by the realization that they are very much alike indeed.

Word spreads fast about the fight, and Livvie hears rumors that she had been the cause. She says in tremendous understatement: "That surprised me very much. I don't know what the remark was, but Errol might have tried to provoke John."[29]

Livvie is almost 30, and professionally she has seen tremendous highs and desperate lows. She must wonder by this point if she has made a mistake bucking the system at script-rich Warner Bros., because look what her first outside venture had gotten her: Ray Milland and *The Well-Groomed Bride*. But Paramount's bravery in hiring her, and Livvie's in making the best of a bad script, is rewarded when a new script is messengered over; a script for one of those glossy women's dramas that had been popular in the 1930s with Kay Francis and Barbara Stanwyck—tough girls paying for indiscretions—the kind of picture now about to be reborn with *Mildred Pierce* starring Joan Crawford, which will be made, ironically enough, at Warner Bros.

The script is called *To Each His Own*, and says Livvie: "I knew immediately it was a part I had to do. It was a very long part and it offered a lot of opportunities for an actress."[30] The story is incredible: young small-town girl has a one-night stand with an heroic World War I Army flier that results in a baby she must give up. The flier is killed in the war and she spends the rest of the picture paying for her sins, watching her bastard son grow to manhood from a distance.

Even as Livvie reads the script, "I knew it would be difficult to make a sentimental story such as this believable."[31] The story of *To Each His Own* is indeed gentle and nostalgic, and poles apart from the over-the-top mean-spiritedness of J.L.'s *Mildred Pierce*. Livvie has always sought this type of script—she appears in almost every scene, and her character is shown as a harsh spinster at first, and then revealed through flashbacks as an idealistic teenager and finally a loving mother.

With one offer, de Havilland feels validated for her long battle with J.L. *To Each His Own* becomes a watershed experience, earning her a Best Actress Academy Award. She hits her 30th birthday achieving the kind of professional fulfillment first tasted with *Gone With the Wind*. But back then she had paid such a high price for it—J.L.'s endless punishment. Now, there is no one to answer to, not professionally and not personally.

Her love life has been marked by playing the field and sowing her wild oats. Until Major Joe McKeon, all

In this staged moment, Olivia sits with husband Marcus Goodrich, who casts a wary eye at Livvie's beloved airedale Shadrack (possibly because he had been a gift from John Huston years earlier). Former U.S. Navy Commander Goodrich runs a tight ship, as had Livvie's stepfather G.M. Fontaine. For Marcus, Olivia gives up cigarettes, alcohol, sweets, and career control, until life becomes impossible.

her significant relationships have been with ladies' men—and the two most self-destructive of these have gone at each other, fighting over her.

Next, she accepts a script from the neighbor of Warner Bros., Universal Pictures, and explores film noir. In *A Stolen Life* at Warner Bros., Bette Davis portrays twins, and while *A Stolen Life* is in release, Olivia follows the formula at Universal in the thriller *The Dark Mirror*, also playing twins, one good and one murderously evil. The script and direction are a little shaky, but de Havilland's notices are strong, and now she decides to get away from it all by heading east to fulfill another personal goal, returning to the stage. She takes the lead in *What Every Woman Knows* by James M. Barrie, and in Westport, Connecticut, she begins keeping company with a very proper ad man named Marcus Goodrich, whose main claim to fame has been *Delilah*, a novel published in 1941.

On the road, Livvie is knocked off her pins by news that John Huston has married her old colleague Evelyn Keyes on a whim—this is the same John Huston that Livvie couldn't pin down. Her bearings off, she dumps war hero McKeon and marries Goodrich, whose temperament uncomfortably matches that of G.M. Fontaine—as if this move can somehow disturb Huston.

Eighteen years her senior and a rigid intellectual with a hot and violent temper, Goodrich proceeds to set Hollywood on its ear by his lack of civility, business acumen, and ability to play ball. As the Kafkaesque drama progresses, Livvie gives up liquor, cigarettes, and candy, fires her agent and staff, and makes Marcus her business manager, which further confounds the picture community since the man has no track record at much of anything, least of all at Hollywood career strategy and motion picture contracts.

And now the final plot twist: After they are man and wife, Livvie learns that her new husband has been married four times before—and failed to tell her! Quips Joanie: "It's too bad that Olivia's husband has had so many wives and only one book."[32]

Well! The on-again, off-again sisters are now very much off again. *To Each His Own* earns Livvie her third Academy Award nomination, and on March 13, 1947, she wins the Oscar as Best Actress of 1946. As Livvie walks off the dais holding the hard-earned statuette, Joanie approaches her with outstretched hand. Livvie does an about-face and hurries off muttering, "I don't know why she does that when she knows how I feel?"[33] Winning the Academy Award is Livvie's most profound professional moment, the culmination of everything she has worked for—with the exultation wrapped in a personal disaster as Joan insists on muscling into the spotlight.

And yet, Livvie's travails are a picnic compared to the life of Errol Flynn, who seems to make a concerted effort to sabotage production after production. His behavior exasperates the Boss, who tries to appeal to Flynn's professionalism, and then his pride, and then his pocketbook. But in the end J.L. does nothing because, against all odds, Errol Flynn pictures continue to attract stacks of cash.

So the years pass and Flynn drinks, Flynn uses drugs, and Flynn watches his career slip and slide and his looks melt into the Mulholland carpet. His second novel, *Showdown*, is released to decent sales but unkind reviews. He makes a series of mostly undistinguished pictures, all at Warner Bros., the most important of which is a swashbuckling, Technicolor homage to the Flynn persona, *Adventures of Don Juan*, an exercise in how not to make a motion pic-

Far from the elegant couple seen in 1945, Nora seems to have been crying and tension is etched in Errol's face as they sit in the restaurant of the Ambassador East Hotel in Chicago on May 20, 1948. Their tortured relationship has only months to live.

ture that witnesses the breakdown of the star and of the director, Vincent Sherman, in a production that takes four times longer than normal to complete. Despite its problems, the final film is beautiful and lush, and Flynn's charm and characterization provide a bittersweet glimpse into the life of a man who is trapped inside his reputation, a man who has doomed himself to loneliness and unfulfillment.

In *Adventures of Don Juan*, the famous lover returns to Spain and there falls in love with his ideal, a woman he cannot have, the Queen, played by Swedish actress Viveca Lindfors. Don Juan knows that if they stay together, unhappiness will result. The theme mirrors his own life and the women he adores completely, women he respects too much to marry and disappoint, Ann Sheridan and Ida Lupino— and just perhaps, Olivia de Havilland.

Lindfors sees the tragedy in her co-star and compares Errol to Marilyn Monroe, believing that he was "taken advantage of by the studio for his charm, his sex appeal, his body, as much as she was; and he was as vulnerable as she and knew as little as she about how to defend himself against the system. He ended up in his own little beauty-box prison, just as she did. And he drank himself to death to get out of there."[34]

Flynn's last lavish swashbuckler, *Adventures of Don Juan*, is the Warner Christmas release of 1948. Here Errol portrays himself—the world-weary globe-trotting lover. Leading lady Viveca Lindfors brings a sweet vulnerability to her role of Queen Margaret of Spain, who is moved to passion by Don Juan. Lindfors sees up close the tragedy of a man slowly drinking himself to death because he can no longer stand to *be* Errol Flynn.

Says former child actor Dean Stockwell, who will work with Flynn the next year: "He was what he was: a truly profound, non-superficial sex symbol." Stockwell also calls him "the ultimate father figure."[35]

Unlike Flynn, de Havilland lives within her means and doesn't feel the need to serve the system and churn out the pictures. She waits for good roles: "Does that person interest me?" she explains. "Do I want to live that person? To express that person? To communicate that person to an audience. That's the basis on which I choose a part."[36]

Livvie's interest in the art of character is rewarded again, this time when Twentieth Century-Fox approaches her to portray a mentally ill young woman named Virginia Cunningham in a new project, *The Snake Pit*. Says Tony Thomas, "...in 1948 it was more than a brave venture: It was highly risky as screen entertainment for the masses and the first time the subject of mental illness was treated in an intelligent and extended fashion in Hollywood."[37]

In preparation, she reads *The Psychology of Insanity* by Bernard Hart, recommended by hubby Marcus, and visits psychiatric wards. There she meets a patient who "had developed a relationship with her doctor, such as Virginia had…. Like Virginia Cunningham, the patient was, too, very engaging and very appealing and it never occurred to me before that someone suffering from so severe a mental malady could be those things."[38] While Flynn is pulling his old stunts at the old studio—calling in sick often, retreating to his boat, banging female extras in his dressing room, and drinking himself into a stupor on set and off—de Havilland is throwing herself into good work and doing it well. *The Snake Pit* is engaging from the start as it tosses the audience into the middle of Virginia's insanity and then together all solve the mystery of the madness. Comic touches infuse Livvie's characterization with sympathy, and soon she has earned another Best Actress Academy Award nomination, as well as a New York Film Critics Award. When accepting this one, she is forced to pose for pictures with the Best Director of 1948, John Huston, who wins for *The Treasure of the Sierra Madre*.

The next year she hits her peak as an actress, proving her skill by successfully capturing in *The*

Heiress the magnificent personal growth of her character, Catherine Sloper, opposite Ralph Richardson and Montgomery Clift. Her fifth Academy Award nomination results in a second Oscar as Best Actress. There is no doubt now: Livvie had been right to buck the system. She has blazed the trail for new generations of actors who will be free to make the pictures they want to, in deals negotiated project by project. She has helped to shape life after the studio system for all involved in the business.

But after several very good moves, Livvie makes a bad one. Director Elia Kazan offers her the role of Blanche Dubois in *A Streetcar Named Desire*, soon to commence shooting at Warner Bros. But de Havilland feels no desire to return to Burbank and no sympathy for Blanche, believing her to be "psychologically unsound." She says, "Elia Kazan wanted to see me and discuss it with me. He wrote me a letter, but I wouldn't see him. I said, 'Nothing's going to change my mind.'"[39] Ironically, de Havilland's old colleague Vivien Leigh will get the part and the resulting Best Actress Academy Award will revive Leigh's flagging career.

A few miles of hairpin turns away from Livvie's apartment, Errol Flynn of Mulholland Farm continues his downward spiral. By early 1949 his union with Nora, which has taken on water for years, finally sinks. Scripts keep coming at Flynn and Flynn keeps showing up at Warner Bros., despite his utter disinterest, only because he needs the money. His yacht, farm, two ex-wives, and three children are expensive! In 1949 he travels to India to make a picture on loanout to MGM, and on the trip home meets Irene Ghika, a leggy Romanian teenager of royal lineage. He brings Irene back to the United States just as he had brought back 19-year-old Blanca Welter seven years earlier.

A few months later, in May 1950, on location for his new picture, *Rocky Mountain*, he becomes interested in singer-actress Patrice Wymore, young, long-legged, and not at all interested in Flynn. Errol, Irene, and Patrice are observed in a hotel bar on location in New Mexico by Ivan Hayes, one of Flynn's pals. "Pat's very tall and blind as a bat. In person, without makeup, she's quite plain and very

For short stretches, Flynn could shake free of depression, clean himself up, and fly right. Here he dances with another conquest, tall, redheaded Patrice Wymore, wife number three.

shy. She was never one of the guys. I was surprised because Errol liked his women to be one of the guys, and she wasn't like that. She didn't respond to him the way most women did. I spent half the night in the bar and saw them together, but I thought she was rather standoffish. I was stunned, but maybe that was it with him—the thing that you can't have, you want. Irene was 19, and a gorgeous brunette, and adored him, but he just couldn't keep still."

Hayes confirms of Flynn and his women, "With Errol it's the chase. I understand it because I'm that way. I enjoy Porsche automobiles, and they're never as good when you get them as you think they're going to be when you want them. Errol said to me, 'I like going after things. Even as a little boy, I would want something and get it and then want something else.'"[40]

Following his old pattern, Flynn begins an ardent pursuit of the disdainful Patrice Wymore, 17 years his junior, then doesn't know what to do with Pat when she becomes Mrs. Errol Flynn number three a few months later in Marseilles. And just now, embarking on a new life, Flynn's

187

world collapses house-of-cards-like. Independent productions go wrong—including *Adventures of Captain Fabian*, *Crossed Swords*, and his CinemaScope gamble, *William Tell*—back taxes come due, alimony piles up, and his business manager dies, revealing in correspondence that he has been ripping Flynn off for years.

A desperate Errol packs up, leaves his beloved Mulholland Farm behind, and seeks exile in Europe with the new Mrs. Flynn at just about the time that Livvie has had enough of the controlling Marcus Goodrich and files for divorce. Like nearly all the other stars of the Golden Era, her career has hit the skids—the time in the sun after the de Havilland Decision had been too brief.

It is a period of sweeping change in Hollywood and at Warner Bros., where J.L. divests himself of all his one-time superstars. By 1950 the headache-producing Bette Davis and cantankerous Humphrey Bogart are gone. Budgets for Joan Crawford's pictures are reduced. The Boss sticks with Flynn longer than anybody and provides the aging swashbuckler with one last opportunity to wield a sword in a Technicolor adventure, *The Master of Ballantrae*, shot in England in 1953.

"These actors who were so anxious to get out of Warners," says John McElwee, "Cagney and Davis—it was disastrous when they left. With de Havilland, if she had just bided her time and played out her contract, she could have made a much smoother transition to someplace else and might have been better off."[41]

As an independent, she *has* made good pictures and cemented her place in Hollywood history with two quick Oscars, but, inevitably, the new reality catches up with Livvie. Good screen roles dwindle, so she turns to the stage, where a different crop of reviewers from the theater notice her limited range and note that she isn't up to the roles she takes on, including Juliet on Broadway.

"With Olivia de Havilland taking the long step from Hollywood for her Broadway debut as Juliet," writes the New York *Times*, "...her intensity comes and goes through her acting in a thin and mechanical ripple. Her performance is poorly paced; she reaches her height of feeling early, and she has nowhere to go thereafter except beyond controlled reality into wild and breathy protests."[42] *Time* magazine says simply, "For Hollywood's Olivia de Havilland Juliet was a gallant try but a double miss. She is neither a good enough actress nor a magical enough Juliet."[43]

That's the thing with de Havilland—she *does* make the gallant try, embracing the challenge of her craft and sometimes paying a price for it, but pushing ahead to the next challenge without second guessing.

In 1953, Flynn is in Italy making his own gallant try with the CinemaScope epic, *William Tell*, which will be his last stand as an independent producer. At the same time, de Havilland receives an invitation from the Academy of Motion Picture Arts and Sciences to attend the Cannes Film Festival. As a two-time Oscar recipient, she is offered the opportunity to present a special Academy Award in France to aged Henri Chretien, inventor of the CinemaScope lens that had so altered the history of the motion picture.

"I'd never been to France," she remembers, "and I'd never been to a festival, and after a fifth of a second of solemn deliberation I decided to accept."[44] In Paris she meets Pierre Galante, an executive editor of the Paris *Match*, and Galante begins an intercontinental pursuit of Livvie that blossoms into romance and concludes with a French wedding, the birth of daughter Gisele to go with son (by Marcus) Benjy, and life in exile as a Parisian housewife.

"By then," she says, "the Hollywood I knew was gone; ...television was casting a terrible shadow on the film industry, which was disintegrating. You can't imagine how depressing life was here in the early '50s. Studios that had made 75 pictures a year were making 10. It was no longer the Hollywood I knew.... I was lucky. I had the good luck of being driven out of Hollywood by the disintegration of the business. The luck of being in Paris."[45]

Her performance as one-eyed Ana de Mendoza in the medieval costume picture *That Lady* is poorly received, and her next film, the medical drama, *Not as a Stranger*, comes and goes. By this time Livvie welcomes the safety of exile in France with her new husband. Flynn is already hiding out in Europe, having lost the remainder of his meager fortune making *William Tell*, which falls apart in mid-production. For Flynn the low point is seeing his family's clothes seized to pay back wages for actor Bruce Cabot—even Errol's best friend now turns on him.

Vagabonding through Europe, one of Flynn's stops with Patrice and their infant daughter, Arnella, is Bad

Soden, Germany. There an ardent, 20-year-old fan, Gertrud Seipmann, hangs out in a hotel lobby holding a bouquet of flowers for her hero, Errol Flynn. She waits a long time to spot him: "Finally, when I was almost ready to give up, a couple came down a long corridor, towards the lobby where I was standing. I recognized Patrice immediately. Pert and pretty, beautifully dressed, carrying the baby. I did not recognize Flynn at first. He was taller than I had imagined him, and much thinner—almost frail looking. His face was still beautiful, but so unexpectedly sad and weary that it shocked me—and broke my heart. I caught his eye and his face brightened, for just a moment. He smiled at me and I smiled back. And then he was gone, and I stood there for a long time with my wilted flowers, tears welling up and quietly running down my cheeks."[46]

Errol Flynn has become a heartbroken shell of himself. He goes on to make pictures in England and elsewhere, ever so slowly climbing out of the financial hole with a dedication that shows, for the bad boy, remarkable maturity and restraint. In 1956 he appreciates an offer received from Universal to return to Hollywood and resume his career as a leading man in the CinemaScope adventure drama, *Istanbul*, and then he appears in supporting roles in two Darryl F. Zanuck epics, *The Sun Also Rises*, set in Spain, and *The Roots of Heaven*, set in Africa. Errol makes these pictures as an excuse to kill time, to travel to exotic locations, and to make a quick buck. His soul is no longer in the business, and his health is shot, with cirrhosis of the liver, heart attacks, a broken back, and cancer of the mouth—all in a man of 48.

Late in 1957, Olivia de Havilland returns to Hollywood also needing to earn a living. She appears in her first picture in two years, *The Proud Rebel* for Samuel Goldwyn Jr. This western is directed by her old antagonist, Mike Curtiz, now tamed by cancer that confines him to a wheelchair.

An event hosted by *The Proud Rebel* costume department will produce the last act in the 22-year-long drama between Olivia de Havilland and Errol Flynn. Jowly, paunchy but still proud Flynn is appearing in the Diana Barrymore biopic, *Too Much, Too Soon*, at—of all places—Warner Bros. of Burbank.

Says J.L., "When we talked about casting the role of John Barrymore, who had literally boozed himself into the grave, I immediately thought of Errol. Frankly, I missed his gaiety and taunting laughter and the excitement he generated on the set."

So Flynn sets foot on his old home lot once again, and the Boss is devastated by what he sees. "I could not bear to watch him struggle through take after take. The once strong and handsome face was puffy and gray, the dancing shimmer was gone from his eyes, and there was no longer a spring in his step.... He was one of the living dead."[47]

In this frame of mind, Flynn spots the last great conquest in his legendary love life. She is a natural blonde, dark-eyed dancer with legs up to here and killer ankles, glimpsed as she walks among the soundstages. Flynn guesses she can't be much older than 18, which is fine because he likes them young now more than ever. In no time he swoops in and snaps up luscious Beverly Aadland, discovering in short order that she is an early blooming 15-year-old actress wannabe. For two years they will be inseparable and live under a cloud of scandal everywhere in the world that they travel. So self-destructive is Flynn at this time, so uncaring of his personal and professional reputation, that he will promote himself as the "ideal actor" to portray Professor Humbert Humbert in the film version of Vladimir Nabokov's controversial novel *Lolita*, with Aadland in the starring role.[48]

While *Too Much, Too Soon* is still in production, Flynn happens to hear of a party for *The Proud Rebel* across town and decides in his booze-soaked haze that it would be fun to surprise his one-time love, Olivia. Errol doesn't remember, or no longer cares about, the whatever-it-was that had caused their estrangement more than 15 years earlier. Still the swashbuckling soldier of fortune, he makes a grand entrance at *The Proud Rebel* party and charms the revelers as all await Livvie's fashionably late arrival.

In a short while, the lady makes her entrance. What does Flynn notice first—that she is in some ways better looking than ever? That she is a smaller woman than he remembers, and a more shapely one? That she has more grace? That she is the same bundle of energy, with a firm step, wide smile, and those giant, inviting brown eyes? He wastes no time making his move, staging one more practical joke, just like that day at the lake when he put the snake in her pantalettes.

Still quite the dish at 42, de Havilland poses for publicity stills in support of *The Proud Rebel*. This well-cared-for face stared into *that* face (opposite) in shock, wondering what in the world had happened to her old flame.

"As I was walking in," says Olivia, "somebody kissed the back of my neck. I whirled around in anger and said, 'Do I know you?'"[49] In most accounts, the pint-sized Livvie does a quick 180 and slaps the tall stranger.

"It's Errol," says the stunned man, red-faced and rocking on his heels.

"He had changed so much," she says. "His eyes were so sad. I had stared into them in enough movies to know his spirit was gone. They used to be full of mischief, with little brown and green glints. They were totally different. I didn't recognize the person behind the eyes."[50]

She will invite him to lunch out of guilt over the slap, and they will sit and talk of old times for a couple of hours, and for a time at least get beyond whatever issue had led to their secret estrangement in 1942. But in short order she heads back to Paris, and Flynn takes off for Africa to make a film version of the popular novel *The Roots of Heaven* for, of all people, John Huston. With Flynn nearing 50 and Huston just past it, neither man is up to fistfights, and in equatorial Africa they become friends in the course of surviving a brutal months-long shoot in 130-degree heat that boils up sunstroke and dysentery and makes location work for *The Charge of the Light Brigade* look like a literal and figurative picnic. Huston's fondest memory of the experience is allowing Errol to go on safari—only if he promises to cut the boozing and drugs.

Says Huston: "Often we'd come back to camp from a long haul and there would be Errol, not drunk, and all excitement over his day. I thanked heaven I'd taken him. I do to this day."[51] Flynn will not be shy in saying that he has the time of his life on safari with John Huston in Africa.

The next year, in the autumn of 1959, Livvie takes her son Benjy and daughter Gisele to see *The Adventures of Robin Hood* at a theater in Paris—a picture she had gone to great lengths to avoid in April 1938. "I was sort of afraid to see it," she says. "You know, you are always afraid of not being any good, terrified of it. So I hadn't seen that film, and…my son was 10 years old, and…it was a Saturday afternoon and I didn't know what to do with him, what amusement to arrange for him, so I took him to see *Robin Hood*.… I thought the film was adorable. I had no idea it was so good. It was enchanting and I thought, good gracious, it's a classic, it really is a classic! When we made those films we had no idea what we were making, that we were making the best of their kind."

She and her children sit through the picture twice, and she hurries home and pens a letter to Errol. "I said, 'If you haven't seen the film recently, run it. You will be so proud of it, so glad that you *were* Robin Hood.' Then I thought perhaps I shouldn't send it. It's sentimental. Perhaps I shouldn't, and I didn't."[52]

Errol and Beverly have been in Jamaica, collaborating with writer Earl Conrad on Flynn's memoirs. The experience has been horrible for Errol. Once he had been able to write. It had never been easy, but he had coaxed two books out of himself in the old days, and now the words will not come, which necessitates Conrad's involvement.

Dictating his story, he reveals the intensity of his feelings for co-star Olivia de Havilland. He speaks of her warmly; there are not many warm remembrances in his memoirs of the women he has known. The affection he reveals is the essence of courtly love. "Olivia was lovely—and distant," he says. He recounts his practical jokes and adolescent behavior and sums it up by saying, "I had a lot to learn about the sensibilities of young ladies."[53]

Livvie will say at various times after reading of his love for her in *My Wicked, Wicked Ways* that she had been unaware of the depth of his feelings. The decades are bound to dim the recollections of the moment he proposed to her and she rebuffed him until such time as he had rid himself of Lili; of the jealousy he had displayed on the set of *Santa Fe Trail*; of the key moment she learned that he had gone to bat for her with Warner; of the "afternoon delight" at the studio. All had been expressions of Errol's deep feelings for Olivia, and hers for him.

While still working out the details of his autobiography with Conrad, Flynn and his paramour go adventuring in Cuba with a young upstart named Fidel Castro who is fighting The Man, the dictator Batista then in charge of the island nation. In Flynn's eyes Castro is a hero who will soon bring freedom and democracy to the Cuban people. In Castro's eyes Flynn is a washed-up dupe who is ripe for manipulation. The unbalanced situation results in Errol Flynn making a mockery of his own reputation by backing a future dictator. He goes on television in the States, on many talk shows and game shows, and speaks glowingly of Cuban revolutionaries who will soon prove to be Marxist Communists. Right about now, diseased, bankrupt again, and dying, he could use a friendly word of the kind that de Havilland had penned.

"I wish I had sent that letter," says Livvie. "It would have pleased him after all those years, but I didn't."

A few weeks later, at home in Paris, the telephone rings.

"Miss de Havilland?" says a French journalist. "We have some very sad news."

"What is it?"

"Your partner, Errol Flynn, is dead."

The memories kaleidoscope before her. The first test, Lake Sherwood, the Cocoanut Grove, necking on the *Robin Hood* balcony, Modesto, the train ride out of Needles, and that beautiful scene when Lt. Custer proposes to Libbie. *It all just happened! It was all just yesterday!*

She says, "I felt a great sense of grief and loss."[55]

But of all the memories, the last are by far the most unsettling—a 15-year estrangement, and then slapping his face, and melting into shocked, tortured eyes. Those sad brown eyes of Errol's will always haunt her as she lives for five more decades, and beyond.

When Olivia spun on her heel and looked up into the face of the man who had kissed her neck, this is what she saw; hardly the dashing visage of Robin Hood. She felt that the life was gone from his eyes; J.L. noted that those once-vibrant eyes had lost their "dancing shimmer."

191

By 1964 Olivia had been swept up in the new cynicism of the picture business that brought back aging leading ladies to take on garish roles in thrillers like *Hush Hush, Sweet Charlotte* and *Lady in a Cage*. She would lament in her book that Old Hollywood was gone.

11 LIFE AFTER FLYNN

Olivia de Havilland remains in Paris through the funeral of Flynn. J.L. of all people eulogizes Errol at a modest Forest Lawn ceremony that may compel Errol to turn over even before he reaches the grave. He had wanted to be buried in Jamaica, not in Hollywood, and the last guy he would giving a sentimental speech over his powerless-to-resist body is The Man, Jack L. Warner.

It's now the time of television, and the Boss has been embracing the medium with successful westerns like *Cheyenne* and *Maverick*. In 1956 Jack had snookered honest, hard-working brothers Harry and Al out of their shares of Warner Bros.—neither would ever speak to him again. Then a car crash had almost killed J.L. in 1958, but he hadn't approved that particular script, so he pulls through to wax rhapsodic over his old nemesis Flynn and to reign over an ever-nimble studio. He secures a hit with *My Fair Lady* in 1964 and is dubbed the Last of the Moguls because he has stayed in power longer than Mayer, Cohn, Selznick, and the others, but finally the magic runs out for Jack Warner with screen versions of the musicals *Camelot* and *1776* amidst what may have been early Alzheimer's. He leaves Warner Bros. in 1969 and sells 1.6 million shares of stock to Seven Arts Productions for $32 million. But he has little time to enjoy his money or retirement; J.L.'s health declines through the 1970s and the Last of the Moguls takes his final breath on September 9, 1978.

Warner's former right-hand-man-turned-independent-producer Hal Wallis fares better than the Boss. Wallis leaves Burbank with the levelheadedness that had made stars and produces dozens of profitable pictures with Martin and Lewis, Elvis Presley, and John Wayne, including *True Grit*, which earns the Duke an Oscar as Best Actor. Hal Wallis never gets over J.L.'s *Casablanca* stunt, and Wallis notes in his 1980 autobiography *Starmaker* that even though he had made Warner Bros. millions by crafting a catalog of strong pictures, "Jack wrote a very lengthy anecdotal memoir [*My First Hundred Years in Hollywood*] without once mentioning my name."[1]

Hal Wallis dies one month after his 87th birthday, outliving Jack Warner by eight years.

One of the Boss's misguided moves had been to sell all his pre-1950 pictures to the company that would become United Artists for what amounts to a song. The move will both relieve the studio of vaults of old celluloid and estrange Jack from brother Harry. Then, as the sands of popular culture shift, cynical, hard-as-brass Humphrey Bogart and upstart James Cagney are re-discovered by the intellectual crowd and live again in revival houses. In 1976 United Artists realizes it has a gold mine in its cans of old features and stages a grand theatrical re-release of a package of Warner Bros. pictures, including many starring Errol Flynn and Olivia de Havilland, in seven U.S. cities over eleven weeks. To mark the event, radiant Livvie is brought across the pond to pose before a giant, smirking portrait of Flynn in New York.

A few years later, after many books had already appeared on Flynn, a biographer seeking to sell out the first run at any cost uses the fact that a dead person can't be slandered to claim that Errol (who couldn't see past the nearest pretty pair of ankles or concentrate on any task to save his life) had been a spy for the Germans and Japanese during World War II. The evidence? Flynn had been pals with Dr. Hermann Erben, who had indeed belonged to the Nazi Party. So, circumstantially, Flynn is presumed guilty. Among those springing to Flynn's defense in a broad counterattack that includes friends, British dignitaries, Nazi hunters, and the U.S. government, is Olivia de Havilland.

From 1938 through 1940 she had been exasperated with Flynn and at wit's end. Beginning in the 1970s, she reexamines the man she had cursed in 1940, given up in 1942, and slapped in 1957. The world now seems to be turning on a different axis. Olivia's work is fading into cinema history, but the force of Flynn's personality, and yes, his talent, is proving more durable. Where once she had been loathe to speak his name because of embarrassment over endless roles as the love interest in those juvenile Flynn pictures, so devoid of prestige, now she begins to look back warmly, with time-tempered affection and an understanding that revisiting the memories of Errol Flynn is a way to keep their love alive. After Flynn's death, her career continues in a variety of pictures—beautiful pictures like *Light in the Piazza*; brutal pictures like *Lady in a Cage* and *Hush, Hush, Sweet Charlotte*; ill-conceived pictures like *The Adventurers*, *The Swarm*, and *The Fifth Musketeer*.

Olivia will take up writing, as Errol had done, and release an effervescent memoir in 1962 entitled *Every Frenchman Has One*, about the culture shock of leaving Hollywood for Paris. She will also write lively articles for magazines. She begins to contemplate an autobiography that spans her career, as Flynn and Warner had done. Errol's book had revealed his soul, while J.L.'s memoir had only stumbled on the truth as if in the dark, by accident.

Livvie begins to mention her autobiography in interviews, but Joanie beats her to the punch with the candid *No Bed of Roses* in 1978. After that the gears in de Havilland's brain begin to grind. She sequesters herself in hotel rooms and writes, and then misses her deadline for submitting a first draft to Dutton on December 31, 1980. She asks for more time to complete what is "a far bigger project than I had realized." She declares to the Los Angeles *Times* that, "It's going to take a long time." Obviously Flynn will be an important element of her book; she admits to Mann, "... for three years I don't suppose I thought of anyone else."[2]

More years go by and no autobiography appears. This author asks in 1986 if she would like help getting the memoir together. She doesn't want to talk about it because she's superstitious, but does allow, "It is a project, like *Every Frenchman Has One*, which will be entirely my own."[3] Thirty years after her missed Dutton deadline, there is still no memoir.

She does, however, revisit in the flesh her association with John Huston,

The lovers make a rare appearance together in New York City in June 1976 to kick off a multi-city Warner Bros. festival of classic pictures.

for whom she has carried a torch for two decades. In January 1967 she reaches out to him in a note that recounts her experience at seeing the new release, *The Bible*: "...I heard your voice. It was an extraordinary experience, for no one had told me that you had done the soundtrack, and, of course, with the first word I knew it was you speaking. It brought back, with a rush, the year of 1942 and the Aleutians, and the film you made there, that beautiful film, and 'I've Got Sixpence,' and your voice on the soundtrack for that picture, and, well, many things. I hope all goes well with you—I always have, I always will."[4]

This note leads Huston to invite her to visit him in Ireland. Olivia's marriage to Pierre is now over, "And I went. For five days—I only lasted three. And I escaped. So I think, although I didn't have my heart's greatest desire, which was marriage with him..., I was lucky."[5]

John Huston, three years older than Flynn, goes on to outlive him by almost 30 years, and takes great pride in brawling with Errol and later becoming his friend. And like Flynn, he would never find lasting happiness with any single woman, including Olivia de Havilland.

Neither could Livvie have made a go of it with Huston any more than she could have with the mercurial Flynn, who always scanned the horizon for his next bedmate and who was an unhappy soul, as she was at times an unhappy soul. In fact, looking back on her life, and considering her relationships with Jimmy Stewart, and Joe McKeon, and two husbands, and her first great love, Flynn, and her second, Huston, she would ultimately admit, "I don't think there was anyone I did meet or could have met with whom I could have had a lasting marriage."[6]

Olivia has by far had the most to say about Flynn, of all her men, and over the generations her reminiscences have been painted in ever warmer hues. "What I felt for Errol Flynn was not a trivial matter at all," she tells an Irish newspaper in June 2009. "I felt terribly attracted to him. And do you know, I still feel it? I still feel very close to him to this day."[7] Why such an admission for a man she had not seen for years when he was alive? A man from whom she was secretly estranged for 15 years?

Perhaps their last picture together and the genuine friendship it engendered conquers all. Perhaps their physical relationship means more in retrospect than she realized at the time. Perhaps the slap had produced guilt she has never reconciled. Or just perhaps she recognizes now how alike she and Flynn always were—each wounded by a domineering parent; each living successfully but unhappily; each unsuccessful at marriage; and each a wandering soul tossed about by the Hollywood system.

Whatever the reason, Olivia now remembers Errol in vivid Technicolor and holds him in high esteem, right up there with Melanie Hamilton and *Gone With the Wind*. As she says, putting their relationship in perspective: "...We *did* have a life together, as Peter Blood and Arabella Bishop, as Maid Marian and Robin Hood, as General Custer and his Libbie, and those were happy lives, and perhaps that was enough."[8] For a person inclined to exhibit control over that which cannot be controlled, what else can she say?

She looks back now over a great distance at a time when two young Hollywood stars created magic onscreen—sometimes against their wills—and couldn't begin to handle life together off it. In a sense they both squandered their salad days in the picture business and *went Hollywood* at just the wrong time, making themselves, and those around them, miserable. But for the span of six years they were, and remain today for what survives onscreen, a beautiful and romantic couple for the ages.

Says Flynn historian Michael Mazzone: "I feel frustration that in the body of their work, all their films, only in the last one are they a married couple, sitting down, eating a meal together, going through life together. In eight pictures, they only did it *that one time*."[9]

Maybe Warner and Wallis had it right all along—with these two sexy kids, the chase was the thing. And the kids believed it too, until they finally realized that neither was the answer for the other. They would live the remainder of their lives melancholy over this fact, and go on loving each other, because the ultimate reality is that each could say, *We'll always have Paris*. Paris to Errol and Olivia would include many happy memories to offset the sour notes, and of course they would always have the summer of 1941 when Errol had gone to bat for Olivia and turned real-life hero, and she had let herself love him all over again for doing it, and allowed herself to understand, finally, the pressures he felt *being* Errol Flynn. That love had endured for his lifetime, and it has endured for hers.

End Notes

Chapter 1: Voyages to Port Royal
1. Errol Flynn. *My Wicked, Wicked Ways.*
2. Academy of Achievement. "The Last Belle of Cinema: Olivia de Havilland Interview."
3. Joan Fontaine. *No Bed of Roses.*
4. Academy of Achievement.
5. Hedda Hopper. Olivia de Havilland interview, raw transcript, September 10, 1952.
6. Errol Flynn letters to Mary White, 1922.
7. John Hammond Moore. *The Young Errol: Flynn Before Hollywood.*
8. Fontaine. *No Bed of Roses.*
9. Hopper. De Havilland interview.
10. Fontaine. *No Bed of Roses.*
11. Lilian de Havilland. *Motion Picture.* 1947.
12. Fontaine. *No Bed of Roses.*
13. Moore. *The Young Errol.*
14. Academy of Achievement.
15. Hopper. De Havilland interview.
16. Fontaine. *No Bed of Roses.*
17. Richard G. Hubler. "Olivia—the Bellicose Belle." *Coronet,* July 1958.
18. Academy of Achievement.
19. Moore. *The Young Errol.*
20. Gerry Connelly. *Errol Flynn in Northampton.*
21. Connelly. *Errol Flynn in Northampton.*
22. Tony Thomas, Rudy Behlmer, and Clifford McCarty. *The Films of Errol Flynn.*
23. Turner Home Entertainment. *The Adventures of Errol Flynn* [Documentary]. 2005.
24. Academy of Achievement.
25. Academy of Achievement.
26. Academy of Achievement.
27. James V. D'Arc. "Perfect Manners: An Interview with Olivia de Havilland." *American Classic Screen,* January/February 1979.
28. Tony Thomas. *The Films of Olivia de Havilland.*
29. Robert Matzen. Rudy Behlmer interview, January 27, 2010.
30. Hal Wallis. *Starmaker.*
31. Hal Wallis memo to William Dieterle, February 15, 1935.
32. Wallis memo to Henry Blanke, March 7, 1935.
33. Flynn. *My Wicked, Wicked Ways.*
34. Flynn. *My Wicked, Wicked Ways.*
35. Flynn. *My Wicked, Wicked Ways.*
36. Thomas. *The Films of Olivia de Havilland.*
37. Academy of Achievement.
38. Thomas. *The Films of Olivia de Havilland.*

Chapter 2: The Coup de Foudre
1. Harry Joe Brown memo to Wallis, June 11, 1935.
2. Jack Warner memo to Hal Wallis, April 16, 1935.
3. Wallis memo to Michael Curtiz, June 20, 1935.
4. Warner memo to Wallis.
5. Jack L. Warner. *My First Hundred Years in Hollywood.*
6. Wallis. *Starmaker.*
7. Academy of Achievement.
8. Thomas. *The Films of Olivia de Havilland.*
9. Robert Matzen. Michael Mazzone interview, April 1, 2010.
10. "Nothing Short of a Miracle." *Silver Screen,* March 1937.
11. Leon Surmelian. "She's No Unkissed Peach." *Picture Play,* February 1938.
12. Hal Boyle. "Actress Olivia de Havilland with Fame at Her Feet Still has Problem." Orlando *Evening Star,* March 11, 1965.
13. Flynn. *My Wicked, Wicked Ways.*
14. Marjorie Pierce. "Olivia de Havilland Returns to Saratoga." San Jose *Mercury,* October 18, 1979.
15. Wallis memo to Curtiz, September 9, 1935.
16. James R. Silke. *Here's Looking at You, Kid.*
17. Wallis memo to Curtiz, August 27, 1935.
18. Wallis memo to Curtiz, August 27, 1935.
19. Wallis memo to Curtiz, August 28, 1935.
20. Wallis memo to George Amy, September 4, 1935.
21. Wallis memo to Curtiz, August 28, 1935.
22. Wallis memo to Curtiz, September 4, 1935.
23. Wallis memo to Koenig, September 10, 1935.
24. Wallis memo to Brown, September 10, 1935.
25. Wallis memo to Koenig, September 19, 1935.
26. Wallis memo to Curtiz, September 30, 1935.
27. Wallis memo to Curtiz, September 30, 1935.
28. Wallis. *Starmaker.*
29. Wallis memo to Harry Joe Brown, November 7, 1935.
30. Wallis memo to Koenig, October 24, 1935.

Chapter 3: Flashman and the Lady
1. Errol Flynn. *Beam Ends.*
2. Moore. *The Young Errol.*
3. Wallis telegram to Warner, March 3, 1936.
4. Mary Decker. "Taking Everything in Stride." *Motion Picture,* January 1937.
5. James Reid. "Can Hollywood Hold Errol Flynn?" *Motion Picture,* August 1936.

6. Michael Sheridan. "Objectively Olivia." *Motion Picture*, October 1946.
7. American Film Institute (AFI). "Dialogue on Film: Olivia de Havilland." December 1974.
8. Matzen. Rudy Behlmer interview.
9. Warner telegram to Wallis, March 27, 1936.
10. Rowland Leigh memo to Wallis, March 28, 1936.
11. David Niven. *Bring on the Empty Horses*.
12. Wallis. *Starmaker*.
13. Flynn. *My Wicked, Wicked Ways*.
14. Frank Mattison production report, April 1936.
15. Warner memo to Wallis, March 10, 1936.
16. Mattison production report, April 1936.
17. Wallis memo to Curtiz, April 17, 1936.
18. Sheridan. "Objectively Olivia."
19. AFI.
20. Dinah Shore. Olivia de Havilland interview. *Dinah!*, 1977.
21. Flynn. *My Wicked, Wicked Ways*.
22. Niven. *Bring on the Empty Horses*.
23. D'Arc. "Perfect Manners."
24. "The Charge of the Light Brigade." *Hollywood*. September 1936.
25. Judith M. Kass. *Olivia de Havilland*.
26. Gladys Hall. *Modern Screen*, March 1937.
27. Wallis memo to Curtiz, June 26, 1936.

Chapter 4: The Big Dance
1. Tony Thomas. *From a Life of Adventure: The Writings of Errol Flynn*.
2. Thomas McNulty. *The Life and Career of Errol Flynn*.
3. Flynn. *My Wicked, Wicked Ways*.
4. Matzen. Rudy Behlmer interview.
5. Josef Fegerl. *Errol Flynn & Dr. Hermann F. Erben: A Friendship of Two Adventurers 1933-1940*.
6. Errol Flynn. Diary from the Spanish Civil War. Unpublished.
7. Flynn. Spanish diary.
8. McNulty. *The Life and Career of Errol Flynn*.
9. Flynn. Spanish diary.
10. Flynn. Spanish diary.
11. Flynn. Spanish diary.
12. Flynn. Spanish diary.
13. Errol Flynn. "What Really Happened to Me in Spain. *Photoplay*, July 1937.
14. Flynn. "What Really Happened to Me in Spain."
15. Flynn. "What Really Happened to Me in Spain."
16. Hedda Hopper collection. Academy of Motion Pictures Arts and Sciences.
17. Shore. De Havilland interview.
18. Shore. De Havilland interview.
19. Flynn. *My Wicked, Wicked Ways*.
20. Niven. *Bring on the Empty Horses*.
21. Shore. De Havilland interview.
22. Dotson Rader. "Rewards and Regrets: Olivia de Havilland Talks About Montgomery Clift, Errol Flynn and Herself." *Parade*, September 7, 1986.
23. Turner. *The Adventures of Errol Flynn*.
24. Rudy Behlmer. *Inside Warner Bros. (1935-1951)*.
25. Robert Matzen. Robert Florczak interview, October 24, 2009.

26. Behlmer. *Inside Warner Bros.*
27. Al Alleborn memo to Wright, September 27, 1937.
28. Wallis memo to William Keighley, October 6, 1937.
29. Mary Parkes. "It's Been too Easy." *Modern Screen*, March 1938.
30. Patric Knowles. "Rebuttal for a Friend." Epilogue to *Errol Flynn: The Spy Who Never Was* by Tony Thomas.
31. Wallis telegram to Alleborn, October 22, 1937.
32. Knowles. "Rebuttal for a Friend."
33. Wallis memo to Keighley, November 2, 1937.
34. Silke. *Here's Looking at You, Kid*.
35. AFI.
36. Thomas. *From a Life of Adventure*.
37. Knowles. "Rebuttal for a Friend."
38. Wallis telegram to Knowles, October 25, 1937.
39. Wallis telegram to Keighley, October 26, 1937.
40. Wallis memo to Blanke, November 3, 1937.
41. Parkes. "It's Been too Easy."
42. Turner. *The Adventures of Errol Flynn*.
43. Parkes. "It's Been too Easy."
44. Wallis. *Starmaker*.
45. Alleborn production report, December 7, 1937.
46. Alleborn production report, December 7, 1937.
47. AFI.
48. Matzen. Michael Mazzone interview.
49. AFI.

Chapter 5: The Sure Thing
1. Flynn. *My Wicked, Wicked Ways*.
2. Robert Matzen. John McElwee interview, June 14, 2009.
3. Robert Matzen. Steven Hayes interview, March 29, 2008.
4. AFI.
5. Lynn Kear and John Rossman. *Kay Francis: A Passionate Life and Career*.
6. Wallis memo to Curtiz, February 10, 1938.
7. Wallis memo to Curtiz, February 24, 1938.
8. AFI.
9. Wallis. *Starmaker*.
10. AFI.
11. "Galaxy of Stars Busy on 'Robin Hood' Location." *Chico Enterprise*, October 1937.
12. Wallis memo to Orry-Kelly, February 11, 1938.

Chapter 6: Gone Hollywood
1. Behlmer, editor. *Inside Warner Bros.*
2. Robert Matzen. Carole Sampeck interview, February 2, 2010.
3. Rudy Behlmer, editor. *Memo from David O. Selznick*.
4. Ronald Haver. *David O. Selznick's Hollywood*.
5. Matzen. Carole Sampeck interview.
6. Behlmer. *Memo from David O. Selznick*.
7. Matzen. Carole Sampeck interview.
8. Matzen. Rudy Behlmer interview.
9. Matzen. Carole Sampeck interview.
10. Matzen. Rudy Behlmer interview.
11. Behlmer. *Memo from David O. Selznick*.
12. Behlmer. *Memo from David O. Selznick*.
13. Warner memo to MacEwen, February 1, 1938.
14. Behlmer. *Inside Warner Brothers*.
15. Robert Lord memo to Wallis, July 7, 1938.

16. Behlmer. *Inside Warner Bros.*
17. Behlmer. *Memo from David O. Selznick.*
18. AFI.
19. Silke. *Here's Looking at You, Kid.*
20. Dan Camp. "What's Biting Errol Flynn?" *Motion Picture*, December 1938.
21. John Lichfield. "Golden Girl: The Divine Olivia de Havilland." *The Independent*, July 14, 2009.
22. Matzen. John McElwee interview.
23. Silke. *Here's Looking at You, Kid.*
24. AFI.
25. Academy of Achievement.
26. Peter Harry Brown and Pat H. Broeske. *Howard Hughes: The Untold Story.* New York: Viking Press, 1996.
27. Academy of Achievement.
28. Matzen. John McElwee interview.
29. Mary C. McCall Jr. "Hollywood Corruption." *Motion Picture*, November 1943.
30. Matzen. John McElwee interview.
31. Parkes. "It's Been too Easy."
32. Turner Home Entertainment. *Melanie Remembers: Reflections by Olivia de Havilland* [Documentary]. 2004.
33. AFI.
34. Jack L. Warner. *My First Hundred Years in Hollywood.*
35. Wallis memo to Lord, December 23, 1938.
36. Wallis memo to Curtiz and Lord, December 14, 1938.
37. Mattison production report, December 1938.
38. Wallis memo to Lord, December 27, 1938.
39. Wallis memo to Curtiz, January 10, 1939.
40. Mattison memo to Wallis, January 6, 1939.
41. "Howard Hughes." *True the Man's Magazine,* May 1966.
42. Matzen. Carole Sampeck interview.
43. Jimmy Starr. *Barefoot on Barbed Wire: An Autobiography of a Forty-Five Year Hollywood Balancing Act.*

Chapter 7: Dysfunction Junction
1. AFI.
2. AFI.
3. Haver. *David O. Selznick's Hollywood.*
4. Haver. *David O. Selznick's Hollywood.*
5. Haver. *David O. Selznick's Hollywood.*
6. Matzen. Carole Sampeck interview.
7. Haver. *David O. Selznick's Hollywood.*
8. Parkes. "It's Been too Easy."
9. AFI.
10. Haver. *David O. Selznick's Hollywood.*
11. AFI.
12. Michael Sragow. *Victor Fleming: An American Movie Master.*
13. Wallis memo to Lord, March 20, 1939.
14. De Havilland letter to Warner, July 18, 1939.
15. Trilling memo to Warner and Wallis, April 10, 1939.
16. Wallis memo to Lord, April 27, 1939.
17. Wallis memo to Lord, May 4, 1939.
18. Behlmer. *Inside Warner Bros.*
19. Behlmer. *Inside Warner Bros.*
20. Wallis memo to Obringer, April 11, 1939.
21. Mattison production report, May 16, 1939.
22. Flynn. *My Wicked, Wicked Ways.*
23. AFI.
24. Glenn Kenny. "Olivia de Havilland." *Premiere*, October 2004.
25. Mattison production report, May 25, 1939.
26. Matzen. Carole Sampeck interview.
27. Olivia de Havilland. "The Dream That Never Died: Gone With the Wind." *Look*, December 12, 1967.
28. Kenny. "Olivia de Havilland."
29. Gladys Hall. "Olivia Decides on a Fling for Herself." *Silver Screen*, January 1941.
30. Sheridan. "Objectively Olivia."
31. Mattison production report, June 7, 1939.
32. Mattison production report, June 10, 1939.
33. Mattison production report, June 12, 1939.
34. Mattison production report, June 14, 1939.
35. Mattison production report, July 3, 1939.
36. Behlmer. *Inside Warner Bros.*
37. Behlmer. *Inside Warner Bros.*

Chapter 8: Bored to Death
1. AFI.
2. Gregory Orr Productions. *Jack L. Warner: The Last Mogul* [Documentary]. 1993.
3. De Havilland. "The Dream That Never Died."
4. Obringer telegram to de Havilland, December 12, 1939.
5. Matzen. Carole Sampeck interview.
6. Frank S. Nugent. "The Screen in Review." The New York *Times*, December 20, 1939.
7. Jhan Robbins. *Everybody's Man: A Biography of Jimmy Stewart.*
8. Robbins. *Everybody's Man.*
9. AFI.
10. AFI.
11. Matzen. John McElwee interview.
12. Warner telegram to de Havilland, December 18, 1939.
13. Obringer memo to Warner, December 19, 1939.
14. AFI.
15. Robbins. *Everybody's Man.*
16. Academy of Achievement.
17. AFI.
18. Ronald Reagan. *Where's the Rest of Me?*
19. Mattison memo to Wright, August 16, 1940.
20. Obringer memo to Wright, August 16, 1940.
21. Wallis memo to Curtiz, September 4, 1940.
22. Screen Actors Guild. "The Olivia de Havilland Interview." 1994.
23. Reagan. *Where's the Rest of Me?*
24. Irene Zarat. "I Feel Like a Heel About Errol." *Photoplay*, January 1942.
25. Wright memo to Robert Fellows, September 10, 1940.
26. Fellows memo to Wright, September 10, 1940.
27. Mattison memo to Wright, September 12, 1940.
28. Wallis memo to Fellows, September 11, 1940.
29. Mattison memo to Wright, September 16, 1940.
30. Zarat. "I Feel Like a Heel About Errol."

Chapter 9: Life Is Full of Surprises
1. Flynn. *My Wicked, Wicked Ways.*
2. Zarat. "I Feel Like a Heel About Errol."

3. Mary Hale. "Olivia de Havilland's Extra Pounds Shake Studio Foundations." The Tampa *Daily Times*, July 26, 1941.
4. Behlmer. *Inside Warner Bros.*
5. Flynn. *My Wicked, Wicked Ways.*
6. Turner. *The Adventures of Errol Flynn.*
7. Reagan. *Where's the Rest of Me?*
8. Flynn. *My Wicked, Wicked Ways.*
9. Matzen. Rudy Behlmer interview.
10. Behlmer. *Inside Warner Bros.*
11. Jimmy Townsend phone call to Warner Bros., June 18, 1941.
12. Fellows memo to Trilling, June 21, 1941
13. Zarat. "I Feel Like a Heel About Errol."
14. Fellows memo to Wallis, June 23, 1941.
15. Warner memo to Wallis, June 21, 1941.
16. Wallis memo to Milo Anderson, July 1, 1941.
17. Matzen. Rudy Behlmer interview.
18. Mattison production report, July 30, 1941.
19. Mattison production report, August 5, 1941.
20. Buster Wiles with William Donati. *My Days with Errol Flynn.*
21. Warner letter to Wright, August 8, 1941.
22. Mattison production report, August 12, 1941.
23. Mattison production report, August 18, 1941.
24. AFI.
25. Michael Caine. *What's It All About?*
26. Matzen. John McElwee interview.
27. John Lichfield. "Golden Girl."
28. Fellows memo to Wallis, August 22, 1941.
29. Wright memo to Wallis, August 25, 1941.
30. Thomas. *The Films of Olivia de Havilland.*
31. Thomas. *The Films of Olivia de Havilland.*
32. "Inside Stuff." *Photoplay*, June 1942.
33. Hopper. De Havilland interview.
34. Hopper. De Havilland interview.
35. Fontaine. *No Bed of Roses.*
36. Robert Matzen. Andrew Parks interview, March 9, 2010.
37. Robert Matzen. Phone conversation with Joan Fontaine, October 5, 2009.

Chapter 10: Lovers in Exile
1. Evelyn Keyes. *Scarlett O'Hara's Younger Sister.*
2. Lawrence Grobel. *The Hustons.*
3. Matzen. Rudy Behlmer interview.
4. Grobel. *The Hustons.*
5. Keyes. *Scarlett O'Hara's Younger Sister.*
6. Grobel. *The Hustons.*
7. Rader. "Rewards and Regrets."
8. Grobel. *The Hustons.*
9. John Arnett. "Errol Flynn's Last Interview: Vivid Memories and No Regrets." New York *Post*, October 15, 1959.
10. Fontaine. *No Bed of Roses.*
11. Oliver O. Jensen. "Sisters." *Life*, May 15, 1942.
12. Grobel. *The Hustons.*
13. Rader. "Rewards and Regrets."
14. McCall. "Hollywood Corruption."
15. Turner. *The Adventures of Errol Flynn.*
16. Linda Christian. *Linda: My Own Story.*
17. Flynn. *My Wicked, Wicked Ways.*
18. Nancy Winslow Squire. "Errol Flynn Exposed." *Modern Screen*, November 1943.
19. Olivia de Havilland as told to Sara Hamilton. "Things I Don't Like About Myself." *Photoplay*, February 1943.
20. AFI.
21. Behlmer. *Inside Warner Bros.*
22. AFI.
23. AFI.
24. Turner. *The Adventures of Errol Flynn.*
25. Wallis. *Starmaker.*
26. John Huston. *An Open Book.*
27. Grobel. *The Hustons.*
28. Huston. *An Open Book.*
29. Grobel. *The Hustons.*
30. AFI.
31. AFI.
32. Thomas. *The Films of Olivia de Havilland.*
33. Kass. *Olivia de Havilland.*
34. Viveca Lindfors. *Viveka...Viveca.*
35. Dick Moore. "Kid Stars Look Back at Uglies, Beauties." Chicago *Sun Times*, November 5, 1984.
36. AFI.
37. Thomas. *The Films of Olivia de Havilland.*
38. AFI.
39. Hopper. De Havilland raw interview.
40. Matzen. Steven Hayes interview.
41. Matzen. John McElwee interview.
42. "Romeo and Juliet." New York *Times* theater review, March 1951.
43. The Theater: Old Play in Manhattan. *Time*, March 19, 1951.
44. Olivia de Havilland. *Every Frenchman Has One.*
45. De Havilland. *Every Frenchman Has One.*
46. Trudy McVicker. "My Encounter with Errol Flynn." Unpublished.
47. Warner. *My First Hundred Years in Hollywood.*
48. John Arnett. "Errol Flynn's Last Interview."
49. Pierce. "Olivia de Havilland Returns to Saratoga."
50. Erskine Johnson. "Olivia Recalls 2 Private Wars." Los Angeles *Mirror*, June 26, 1961.
51. Huston. *An Open Book.*
52. Turner. *The Adventures of Errol Flynn.*
53. Flynn. *My Wicked, Wicked Ways.*

Chapter 11: Life After Flynn
1. Wallis. *Starmaker.*
2. Roderick Mann. "Olivia Keeps Publisher Waiting." Los Angeles *Times*, December 30, 1980.
3. De Havilland letter to Matzen, October 4, 1986.
4. De Havilland letter to John Huston, January 20, 1967. John Huston collection. Academy of Motion Picture Arts and Sciences.
5. Rader. "Rewards and Regrets."
6. Rader. "Rewards and Regrets."
7. Lichfield. "Golden Girl."
8. Turner. *The Adventures of Errol Flynn.*
9. Matzen. Michael Mazzone interview.

Selected Book-Length Sources

Balio, Tino, General Editor. *The Adventures of Robin Hood*. Madison: The University of Wisconsin Press, 1979.

Behlmer, Rudy, Editor. *Inside Warner Bros. (1935-1951)*. New York: Viking Penguin, Inc., 1985.

Behlmer, Rudy, Editor. *Memo from David O. Selznick*. New York: The Viking Press, 1972.

Cagney, James. *Cagney by Cagney*. Garden City: Doubleday & Company, Inc., 1976.

Caine. Michael. *What's It All About? An Autobiography*. New York: Turtle Bay Books, 1992.

Christian, Linda. *Linda: My Own Story*. New York: Dell Publishing Co., Inc., 1962.

Conrad, Earl. *Errol Flynn: A Memoir*. New York: Dodd, Mead & Company, 1978.

De Havilland, Olivia. *Every Frenchman Has One*. New York: Random House, 1962.

Eyman, Scott. *Lion of Hollywood: The Life and Legend of Louis B. Mayer*. New York: Simon & Schuster, 2005.

Fegerl, Josef. *Errol Flynn Dr. Hermann F. Erben: A Friendship of Two Adventurers 1933-1940*. Vienna: Peter Pospischil, 1985.

Flynn, Errol. *Beam Ends*. New York: Longmans, Green and Co., 1937.

Flynn, Errol. *My Wicked, Wicked Ways*. New York: G.P. Putnam's Sons, 1959.

Grobel, Lawrence. *The Hustons*. New York: Charles Scribner's Sons, 1989.

Haver, Ronald. *David O. Selznick's Hollywood*. New York: Bonanza Books, 1980.

Huston, John. *An Open Book*. New York: Alfred A. Knopf, 1980.

Kass, Judith M. *Olivia de Havilland*. New York: Pyramid Communications, Inc., 1976.

Kear, Lynn and Rossman, John. *Kay Francis: A Passionate Life and Career*. Jefferson, NC: McFarland & Company, Inc., 2006.

Keyes, Evelyn. *Scarlett O'Hara's Younger Sister*. Secaucus: Lyle Stuart Inc., 1977.

Lindfors, Viveca. *Viveka...Viveca*. New York: Everest House, 1981.

Matzen, Robert and Mazzone, Michael. *Errol Flynn Slept Here: The Flynns, the Hamblens, Rick Nelson, & the Most Notorious House in Hollywood*. Pittsburgh: GoodKnight Books, 2009.

McNulty, Thomas. *The Life and Career of Errol Flynn*. Jefferson, NC: MacFarland & Company, 2004.

Niven, David. *Bring on the Empty Horses*. New York: G.P. Putnam's Sons, 1975.

Reagan, Ronald with Hubler, Richard G. *Where's the Rest of Me?* New York: Dell, Sloan and Pearce, 1965.

Robbins, Jhan. *Everybody's Man: A Biography of Jimmy Stewart*. New York: G.P. Putnam's Sons, 1985.

Silke, James R. *Here's Looking at You, Kid: 50 Years of Fighting, Working and Dreaming at Warner Bros*. Boston: Little, Brown & Co., 1976.

Sragow, Michael. *Victor Fleming: An American Movie Master*. New York: Pantheon Books, 2008.

Thomas, Tony, Rudy Behlmer, and Clifford McCarty. *The Films of Errol Flynn*. Secaucus: The Citadel Press, 1969.

Thomas, Tony. *The Films of Olivia de Havilland*. Secaucus: The Citadel Press, 1983.

Thomas, Tony, Editor. *From a Life of Adventure: The Writings of Errol Flynn*. Secaucus: The Citadel Press, 1980.

Thomas, Tony. *Errol Flynn: The Spy Who Never Was*. New York: Carol Publishing Group, 1990.

Wallis, Hal B. *Starmaker: The Autobiography of Hal Wallis*. New York: Macmillan Publishing Co., Inc., 1980.

Warner, Jack L. *My First Hundred Years in Hollywood: An Autobiography*. New York: Random House, 1964.

Wiles, Buster with Donati, William. *My Days With Errol Flynn*. Santa Monica: Roundtable Publishing, Inc., 1988.

Index

Aadland, Beverly 189, 190
Abe Lincoln in Illinois 118
Across the Pacific 178
Adventures of Captain Fabian 188
Adventures of Don Juan 185-186
Adventures of Robin Hood, The 46, 55, 56-75, 78, 80, 81, 84, 85, 90, 96, 99, 101, 111, 114, 116, 117, 136, 138, 144, 167, 168, 190
Affectionately Yours 152, 180
Aherne, Brian 16, 50, 54, 84, *91*, 114, 139, *152*, 170, 178
Albert, Eddie 135
Alexander, Ross 12, 17, *25*
Alibi Ike 11, 12
All Rights Reserved/Four's a Crowd 76-85, 92
Alleborn, Al 62, 64, 66, 69
Ambassador Hotel 52, 53, 54, 135
Ameche, Don 108
Amy, George 23, 101, 107
Anderson, Maxwell 119, 131, 134
Anderson, Milo 56, 157, 160
Angels with Dirty Faces 91
The Animal Kingdom/One More Tomorrow 180
Another Dawn 47, 80
Anthony Adverse 32, 34, 35
Arno (the dog) 62, *96*, 97, 147, 176
Asher, Irving 9
Astaire, Fred 173
Astor, Mary 178
Atwill, Lionel 17, 23
Aviator, The 53, 102

Bainter, Fay 90
Bankhead, Tallulah 88, 114
Barbier, George 161
Barkleys of Broadway, The 173
Barrymore, John 17, 113, 189
Beam Ends 31, 47
Behlmer, Rudy 12, 34, 48, 68, 88, 154, 161, 174
Bellamy, Ralph 81
Bern, Paul 102
Blanke, Henry 12, 13, 64, 70, 71, 74
Blondell, Gloria 81
Blondell, Joan 51, 78, 81

Bluebeard's Eighth Wife 91
Bogart, Humphrey 91, 108, *109*, 131, 154, 178, 188, 193
Borzage, Frank 31, 36
Bounty, HMS and Errol Flynn ancestry 6
Boy Meets Girl 91
Boyer, Charles 34
Brent, George 9, 17, 173
Brown, Harry Joe 18, 26
Brown, Joe E. 11, *12*, 32, 131
Brown, Kay 87
Bruce, Nigel *53*, 54
Bruce, Virginia 114
Bryan, Jane 92
Brynner, Yul 67
Buccaneer, The 78, 89, 90
Buck, Frank 38
Buckner, Robert 105, 106, 136, 137
Budlong, Ralph 161
Bullets or Ballots 60

Cabot, Bruce 189
Cagney, James 10, 11, 13, 17, 19, 60, 81, 91, 94, 131, 136, 147, 154, 171, 188, 193
Cain and Mabel 19
Caine, Michael 164-165
Call It a Day 50
Camp, Dan 95, 96
Campbell, Colin *67, 70*
Captain Blood 14-29, 31, 35, 37, 44, 72, 77, 85, 116, 144
Carnahan, Suzanne (Susan Peters) 143, 157
Casablanca 105, 182, 183, 193
Case of the Curious Bride, The 18
Castro, Fidel 191
Charge of the Light Brigade, The 31, 36-43, 50, 81, 85, 88, 105, 190
Chateau des Fleurs *9*, 13, 21
Chauvel, Charles 6
Christian, Fletcher 6
Christian, Linda (Blanca Rosa Welter) 180, 187
CinemaScope 188, 189
Clift, Montgomery 187
Clive, Colin 17
Cocoanut Grove 52, 53, 54, 135

203

Coffee, Lenore *156*, 157-158, 160, 161, 164, 167, 168
Colbert, Claudette 34, 91, 114
Coleman, Nancy 155
Colman, Ronald 8, 16, 31, 88
Columbia Pictures 77, 81
Connolly, Walter *82*, 84
Conrad, Earl 190, 191
Constant Nymph, The 153
Cooper, Gary 91
Cooper, Melville 61, *64*, *73*, 85
Cosmopolitan Productions 19
Count of Monte Cristo, The 15
Crawford, Joan 53, 80, 184, 188
Crisp, Donald 39, 124, *147*
Crossed Swords 188
Crusades, The 11
Cruze, James 116
Cukor, George 88, 94, 104, 111, 112, 115, 117, 171
Curtiz, Michael: and *The Adventures of Robin Hood* 72-73, 74, 75; biography 17-18; and *Captain Blood* 16, 17, 18, 22, 23, 24, *25*, 26, 27; and *The Charge of the Light Brigade* 36, 37, 39, 40, 41, 43; and Olivia de Havilland 55, 74, 112, 121, 122, 123, 127, 128, 165, 173, 189; and *Dodge City* 95, 96, 97, *98*, 99, 104, 105, 106, 107; and Errol Flynn *18*, 19, 21, 22, 31, 32, 37, 60, 61, 81, 111, 129, 137, *140*, 141, 142, 153-154; and *Four's a Crowd* 81, 82, 85; and Wallis 17-18, 23, 24, 25, 26, 36, 39, 43, 72-73, 74, 81, 99, 105, 106, 139; and *The Private Lives of Elizabeth and Essex* 119, *120*, 121, 122, 123, 125, 127, 128, 129; and *Santa Fe Trail* 136, 137, 139, 140, 141, 142; and *They Died with Their Boots On* 153-154, 159
Custer, Elizabeth Bacon *154*, 155, 157, 158
Custer, George Armstrong 146, 153, *154*, 155, 157, 158, 159, *166*
Damita, Lili *5*, *8*, 9, 12-13, 18, *19*, 21, 31, 36, 37, 38, 41-42, 47, *48*, *49*, 51, 54, 55, *63*, 65-*66*, 67, 68, 71, 72, 97, 100, 147, 176, 191
Daniell, Henry 124, 126
Dark Mirror, The 185
Dark Victory 135
Datig, Fred 11
Daves, Delmer 9
Davies, Marion 16, 19
Davis, Bette 16, 17, 34, 50, 65, 77, 80, 87, 89, 90, 113, 114, 117, 119, *120*, 121-122, 124, *125*, *126*, *127*, *128*, *129*, 131, *133*, 136, 173, 174, 175, 178, 185, 188
Dawn Patrol, The 91, 92
de Cordoba, Pedro 23
de Havilland Decision 181, 182, 188
de Havilland, Lilian 2, 3, 4, 9, 13, 21, 50, 107, 124, 178, 180
de Havilland, Olivia: Academy Awards 135, 138, 171, 178, 184, 185, 187; angles for role in *Gone With the Wind* 93-95, 102-104; childhood and adolescence 2, 3-5, 6-8; conflicts with Mike Curtiz 40-41, 73, 74, 82; dating Errol Flynn 52-53, 54-55, 171; de Havilland vs. Warner Bros. (court case) 181-182; depression 95; doesn't know herself 6, 34, 71, 124; feelings about film roles 13, 34, 42, 65, 67, 81-82, 83, 101, 117, 121, 124, 131; illnesses 2, 81, 92, 100, 107, 148-150, 152; landing of *Captain Blood* role with Flynn 18-19; literary career 194; packaged as a sex object 28-29, 44-45; profanity 78-79; stage career 4, 6, 7, 10-11, 188; suspensions 134, 136, 152, 180-181; and Jack Warner 11, 13, 18-19, 32-33, 35, 39, 56, 83, 93, 107, 155, 156; Warner feud 93-95, 104, 115-116, 117-118, 122-123, 124, 127, 131, 132, 133-134, 136, 152, 180-181; upstaging by Flynn 67-68, 98, 99-101; Warner Bros. contracts 11, 32-33, 39, 180-181; sensitivity over weight 52-53, 152
de Havilland, Walter 2, 8
DeMille, Cecil B. 11, 89, 90, 91, 107
Desperate Journey/Forced Landing 175, 176, 183
Destry Rides Again 133
Dibbs, Naomi 3, 5, 7
DiCaprio, Leonardo 53
Dieterle, William 11, 12, 80, 81
Dietrich, Marlene 65, 133
Dive Bomber 154, 155
Doctor X 17
Dodge City 90-92, 93, 95-107, 111, 115, 117, 139, 168
Donat, Robert 9, 11, 15, 16
Dunne, Irene 77, 114

Earp, Wyatt 89, 90
Eason, B. Reeves 43, 70, 138, 140
Eddington, Nora *179*, 180, 182, 183, *185*, 187
Edge of Darkness 182
Einfeld, Charlie 108, 147, 149
Erben, Hermann F. 7, 47, 48, *49*, 50, 51, 175, 194
Errol Flynn Slept Here 75, 165
Eyman, Scott 102

Fabray, Nanette 122, *126*, 127
Fairbanks, Douglas Jr. 114
Farmer, Francis 136
Farrell, Charles 9
Faye, Alice 108
Fellows, Robert 140, 153, 156-157, 159, 167
Ferber, Edna 175
Fields, W.C. 10
Fire Over England 114
Fleming, Victor 112-*113*, 116-117, 118, 121, 123, 171
Flight Eight/Flight Angels 134, 136, 180
Florczak, Robert 58-59
Flynn, Arnella 189
Flynn, Deirdre 182
Flynn, Errol: childhood and adolescence 1, 2-3; conflicts with Mike Curtiz 18, 21, 22, 37, 73, 74, 120, 140, 153-154; considered for Rhett Butler in *Gone With the Wind* 88-89; dating Olivia de Havilland 52-53, 54-55, 139, 171; dealings with mother 1, 3-4, 8, 19, 96; depression 180, 182, 189; fistfight with John Huston 183-184; flying airplanes 66, 68-70; illnesses 81, 160, 161, 162, 175; "in like Flynn" 181-182; jealousy over de Havilland 139-

204

140, 165, 183-184; landing of *Captain Blood* lead 17, 18; learning disability 3, 37-38, 39-40, 97; literary career 31, 47, 190-191; packaged as a sex object 28-29, 44-45, 186; rape trial 177, 178, 179-180; Spanish adventure (1937) 47-51; stage career 8-9; and Jack Warner 12, 13, 14, 17, 18, 19, 37, 48, 50, 51, 78, 107, 115, 140, 153, 155, 160, 173, 179-180, 184, 185, 189, 191, 193

Flynn, Lily Mary 1, 2, 3, 6, 8, 21, 41, 42
Flynn, Rory 182
Flynn, Sean Leslie 155
Flynn, Theodore Leslie 1, 2
Fonda, Henry 114, 173
Fontaine, George Milan 3, 4, 7, 57, 178, 185
Fontaine, Joan de Beauvoir de Havilland 2, 3, 4, 5, 7, 8, 9, 21, 42, 50, 79, 84, 91, 97, 124, 134, *152*, 155, *170-171*, 178, 180, 185, 194
Fools for Scandal 78
Footsteps in the Dark 147, 148, 153
Four's a Crowd/All Rights Reserved 76-85, 92, 133
Forced Landing/Desperate Journey 175, 176
Francis, Kay 15, 17, 47, 80, 81, 184
Franklin, Dwight 25
Fraser, George MacDonald 31
Frontier Marshal 90

G-Men 56
Gable, Clark 16, 77, 88, 93, 108, *109*, 111, *112*, 113, 117, 118, 121, *123-124*, 132, 135, 154, 171
Galante, Gisele 171, 188, 190
Galante, Pierre 188, 190
Gang, Martin 181
Garbo, Greta 88
Garden of Allah, The 13, 36
Gardner, Ava 79
Garfield, John 131, 134, 155
Garrett, Betty 67
Garson, Greer 102, 178
Gaudio, Tony *33*, 73
Gay Sisters, The 152, 180
Gentleman Jim 183
George Washington Slept Here 176
Ghika, Irene 187
Gibson, Hoot 108
Goddard, Paulette 183
God's Country and the Woman 56
Gold Diggers of 1933 32
Gold Is Where You Find It 55, 56, 65
Goldwyn, Samuel Productions 118, 131, 134, 153
Goldwyn, Samuel Jr. Productions 189
Gone With the Wind (book) 87, 88
Gone With the Wind (motion picture) 88, 89-90, 92, 93, 94, 95, 98, 101, 102, 103, 104, 105, 108, 111-113, 116, 117, 118, 121, 122, 123, 127, 131, 132, 133, 134, 135, 136, 154, 157, 173, 176, 184
Goodrich, Benjamin 188
Goodrich, Marcus 171, *184*, 185, 186, 188

Grahame, Margot 114
Grand National Pictures 91
Grant, Cary 54, 77
Grapewin, Charlie *168*
Great Garrick, The 50, 84
Green Light 47, 56
Greenstreet, Sidney 161
Gurney, Noll 92

Hale, Alan *58*, 61, *62*, 63, 65, 97, *100*, 101, 105, 108, 121, 129
Haller, Ernest 90, 116
Hansen, Betty 178
Hard to Get 92
Harlow, Jean 77, 80, 102
Haver, Ronald 112, 113
Hawks, Howard 116
Hayes, Helen 114
Hayes, Ivan (Steven) 79, 187
Hayworth, Rita 147, 152
Head, Edith 152
Hearst, William Randolph 16, 19
Hecht, Ben 113
Heiress, The 68, 187
Hell's Angels 116
Henreid, Paul 79
Hepburn, Katharine 77, 102, 114
Herzig, Sig 83, 84
High Sierra 154
Hill, Howard 66, 121
Hold Back the Dawn 152, 155, 176
Hollywood Bowl 10, 11
Hopkins, John *177*
Hopkins, Miriam 78, 88, 114
Hopkins, Samuel 51
Hopper, Hedda 51, 108, 170, 171
Howard, Leslie 9, 15, 16, 50, 68, 111, 118
Hughes, Howard *101*, 102-103, 107, 116, 118, 133, 139
Hunter, Ian 17, 65
Huntley, G.P. Jr. 36, 157, 168
Huston, John 134, 161, 167, 173-175, *176*, 178, 179, 181, 182, 183-184, 185, 186, 190, 194-195

I Adore You! 8
In the Wake of the Bounty 6
In This Our Life 173, 174, 175
Inside Warner Bros. (1935-1951) 12
Invisible Man, The 10
Irish in Us, The 13
Istanbul 189
It Happened One Night 51, 77, 84
It's a Gift 10
It's Love I'm After 50, 77
It's a Wonderful Life 104

Jacoby, Michel 34
Jazz Singer, The 9
Jezebel 87, 90
Jones, Buck 108
Juarez 114, 159

Kahn, Ivan Agency 32-33, 34
Kazan, Elia 187
Keeler, Ruby 31
Keighley, William 56, 60, *62*, 63, 64, 65, 67, 70, 72, 74, 80
Kennedy, Arthur 157, 159, 168
Keyes, Evelyn 174, 175, 185
Kibbee, Guy 20
Kline, Wallace 153, 159
Knowles, Patric *36*, 42, 50, 61, 62, 63, 64, 65, 66, *68*, 69, 70, 75, *79*, 80, 81, *83*, 85, 137
Knute Rockne, All American 136
Koch, Howard 174
Korda, Alexander 129
Korngold, Erich Wolfgang 129

Lane, Priscilla 92, 108, 155
Lane, Rosemary 108
Law, Jude 53
Lee, Christopher 26
Leigh, Vivien 111, *112*, *113*, 116, 117, *118*, 135, 187
Leigh, Rowland 34
Leisen, Mitchell 185
LeRoy, Mervyn 32, *33*, 170
Leslie, Joan *155*, 156
Libeled Lady 77, 82, 84, 85
Life magazine 161, 173, 178
Life of Emil Zola, The 34, 80
Lilly, Doris 179
Lindfors, Viveca *186*
Lindsay, Margaret *73*, 114
Lion of Hollywood 102
Little Caesar 9, 15, 32
Lives of a Bengal Lancer 34
Lloyd, Frank 116
Lockhart, Gene 162, 164, 165, 167
Lolita 189
Lombard, Carole 31, 78, 80, 108, *109*, 113, 132
Lord, Robert 91, 92, 97, 105, 115, 117, 119, 122
Louise, Anita 16, 35, 50, 56, 114
Loy, Myrna 82, 85, 153
Lundigan, William 97
Lupino, Ida 94, 114, 186
Lynn, Jeffrey 136

MacEwen, Walter 23, 85, 90
MacKenzie, Aneas 153, 159
MacMurray, Fred 155

Mad Genius, The 17
Magnificent Seven, The 68
Male Animal, The 167, 173, 174
Maltese Falcon, The 161, 174
March, Fredric 16, 32, *33*, 78, 80, 81, 82, *89*, 90, 114, 115
Mark of Zorro, The 26
Married, Pretty and Poor/Saturday's Children 131, 133, 134, 136, 180
Marshall, Brenda 136, 147, *153*
Marx Brothers 77
Massey, Raymond 142, 149
Master of Ballantrae, The 188
Mattison, Frank 37, 106, 107, 119, 121, 122, 126, 127, 128, 139, 140-141, 161, 162
Mayer, Louis B. 88, 93, 112, 133
Mazzone, Michael 19, 75, 195
McDaniel, Hattie *123*, 132, 135, 157, 161, 162, *164*, 167, 168
McElwee, John 79, 97, 102, 103, 134, 150, 165, 188
McEvoy, Fred 176
McHugh, Frank *100*, 108
McKeon, Joe *182*, 183, 184, 185
McLaglen, Victor 183
McNulty, Thomas 47
McQueen, Butterfly 111
McQueen, Steve 67-68
McCrea, Joel 81, 91, 114
McVicker, Trudy (Gertrud Seipmann) 189
Memo from David O. Selznick 88
Meredith, Burgess 170
Methot, Mayo *109*
Metro Goldwyn Mayer Studios 15, 77, 80, 84, 88, 93, 94, 102, 112, 113, 133, 187
Midsummer Night's Dream, A (film version) 11, 12, 34, 80
Midsummer Night's Dream, A (stage version) 6, 10-11
Mildred Pierce 184
Milestone, Lewis 116
Milland, Ray 114, 183, 184
Mitchell, Margaret 87, 88, 90, 113, 117, 132, 137
Moore, John Hammond 3, 31
Morgan, Dennis 119, 136, 152, 173
Morris, Wayne 108
Mr. Smith Goes to Washington 135
Muir, Jean 16, 17, 18
Mundin, Herbert 65
Muni, Paul 17, 34, 68, 114
Munson, Ona 118, 124
Murder at Monte Carlo 9
Mutiny on the Bounty 15
My Love Came Back 136
My Wicked, Wicked Ways 1, 49, 50, 121, 176, 191
Mystery of the Wax Museum 17

Naish, J. Carrol 25
Niven, David 36, *40*, 41, 43, 51, *52*, 53, 54, 61, 78, 91, 131, 137, 181

No Bed of Roses 170
Northampton Repertory Theatre 8
Not as a Stranger 188
Nothing Sacred 78, 84, 113

O'Brien, Pat 10, 13, 78, 91, 171
O'Connor, Una 71
O'Neill, Henry 138, 140, 141
O'Shea, Daniel 88, 93, 155
Objective, Burma! 182
Obringer, R.J. 33, 38, 121, 132, 139, 152, 181
Of Mice and Men 135
Oklahoma Kid, The 91
Old Dark House, The 10
Olivier, Laurence 114, 115,
One More Tomorrow/The Animal Kingdom 180
Onyx (the horse) 108
Orry-Kelly 84

Pallette, Eugene 59, 61, 62, 65
Paramount Pictures 78, 80, 87, 90, 91, 107, 152, 183, 184
Park, Jackie 131
Parkes, Mary 71
Parks, Andrew 67, 68, 171
Parks, Larry 67
Parsons, Louella O. 108, 120
Patrick, Gail 114
Payne, John 92, 131
Perfect Specimen, The 51, 60, 183
Peters, Susan (Suzanne Carnahan) 143, 157
Photoplay magazine 42, 51, 170
Polito, Sol 73
Powell, Dick 10, 31, 92, 131
Powell, William 15, 17, 77, 82, 148, 153
Power, Tyrone 26, 91
Price, Vincent 114
Prince and the Pauper, The 47, 51, 56
Princess O'Rourke, The 176
Private Lives of Elizabeth and Essex, The 113-115, 116, 117, 118-120, 131, 133, 138, 154
Proud Rebel, The 189, 190
Public Enemy, The 9, 15, 17

Quiet Man, The 183
Quinn, Anthony 89

Rabwyn, Marcella 116
Raffles 118, 131, 134, 136
Raine, Norman Reilly 55
Rathbone, Basil 24, 25, 26, 53, 54, 60, 61, 64, 65, 66, 67, 92
Reagan, Ronald 135, 136, 137, 138, 139, 140, 141, 142, 143, 148, 153, 154, 165, 175
Rebecca 155

Reinhardt, Max 10-12, 34, 170
Return of Dr. X, The 131
Richardson, Ralph 68
RKO Radio Pictures 77, 97, 118
Robinson, Casey 26, 77, 83, 84
Robinson, Edward G. 56
Robson, May 149
Rocky Mountain 187
Rogers, Ginger *101*, 103, 133, 173
Rogers, Roy 70
Roosevelt, Franklin Delano (FDR) 185
Roots of Heaven, The 189, 190
Russell, Rosalind 51, 79, 81, *83*, 85, 133
Rutherford, Ann 116

Sampeck, Carole 88, 108, 113, 123, 132
Santa Fe Trail 136-143, 147, 153, 154, 155, 191
Saratoga Trunk 175
Satterlee, Peggy 177, 178
Saturday's Children/Married, Pretty and Poor 131, 133, 134, 136, 180
Sawyer, Joe 159
Scarlet Pimpernel, The 9, 15
Scott, Randolph 87
Sea Hawk, The 131, 138
Sears, Gradwell 119, 129
Seipmann McVicker, Gertrud (Trudy) 189
Selznick, David O.: purchasing *GWTW* 87; casting *GWTW* 88-89, 92-94, 103-104, 118; and Olivia de Havilland 93-94, 100, 104, 111, 112, 115, 121, 124, 132-133, 135, 171; and Errol Flynn 88-89, 183-184; producing *GWTW* 112, 113, 116, 117, 118, 121, 131-132; and Jack Warner 89, 90, 94-95, 103-104, 108-109, 193
Selznick, Irene 133
Selznick International Pictures 84, 94, 111, 112, 116, 117, 120, 121, 122, 123, 124, 128, 131, 155
Selznick, Myron 88, 89, 92
Sergeant York 153, 156, 157, 159
Shearer, Norma 102, 114, 133
Sheridan, Ann 93, *94, 103*, 105, 108, 109, 118, 154, 180, 186
Sherman, Vincent 131
Shourds, Sherry 119
Showdown 185
Sirocco (I; cutter) 31
Sirocco (II; ketch) 74, 96, 176
Sisters, The 114
Snake Pit, The 186-187
So Red the Rose 87
Sondergaard, Gale 114
Sons of Liberty 112
Squire, Nancy Winslow 180
Stackpole, Peter 161
Stagecoach 91, 135
Stanwyck, Barbara 91, 114, 184
Star is Born, A 90

Starr, Jimmy 109
Steiner, Max 90
Stephenson, Henry 24, 25
Stewart, James 104, 107, *132*, *133*, 134, 135, 137, 138, 139, 144, 148, 170, 174, 176, 178, 194, 195
Stockwell, Dean 186
Stolen Life, A 185
Story of Alexander Graham Bell, The 108
Story of Louis Pasteur, The 34, 80
Strawberry Blonde, The 147, 154
Streetcar Named Desire, A 187
Stuart, Gloria 10
Sullavan, Margaret 87, 114
Sullivan, Ed 89
Sullivan, Wallace 77
Sun Also Rises, The 189
Sutton, John 126
Swarm, The 164

Tamiroff, Akim *89*
Taplinger, Robert 85, 90, 108
Technicolor 48, 55, 56, 58, 62, 64, 65, 96, 98, 107, 112, 114, 117, 119, 127, 154
Thalberg, Irving 102
That Lady 188
Thau, Benny 102
They Died with Their Boots On 153-169, 173, 176, 186
Thomas, Tony 13, 19, 168, 169, 186
Three Musketeers, The 15
Titanic 10
To Each His Own 171, 184, 185
Toler, Sidney 161
Too Much, Too Soon 189
Tovarich 34
Townsend, Jimmie 152, 181
Tracy, Spencer 77
Travers, Henry *100*, 104
Treasure Island 15
Treasure of the Sierra Madre, The 187
Trigger (the horse) 70
Trilling, Steve 117, 118, 156
Trump, Donald 53
Turner, Don 84
Twentieth Century 113
Twentieth Century-Fox 108, 186

Uncertain Glory 182
Union Pacific 107
United Artists 91
Universal Pictures 87, 119, 185
Venable, Evelyn *6*
Vidor, King 87
Virginia City 131, 138, 154

Wald, Jerry 134
Wallis, Hal: and *The Adventures of Robin Hood* 55, 56, 60, 61, 64-65, 66, 67, 68, 69, 70-71, 72, 73, 74, 75; biography 11-12; and *Captain Blood* 17-19, 22, 23, 24, 25, 26, 27; and *The Charge of the Light Brigade* 35, 36, 37, 39, 43, criticizing de Havilland 10, 12, 21, 23, 56, 106, 117, 131, 137, 138, 139, 141, 152; and Michael Curtiz 17-18, 23, 24, 25, 26, 36, 39, 43, 72-73, 74, 81, 99, 105, 106, 139; de Havilland contract 32-33; de Havilland discovery 11; and *Dodge City* 91, *92*, 94, 95, 97, 99, 100, 105, 106, 107; and Errol Flynn 47, 60, 66, 67, 81, 140, 195; and *Four's a Crowd* 77, 78, 80, 81; and *Gone With the Wind* 87, 89, 117, 118, 121, 132; and *The Private Lives of Elizabeth and Essex* 113-114, 115, 117, 119, 121, 122, 126, 128; replacing Keighley with Curtiz 72-73; and *Santa Fe Trail* 136, 137, 138, 139, 140, 141, 143; and *They Died with Their Boots On* 153, 154, 155, 156, 157, 158, 159, 160, 167; and Jack Warner 182-183, 193
Walsh, Raoul 154, 159, 160, 161, *163*, 164, 165, 167
Wanger, Walter 90, 91
Warner, Albert 9, 193
Warner, Ann Alvarado 103, 104, 107
Warner, Harry 9, 17, 89, 193
Warner, Jack L.: and *The Adventures of Robin Hood* 46, 48, 56, 60, 73; biography 9, 193; and brothers 9, 188, 193; as a businessman 13, 14, 15, 16-19, 32-33, 34-35, 36, 37, 39, 44, 46, 48, 56, 73, 77, 87, 89, 91, 92, 108, 118, 126, 127, 131, 153, 155, 156, 157, 175, 185, 188, 193; and *Captain Blood* 15, 16-17, 18-19; and *The Charge of the Light Brigade* 34, 35, 36, 37; and *Dodge City* 90, 91, 92, 107; and *Four's a Crowd* 78, 80, 81, 82, 83, 85; and Olivia de Havilland 11, 13, 18-19, 32-33, 35, 39, 56, 83, 93, 107, 155, 156; and de Havilland feud 93-95, 104, 115-116, 117-118, 122-123, 124, 127, 131, 132, 133-134, 136, 152, 180-181; discovering de Havilland 11; discovering Flynn 9-10; and Errol Flynn 12, 13, 14, 17, 18, 19, 37, 48, 50, 51, 78, 107, 115, 140, 153, 155, 160, 173, 179-180, 184, 185, 189, 191, 193; and *Gone With the Wind* 87, 89, 90, 93, 94, 103, 104, 108-109, 118, 121, 132; and *The Private Lives of Elizabeth and Essex* 113-114, 117, 119-120, 126, 129; relationships with contract players 11, 13, 80, 119-120, 129, 157, 188; and *Santa Fe Trail* 137, 140; and David O. Selznick 89-90, 94, 108-109, 115, 118, 133; and *They Died with Their Boots On* 153, 155, 156, 159, 160, 168; and Hal Wallis 11, 13, 16, 17, 18, 19, 32, 35, 37, 56, 60, 73, 78, 80, 81, 82, 83, 113, 115-116, 118, 119, 121, 126, 131, 132, 134, 140, 152, 153, 155, 156, 157, 159, 182, 193; and Warner Bros. Studio 1, 9, 16, 27, 188, 193
Warner, Samuel 9
Warwick, Robert 121
Wayne, John 91, 183
Weissberger, Felix 10
Welbourne, Scotty 143, 144
Well-Groomed Bride, The 183, 184
Welter, Blanca Rosa (Linda Christian) 180, 187
Westmore, Perc 119
Whale, James 170

What Every Woman Knows 185
Whitney, John Hay "Jock" 87
Wiles, Buster 101, 161, 168
William Tell 188, 189
William, Warren 12
Williams, Guinn "Big Boy" 101, 105, 108, 109
Wings of the Navy 92
Winn, Marcia 103
Witherspoon, Cora 106
Wizard of Oz, The 112, 135
Wood, Sam 118, 121
Wuthering Heights 135

Wray, Fay 17
Wright, Tenny 56, 62, 63, 121, 122, 139, 140, 141, 161, 167
Wyler, Margaret Tallichet 175
Wyler, William 175
Wyman, Jane 108, 136
Wymore, Patrice *187*, 188, 189

Young, Edward 6
Young Errol, The 3

Zaca (the schooner) 180, 182
Zanuck, Darryl F. 12, 87, 189